ANSI
Common Lisp

 **PRENTICE HALL SERIES
IN ARTIFICIAL INTELLIGENCE**
Stuart Russell and Peter Norvig, Editors

ANSI
Common Lisp

Paul Graham

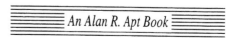
An Alan R. Apt Book

Prentice Hall, Englewood Cliffs, New Jersey 074623

Library of Congress Cataloging-in-Publication Data

Graham, Paul.
    ANSI common lisp. / Paul Graham.
        p.   cm.
    "An Alan R. Apt book."
    Includes bibliographical references and index.
    ISBN 0-13-370875-6
    1. COMMON LISP (Computer program language) I. Title.
QA76.73.C28G69   1996
005.13'3–dc20   95-45017
                                                       CIP

Publisher: Alan Apt
Production Editor: Mona Pompili
Cover Designer: Gino Lee
Copy Editor: Shirley Michaels
Production Coordinator: Donna Sullivan
Editorial Assistant: Shirley McGuire
Cover Photo: Ed Lynch

 © 1996 by Prentice-Hall, Inc.
Simon & Schuster/A Viacom Company
Englewood Cliffs, New Jersey 07632

The author and publisher of this book have used their best efforts in preparing this book.
These efforts include the development, research, and testing of the theories and programs
to determine their effectiveness. The author and publisher shall not be liable in any event
for incidental or consequential damages in connection with, or arising out of, the furnishing,
performance, or use of these programs.

Printed in the United States of America

10 9 8 7 6 5 4 3 2

ISBN   0-13-370875-6

Prentice-Hall International (UK) Limited, *London*
Prentice-Hall of Australia Pty. Limited, *Sydney*
Prentice-Hall Canada, Inc., *Toronto*
Prentice-Hall Hispanoamericana, S.A., *Mexico*
Prentice-Hall of India Private Limited, *New Delhi*
Prentice-Hall of Japan, Inc., *Tokyo*
Simon & Schuster Asia Pte. Ltd, *Singapore*
Editora Prentice-Hall do Brasil, Ltda., *Rio de Janeiro*

TO RTM

Half lost on my firmness gains to more glad heart,
Or violent and from forage drives
A glimmering of all sun new begun
Both harp thy discourse they march'd,
Forth my early, is not without delay;
For their soft with whirlwind; and balm.
Undoubtedly he scornful turn'd round ninefold,
Though doubled now what redounds,
And chains these a lower world devote, yet inflicted?
Till body or rare, and best things else enjoy'd in heav'n
To stand divided light at ev'n and poise their eyes,
Or nourish, lik'ning spiritual, I have thou appear.

—Henley

Preface

The aim of this book is to teach you Common Lisp quickly and thoroughly. It is really two books. The first half is a tutorial that explains, with plenty of examples, all the essential concepts of Lisp programming. The second half is an up-to-date summary of ANSI Common Lisp, describing every operator in the language.

Audience

ANSI Common Lisp is intended for both students and professional programmers. It assumes no prior knowledge of Lisp. Experience writing programs in some other language would be helpful, but not absolutely necessary. The book begins with the most basic concepts, and pays special attention to the points that tend to confuse someone seeing Lisp for the first time.

This book could be used by itself as the textbook in a course on Lisp programming, or to teach Lisp as part of a course on artificial intelligence or programming languages. Professional programmers who want to learn Lisp will appreciate the direct, practical approach. Those who already use Lisp will find it a useful source of examples, and a convenient reference for ANSI Common Lisp.

How to Use This Book

The best way to learn Lisp is to use it. It's also *more fun* to learn a language by writing programs in it. This book is designed to get you started as quickly as possible. After a brief Introduction,

- Chapter 2 explains, in 21 pages, everything you need to start writing Lisp programs.

- Chapters 3–9 introduce the essential elements of Lisp programming. These chapters pay special attention to critical concepts like the role of pointers in Lisp, the use of recursion to solve problems, and the significance of first-class functions.

For readers who want a thorough grounding in Lisp techniques,

- Chapters 10–14 cover macros, CLOS, operations on list structure, optimization, and advanced topics like packages and read-macros.

- Chapters 15–17 sum up the lessons of the preceding chapters in three examples of real applications: a program for making logical inferences, an HTML generator, and an embedded language for object-oriented programming.

The last part of the book consists of four appendices, which should be useful to all readers:

- Appendices A–D include a guide to debugging, source code for 58 Common Lisp operators, a summary of the differences between ANSI Common Lisp and previous versions of the language,° and a reference describing every operator in ANSI Common Lisp.

The book concludes with a section of notes. The notes contain clarifications, references, additional code, and occasional heresies. Notes are indicated in the text by a small circle, like this.°

The Code

Although it describes ANSI Common Lisp, this book has been designed so that you can use it with any version of Common Lisp. Examples that depend on newer features are usually accompanied by notes showing how they would be rendered in older implementations.

All the code in this book is available online. You can find it, along with links to free software, historic papers, the Lisp FAQ, and a variety of other resources, at:

http://www.eecs.harvard.edu/onlisp/

The code is also available by anonymous FTP from:

ftp://ftp.eecs.harvard.edu:/pub/onlisp/

Questions and comments can be sent to pg@eecs.harvard.edu.

On Lisp

Throughout this book I've tried to point out the unique qualities that make Lisp Lisp, and the new things that this language will let you do. Macros, for example: Lisp programmers can, and often do, write programs to write their programs for them. Lisp is the only major language in which this is a routinely used technique, because Lisp is the only major language to provide the abstractions that make it convenient. I would like to invite readers who are interested in learning more about macros and other advanced techniques to read the companion volume, *On Lisp*.

Acknowledgements

Of all the friends who have helped me during the writing of this book, I owe special thanks to Robert Morris. The whole book reflects his influence, and is very much the better for it. Several of the examples are derived from programs he originally wrote, including Henley (page 138) and the pattern-matcher on page 249.

I was fortunate to have a first-rate team of technical reviewers: Skona Brittain, John Foderaro, Nick Levine, Peter Norvig, and Dave Touretzky. There is hardly a page of the book that did not benefit in some way from their suggestions. John Foderaro even rewrote some of the code in Section 5.7.

Several other people consented to read all or part of the manuscript, including Ken Anderson, Tom Cheatham, Richard Fateman, Steve Hain, Barry Margolin, Waldo Pacheco, Wheeler Ruml, and Stuart Russell. Ken Anderson and Wheeler Ruml, in particular, made many useful comments.

I'm grateful to Professor Cheatham, and Harvard generally, for providing the facilities used to write this book. Thanks also to the staff at Aiken Lab, including Tony Hartman, Dave Mazieres, Janusz Juda, Harry Bochner, and Joanne Klys.

I'm glad to have had the chance to work with Alan Apt again. The people at Prentice Hall—Alan, Mona Pompili, Shirley McGuire, and Shirley Michaels—are really a pleasure to work with.

The cover is again the work of the incomparable Gino Lee, of the Bow & Arrow Press, Cambridge.

This book was typeset using LaTeX, a language written by Leslie Lamport atop Donald Knuth's TeX, with additional macros by L. A. Carr, Van Jacobson, and Guy Steele. The diagrams were done with Idraw, by John Vlissides and Scott Stanton. The whole was previewed with Ghostview, by Tim Theisen, which is built on Ghostscript, by L. Peter Deutsch.

I owe thanks to many others, including Henry Baker, Kim Barrett, Ingrid Bassett, Trevor Blackwell, Paul Becker, Gary Bisbee, Frank Deutschmann, Frances Dickey, Rich and Scott Draves, Bill Dubuque, Dan Friedman, Jenny

Graham, Alice Hartley, David Hendler, Mike Hewett, Glenn Holloway, Brad Karp, Sonya Keene, Ross Knights, Mutsumi Komuro, Steffi Kutzia, David Kuznick, Madi Lord, Julie Mallozzi, Paul McNamee, Dave Moon, Howard Mullings, Mark Nitzberg, Nancy Parmet and her family, Robert Penny, Mike Plusch, Cheryl Sacks, Hazem Sayed, Shannon Spires, Lou Steinberg, Paul Stoddard, John Stone, Guy Steele, Steve Strassmann, Jim Veitch, Dave Watkins, Idelle and Julian Weber, the Weickers, Dave Yost, and Alan Yuille.

Most of all, I'd like to thank my parents, and Jackie.

Donald Knuth called his classic series *The Art of Computer Programming.* In his Turing Award Lecture, he explained that this title was a conscious choice—that what drew him to programming was "the possibility of writing beautiful programs."

Like architecture, programming has elements of both art and science. A program has to live up to mathematical truth in the same way that a building has to live up to the laws of physics. But the architect's aim is not simply to make a building that doesn't fall down. Almost always the real aim is to make something beautiful.

Many programmers feel, like Donald Knuth, that this is also the real aim of programming. Almost all Lisp hackers do. The spirit of Lisp hacking can be expressed in two sentences. Programming should be fun. Programs should be beautiful. That's the spirit I have tried to convey in this book.

Paul Graham

Contents

ANSI
Common Lisp

1

Introduction

John McCarthy and his students began work on the first Lisp implementation in 1958. After FORTRAN, Lisp is the oldest language still in use.° What's more remarkable is that it is still in the forefront of programming language technology. Programmers who know Lisp will tell you, there is something about this language that sets it apart.

Part of what makes Lisp distinctive is that it is designed to evolve. You can use Lisp to define new Lisp operators. As new abstractions become popular (object-oriented programming, for example), it always turns out to be easy to implement them in Lisp. Like DNA, such a language does not go out of style.

1.1 New Tools

Why learn Lisp? Because it lets you do things that you can't do in other languages. If you just wanted to write a function to return the sum of the numbers less than n, say, it would look much the same in Lisp and C:

```
; Lisp                   /* C */
(defun sum (n)           int sum(int n){
  (let ((s 0))             int i, s = 0;
    (dotimes (i n s)        for(i = 0; i < n; i++)
      (incf s i))))            s += i;
                            return(s);
                         }
```

If you only need to do such simple things, it doesn't really matter which language you use. Suppose instead you want to write a function that takes a

1

number *n*, and returns a function that adds *n* to its argument:

```
; Lisp
(defun addn (n)
  #'(lambda (x)
      (+ x n)))
```

What does addn look like in C? You just can't write it.

You might be wondering, when does one ever want to do things like this? Programming languages teach you not to want what they cannot provide. You have to think in a language to write programs in it, and it's hard to want something you can't describe. When I first started writing programs—in Basic—I didn't miss recursion, because I didn't know there was such a thing. I thought in Basic. I could only conceive of iterative algorithms, so why should I miss recursion?

If you don't miss lexical closures (which is what's being made in the preceding example), take it on faith, for the time being, that Lisp programmers use them all the time. It would be hard to find a Common Lisp program of any length that did not take advantage of closures. By page 112 you will be using them yourself.

And closures are only one of the abstractions we don't find in other languages. Another unique feature of Lisp, possibly even more valuable, is that Lisp programs are expressed as Lisp data structures. This means that you can write programs that write programs. Do people actually *want* to do this? Yes—they're called macros, and again, experienced programmers use them all the time. By page 173 you will be able to write your own.

With macros, closures, and run-time typing, Lisp transcends object-oriented programming. If you understood the preceding sentence, you probably should not be reading this book. You would have to know Lisp pretty well to see why it's true. But it is not just words. It is an important point, and the proof of it is made quite explicit, in code, in Chapter 17.

Chapters 2–13 will gradually introduce all the concepts that you'll need in order to understand the code in Chapter 17. The reward for your efforts will be an equivocal one: you will feel as suffocated programming in C++ as an experienced C++ programmer would feel programming in Basic. It's more encouraging, perhaps, if we think about where this feeling comes from. Basic is suffocating to someone used to C++ because an experienced C++ programmer knows techniques that are impossible to express in Basic. Likewise, learning Lisp will teach you more than just a new language—it will teach you new and more powerful ways of thinking about programs.

1.2 New Techniques

As the preceding section explained, Lisp gives you tools that other languages don't provide. But there is more to the story than this. Taken separately, the new things that come with Lisp—automatic memory management, manifest typing, closures, and so on—each make programming that much easier. Taken together, they form a critical mass that makes possible a new way of programming.

Lisp is designed to be extensible: it lets you define new operators yourself. This is possible because the Lisp language is made out of the same functions and macros as your own programs. So it's no more difficult to extend Lisp than to write a program in it. In fact, it's so easy (and so useful) that extending the language is standard practice. As you're writing your program down toward the language, you build the language up toward your program. You work bottom-up, as well as top-down.

Almost any program can benefit from having the language tailored to suit its needs, but the more complex the program, the more valuable bottom-up programming becomes. A bottom-up program can be written as a series of layers, each one acting as a sort of programming language for the one above. TEX was one of the earliest programs to be written this way. You can write programs bottom-up in any language, but Lisp is far the most natural vehicle for this style.

Bottom-up programming leads naturally to extensible software. If you take the principle of bottom-up programming all the way to the topmost layer of your program, then that layer becomes a programming language for the user. Because the idea of extensibility is so deeply rooted in Lisp, it makes the ideal language for writing extensible software. Three of the most successful programs of the 1980s provide Lisp as an extension language: Gnu Emacs, Autocad, and Interleaf.

Working bottom-up is also the best way to get reusable software. The essence of writing reusable software is to separate the general from the specific, and bottom-up programming inherently creates such a separation. Instead of devoting all your effort to writing a single, monolithic application, you devote part of your effort to building a language, and part to writing a (proportionately smaller) application on top of it. What's specific to this application will be concentrated in the topmost layer. The layers beneath will form a language for writing applications like this one—and what could be more reusable than a programming language?

Lisp allows you not just to write more sophisticated programs, but to write them faster. Lisp programs tend to be short—the language gives you bigger concepts, so you don't have to use as many. As Frederick Brooks has pointed out, the time it takes to write a program depends mostly on its length.° So this fact alone means that Lisp programs take less time to write. The effect is

amplified by Lisp's dynamic character: in Lisp the edit-compile-test cycle is
so short that programming is real-time.

Bigger abstractions and an interactive environment can change the way
organizations develop software. The phrase *rapid prototyping* describes a
kind of programming that began with Lisp: in Lisp, you can often write a
prototype in less time than it would take to write the spec for one. What's
more, such a prototype can be so abstract that it makes a better spec than one
written in English. And Lisp allows you to make a smooth transition from
prototype to production software. When Common Lisp programs are written
with an eye to speed and compiled by modern compilers, they run as fast as
programs written in any other high-level language.

Unless you already know Lisp quite well, this introduction may seem a
collection of grand and possibly meaningless claims. Lisp transcends object-
oriented programming? You build the language up toward your programs?
Lisp programming is real-time? What can such statements mean? At the
moment, these claims are like empty lakes. As you learn more of the actual
features of Lisp, and see examples of working programs, they will fill with
real experience and take on a definite shape.

1.3   A New Approach

One of the aims of this book is to explain not just the Lisp language, but the
new approach to programming that Lisp makes possible. This approach is one
that you will see more of in the future. As programming environments grow
in power, and languages become more abstract, the Lisp style of programming
is gradually replacing the old plan-and-implement model.

In the old model, bugs are never supposed to happen. Thorough specifications, painstakingly worked out in advance, are supposed to ensure that
programs work perfectly. Sounds good in theory. Unfortunately, the specifications are both written and implemented by humans. The result, in practice,
is that the plan-and-implement method does not work very well.

As manager of the OS/360 project, Frederick Brooks was well acquainted
with the traditional approach. He was also acquainted with its results:

> Any OS/360 user is quickly aware of how much better it should
> be... Furthermore, the product was late, it took more memory
> than planned, the costs were several times the estimate, and it
> did not perform very well until several releases after the first.°

And this is a description of one of the most successful systems of its era.

The problem with the old model was that it ignored human limitations. In
the old model, you are betting that specifications won't contain serious flaws,
and that implementing them will be a simple matter of translating them into

code. Experience has shown this to be a very bad bet indeed. It would be safer to bet that specifications will be misguided, and that code will be full of bugs.

This is just what the new model of programming does assume. Instead of hoping that people won't make mistakes, it tries to make the cost of mistakes very low. The cost of a mistake is the time required to correct it. With powerful languages and good programming environments, this cost can be greatly reduced. Programming style can then depend less on planning and more on exploration.

Planning is a necessary evil. It is a response to risk: the more dangerous an undertaking, the more important it is to plan ahead. Powerful tools decrease risk, and so decrease the need for planning. The design of your program can then benefit from what is probably the most useful source of information available: the experience of implementing it.

Lisp style has been evolving in this direction since the 1960s. You can write prototypes so quickly in Lisp that you can go through several iterations of design and implementation before you would, in the old model, have even finished writing out the specifications. You don't have to worry so much about design flaws, because you discover them a lot sooner. Nor do you have to worry so much about bugs. When you program in a functional style, bugs can only have a local effect. When you use a very abstract language, some bugs (e.g. dangling pointers) are no longer possible, and what remain are easy to find, because your programs are so much shorter. And when you have an interactive environment, you can correct bugs instantly, instead of enduring a long cycle of editing, compiling, and testing.

Lisp style has evolved this way because it yields results. Strange as it sounds, less planning can mean better design. The history of technology is full of parallel cases. A similar change took place in painting during the fifteenth century. Before oil paint became popular, painters used a medium, called *tempera*, that cannot be blended or overpainted. The cost of mistakes was high, and this tended to make painters conservative. Then came oil paint, and with it a great change in style. Oil "allows for second thoughts."° This proved a decisive advantage in dealing with difficult subjects like the human figure.

The new medium did not just make painters' lives easier. It made possible a new and more ambitious kind of painting. Janson writes:

> Without oil, the Flemish Masters' conquest of visible reality would have been much more limited. Thus, from a technical point of view, too, they deserve to be called the "fathers of modern painting," for oil has been the painter's basic medium ever since.°

As a material, tempera is no less beautiful than oil. But the flexibility of oil
paint gives greater scope to the imagination—that was the deciding factor.

Programming is now undergoing a similar change. The new medium is
the "object-oriented dynamic language"—in a word, Lisp. This is not to
say that all our software is going to be written in Lisp within a few years.
The transition from tempera to oil did not happen overnight; at first, oil was
only popular in the leading art centers, and was often used in combination
with tempera. We seem to be in this phase now. Lisp is used in universities,
research labs, and a few leading-edge companies. Meanwhile, ideas borrowed
from Lisp increasingly turn up in the mainstream: interactive programming
environments, garbage collection, and run-time typing, to name a few.

More powerful tools are taking the risk out of exploration. That's good
news for programmers, because it means that we will be able to undertake
more ambitious projects. The use of oil paint certainly had this effect. The
period immediately following its adoption was a golden age for painting.
There are signs already that something similar is happening in programming.

2

Welcome to Lisp

This chapter aims to get you programming as soon as possible. By the end of it you will know enough Common Lisp to begin writing programs.

2.1 Form

It is particularly true of Lisp that you learn it by using it, because Lisp is an interactive language. Any Lisp system will include an interactive front-end called the *toplevel*. You type Lisp expressions into the toplevel, and the system displays their values.

Lisp usually displays a prompt to tell you that it's waiting for you to type something. Many implementations of Common Lisp use > as the toplevel prompt. That's what we'll use here.

One of the simplest kinds of Lisp expression is an integer. If we enter 1 after the prompt,

```
> 1
1
>
```

the system will print its value, followed by another prompt, to say that it's ready for more.

In this case, the value displayed is the same as what we typed. A number like 1 is said to evaluate to itself. Life gets more interesting when we enter expressions that take some work to evaluate. For example, if we want to add two numbers together, we type something like:

7

```
> (+ 2 3)
5
```

In the expression (+ 2 3), the + is called the *operator*, and the numbers 2 and 3 are called the *arguments*.

In everyday life, we would write this expression as 2 + 3, but in Lisp we put the + operator first, followed by the arguments, with the whole expression enclosed in a pair of parentheses: (+ 2 3). This is called *prefix* notation, because the operator comes first. It may at first seem a strange way to write expressions, but in fact this notation is one of the best things about Lisp.

For example, if we want to add three numbers together, in ordinary notation we have to use + twice,

```
2 + 3 + 4
```

while in Lisp we just add another argument:

```
(+ 2 3 4)
```

The way we ordinarily use +, it must have exactly two arguments: one on the left and one on the right. The flexibility of prefix notation means that, in Lisp, + can take any number of arguments, including none:

```
> (+)
0
> (+ 2)
2
> (+ 2 3)
5
> (+ 2 3 4)
9
> (+ 2 3 4 5)
14
```

Because operators can take varying numbers of arguments, we need parentheses to show where an expression begins and ends.

Expressions can be nested. That is, the arguments in an expression may themselves be complex expressions:

```
> (/ (- 7 1) (- 4 2))
3
```

In English, this is seven minus one, divided by four minus two.

Another beauty of Lisp notation is: this is all there is. All Lisp expressions are either *atoms*, like 1, or *lists*, which consist of zero or more expressions enclosed in parentheses. These are valid Lisp expressions:

2   (+ 2 3)   (+ 2 3 4)   (/ (- 7 1) (- 4 2))

As we will see, all Lisp code takes this form. A language like C has a more complicated syntax: arithmetic expressions use infix notation; function calls use a sort of prefix notation, with the arguments delimited by commas; expressions are delimited by semicolons; and blocks of code are delimited by curly brackets. In Lisp, we use a single notation to express all these ideas.

2.2 Evaluation

In the previous section, we typed expressions into the toplevel, and Lisp displayed their values. In this section we take a closer look at how expressions are evaluated.

In Lisp, + is a function, and an expression like (+ 2 3) is a function call. When Lisp evaluates a function call, it does so in two steps:

1. First the arguments are evaluated, from left to right. In this case, each argument evaluates to itself, so the values of the arguments are 2 and 3, respectively.

2. The values of the arguments are passed to the function named by the operator. In this case, it is the + function, which returns 5.

If any of the arguments are themselves function calls, they are evaluated according to the same rules. So when (/ (- 7 1) (- 4 2)) is evaluated, this is what happens:

1. Lisp evaluates (- 7 1): 7 evaluates to 7 and 1 evaluates to 1. These values are passed to the function -, which returns 6.

2. Lisp evaluates (- 4 2): 4 evaluates to 4 and 2 evaluates to 2. These values are passed to the function -, which returns 2.

3. The values 6 and 2 are sent to the function /, which returns 3.

Not all the operators in Common Lisp are functions, but most are. And function calls are always evaluated this way. The arguments are evaluated left-to-right, and their values are passed to the function, which returns the value of the expression as a whole. This is called the *evaluation rule* for Common Lisp.

GETTING OUT OF TROUBLE

If you type something that Lisp can't understand, it will display an error
message and put you into a version of the toplevel called a *break loop*.
The break loop gives experienced programmers a chance to figure out what
caused an error, but initially the only thing you will want to do in a break
loop is get out of it. What you have to type to get back to the toplevel
depends on your implementation of Common Lisp. In this hypothetical
implementation, :abort does it:

```
> (/ 1 0)
Error: Division by zero.
        Options: :abort, :backtrace
>> :abort
>
```

Appendix A shows how to debug Lisp programs, and gives examples of
some of the most common errors.

One operator that doesn't follow the Common Lisp evaluation rule is
quote. The quote operator is a *special operator*, meaning that it has a
distinct evaluation rule of its own. And the rule is: do nothing. The quote
operator takes a single argument, and just returns it verbatim:

```
> (quote (+ 3 5))
(+ 3 5)
```

For convenience, Common Lisp defines ' as an abbreviation for quote.
You can get the effect of calling quote by affixing a ' to the front of any
expression:

```
> '(+ 3 5)
(+ 3 5)
```

It is much more common to use the abbreviation than to write out the whole
quote expression.

Lisp provides the quote as a way of *protecting* expressions from evaluation. The next section will explain how such protection can be useful.

2.3   Data

Lisp offers all the data types we find in most other languages, along with
several others that we don't. One data type we have used already is the

integer, which is written as a series of digits: 256. Another data type Lisp
has in common with most other languages is the *string,* which is represented
as a series of characters surrounded by double-quotes: `"ora et labora"`.
Integers and strings both evaluate to themselves.

Two Lisp data types that we don't commonly find in other languages
are symbols and lists. *Symbols* are words. Ordinarily they are converted to
uppercase, regardless of how you type them:

```
> 'Artichoke
ARTICHOKE
```

Symbols do not (usually) evaluate to themselves, so if you want to refer to a
symbol, you should quote it, as above.

Lists are represented as zero or more elements enclosed in parentheses.
The elements can be of any type, including lists. You have to quote lists, or
Lisp would take them for function calls:

```
> '(my 3 "Sons")
(MY 3 "Sons")
> '(the list (a b c) has 3 elements)
(THE LIST (A B C) HAS 3 ELEMENTS)
```

Notice that one quote protects a whole expression, including expressions
within it.

You can build lists by calling `list`. Since `list` is a function, its arguments
are evaluated. Here we see a call to + within a call to `list`:

```
> (list 'my (+ 2 1) "Sons")
(MY 3 "Sons")
```

We are now in a position to appreciate one of the most remarkable features
of Lisp. *Lisp programs are expressed as lists.* If the arguments of flexibility
and elegance did not convince you that Lisp notation is a valuable tool, this
point should. It means that Lisp programs can generate Lisp code. Lisp
programmers can (and often do) write programs to write their programs for
them.

Such programs are not considered till Chapter 10, but it is important even
at this stage to understand the relation between expressions and lists, if only
to avoid being confused by it. This is why we need the quote. If a list is
quoted, evaluation returns the list itself; if it is not quoted, the list is treated
as code, and evaluation returns its value:

```
> (list '(+ 2 1) (+ 2 1))
((+ 2 1) 3)
```

Here the first argument is quoted, and so yields a list. The second argument is not quoted, and is treated as a function call, yielding a number.

In Common Lisp, there are two ways of representing the empty list. You can represent it as a pair of parentheses with nothing between them, or you can use the symbol nil. It doesn't matter which way you write the empty list, but it will be displayed as nil:

```
> ()
NIL
> nil
NIL
```

You don't have to quote nil (though it wouldn't hurt) because nil evaluates to itself.

2.4 List Operations

The function cons builds lists. If its second argument is a list, it returns a new list with the first argument added to the front:

```
> (cons 'a '(b c d))
(A B C D)
```

We can build up lists by consing new elements onto an empty list. The list function that we saw in the previous section is just a more convenient way of consing several things onto nil:

```
> (cons 'a (cons 'b nil))
(A B)
> (list 'a 'b)
(A B)
```

The primitive functions for extracting the elements of lists are car and cdr.° The car of a list is the first element, and the cdr is everything after the first element:

```
> (car '(a b c))
A
> (cdr '(a b c))
(B C)
```

You can use combinations of car and cdr to reach any element of a list. If you want to get the third element, you could say:

```
> (car (cdr (cdr '(a b c d))))
C
```

However, you can do the same thing more easily by calling `third`:

```
> (third '(a b c d))
C
```

2.5   Truth

In Common Lisp, the symbol t is the default representation for truth. Like
nil, t evaluates to itself. The function `listp` returns true if its argument is
a list:

```
> (listp '(a b c))
T
```

A function whose return value is intended to be interpreted as truth or falsity
is called a *predicate*. Common Lisp predicates often have names that end
with p.

Falsity in Common Lisp is represented by `nil`, the empty list. If we give
`listp` an argument that isn't a list, it returns `nil`:

```
> (listp 27)
NIL
```

Because `nil` plays two roles in Common Lisp, the function `null`, which
returns true of the empty list,

```
> (null nil)
T
```

and the function `not`, which returns true if its argument is false,

```
> (not nil)
T
```

do exactly the same thing.

The simplest conditional in Common Lisp is `if`. It usually takes three
arguments: a *test* expression, a *then* expression, and an *else* expression. The
test expression is evaluated. If it returns true, the *then* expression is evaluated
and its value is returned. If the *test* expression returns false, the *else* expression
is evaluated and its value is returned:

```
> (if (listp '(a b c))
      (+ 1 2)
      (+ 5 6))
3
> (if (listp 27)
      (+ 1 2)
      (+ 5 6))
11
```

Like quote, if is a special operator. It could not possibly be implemented as a function, because the arguments in a function call are always evaluated, and the whole point of if is that only one of the last two arguments is evaluated.

The last argument to if is optional. If you omit it, it defaults to nil:

```
> (if (listp 27)
      (+ 2 3))
NIL
```

Although t is the default representation for truth, everything except nil also counts as true in a logical context:

```
> (if 27 1 2)
1
```

The logical operators and and or resemble conditionals. Both take any number of arguments, but only evaluate as many as they need to in order to decide what to return. If all its arguments are true (that is, not nil), then and returns the value of the last one:

```
> (and t (+ 1 2))
3
```

But if one of the arguments turns out to be false, none of the arguments after that get evaluated. Similarly for or, which stops as soon as it finds an argument that is true.

These two operators are *macros*. Like special operators, macros can circumvent the usual evaluation rule. Chapter 10 explains how to write macros of your own.

2.6   Functions

You can define new functions with defun. It usually takes three or more arguments: a name, a list of parameters, and one or more expressions that will make up the body of the function. Here is how we might define third:

```
> (defun our-third (x)
    (car (cdr (cdr x))))
OUR-THIRD
```

The first argument says that the name of this function will be our-third. The second argument, the list (x), says that the function will take exactly one argument: x. A symbol used as a placeholder in this way is called a *variable*. When the variable represents an argument to a function, as x does, it is also called a *parameter.*

The rest of the definition, (car (cdr (cdr x))), is known as the *body* of the function. It tells Lisp what it has to do to calculate the return value of the function. So a call to our-third returns (car (cdr (cdr x))), for whatever x we give as the argument:

```
> (our-third '(a b c d))
C
```

Now that we've seen variables, it's easier to understand what symbols are. They are variable names, existing as objects in their own right. And that's why symbols, like lists, have to be quoted. A list has to be quoted because otherwise it will be treated as code; a symbol has to be quoted because otherwise it will be treated as a variable.

You can think of a function definition as a generalized version of a Lisp expression. The following expression tests whether the sum of 1 and 4 is greater than 3:

```
> (> (+ 1 4) 3)
T
```

By replacing these particular numbers with variables, we can write a function that will test whether the sum of any two numbers is greater than a third:

```
> (defun sum-greater (x y z)
    (> (+ x y) z))
SUM-GREATER
> (sum-greater 1 4 3)
T
```

Lisp makes no distinction between a program, a procedure, and a function. Functions do for everything (and indeed, make up most of the language itself). If you want to consider one of your functions as the *main* function, you can, but you will ordinarily be able to call any function from the toplevel. Among other things, this means that you will be able to test your programs piece by piece as you write them.

2.7   Recursion

The functions we defined in the previous section called other functions to do some of their work for them. For example, sum-greater called + and >. A function can call any function, including itself.

A function that calls itself is *recursive*. The Common Lisp function member tests whether something is an element of a list. Here is a simplified version defined as a recursive function:

```
(defun our-member (obj lst)
  (if (null lst)
      nil
      (if (eql (car lst) obj)
          lst
          (our-member obj (cdr lst)))))
```

The predicate eql tests whether its two arguments are identical; aside from that, everything in this definition is something we have seen before. Here it is in action:

```
> (our-member 'b '(a b c))
(B C)
> (our-member 'z '(a b c))
NIL
```

The definition of our-member corresponds to the following English description. To test whether an object obj is a member of a list lst, we

1. First check whether lst is empty. If it is, then obj is clearly not a member of it, and we're done.

2. Otherwise, if obj is the first element of lst, it is a member.

3. Otherwise obj is only a member of lst if it is a member of the rest of lst.

When you want to understand how a recursive function works, it can help to translate it into a description of this kind.

Many people find recursion difficult to understand at first. A lot of the difficulty comes from using a mistaken metaphor for functions. There is a tendency to think of a function as a sort of machine. Raw materials arrive as parameters; some of the work is farmed out to other functions; finally the finished product is assembled and shipped out as the return value. If we use this metaphor for functions, recursion becomes a paradox. How can a machine farm out work to itself? It is already busy.

A better metaphor for a function would be to think of it as a *process* one goes through. Recursion is natural in a process. We often see recursive processes in everyday life. For example, suppose a historian was interested in population changes in European history. The process of examining a document might be as follows:

1. Get a copy of the document.

2. Look for information relating to population changes.

3. If the document mentions any other documents that might be useful, examine them.

This process is easy enough to understand, yet it is recursive, because the third step could entail one or more applications of the same process.

So don't think of our-member as a machine that tests whether something is in a list. Think of it instead as the rules for determining whether something is in a list. If we think of functions in this light, the paradox of recursion disappears.°

2.8 Reading Lisp

The pseudo-member defined in the preceding section ends with five parentheses. More elaborate function definitions might end with seven or eight. People who are just learning Lisp find the sight of so many parentheses discouraging. How is one to read, let alone write, such code? How is one to see which parenthesis matches which?

The answer is, one doesn't have to. Lisp programmers read and write code by indentation, not by parentheses. When they're writing code, they let the text editor show which parenthesis matches which. Any good editor, particularly if it comes with a Lisp system, should be able to do paren-matching. In such an editor, when you type a parenthesis, the editor indicates the matching one. If your editor doesn't match parentheses, stop now and figure out how to make it, because it is virtually impossible to write Lisp code without it.[1]

With a good editor, matching parentheses ceases to be an issue when you're writing code. And because there are universal conventions for Lisp indentation, it's not an issue when you're reading code either. Because everyone uses the same conventions, you can read code by the indentation, and ignore the parentheses.

Any Lisp hacker, however experienced, would find it difficult to read the definition of our-member if it looked like this:

---

[1] In vi, you can turn on paren-matching with :set sm. In Emacs, M-x lisp-mode is a good way to get it.

```
(defun our-member (obj lst) (if (null lst) nil (if
(eql (car lst) obj) lst (our-member obj (cdr lst)))))
```

But when the code is properly indented, one has no trouble. You could omit most of the parentheses and still read it:

```
defun our-member (obj lst)
  if null lst
    nil
    if eql (car lst) obj
      lst
      our-member obj (cdr lst)
```

Indeed, this is a practical approach when you're writing code on paper. Later, when you type it in, you can take advantage of paren-matching in the editor.

2.9   Input and Output

So far we have done I/O implicitly, by taking advantage of the toplevel. For real interactive programs this is not likely to be enough. In this section we look at a few functions for input and output.

The most general output function in Common Lisp is format. It takes two or more arguments: the first indicates where the output is to be printed, the second is a string template, and the remaining arguments are usually objects whose printed representations are to be inserted into the template. Here is a typical example:

```
> (format t "~A plus ~A equals ~A.~%" 2 3 (+ 2 3))
2 plus 3 equals 5.
NIL
```

Notice that two things get displayed here. The first line is displayed by format. The second line is the value returned by the call to format, displayed in the usual way by the toplevel. Ordinarily a function like format is not called directly from the toplevel, but used within programs, so the return value is never seen.

The first argument to format, t, indicates that the output is to be sent to the default place. Ordinarily this will be the toplevel. The second argument is a string that serves as a template for output. Within this string, each ~A indicates a position to be filled, and the ~% indicates a newline. The positions are filled by the values of the remaining arguments, in order.

The standard function for input is read. When given no arguments, it reads from the default place, which will usually be the toplevel. Here is a function that prompts the user for input, and returns whatever is entered:

```
(defun askem (string)
  (format t "~A" string)
  (read))
```

It behaves as follows:

```
> (askem "How old are you? ")
How old are you? 29
29
```

Bear in mind that `read` will sit waiting indefinitely until you type something and (usually) hit return. So it's unwise to call `read` without printing an explicit prompt, or your program may give the impression that it is stuck, while in fact it's just waiting for input.

The second thing to know about `read` is that it is very powerful: `read` is a complete Lisp parser. It doesn't just read characters and return them as a string. It parses what it reads, and returns the Lisp object that results. In the case above, it returned a number.

Short as it is, the definition of `askem` shows something we haven't seen before in a function. Its body contains more than one expression. The body of a function can have any number of expressions. When the function is called, they will be evaluated in order, and the function will return the value of the last one.

In all the sections before this, we kept to what is called "pure" Lisp—that is, Lisp without side-effects. A side-effect is some change to the state of the world that happens as a consequence of evaluating an expression. When we evaluate a pure Lisp expression like (+ 1 2), there are no side-effects; it just returns a value. But when we call `format`, as well as returning a value, it prints something. That's one kind of side-effect.

When we are writing code without side-effects, there is no point in defining functions with bodies of more than one expression. The value of the last expression is returned as the value of the function, but the values of any preceding expressions are thrown away. If such expressions didn't have side-effects, you would have no way of telling whether Lisp bothered to evaluate them at all.

2.10 Variables

One of the most frequently used operators in Common Lisp is `let`, which allows you to introduce new local variables:

```
> (let ((x 1) (y 2))
    (+ x y))
3
```

A let expression has two parts. First comes a list of instructions for creating variables, each of the form (*variable expression*). Each *variable* will initially be set to the value of the corresponding *expression*. So in the example above, we create two new variables, x and y, which are initially set to 1 and 2, respectively. These variables are valid within the body of the let.

After the list of variables and values comes a body of expressions, which are evaluated in order. In this case there is only one, a call to +. The value of the last expression is returned as the value of the let. Here is an example of a more selective version of askem written using let:

```
(defun ask-number ()
  (format t "Please enter a number. ")
  (let ((val (read)))
    (if (numberp val)
        val
        (ask-number))))
```

This function creates a variable val to hold the object returned by read. Because it has a handle on this object, the function can look at what you entered before deciding whether or not to return it. As you probably guessed, numberp is a predicate that tests whether its argument is a number.

If the value entered by the user isn't a number, ask-number calls itself. The result is a function that insists on getting a number:

```
> (ask-number)
Please enter a number. a
Please enter a number. (ho hum)
Please enter a number. 52
52
```

Variables like those we have seen so far are called *local* variables. They are only valid within a certain context. There is another kind of variable, called a *global* variable, that can be visible everywhere.[2]

You can create a global variable by giving a symbol and a value to defparameter:

```
> (defparameter *glob* 99)
*GLOB*
```

Such a variable will then be accessible everywhere, except in expressions that create a new local variable with the same name. To avoid the possibility of this happening by accident, it's conventional to give global variables names

---

[2]The real distinction here is between lexical and special variables, but we will not need to consider this until Chapter 6.

that begin and end with asterisks. The name of the variable we just created would be pronounced "star-glob-star".

You can also define global constants, by calling defconstant:

```
(defconstant limit (+ *glob* 1))
```

There is no need to give constants distinctive names, because it will cause an error if anyone uses the same name for a variable. If you want to check whether some symbol is the name of a global variable or constant, use boundp:

```
> (boundp '*glob*)
T
```

2.11   Assignment

In Common Lisp the most general assignment operator is setf. We can use it to do assignments to either kind of variable:

```
> (setf *glob* 98)
98
> (let ((n 10))
    (setf n 2)
    n)
2
```

When the first argument to setf is a symbol that is not the name of a local variable, it is taken to be a global variable:

```
> (setf x (list 'a 'b 'c))
(A B C)
```

That is, you can create global variables implicitly, just by assigning them values. In source files, at least, it is better style to use explicit defparameters.

You can do more than just assign values to variables. The first argument to setf can be an expression as well as a variable name. In such cases, the value of the second argument is inserted in the *place* referred to by the first:

```
> (setf (car x) 'n)
N
> x
(N B C)
```

The first argument to setf can be almost any expression that refers to a particular place. All such operators are marked as "settable" in Appendix D.

You can give any (even) number of arguments to `setf`. An expression of the form

```
(setf a b
      c d
      e f)
```

is equivalent to three separate calls to `setf` in sequence:

```
(setf a b)
(setf c d)
(setf e f)
```

2.12   Functional Programming

Functional programming means writing programs that work by returning values, instead of by modifying things. It is the dominant paradigm in Lisp. Most built-in Lisp functions are meant to be called for the values they return, not for side-effects.

The function `remove`, for example, takes an object and a list and returns a new list containing everything but that object:

```
> (setf lst '(c a r a t))
(C A R A T)
> (remove 'a lst)
(C R T)
```

Why not just say that `remove` removes an object from a list? Because that's not what it does. The original list is untouched afterwards:

```
> lst
(C A R A T)
```

So what if you really do want to remove something from a list? In Lisp you generally do such things by passing the list as an argument to some function, and using `setf` with the return value. To remove all the as from a list x, we say:

```
(setf x (remove 'a x))
```

Functional programming means, essentially, avoiding `setf` and things like it. At first sight it may be difficult to imagine how this is even possible, let alone desirable. How can one build programs just by returning values?

It would be inconvenient to do without side-effects entirely. However, as you read further, you may be surprised to discover how few you really need. And the more side-effects you do without, the better off you'll be.

One of the most important advantages of functional programming is that it allows *interactive testing*. In purely functional code, you can test each function as you write it. If it returns the values you expect, you can be confident that it is correct. The added confidence, in the aggregate, makes a huge difference. You have instant turnaround when you make changes anywhere in a program. And this instant turnaround enables a whole new style of programming, much as the telephone, as compared to letters, enabled a new style of communication.

2.13 Iteration

When we want to do something repeatedly, it is sometimes more natural to use iteration than recursion. A typical case for iteration is to generate some sort of table. This function

```
(defun show-squares (start end)
  (do ((i start (+ i 1)))
      ((> i end) 'done)
    (format t "~A ~A~%" i (* i i))))
```

prints out the squares of the integers from start to end:

```
> (show-squares 2 5)
2 4
3 9
4 16
5 25
DONE
```

The do macro is the fundamental iteration operator in Common Lisp. Like let, do can create variables, and the first argument is a list of variable specifications. Each element of this list can be of the form

(*variable initial update*)

where *variable* is a symbol, and *initial* and *update* are expressions. Initially each *variable* will be set to the value of the corresponding *initial*; on each iteration it will be set to the value of the corresponding *update*. The do in show-squares creates just one variable, i. On the first iteration i will be set to the value of start, and on successive iterations its value will be incremented by one.

The second argument to do should be a list containing one or more expressions. The first expression is used to test whether iteration should stop. In the case above, the test expression is (> i end). The remaining expressions in this list will be evaluated in order when iteration stops, and the value of the last will be returned as the value of the do. So show-squares will always return done.

The remaining arguments to do comprise the body of the loop. They will be evaluated, in order, on each iteration. On each iteration the variables are updated, then the termination test is evaluated, and then (if the test failed) the body is evaluated.

For comparison, here is a recursive version of show-squares:

```
(defun show-squares (i end)
  (if (> i end)
      'done
      (progn
        (format t "~A ~A~%" i (* i i))
        (show-squares (+ i 1) end))))
```

The only thing new in this function is progn. It takes any number of expressions, evaluates them in order, and returns the value of the last.

Common Lisp has simpler iteration operators for special cases. To iterate through the elements of a list, for example, you would be more likely to use dolist. Here is a function that returns the length of a list:

```
(defun our-length (lst)
  (let ((len 0))
    (dolist (obj lst)
      (setf len (+ len 1)))
    len))
```

Here dolist takes an argument of the form (*variable expression*), followed by a body of expressions. The body will be evaluated with *variable* bound to successive elements of the list returned by *expression*. So the loop above says, for each obj in lst, increment len.

The obvious recursive version of this function would be:

```
(defun our-length (lst)
  (if (null lst)
      0
      (+ (our-length (cdr lst)) 1)))
```

Or, if the list is empty, its length is zero; otherwise it is the length of the cdr plus one. This version of our-length is cleaner, but because it's not tail-recursive (Section 13.2), it won't be as efficient.

2.14   Functions as Objects

In Lisp, functions are regular objects, like symbols or strings or lists. If we give the name of a function to `function`, it will return the associated object. Like `quote`, `function` is a special operator, so we don't have to quote the argument:

```
> (function +)
#<Compiled-Function + 17BA4E>
```

This strange-looking return value is the way a function might be displayed in a typical Common Lisp implementation.

    Until now we have only dealt with objects that look the same when Lisp displays them as when we typed them in. This convention does not apply to functions. Internally, a built-in function like + is likely to be a segment of machine language code. A Common Lisp implementation may choose whatever external representation it likes.

    Just as we can use ' as an abbreviation for `quote`, we can use #' as an abbreviation for `function`:

```
> #'+
#<Compiled-Function + 17BA4E>
```

This abbreviation is known as sharp-quote.

    Like any other kind of object, we can pass functions as arguments. One function that takes a function as an argument is `apply`. It takes a function and a list of arguments for it, and returns the result of applying the function to the arguments:

```
> (apply #'+ '(1 2 3))
6
> (+ 1 2 3)
6
```

It can be given any number of arguments, so long as the last is a list:

```
> (apply #'+ 1 2 '(3 4 5))
15
```

The function `funcall` does the same thing but does not need the arguments to be packaged in a list:

```
> (funcall #'+ 1 2 3)
6
```

WHAT IS LAMBDA?

The `lambda` in a lambda expression is not an operator. It is just a symbol.°
In earlier dialects of Lisp it had a purpose: functions were represented
internally as lists, and the only way to tell a function from an ordinary list
was to check if the first element was the symbol `lambda`.
In Common Lisp, you can express functions as lists, but they are represented internally as distinct function objects. So `lambda` is no longer really
necessary. There would be no inconsistency in requiring that functions be
denoted as

```
((x) (+ x 100))
```

instead of

```
(lambda (x) (+ x 100))
```

but Lisp programmers were used to beginning functions with the symbol
`lambda`, so Common Lisp retained it for the sake of tradition.

The `defun` macro creates a function and gives it a name. But functions
don't have to have names, and we don't need `defun` to define them. Like
most other kinds of Lisp objects, we can refer to functions literally.

To refer literally to an integer, we use a series of digits; to refer literally to
a function, we use what's called a *lambda expression*. A lambda expression
is a list containing the symbol `lambda`, followed by a list of parameters,
followed by a *body* of zero or more expressions.

Here is a lambda expression representing a function that takes two numbers and returns their sum:

```
(lambda (x y)
  (+ x y))
```

The list (x y) is the parameter list, and after it comes the body of the function.

A lambda expression can be considered as the name of a function. Like
an ordinary function name, a lambda expression can be the first element of a
function call,

```
> ((lambda (x) (+ x 100)) 1)
101
```

and by affixing a sharp-quote to a lambda expression, we get the corresponding
function,

```
> (funcall #'(lambda (x) (+ x 100))
           1)
101
```

Among other things, this notation allows us to use functions without naming them.

2.15   Types

Lisp has an unusually flexible approach to types. In many languages, variables are what have types, and you can't use a variable without specifying its type. In Common Lisp, values have types, not variables. You could imagine that every object had a label attached to it, identifying its type. This approach is called *manifest typing*. You don't have to declare the types of variables, because any variable can hold objects of any type.

Though type declarations are never required, you may want to make them for reasons of efficiency. Type declarations are discussed in Section 13.3.

The built-in Common Lisp types form a hierarchy of subtypes and super-types. An object always has more than one type. For example, the number 27 is of type fixnum, integer, rational, real, number, atom, and t, in order of increasing generality. (Numeric types are discussed in Chapter 9.) The type t is the supertype of all types, so everything is of type t.

The function typep takes an object and a type specifier, and returns true if the object is of that type:

```
> (typep 27 'integer)
T
```

We will mention the various built-in types as we encounter them.

2.16   Looking Forward

In this chapter we have barely scratched the surface of Lisp. And yet a portrait of a very unusual language is beginning to emerge. To start with, the language has a single syntax to express all program structure. This syntax is based on the list, which is a kind of Lisp object. Functions, which are Lisp objects in their own right, can be expressed as lists. And Lisp is itself a Lisp program, made almost entirely of Lisp functions no different from the ones you can define yourself.

Don't worry if the relations between all these ideas are not entirely clear. Lisp introduces so many novel concepts that it takes some time to get used to all the new things you can do with it. One thing should be clear at least: there are some startlingly elegant ideas here.

Richard Gabriel once half-jokingly described C as a language for writing Unix.° We could likewise describe Lisp as a language for writing Lisp. But this is a different kind of statement. A language that can be written in itself is fundamentally different from a language good for writing some particular class of applications. It opens up a new way of programming: as well as writing your program in the language, you can improve the language to suit your program. If you want to understand the essence of Lisp programming, this idea is a good place to begin.

Summary

1. Lisp is an interactive language. If you type an expression into the toplevel, Lisp will display its value.

2. Lisp programs consist of expressions. An expression can be an atom, or a list of an operator followed by zero or more arguments. Prefix syntax means that operators can take any number of arguments.

3. The evaluation rule for Common Lisp function calls: evaluate the arguments left to right, and pass them to the function denoted by the operator. The `quote` operator has its own evaluation rule, which is to return the argument unchanged.

4. Along with the usual data types, Lisp has symbols and lists. Because Lisp programs are expressed as lists, it's easy to write programs that write programs.

5. The three basic list functions are `cons`, which builds a list; `car`, which returns the first element; and `cdr`, which returns everything after the first element.

6. In Common Lisp, `t` represents true and `nil` represents false. In a logical context, anything except `nil` counts as true. The basic conditional is `if`. The `and` and `or` operators resemble conditionals.

7. Lisp consists mainly of functions. You can define new ones with `defun`.

8. A function that calls itself is recursive. A recursive function should be considered as a process rather than a machine.

9. Parentheses are not an issue, because programmers read and write Lisp by indentation.

10. The basic I/O functions are `read`, which includes a complete Lisp parser, and `format`, which generates output based on templates.

11. You can create new local variables with let, and global variables with defparameter.

12. The assignment operator is setf. Its first argument can be an expression.

13. Functional programming, which means avoiding side-effects, is the dominant paradigm in Lisp.

14. The basic iteration operator is do.

15. Functions are regular Lisp objects. They can be passed as arguments, and denoted by lambda expressions.

16. In Lisp, values have types, not variables.

Exercises

1. Describe what happens when the following expressions are evaluated:

    (a) `(+ (- 5 1) (+ 3 7))`
    (b) `(list 1 (+ 2 3))`
    (c) `(if (listp 1) (+ 1 2) (+ 3 4))`
    (d) `(list (and (listp 3) t) (+ 1 2))`

2. Give three distinct cons expressions that return (a b c).

3. Using car and cdr, define a function to return the fourth element of a list.

4. Define a function that takes two arguments and returns the greater of the two.

5. What do these functions do?

    (a)
    ```
    (defun enigma (x)
      (and (not (null x))
           (or (null (car x))
               (enigma (cdr x)))))
    ```
    (b)
    ```
    (defun mystery (x y)
      (if (null y)
          nil
          (if (eql (car y) x)
              0
              (let ((z (mystery x (cdr y))))
                (and z (+ z 1))))))
    ```

6. What could occur in place of the x in each of the following exchanges?

  (a) > (car (x (cdr '(a (b c) d))))
      B

  (b) > (x 13 (/ 1 0))
      13

  (c) > (x #'list 1 nil)
      (1)

7. Using only operators introduced in this chapter, define a function that takes a list as an argument and returns true if one of its elements is a list.

8. Give iterative and recursive definitions of a function that

  (a) takes a positive integer and prints that many dots.

  (b) takes a list and returns the number of times the symbol a occurs in it.

9. A friend is trying to write a function that returns the sum of all the non-nil elements in a list. He has written two versions of this function, and neither of them work. Explain what's wrong with each, and give a correct version:

  (a) (defun summit (lst)
        (remove nil lst)
        (apply #'+ lst))

  (b) (defun summit (lst)
        (let ((x (car lst)))
          (if (null x)
              (summit (cdr lst))
              (+ x (summit (cdr lst)))))))

3

Lists

Lists are one of the fundamental data structures in Lisp. In the earliest dialects they were the only data structure: the name "Lisp" originally stood for "LISt Processor." But Lisp has long since outgrown this acronym. Common Lisp is a general-purpose programming language with a wide variety of data structures.

The development of Lisp programs often echoes the development of Lisp itself. In the initial version of a Lisp program, you may use a lot of lists. Then in later versions you may switch to faster, specialized data structures. This chapter describes the many things you can do with lists, and uses them to illustrate some general Lisp concepts.

3.1 Conses

Section 2.4 introduced cons, car, and cdr, the primitive list-manipulation functions. What cons really does is combine two objects into a two-part object called a *cons*. Conceptually, a cons is a pair of pointers; the first one is the car and the second is the cdr.

Conses provide a convenient representation for pairs of any type. The two halves of a cons can point to any kind of object, including conses. It is by taking advantage of the latter possibility that we use conses to build lists.

One does not tend to think of lists as pairs, but they can be defined that way. Any nonempty list can be considered as a pair of the first element and the rest of the list. Lisp lists are the embodiment of this idea. We use one half of the cons to point to the first element of the list, and the other to point to the rest of the list (which is either another cons or nil). The convention

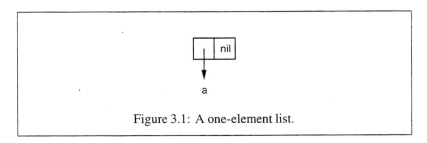

Figure 3.1: A one-element list.

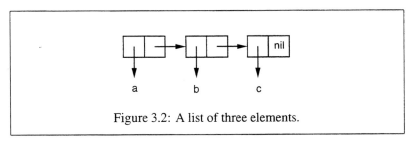

Figure 3.2: A list of three elements.

in Lisp has always been to use the car for the first element and the cdr for the rest of the list. So now car is synonymous with the first element of a list, and cdr with the rest. Lists are not a distinct kind of object, but conses linked together in this way.

When we cons something onto nil,

```
> (setf x (cons 'a nil))
(A)
```

the resulting list consists of a single cons, as shown in Figure 3.1. This way of representing conses is called *box notation*, because each cons is shown as a box, with pointers for the car and cdr. When we call car and cdr, we get back what those pointers point to:

```
> (car x)
A
> (cdr x)
NIL
```

When we build a list with multiple elements, we get a chain of conses:

```
> (setf y (list 'a 'b 'c))
(A B C)
```

The resulting structure is shown in Figure 3.2. Now when we ask for the cdr of this list, it is itself a list of two elements:

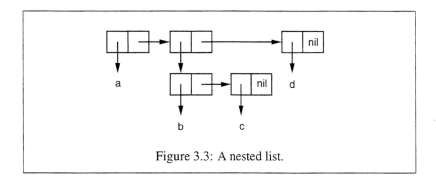

Figure 3.3: A nested list.

```
> (cdr y)
(B C)
```

In a list of several elements, the car pointers get you the elements, and the cdr pointers get you the rest of the list.

A list can have any kind of object as an element, including another list:

```
> (setf z (list 'a (list 'b 'c) 'd))
(A (B C) D)
```

When this happens, the underlying structure is as shown in Figure 3.3; the car pointer of the second cons in the chain also points to a list:

```
> (car (cdr z))
(B C)
```

The last two lists we made both have three elements; it just happens that the second element of z is also a list. Such a list is called a *nested* list, while a list like y that doesn't contain other lists as elements is called a *flat* list.

The function consp returns true if its argument is a cons. So listp could be defined:

```
(defun our-listp (x)
  (or (null x) (consp x)))
```

Since everything that is not a cons is an atom, the predicate atom could be defined:

```
(defun our-atom (x) (not (consp x)))
```

Note that nil is both an atom and a list.

3.2 Equality

Each time you call cons, Lisp allocates a new piece of memory with room
for two pointers. So if we call cons twice with the same arguments, we get
back two values that look the same, but are in fact distinct objects:

```
> (eql (cons 'a nil) (cons 'a nil))
NIL
```

It would be convenient if we could also ask whether two lists had the same
elements. Common Lisp provides another equality predicate for this purpose:
equal. While eql[1] returns true only if its arguments are the same object,

```
> (setf x (cons 'a nil))
(A)
> (eql x x)
T
```

equal, essentially, returns true if its arguments would print the same:

```
> (equal x (cons 'a nil))
T
```

This predicate works for other kinds of structures besides lists, but a
version for lists alone might be defined:

```
(defun our-equal (x y)
  (or (eql x y)
      (and (consp x)
           (consp y)
           (our-equal (car x) (car y))
           (our-equal (cdr x) (cdr y)))))
```

As this definition suggests, if some x and y are eql, they are also equal.

3.3 Why Lisp Has No Pointers

One of the secrets to understanding Lisp is to realize that variables have values
in the same way that lists have elements. As conses have pointers to their
elements, variables have pointers to their values.

You may have used other languages in which pointers were manipulated
explicitly. In Lisp you never have to do this, because the language handles
pointers for you. We've already seen how this happens with lists. Something

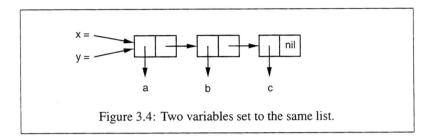

Figure 3.4: Two variables set to the same list.

similar happens with variables. Suppose, for example, we set two variables to the same list:

```
> (setf x '(a b c))
(A B C)
> (setf y x)
(A B C)
```

What actually happens when we set y to the value of x? The location in memory associated with the variable x does not contain the list itself, but a pointer to it. When we assign the same value to y, Lisp copies the pointer, not the list. (Figure 3.4 shows the situation that results.) So whenever you assign one variable the value of another, the two variables will have eql values:

```
> (eql x y)
T
```

The reason Lisp has no pointers is that every value is conceptually a pointer. When you assign a value to a variable or store it in a data structure, what gets stored is actually a pointer to the value. When you ask for the contents of the data structure or the value of the variable, Lisp returns what it points to. But all this happens beneath the surface. You can just put values in structures or "in" variables without thinking about it.

For efficiency, Lisp will sometimes choose to use an immediate representation instead of a pointer. For example, since a small integer takes no more space than a pointer, a Lisp implementation may as well handle small integers directly instead of handling pointers to them. But the bottom line for you, the programmer, is that by default you can put anything anywhere. Unless you have made declarations to the contrary, you will be able to store any kind of object in any kind of data structure, including the structure itself.

---

[1] In earlier dialects of Lisp the role of eql was played by eq. In Common Lisp, eq is a stricter function, and eql is the default predicate for identity. For an explanation of eq, see page 228.

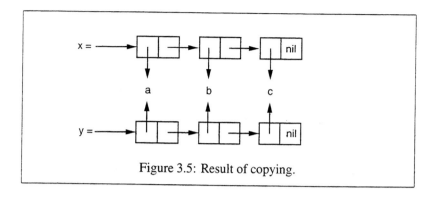

Figure 3.5: Result of copying.

3.4   Building Lists

The function copy-list takes a list and returns a copy of it. The new list
will have the same elements, but contained in new conses:

```
> (setf x '(a b c)
        y (copy-list x))
(A B C)
```

Figure 3.5 shows the structure that results; the return value is like a new bus
with the same passengers. We could think of copy-list as being defined:

```
(defun our-copy-list (lst)
  (if (atom lst)
      lst
      (cons (car lst) (our-copy-list (cdr lst)))))
```

This definition implies that x and (copy-list x) will always be equal,
and never eql unless x is nil.

Finally, the function append returns the concatenation of any number of
lists:

```
> (append '(a b) '(c d) '(e))
(A B C D E)
```

In doing so, it copies all the arguments except the last.

3.5   Example: Compression

As an example, this section shows how to perform a simple form of compression on lists. This algorithm goes by the impressive name of *run-length*

```
(defun compress (x)
  (if (consp x)
      (compr (car x) 1 (cdr x))
      x))

(defun compr (elt n lst)
  (if (null lst)
      (list (n-elts elt n))
      (let ((next (car lst)))
        (if (eql next elt)
            (compr elt (+ n 1) (cdr lst))
            (cons (n-elts elt n)
                  (compr next 1 (cdr lst)))))))

(defun n-elts (elt n)
  (if (> n 1)
      (list n elt)
      elt))
```

Figure 3.6: Run-length encoding: Compression.

encoding. In restaurants, the algorithm works as follows. A waitress approaches a table of four customers.

"What'll ya have?" she asks.

"I'll have the special," the first customer says.

"Me too," says the second.

"Sounds good," says the third.

Everyone looks at the fourth customer. "I'd like a cilantro soufflé," he says quietly.

With a sniff, the waitress turns on her heel and walks back to the counter. "Three specials," she shouts to the cook, "and a cilantro soufflé."

Figure 3.6 shows how to implement this compression algorithm for lists. The function compress takes a list of atoms and returns a compressed representation of it:

```
> (compress '(1 1 1 0 1 0 0 0 0 1))
((3 1) 0 1 (4 0) 1)
```

Whenever the same element occurs several times in a row, the sequence is replaced by a list indicating the element and the number of occurrences.

Most of the work is done by the recursive compr. This function takes three arguments: elt, the element we last saw; n, the number of times in a

```
(defun uncompress (lst)
  (if (null lst)
      nil
      (let ((elt (car lst))
            (rest (uncompress (cdr lst))))
        (if (consp elt)
            (append (apply #'list-of elt)
                    rest)
            (cons elt rest)))))

(defun list-of (n elt)
  (if (zerop n)
      nil
      (cons elt (list-of (- n 1) elt))))
```

Figure 3.7: Run-length encoding: Expansion.

row we've seen it; and lst, the part of the list we've yet to examine. If there is nothing left to examine, we just call n-elts to get something representing n elts. If the first element of lst is still elt, we increment n and keep going. Otherwise we get a compressed list of what we've seen so far, and cons that onto whatever compr returns for the rest of the list.

To reconstitute a compressed list, we call uncompress (Figure 3.7):

```
> (uncompress '((3 1) 0 1 (4 0) 1))
(1 1 1 0 1 0 0 0 0 1)
```

This function works recursively through the compressed list, copying atoms verbatim and expanding lists by calling list-of:

```
> (list-of 3 'ho)
(HO HO HO)
```

We don't really need to write list-of. The built-in make-list can do the same thing—but it uses keyword arguments, which haven't been introduced yet.

In this and other ways, the code in Figures 3.6 and 3.7 is not written the way an experienced Lisp programmer would write it. It's inefficient, it does not compress as tightly as it could, and it only works for lists of atoms. Within a few chapters we'll have seen techniques that would make it possible to fix all these problems.

LOADING PROGRAMS

The code in this section is our first example of a substantial program. When one wants to write functions of more than a couple lines, it's usual to type the code into a file, and then use `load` to get Lisp to read the definitions. If we stored the code in Figures 3.6 and 3.7 in a file called "compress.lisp", then typing

```
(load "compress.lisp")
```

into the toplevel would have the same effect, more or less, as typing the expressions in that file into the toplevel directly.

Note: In some implementations, the extension for Lisp files will be ".lsp" rather than ".lisp".

3.6 Access

Common Lisp has additional access functions defined in terms of `car` and `cdr`. To find the element at a given position in a list we call `nth`,

```
> (nth 0 '(a b c))
A
```

and to find the *n*th cdr, we call `nthcdr`:

```
> (nthcdr 2 '(a b c))
(C)
```

Both `nth` and `nthcdr` are zero-indexed; that is, the elements are numbered starting at zero rather than one. In Common Lisp, whenever you use a number to refer to an element of a data structure, the numbering starts at zero.

The two functions do almost the same thing; `nth` is equivalent to `car` of `nthcdr`. Without error-checking, `nthcdr` could be defined as:

```
(defun our-nthcdr (n lst)
  (if (zerop n)
      lst
      (our-nthcdr (- n 1) (cdr lst))))
```

The function `zerop` just returns true if its argument is zero.

The function `last` returns the last cons in a list:

```
> (last '(a b c))
(C)
```

This is not the same as getting the last element. To get the last element of a list, you would take the car of last.

Common Lisp defines first through tenth as functions that retrieve the corresponding element of a list. These functions are *not* zero-indexed: (second x) is equivalent to (nth 1 x).

In addition, Common Lisp defines functions like caddr, which is an abbreviation for car of cdr of cdr. All the functions of the form c*xr*, where *x* is a string of up to four as or ds, are defined in Common Lisp. With the possible exception of cadr, which refers to the second element, it is not a good idea to use them in code that anyone else is going to read.

3.7 Mapping Functions

Common Lisp provides several functions for calling functions on the elements of a list. The most frequently used is mapcar, which takes a function and one or more lists, and returns the result of applying the function to elements taken from each list, until some list runs out:

```
> (mapcar #'(lambda (x) (+ x 10))
          '(1 2 3))
(11 12 13)
> (mapcar #'list
          '(a b c)
          '(1 2 3 4))
((A 1) (B 2) (C 3))
```

The related maplist takes the same arguments, but calls the function on successive *cdrs* of the lists:

```
> (maplist #'(lambda (x) x)
           '(a b c))
((A B C) (B C) (C))
```

Other mapping functions include mapc, which is discussed on page 88, and mapcan, which is discussed on page 202.

3.8 Trees

Conses can also be considered as binary trees, with the car representing the right subtree and the cdr the left. For example, the list

```
(a (b c) d)
```

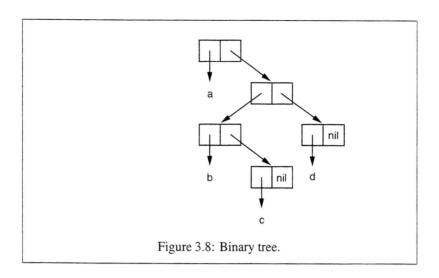

Figure 3.8: Binary tree.

is also the tree represented in Figure 3.8. (If you rotate it 45° counter-clockwise, you'll see that it is the same as Figure 3.3.)

Common Lisp has several built-in functions for use with trees. For example, copy-tree takes a tree and returns a copy of it. It might be defined:

```
(defun our-copy-tree (tr)
  (if (atom tr)
      tr
      (cons (our-copy-tree (car tr))
            (our-copy-tree (cdr tr)))))
```

Compare this to the sketch of copy-list on page 36; copy-tree copies both the car and cdr of each cons, while copy-list copies only the cdr.

Binary trees without interior nodes are not useful for much. Common Lisp includes functions for operating on trees not because one needs trees as such, but because one needs a way to do something to a list and all the lists within it. For example, suppose we have a list like

```
(and (integerp x) (zerop (mod x 2)))
```

and we want to substitute y for x throughout. It won't do to call substitute, which replaces elements in a sequence:

```
> (substitute 'y 'x '(and (integerp x) (zerop (mod x 2))))
(AND (INTEGERP X) (ZEROP (MOD X 2)))
```

This call has no effect because the list has three elements, and none of them are x. What we need here is subst, which replaces elements in a tree:

```
> (subst 'y 'x '(and (integerp x) (zerop (mod x 2))))
(AND (INTEGERP Y) (ZEROP (MOD Y 2)))
```

If we define a version of subst, it comes out looking a lot like copy-tree:

```
(defun our-subst (new old tree)
  (if (eql tree old)
      new
      (if (atom tree)
          tree
          (cons (our-subst new old (car tree))
                (our-subst new old (cdr tree))))))
```

Functions that operate on trees usually have this form, recursing down both the car and cdr. Such functions are said to be *doubly recursive*.

3.9   Understanding Recursion

Students learning about recursion are sometimes encouraged to trace all the invocations of a recursive function on a piece of paper. (A trace of a recursive function can be seen on page 288.) This exercise could be misleading: a programmer defining a recursive function usually does not think explicitly about the sequence of invocations that results from calling it.

If one always had to think of a program in such terms, recursion would be burdensome, not helpful. The advantage of recursion is precisely that it lets us view algorithms in a more abstract way. You can judge whether or not a recursive function is correct without considering all the invocations that result when the function is actually called.

To see if a recursive function does what it's supposed to, all you have to ask is, does it cover all the cases? For example, here is a recursive function for finding the length of a list:

```
(defun len (lst)
  (if (null lst)
      0
      (+ (len (cdr lst)) 1)))
```

We can assure ourselves that this function is correct by verifying two things:

1. That it works for lists of length 0.

2. Given that it works for lists of length n, that it also works for lists of
   length $n+1$.

If we can establish both points, then we know that the function is correct for
all possible lists.

Our definition obviously satisfies the first point: if lst is nil, the function
immediately returns 0. Now suppose that the function works for lists of length
n. We give it a list of length $n+1$. The definition says that the function will
return the len of the cdr of this list, plus 1. The cdr is a list of length n. We
know by our assumption that its len is n. Thus the len of the whole list is
$n+1$.

This is all we need to know. The secret to understanding recursion is
a lot like the secret for dealing with parentheses. How do you see which
parenthesis matches which? You don't have to. How do you visualize all
those invocations? You don't have to.

With more complicated recursive functions, there might be more cases,
but the procedure is the same. For example, with our-copy-tree (page 41)
we would have to consider three cases: atoms, single conses, and trees of
$n+1$ conses.

The first case (here, lists of length 0) is known as the *base case*. When a
recursive function doesn't behave as you intended, it is usually because the
base case is wrong. It is a common error to omit the base case entirely, as in
this incorrect definition of member:[2]

```
(defun our-member (obj lst)                              ; wrong
  (if (eql (car lst) obj)
      lst
      (our-member obj (cdr lst))))
```

We need the initial null test to ensure that the recursion stops when it gets to
the end of the list without finding what it's looking for. This version would
go into an infinite loop if the object we sought wasn't in the list. Appendix A
looks at this kind of problem in more detail.

Being able to judge whether or not a recursive function is correct is only
the first half of understanding recursion. The other half is being able to write
a recursive function that does what you want. Section 6.9 deals with this
question.

3.10   Sets

Lists are a good way to represent small sets. Every element of a list is a
member of the set it represents:

---

[2] The ; wrong in this definition is a *comment*. In Lisp code, everything from a semicolon to
the end of the line is ignored.

```
> (member 'b '(a b c))
(B C)
```

When member returns true, instead of simply returning t, it returns the part of
the list beginning with the object it was looking for. Logically, a cons serves
just as well as t, and this way the function returns more information.

By default, member compares objects using eql. You can override this
default by using something called a *keyword* argument. Many Common Lisp
functions take one or more keyword arguments. The unusual thing about these
arguments is that they are not matched with the corresponding parameters by
their position, but by special tags, called keywords, that must precede them
in the call. A keyword is a symbol preceded by a colon.

One of the keyword arguments accepted by member is a :test argument.
If you pass some function as the :test argument in a call to member, then
that function will be used to test for equality instead of eql. So if we want to
find a member of a list that is equal to a given object, we might say:

```
> (member '(a) '((a) (z)) :test #'equal)
((A) (Z))
```

Keyword arguments are always optional. If any are included in a call, they
come last; if more than one keyword argument is given, their order doesn't
matter.

The other keyword argument accepted by member is a :key argument.
By providing this argument you can specify a function to be applied to each
element before comparison:

```
> (member 'a '((a b) (c d)) :key #'car)
((A B) (C D))
```

In this example, we asked if there was an element whose car was a.

If we wanted to give both keyword arguments, we could give them in
either order. The following two calls are equivalent:

```
> (member 2 '((1) (2)) :key #'car :test #'equal)
((2))
> (member 2 '((1) (2)) :test #'equal :key #'car)
((2))
```

Both ask if there is an element whose car is equal to 2.

If we want to find an element satisfying an arbitrary predicate—like oddp,
which returns true for odd integers—we can use the related member-if:

```
> (member-if #'oddp '(2 3 4))
(3 4)
```

We could imagine a limited version of member-if being written:

```
(defun our-member-if (fn lst)
  (and (consp lst)
       (if (funcall fn (car lst))
           lst
           (our-member-if fn (cdr lst)))))
```

The function adjoin is like a conditional cons. It takes an object and a list, and conses the object onto the list only if it is not already a member:

```
> (adjoin 'b '(a b c))
(A B C)
> (adjoin 'z '(a b c))
(Z A B C)
```

In the general case it takes the same keyword arguments as member.

The operations of set union, intersection, and complement are implemented by the functions union, intersection, and set-difference. These functions expect exactly two lists (but also take the same keyword arguments as member).

```
> (union '(a b c) '(c b s))
(A C B S)
> (intersection '(a b c) '(b b c))
(B C)
> (set-difference '(a b c d e) '(b e))
(A C D)
```

Since there is no notion of ordering in a set, these functions do not necessarily bother to preserve the order of elements found in the original lists. The call to set-difference might just as well have returned (d c a), for example.

3.11 Sequences

Another way to think of a list is as a series of objects in a particular order. In Common Lisp, *sequences* include both lists and vectors. This section introduces some of the sequence functions that are especially applicable to lists. Operations on sequences are covered in more detail in Section 4.4.

The function length returns the number of elements in a sequence:

```
> (length '(a b c))
3
```

We wrote a version of this function (limited to lists) on page 24.

To copy part of a sequence, we use subseq. The second argument (required) is the position of the first element to be included, and the third argument (optional) is the position of the first element not to be included.

```
> (subseq '(a b c d) 1 2)
(B)
> (subseq '(a b c d) 1)
(B C D)
```

If the third argument is omitted, the subsequence goes all the way to the end of the original sequence.

The function reverse returns a sequence with the same elements as its argument, but in the reverse order:

```
> (reverse '(a b c))
(C B A)
```

A *palindrome* is a sequence that reads the same in either direction—for example, (a b b a). If a palindrome has an even number of elements, then the second half will be a mirror of the first. Using length, subseq, and reverse, we can define a function

```
(defun mirror? (s)
  (let ((len (length s)))
    (and (evenp len)
         (let ((mid (/ len 2)))
           (equal (subseq s 0 mid)
                  (reverse (subseq s mid)))))))
```

that detects such palindromes:

```
> (mirror? '(a b b a))
T
```

Common Lisp has a built-in sort function called sort. It takes a sequence and a comparison function of two arguments, and returns a sequence with the same elements, sorted according to the function:

```
> (sort '(0 2 1 3 8) #'>)
(8 3 2 1 0)
```

You have to be careful when using sort, because it's *destructive*. For efficiency reasons, sort is allowed to modify the sequence given to it as an argument. So if you don't want your original sequence modified, pass a copy.°

Using sort and nth, we can write a function that takes an integer *n*, and returns the *n*th greatest element of a list:

```
(defun nthmost (n lst)
  (nth (- n 1)
       (sort (copy-list lst) #'>)))
```

We subtract one from the integer because nth is zero-indexed, but it would be unintuitive if nthmost were.

```
> (nthmost 2 '(0 2 1 3 8))
3
```

With some effort we could write a more efficient version of this function.

The functions every and some take a predicate and one or more sequences. When given just one sequence, they test whether the elements satisfy the predicate:

```
> (every #'oddp '(1 3 5))
T
> (some #'evenp '(1 2 3))
T
```

If they are given more than one sequence, the predicate must take as many arguments as there are sequences, and arguments are drawn one at a time from all the sequences:

```
> (every #'> '(1 3 5) '(0 2 4))
T
```

If the sequences are of different lengths, the shortest one determines the number of tests performed.

3.12   Stacks

The representation of lists as conses makes it natural to use them as pushdown stacks. This is done so often that Common Lisp provides two macros for the purpose: (push x y) pushes x onto the front of the list y, and (pop x) removes and returns the first element of the list x.

Both are defined in terms of setf. It's easy to translate calls if the arguments are constants or variables. The expression

```
(push obj lst)
```

is equivalent to

```
(setf lst (cons obj lst))
```

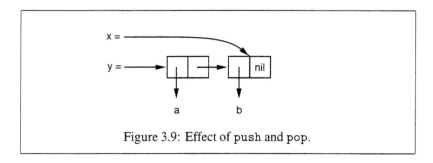

Figure 3.9: Effect of push and pop.

and the expression

```
(pop lst)
```

is equivalent to

```
(let ((x (car lst)))
  (setf lst (cdr lst))
  x)
```

So, for example:

```
> (setf x '(b))
(B)
> (push 'a x)
(A B)
> x
(A B)
> (setf y x)
(A B)
> (pop x)
A
> x
(B)
> y
(A B)
```

All this follows from the equivalences given above. Figure 3.9 shows the structure that remains after these expressions are evaluated.

You could use push to define an iterative version of reverse for lists:

```
(defun our-reverse (lst)
  (let ((acc nil))
    (dolist (elt lst)
      (push elt acc))
    acc))
```

In this version we start with an empty list and push each element of lst onto it. When we're finished, the last element of lst will be on the front.

The pushnew macro is a variant of push that uses adjoin instead of cons:

```
> (let ((x '(a b)))
    (pushnew 'c x)
    (pushnew 'a x)
    x)
(C A B)
```

Here, c gets pushed onto the list, but a, because it is already a member, does not.

3.13   Dotted Lists

The kind of lists that can be built by calling list are more precisely known as *proper lists*. A proper list is either nil, or a cons whose cdr is a proper list. That is, we could define a predicate that would return true only for proper lists as:[3]

```
(defun proper-list? (x)
  (or (null x)
      (and (consp x)
           (proper-list? (cdr x)))))
```

All the lists we've built so far have been proper lists.

Conses are not just for building lists, however. Whenever you need a structure with two fields you can use a cons. You will be able to use car to refer to the first field and cdr to refer to the second.

```
> (setf pair (cons 'a 'b))
(A . B)
```

Because this cons is not a proper list, it is displayed in *dot notation*. In dot notation, the car and cdr of each cons are shown separated by a period. The structure of this cons is shown in Figure 3.10.

A cons that isn't a proper list is called a *dotted list*. This is not a very good name, because conses that aren't proper lists are usually not meant to represent lists at all: (a . b) is just a two-part data structure.

You could express proper lists in dot notation as well, but when Lisp displays a proper list, it will always use regular list notation:

---

[3]This description is a little misleading, because the function would not return nil for everything that wasn't a proper list. If given a cdr-circular list, it would fail to terminate. Circular lists are covered in Section 12.7.

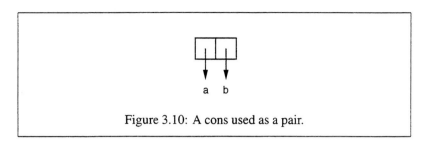

Figure 3.10: A cons used as a pair.

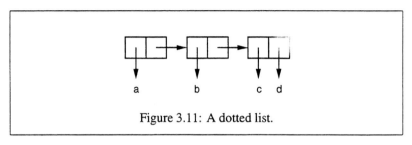

Figure 3.11: A dotted list.

```
> '(a . (b . (c . nil)))
(A B C)
```

Incidentally, notice the correspondence between the way this list looks in dot
notation and the way it looks in box notation in Figure 3.2.

There is an intermediate form of notation, between list notation and pure
dot notation, for dotted lists whose cdrs are conses:

```
> (cons 'a (cons 'b (cons 'c 'd)))
(A B C . D)
```

Such conses are displayed like proper lists, except that the final cdr is shown,
preceded by a period. The structure of this list is shown in Figure 3.11; notice
how similar it is to the structure shown in Figure 3.2.

So there are actually four ways you could denote the list (a b),

```
(a . (b . nil))
(a . (b))
(a b . nil)
(a b)
```

though when Lisp displays this list, it will always use the latter form.

3.14 Assoc-lists

It is also natural to use conses to represent mappings. A list of conses is called an *assoc-list* or *alist*. Such a list could represent a set of translations, for example:

```
> (setf trans '((+ . "add") (- . "subtract")))
((+ . "add") (- . "subtract"))
```

Assoc-lists are slow, but convenient in the first stages of a program. Common Lisp has a built-in function, `assoc`, for retrieving the pair associated with a given key:

```
> (assoc '+ trans)
(+ . "add")
> (assoc '* trans)
NIL
```

If `assoc` doesn't find what it's looking for, it returns `nil`.

We could write a limited version of `assoc` as:

```
(defun our-assoc (key alist)
  (and (consp alist)
       (let ((pair (car alist)))
         (if (eql key (car pair))
             pair
             (our-assoc key (cdr alist))))))
```

Like `member`, the real `assoc` takes keyword arguments, including `:test` and `:key`. Common Lisp also defines an `assoc-if`, which is to `assoc` what `member-if` is to `member`.

3.15 Example: Shortest Path

Figure 3.12 contains a program for finding the shortest path through a network. The function `shortest-path` takes a start node, a destination node, and a network, and returns the shortest path, if there is one.

In this example, nodes are represented as symbols, and networks are represented as assoc-lists with elements of the form

$$(node \;.\; neighbors)$$

So the minimal network shown in Figure 3.13 would be represented as

```
(setf min '((a b c) (b c) (c d)))
```

```
(defun shortest-path (start end net)
  (bfs end (list (list start)) net))

(defun bfs (end queue net)
  (if (null queue)
      nil
      (let ((path (car queue)))
        (let ((node (car path)))
          (if (eql node end)
              (reverse path)
              (bfs end
                   (append (cdr queue)
                           (new-paths path node net))
                   net))))))

(defun new-paths (path node net)
  (mapcar #'(lambda (n)
              (cons n path))
          (cdr (assoc node net))))
```

Figure 3.12: Breadth-first search

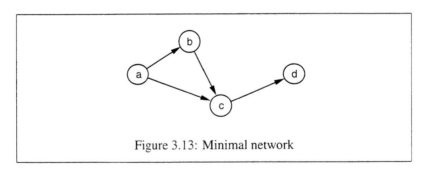

Figure 3.13: Minimal network

and to find the nodes we can reach from a we would say:

```
> (cdr (assoc 'a min))
(B C)
```

The program in Figure 3.12 works by searching the network breadth-first. To search breadth-first you have to maintain a queue of unexplored nodes. Each time you get to a node, you check to see if it is the one you want. If not, you append each of its children to the end of the queue, then take a node from the front of the queue and continue the search there. By always putting deeper nodes at the end of the queue, we ensure that the network gets searched one layer at a time.

The code in Figure 3.12 represents a slight complication of this idea. We don't just want to find the destination, but to keep a record of how we got there. So instead of maintaining a queue of nodes, we maintain a queue of paths we've followed, each of which is a list of nodes. When we take an element from the queue to continue the search, it will not be a node but a list, with the node on the front.

The function `bfs` does the searching. Initially there will be only one element in the queue, a path representing the start node with no history. So `shortest-path` calls `bfs` with `(list (list start))` as the initial queue.

Within `bfs` the first thing to consider is whether there are any nodes left to explore. If the queue is empty, `bfs` returns `nil` to indicate that no path could be found. If there are still nodes to search, `bfs` looks at the element on the front of the queue. If the car is the node we're looking for, we've found a path and we just return it, reversing for readability. If we haven't found the node we're looking for, it might still be a descendant of the current node, so we add each of its children (or paths for each of them) to the end of the queue. Then we call `bfs` recursively to continue searching the rest of the queue.

Because `bfs` searches breadth-first, the first path it finds will be the shortest, or one of the shortest:

```
> (shortest-path 'a 'd min)
(A C D)
```

Here is what the queue looks like in successive calls to `bfs`:

```
((A))
((B A) (C A))
((C A) (C B A))
((C B A) (D C A))
((D C A) (D C B A))
```

The second element in a queue becomes the first element in the next queue. The first element in a queue becomes the cdr of any new elements at the end of the next queue.

The code in Figure 3.12 is not the fastest way to search a network, but it does give an idea of the versatility of lists. In this simple program we use lists in three distinct ways: we use a list of symbols to represent a path, a list of paths to represent the queue used in breadth-first search,[4] and an assoc-list to represent the network itself.

---

[4]Section 12.3 will show how to implement queues more efficiently.

3.16 Garbage

Lists can be slow for several reasons. They offer sequential instead of random access, so retrieving a given element takes longer in a list than an array, for the same reason that it takes longer to find something on a tape than on a disk. Internally, conses tend to be represented as pointers, so traversing a list means traversing a series of pointers, instead of simply incrementing an index, as in an array. But these two costs can be small compared to the cost of allocating and recycling cons cells.

Automatic memory management is one of Lisp's most valuable features. The Lisp system maintains a segment of memory called the *heap*. The system keeps track of unused memory in the heap and doles it out as new objects are created. The function cons, for example, returns a newly allocated cons. Allocating memory from the heap is sometimes generically known as *consing*.

If such memory were never freed, Lisp would run out of space for new objects and have to shut down. So the system must periodically search through the heap, looking for memory that is no longer needed. Memory that is no longer needed is called *garbage*, and the scavenging operation is called *garbage collection*, or GC.

Where does garbage come from? Let's create some:[5]

```
> (setf lst (list 'a 'b 'c))
(A B C)
> (setf lst nil)
NIL
```

Initially we call list, which calls cons, which allocates new cons cells on the heap. In this case we made three. After we set lst to nil, we no longer have any way of reaching the old value of lst, the list (a b c).[5]

Since we have no way of reaching this list, it might as well not exist. Objects that we no longer have any way of reaching are garbage. The system can safely reuse these three cons cells.

This way of managing memory is a great convenience to the programmer. You never have to allocate or deallocate memory explicitly. And this means that you never have to deal with the bugs that come from doing so. Memory leaks and dangling pointers are simply impossible in Lisp.

But, like any technical advance, automatic memory management can work against you if you're not careful. The costs associated with using and recycling heap space are sometimes referred to simply as the costs of consing. This is reasonable, because unless a program never throws anything away,

---

[5]Actually, we do have a way of reaching the list, for a bit. The globals *, **, and *** are always set to the the last three values returned to the toplevel. These variables are useful in debugging.

most of those conses are going to end up as garbage sooner or later. The trouble with consing is, allocating storage and scavenging memory to reclaim it can be expensive compared to the routine operations of a program. Recent research has produced greatly improved garbage collection algorithms, but consing will always cost something, and in some existing Lisp systems, it is quite expensive.

Unless you're careful, it's easy to write programs that cons excessively. For example, remove has to copy all the conses up to the last element removed from a list. You can avoid some of this consing by using destructive functions, which try to re-use most of the structure of the lists passed to them as arguments. Destructive functions are discussed in Section 12.4.

While it's easy to write programs that cons a lot, it's possible to write programs that don't cons at all. The typical approach would be to write the initial version of a program in a purely functional style and using a lot of lists. As the program evolves, you can use destructive operations and/or other data structures in critical portions of the code. But it's hard to give general advice about consing, because some Lisp implementations now do memory management so well that it can sometimes be faster to cons than not to. The whole issue is covered in more detail in Section 13.4.

Consing is ok in prototypes and experiments, at least. And if you take advantage of the flexibility that lists give you in the early stages of a program, you're more likely to produce something that survives to the later stages.

Summary

1. A cons is a two-part data structure. Lists are made of conses linked together.

2. The predicate equal is less strict than eql. Essentially, it returns true if its arguments print the same.

3. All Lisp objects behave like pointers. You never have to manipulate pointers explicitly.

4. You can copy lists with copy-list, and join their elements with append.

5. Run-length encoding is a simple compression algorithm for use in restaurants.

6. Common Lisp has a variety of access functions defined in terms of car and cdr.

7. Mapping functions apply a function to successive elements, or successive tails, of a list.

8. Operations on nested lists are sometimes considered as operations on trees.

9. To judge a recursive function, you only have to consider whether it covers all the cases.

10. Lists can be used to represent sets. Several built-in functions view lists this way.

11. Keyword arguments are optional, and are identified not by position, but by symbolic tags that precede them.

12. Lists are a subtype of sequences. Common Lisp has a large number of sequence functions.

13. A cons that isn't a proper list is called a dotted list.

14. Lists with conses as elements can be used to represent mappings. Such lists are called assoc-lists.

15. Automatic memory management saves you from dealing with memory allocation, but generating excessive garbage can make programs slow.

Exercises

1. Show the following lists in box notation:

    (a) (a b (c d))
    (b) (a (b (c (d))))
    (c) (((a b) c) d)
    (d) (a (b . c) . d)

2. Write a version of union that preserves the order of the elements in the original lists:

    ```
    > (new-union '(a b c) '(b a d))
    (A B C D)
    ```

3. Define a function that takes a list and returns a list indicating the number of times each (eql) element appears, sorted from most common element to least common:

    ```
    > (occurrences '(a b a d a c d c a))
    ((A . 4) (C . 2) (D . 2) (B . 1))
    ```

4. Why does (member '(a) '((a) (b))) return nil?

5. Suppose the function pos+ takes a list and returns a list of each element plus its position:

```
> (pos+ '(7 5 1 4))
(7 6 3 7)
```

Define this function using (a) recursion, (b) iteration, (c) mapcar.

6. After years of deliberation, a government commission has decided that lists should be represented by using the cdr to point to the first element and the car to point to the rest of the list. Define the government versions of the following functions:

   (a) cons

   (b) list

   (c) length (for lists)

   (d) member (for lists; no keywords)

7. Modify the program in Figure 3.6 to use fewer cons cells. (Hint: Use dotted lists.)

8. Define a function that takes a list and prints it in dot notation:

```
> (showdots '(a b c))
(A . (B . (C . NIL)))
NIL
```

9. Write a program to find the *longest* finite path through a network represented as in Section 3.15. The network may contain cycles.

4

Specialized Data Structures

The preceding chapter discussed the list, Lisp's most versatile data structure. This chapter shows how to use Lisp's other data structures: arrays (including vectors and strings), structures, and hash tables. They may not be as flexible as lists, but they can make access faster, and take up less space.

Common Lisp has one other data structure: the instance. Instances are covered in Chapter 11, which describes CLOS.

4.1 Arrays

In Common Lisp, you can make an array by calling `make-array` with a list of dimensions as the first argument. To make a 2×3 array we would say:

```
> (setf arr (make-array '(2 3) :initial-element nil))
#<Simple-Array T (2 3) BFC4FE>
```

Arrays in Common Lisp can have at least seven dimensions, and each dimension can have at least 1023 elements.

The `:initial-element` argument is optional. If it is provided, the whole array will be initialized to that value. The consequences of trying to retrieve an element of an uninitialized array are undefined.

To retrieve an array element we call `aref`. As usual for Common Lisp access functions, `aref` is zero-indexed:

```
> (aref arr 0 0)
NIL
```

To replace some element of an array, we use setf with aref:

```
> (setf (aref arr 0 0) 'b)
B
> (aref arr 0 0)
B
```

To denote a literal array, we use the #*n*a syntax, where *n* is the number of dimensions in the array. For example, we could denote an array equivalent to arr as:

```
#2a((b nil nil) (nil nil nil))
```

If the global *print-array* is t, arrays will be displayed in this form:

```
> (setf *print-array* t)
T
> arr
#2A((B NIL NIL) (NIL NIL NIL))
```

If you want just a one-dimensional array, you can give an integer instead of a list as the first argument to make-array:

```
> (setf vec (make-array 4 :initial-element nil))
#(NIL NIL NIL NIL)
```

A one-dimensional array is also called a *vector.* You can create and fill one in a single step by calling vector, which will return a vector of whatever arguments you give it:

```
> (vector "a" 'b 3)
#("a" B 3)
```

A literal vector can be expressed using this syntax, just as a literal array can be expressed using #*n*a.

You can use aref for vector access, but there is a faster function called svref for use with vectors.

```
> (svref vec 0)
NIL
```

The "sv" in the name stands for "simple vector," which is what all vectors are by default.[1]

---

[1] A simple array is one that is neither adjustable, nor displaced, nor has a fill-pointer. Arrays are simple by default. A simple vector is a simple array of one dimension that can contain elements of any type.

```
(defun bin-search (obj vec)
  (let ((len (length vec)))
    (and (not (zerop len))
         (finder obj vec 0 (- len 1)))))

(defun finder (obj vec start end)
  (let ((range (- end start)))
    (if (zerop range)
        (if (eql obj (aref vec start))
            obj
            nil)
        (let ((mid (+ start (round (/ range 2)))))
          (let ((obj2 (aref vec mid)))
            (if (< obj obj2)
                (finder obj vec start (- mid 1))
                (if (> obj obj2)
                    (finder obj vec (+ mid 1) end)
                    obj)))))))
```

Figure 4.1: Searching a sorted vector.

4.2   Example: Binary Search

As an example, this section shows how to write a function to search for an object in a sorted vector. If we know that a vector is sorted, we can do better than find (page 65), which must look at each element in turn. Instead we jump right into the middle of the vector. If the middle element is the object we're looking for, then we're done. Otherwise, we continue searching in either the left or right half of the vector, depending on whether the object was less than or greater than the middle element.

Figure 4.1 contains a function that works this way. Two functions actually: bin-search sets the initial bounds and sends control to finder, which searches for obj between the startth and endth elements of a vector vec.

If the range to be searched has narrowed to one element, then finder returns that element if it is obj, and nil otherwise. If the range includes several elements, we find the middle (round returns the nearest integer to its argument) and look at the element there (obj2). If obj is less than obj2, the search continues recursively in the left half of the vector. If it's greater, the search continues in the right half of the vector. The only remaining alternative is that obj = obj2, in which case we've found what we were looking for, and simply return it.

COMMENTING CONVENTIONS

In Common Lisp code, anything following a semicolon is treated as a comment. Some Lisp programmers use multiple semicolons to indicate the level of the comment: four semicolons in a heading, three in a description of a function or macro, two to explain the line below, and one when a comment is on the same line as the code it applies to. Using this convention, Figure 4.1 might begin:

```
;;;; Utilities for operations on sorted vectors.

;;; Finds an element in a sorted vector.

(defun bin-search (obj vec)
  (let ((len (length vec)))
    ;; if a real vector, send it to finder
    (and (not (zerop len)) ; returns nil if empty
         (finder obj vec 0 (- len 1)))))
```

For extensive comments, it may be preferable to use the #|...|# read-macro. Everything between a #| and |# is ignored by read.°

If we insert the following line at the beginning of finder,

```
(format t "~A~%" (subseq vec start (+ end 1)))
```

then we can watch as the number of elements left to be searched is halved in each step:

```
> (bin-search 3 #(0 1 2 3 4 5 6 7 8 9))
#(0 1 2 3 4 5 6 7 8 9)
#(0 1 2 3)
#(3)
3
```

4.3 Strings and Characters

Strings are vectors of characters. We denote a constant string as a series of characters surrounded by double-quotes, and an individual character c as #\c.

Each character has an associated integer—usually, but not necessarily, the ASCII number. In most implementations, the function char-code returns the number associated with a character, and code-char returns the character associated with a number.°

The functions char< (less than), char<= (less than or equal), char= (equal), char>= (greater than or equal), char> (greater than), and char/= (different) compare characters. They work like the numeric comparison operators described on page 146.

```
> (sort "elbow" #'char<)
"below"
```

Because strings are vectors, both sequence functions and array functions work on them. You could use aref to retrieve elements, for example,

```
> (aref "abc" 1)
#\b
```

but with a string you can use the faster char:

```
> (char "abc" 1)
#\b
```

You can use setf with char (or aref) to replace elements:

```
> (let ((str (copy-seq "Merlin")))
    (setf (char str 3) #\k)
    str)
"Merkin"
```

If you want to compare two strings, you can use the general equal, but there is also a function string-equal that ignores case:

```
> (equal "fred" "fred")
T
> (equal "fred" "Fred")
NIL
> (string-equal "fred" "Fred")
T
```

Common Lisp provides a large number of functions for comparing and manipulating strings. They are listed in Appendix D, starting on page 364.

There are several ways of building strings. The most general is to use format. Calling format with nil as the first argument makes it return as a string what it would have printed:

```
> (format nil "~A or ~A" "truth" "dare")
"truth or dare"
```

But if you just want to join several strings together, you can use `concatenate`, which takes a symbol indicating the type of the result, plus one or more sequences:

```
> (concatenate 'string "not " "to worry")
"not to worry"
```

4.4   Sequences

In Common Lisp the type `sequence` includes both lists and vectors (and therefore strings). Some of the functions that we have been using on lists are actually sequence functions, including `remove`, `length`, `subseq`, `reverse`, `sort`, `every`, and `some`. So the function that we wrote on page 46 would also work with other kinds of sequences:

```
> (mirror? "abba")
T
```

We've already seen four functions for retrieving elements of sequences: `nth` for lists, `aref` and `svref` for vectors, and `char` for strings. Common Lisp also provides a function `elt` that works for sequences of any kind:

```
> (elt '(a b c) 1)
B
```

For sequences of specific types, the access functions we've already seen should be faster, so there is no point in using `elt` except in code that is supposed to work for sequences generally.

Using `elt`, we could write a version of `mirror?` that would be more efficient for vectors:

```
(defun mirror? (s)
  (let ((len (length s)))
    (and (evenp len)
         (do ((forward 0 (+ forward 1))
              (back (- len 1) (- back 1)))
             ((or (> forward back)
                  (not (eql (elt s forward)
                            (elt s back))))
              (> forward back))))))
```

This version would work with lists too, but its implementation is better suited to vectors. The frequent calls to `elt` would be expensive with lists, because lists only allow sequential access. In vectors, which allow random access, it is as cheap to reach one element as any other.

Many sequence functions take one or more keyword arguments from the standard set listed in this table:

PARAMETER	PURPOSE	DEFAULT
:key	a function to apply to each element	identity
:test	the test function for comparison	eql
:from-end	if true, work backwards	nil
:start	position at which to start	0
:end	position, if any, at which to stop	nil

One function that takes the full set is position, which returns the position of an element in a sequence, or nil if it is not found. We'll use position to illustrate the roles of the keyword arguments.

```
> (position #\a "fantasia")
1
> (position #\a "fantasia" :start 3 :end 5)
4
```

The second example asks for the position of the first a between the fourth and sixth characters. The :start argument is the position of the first element to be considered, and defaults to the first element of the sequence. The :end argument is the position of the first element, if any, not to be considered.

If we give the :from-end argument,

```
> (position #\a "fantasia" :from-end t)
7
```

we get the position of the a closest to the end. But the position is calculated in the usual way; it does not represent the distance from the end.

The :key argument is a function that is applied to each element of a sequence before it is considered. If we ask something like this,

```
> (position 'a '((c d) (a b)) :key #'car)
1
```

then what we are asking for is the position of the first element whose *car* is the symbol a.

The :test argument is a function of two arguments, and defines what it takes for a successful match. It always defaults to eql. If you're trying to match a list, you might want to use equal instead:

```
> (position '(a b) '((a b) (c d)))
NIL
> (position '(a b) '((a b) (c d)) :test #'equal)
0
```

The :test argument can be any function of two arguments. For example,
by giving <, we can ask for the position of the first element such that the first
argument is less than it:

```
> (position 3 '(1 0 7 5) :test #'<)
2
```

Using subseq and position, we can write functions that take sequences
apart. For example, this function

```
(defun second-word (str)
  (let ((p1 (+ (position #\  str) 1)))
    (subseq str p1 (position #\  str :start p1))))
```

returns the second word in a string of words separated by spaces:

```
> (second-word "Form follows function.")
"follows"
```

To find an element satisfying a predicate of one argument, we use
position-if. It takes a function and a sequence, and returns the position of the first element satisfying the function:

```
> (position-if #'oddp '(2 3 4 5))
1
```

It takes all the keyword arguments except :test.
There are functions similar to member and member-if for sequences.
They are, respectively, find (which takes all the keyword arguments) and
find-if (which takes all except :test):

```
> (find #\a "cat")
#\a
> (find-if #'characterp "ham")
#\h
```

Unlike member and member-if, they return only the object they were looking
for.
Often a call to find-if will be clearer if it is translated into a find with
a :key argument. For example, the expression

```
(find-if #'(lambda (x)
             (eql (car x) 'complete))
         lst)
```

would be better rendered as

```
(find 'complete lst :key #'car)
```

The functions `remove` (page 22) and `remove-if` both work on sequences generally. They bear the same relation to one another as `find` and `find-if`. A related function is `remove-duplicates`, which preserves only the last of each occurrence of any element of a sequence:

```
> (remove-duplicates "abracadabra")
"cdbra"
```

This function takes all the keyword arguments listed in the preceding table.

The function `reduce` is for boiling down a sequence into a single value. It takes at least two arguments, a function and a sequence. The function must be a function of two arguments. In the simplest case, it will be called initially with the first two elements, and thereafter with successive elements as the second argument, and the value it returned last time as the first. The value returned by the last call is returned as the value of the `reduce`. Which means that an expression like

```
(reduce #'fn '(a b c d))
```

is equivalent to

```
(fn (fn (fn 'a 'b) 'c) 'd)
```

We can use `reduce` to extend functions that only take two arguments. For example, to get the intersection of three or more lists, we could write something like

```
> (reduce #'intersection '((b r a d 's) (b a d) (c a t)))
(A)
```

4.5   Example: Parsing Dates

As an example of operations on sequences, this section shows how to write a program to parse dates. We will write a program that can take a string like "16 Aug 1980" and return a list of integers representing the day, month, and year.

```
(defun tokens (str test start)
  (let ((p1 (position-if test str :start start)))
    (if p1
        (let ((p2 (position-if #'(lambda (c)
                                   (not (funcall test c)))
                               str :start p1)))
          (cons (subseq str p1 p2)
                (if p2
                    (tokens str test p2)
                    nil)))
        nil)))

(defun constituent (c)
  (and (graphic-char-p c)
       (not (char= c #\  ))))
```

Figure 4.2: Identifying tokens.

Figure 4.2 contains some general-purpose parsing functions that we'll need in this application. The first, tokens, is for extracting the tokens from a string. Given a string and a test function, it returns a list of the substrings whose characters satisfy the function. For example, if the test function is alpha-char-p, which returns true of alphabetic characters, we get:

```
> (tokens "ab12 3cde.f" #'alpha-char-p 0)
("ab" "cde" "f")
```

All characters that do not satisfy the function are treated as whitespace—they separate tokens but are never part of them.

The function constituent is defined for use as an argument to tokens. In Common Lisp, *graphic characters* are all the characters we can see, plus the space character. So if we use constituent as the test function,

```
> (tokens "ab12 3cde.f
          gh" #'constituent 0)
("ab12" "3cde.f" "gh")
```

then tokens will have the conventional notion of whitespace.

Figure 4.3 contains functions specifically for parsing dates. The function parse-date takes a date in the specified form and returns a list of integers representing its components:

```
(defun parse-date (str)
  (let ((toks (tokens str #'constituent 0)))
    (list (parse-integer (first toks))
          (parse-month   (second toks))
          (parse-integer (third toks)))))

(defconstant month-names
  #("jan" "feb" "mar" "apr" "may" "jun"
    "jul" "aug" "sep" "oct" "nov" "dec"))

(defun parse-month (str)
  (let ((p (position str month-names
                       :test #'string-equal)))
    (if p
        (+ p 1)
        nil)))
```

Figure 4.3: Functions for parsing dates.

```
> (parse-date "16 Aug 1980")
(16 8 1980)
```

It uses tokens to break up a date string, and then calls parse-month and parse-integer to interpret the elements. To find the month, it calls parse-month, which is not case-sensitive because it uses string-equal to match the name of the month. To find the day and year, it calls the built-in parse-integer, which takes a string and returns the corresponding integer.

If we had to write code to parse integers, we might say something like:

```
(defun read-integer (str)
  (if (every #'digit-char-p str)
      (let ((accum 0))
        (dotimes (pos (length str))
          (setf accum (+ (* accum 10)
                          (digit-char-p (char str pos)))))
        accum)
      nil))
```

This definition illustrates how to get from a character to a number in Common Lisp—the function digit-char-p not only tests whether a character is a digit, but returns the corresponding integer.

4.6   Structures

A *structure* can be considered as a deluxe kind of vector. Suppose you had to write a program that kept track of a number of rectangular solids. You might consider representing them as vectors of three elements: height, width, and depth. Your program would be easier to read if, instead of using raw svrefs, you defined functions like

```
(defun block-height (b) (svref b 0))
```

and so on. You can think of a structure as a vector in which all these kinds of functions get defined for you.

To define a structure, we use defstruct. In the simplest case we just give the name of the structure and the names of the fields:

```
(defstruct point
  x
  y)
```

This defines a point to be a structure with two fields, x and y. It also implicitly defines the functions make-point, point-p, copy-point, point-x, and point-y.

Section 2.3 mentioned that Lisp programs could write Lisp programs. This is one of the most conspicuous examples we have seen so far. When you call defstruct, it automatically writes code defining several other functions. With macros you will be able to do the same thing yourself. (You could even write defstruct if you had to.)

Each call to make-point will return a new point. We can specify the values of individual fields by giving the corresponding keyword arguments:

```
> (setf p (make-point :x 0 :y 0))
#S(POINT X 0 Y 0)
```

The access functions for point fields are defined not only to retrieve values, but to work with setf.

```
> (point-x p)
0
> (setf (point-y p) 2)
2
> p
#S(POINT X 0 Y 2)
```

Defining a structure also defines a type of that name. Each point will be of type point, then structure, then atom, then t. So as well as using point-p to test whether something is a point,

```
> (point-p p)
T
> (typep p 'point)
T
```

we can also use general-purpose functions like typep.

We can specify default values for structure fields by enclosing the field name and a default expression in a list in the original definition.

```
(defstruct polemic
  (type (progn
          (format t "What kind of polemic was it? ")
          (read)))
  (effect nil))
```

If a call to make-polemic specifies no initial values for these fields, they will be set to the values of the corresponding expressions:

```
> (make-polemic)
What kind of polemic was it? scathing
#S(POLEMIC TYPE SCATHING EFFECT NIL)
```

We can also control things like the way a structure is displayed, and the prefix used in the names of the access functions it creates. Here is a more elaborate definition for point that does both:

```
(defstruct (point (:conc-name p)
                  (:print-function print-point))
  (x 0)
  (y 0))

(defun print-point (p stream depth)
  (format stream "#<~A,~A>" (px p) (py p)))
```

The :conc-name argument specifies what should be concatenated to the front of the field names to make access functions for them. By default it was point-; now it will be simply p. Not using the default makes your code a little less readable, so you would only want to do this kind of thing if you're going to be using the access functions constantly.

The :print-function is the *name* of the function that should be used to print a point when it has to be displayed—e.g. by the toplevel. This function must take three arguments: the structure to be printed, the place where it is to be printed, and a third argument that can usually be ignored.[2] We will

---

[2] In ANSI Common Lisp, you can give instead a :print-object argument, which only takes the first two arguments. There is also a macro print-unreadable-object, which should be used, when available, to display objects in #<...> syntax.

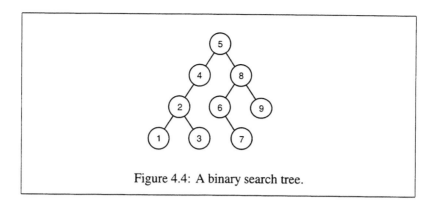

Figure 4.4: A binary search tree.

deal with streams in Section 7.1. For now, suffice it to say that the stream argument can simply be passed on to `format`.

The function `print-point` will display points in an abbreviated form:

```
> (make-point)
#<0,0>
```

4.7   Example: Binary Search Trees

Because `sort` comes built-in, you will rarely, if ever, have to write sort routines in Common Lisp. This section shows how to solve a related problem for which no ready-made solution is provided: maintaining a sorted collection of objects. The code in this section will store objects in *binary search trees*, or BSTs. When balanced, BSTs allow us to find, add, or delete elements in time proportional to log n, where n is the size of the set.

A BST is a binary tree in which, for some ordering function <, the left child of each element is < the element, and the element is < its right child. Figure 4.4 shows an example of a BST ordered according to <.

Figure 4.5 contains functions for inserting and finding objects in BSTs. The fundamental data structure will be the node, which has three fields: one for the object stored at that node, and one each for the left and right children of the node. You could think of a node as a cons cell with one car and two cdrs.

A BST is either `nil`, or a node whose `l` and `r` fields are BSTs. As lists can be built by successive calls to cons, BSTs will be built by successive calls to `bst-insert`. This function takes an object, a BST, and an ordering function, and returns a BST that contains the object. Like cons, `bst-insert` does not modify the BST given as the second argument. Here's how we would use it to build a BST:

```
(defstruct (node (:print-function
                  (lambda (n s d)
                    (format s "#<~A>" (node-elt n)))))
  elt (l nil) (r nil))

(defun bst-insert (obj bst <)
  (if (null bst)
      (make-node :elt obj)
      (let ((elt (node-elt bst)))
        (if (eql obj elt)
            bst
            (if (funcall < obj elt)
                (make-node
                 :elt elt
                 :l   (bst-insert obj (node-l bst) <)
                 :r   (node-r bst))
                (make-node
                 :elt elt
                 :r   (bst-insert obj (node-r bst) <)
                 :l   (node-l bst)))))))

(defun bst-find (obj bst <)
  (if (null bst)
      nil
      (let ((elt (node-elt bst)))
        (if (eql obj elt)
            bst
            (if (funcall < obj elt)
                (bst-find obj (node-l bst) <)
                (bst-find obj (node-r bst) <))))))

(defun bst-min (bst)
  (and bst
       (or (bst-min (node-l bst)) bst)))

(defun bst-max (bst)
  (and bst
       (or (bst-max (node-r bst)) bst)))
```

Figure 4.5: Binary search trees: Lookup and insertion.

```
> (setf nums nil)
NIL
> (dolist (x '(5 8 4 2 1 9 6 7 3))
    (setf nums (bst-insert x nums #'<)))
NIL
```

At this point the structure of nums corresponds to the tree shown in Figure 4.4.

We can use bst-find, which takes the same arguments as bst-insert, to find objects within a BST. The description of the node structure mentioned that it was like a cons cell with two cdrs. The analogy becomes clearer when we compare the definition of bst-find to the definition of our-member on page 16.

Like member, bst-find returns not just the sought-for element, but the subtree of which it is the root:

```
> (bst-find 12 nums #'<)
NIL
> (bst-find 4 nums #'<)
#<4>
```

This allows us to distinguish between failing to find something, and succeeding in finding nil.

Finding the least and greatest elements of a BST is easy. To find the least, we keep following left children, as in bst-min. To find the greatest, we keep following right children, as in bst-max:

```
> (bst-min nums)
#<1>
> (bst-max nums)
#<9>
```

Removing an element from a BST is just as fast, but requires more code. Figure 4.6 shows how to do it. The function bst-remove takes an object, a BST, and an ordering function, and returns a BST like the original one, but without the object. Like remove, it does not modify the BST given as the second argument:

```
> (setf nums (bst-remove 2 nums #'<))
#<5>
> (bst-find 2 nums #'<)
NIL
```

At this point nums might have the structure shown in Figure 4.7. (The other possibility is that 1 took the place of 2.)

```
(defun bst-remove (obj bst <)
  (if (null bst)
      nil
      (let ((elt (node-elt bst)))
        (if (eql obj elt)
            (percolate bst)
            (if (funcall < obj elt)
                (make-node
                  :elt elt
                  :l (bst-remove obj (node-l bst) <)
                  :r (node-r bst))
                (make-node
                  :elt elt
                  :r (bst-remove obj (node-r bst) <)
                  :l (node-l bst)))))))

(defun percolate (bst)
  (cond ((null (node-l bst))
         (if (null (node-r bst))
             nil
             (rperc bst)))
        ((null (node-r bst)) (lperc bst))
        (t (if (zerop (random 2))
               (lperc bst)
               (rperc bst)))))

(defun rperc (bst)
  (make-node :elt (node-elt (node-r bst))
             :l (node-l bst)
             :r (percolate (node-r bst))))

(defun lperc (bst)
  (make-node :elt (node-elt (node-l bst))
             :l (percolate (node-l bst))
             :r (node-r bst)))
```

Figure 4.6: Binary search trees: Deletion.

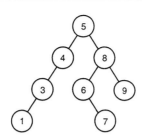

Figure 4.7: Binary search tree after removal of an element.

```
(defun bst-traverse (fn bst)
  (when bst
    (bst-traverse fn (node-l bst))
    (funcall fn (node-elt bst))
    (bst-traverse fn (node-r bst))))
```

Figure 4.8: Binary search trees: Traversal.

Deletion is more work because an object removed from an interior node leaves an empty space that has to be filled by one or the other of the children. This is the purpose of the function `percolate`. It replaces the topmost element of a BST with one of its children, then replaces the child with one of *its* children, and so on.

In order to maintain the balance of the tree, `percolate` chooses randomly if there are two children. The expression `(random 2)` will return either 0 or 1, so `(zerop (random 2))` will return true half the time.

Once we have a collection of objects inserted into a BST, an inorder traversal will yield them in ascending order. This is the purpose of `bst-traverse`, in Figure 4.8:

```
> (bst-traverse #'princ nums)
13456789
NIL
```

(The function `princ` just displays a single object.)

The code given in this section provides a skeleton implementation of BSTs. You would probably want to flesh it out somewhat, depending on the application. For example, the code given here has only a single `elt` field in each node; in many applications, it would make sense to have two fields, key and `value`. The version in this chapter also treats BSTs as sets, in the sense that duplicate insertions are ignored. But the code could easily be modified to handle duplicate elements.

BSTs are not the only way to maintain a sorted collection of objects. Whether they are the best way depends on the application. Generally, BSTs work best when insertions and deletions are evenly distributed. So one of the things they are *not* good for is maintaining priority queues. In a priority queue, the insertions may be evenly distributed, but the deletions will always happen at one end. This would cause a BST to become unbalanced, and our expected $O(\log n)$ insertions and deletions would become $O(n)$ instead. If you used a BST to represent a priority queue, you might as well use an ordinary list, because the BST would end up behaving like one.°

4.8   Hash Tables

Chapter 3 showed that lists could be used to represent both sets and mappings. When either grow to a substantial size (say 10 elements) it will be faster to use hash tables. You create a hash table by calling `make-hash-table`, which has no required arguments:

```
> (setf ht (make-hash-table))
#<Hash-Table BF0A96>
```

Like functions, hash tables are always displayed in #<...> form.

A hash table, like an assoc-list, is a way of associating pairs of objects. To retrieve the value associated with a given key, we call `gethash` with a key and a hash table. By default, `gethash` returns `nil` when there is no value associated with the key.

```
> (gethash 'color ht)
NIL
NIL
```

Here we see for the first time one of the distinctive features of Common Lisp: an expression can return multiple values. The function `gethash` returns two. The first is the value associated with the key, and the second says whether the hash table has any value stored under that key. Because the second value is `nil`, we know that the first `nil` was returned by default, not because `nil` was explicitly associated with `color`.

Most implementations will display all the return values of a call made at the toplevel, but code that expects only one return value will get just the first. Section 5.5 will explain how code can receive multiple return values.

To associate a value with a key, we use `setf` with `gethash`:

```
> (setf (gethash 'color ht) 'red)
RED
```

Now if we call `gethash` again we'll get the value we just inserted:

```
> (gethash 'color ht)
RED
T
```

The second return value proves that now we're getting a real stored object and not just a default.

The objects stored in a hash table or used as keys can be of any type. For example, if we wanted to keep some kind of information about functions, we could use a hash table with functions as keys and strings as entries:

```
> (setf bugs (make-hash-table))
#<Hash-Table BF4C36>
> (push "Doesn't take keyword arguments."
        (gethash #'our-member bugs))
("Doesn't take keyword arguments.")
```

Since `gethash` returns `nil` by default, and `push` is an abbreviation for a `setf`, we can simply push new strings into the entry for a function. (The offending `our-member` is defined on page 16.)

You can use hash tables instead of lists to represent sets. When the sets become large, lookups and deletions should be much faster with hash tables. To add a member to a set represented as a hash table, `setf` the `gethash` of it to `t`:

```
> (setf fruit (make-hash-table))
#<Hash-Table BFDE76>
> (setf (gethash 'apricot fruit) t)
T
```

Then to test for membership you just call `gethash`:

```
> (gethash 'apricot fruit)
T
T
```

Since `gethash` returns `nil` by default, a new-made hash table is also, conveniently, an empty set.

To remove an object from a set, you would call `remhash`, which removes an entry from a hash table:

```
> (remhash 'apricot fruit)
T
```

The return value shows whether there was an entry to remove; in this case there was.

There is an iteration function for hash tables: maphash, which takes a function of two arguments and a hash table. The function will be called on every key/value pair in the table, in no particular order:

```
> (setf (gethash 'shape ht) 'spherical
        (gethash 'size  ht) 'giant)
GIANT
> (maphash #'(lambda (k v)
                (format t "~A = ~A~%" k v))
            ht)
SHAPE = SPHERICAL
SIZE = GIANT
COLOR = RED
NIL
```

It always returns nil, but you can save the values by passing a function that will accumulate them in a list.

Hash tables can accommodate any number of elements, because they are expanded when they run out of space. If you want to ensure that a hash table starts with room for a particular number of elements, you can give the optional :size argument to make-hash-table. There are two reasons to do this: because you know the hash table is going to be huge, and you want to avoid expanding it; or because you know the hash table is going to be small, and you don't want to waste memory. The :size argument specifies not the number of spaces in the hash table, but the number of elements, on the average, it will be able to accommodate before being expanded. So

```
(make-hash-table :size 5)
```

would return a hash table intended to hold up to five elements.

Like any structure involved in lookups, hash tables must have some notion of equality for keys. By default they use eql, but you can specify that a hash table should use eq, equal, or equalp instead by providing the optional :test argument:

```
> (setf writers (make-hash-table :test #'equal))
#<Hash-Table C005E6>
> (setf (gethash '(ralph waldo emerson) writers) t)
T
```

This is one of the trade-offs we have to make for the efficiency of hash tables. With lists, we could specify the equality predicate in the call to member. With hash tables we have to decide ahead of time, and specify it when the hash table is created.

Most of the trade-offs in Lisp programming (or life, for that matter) have this character. Initially you try to keep things fluid, even at the cost of efficiency. Later, as the program hardens, you can sacrifice some flexibility for speed.

Summary

1. Common Lisp supports arrays of at least 7 dimensions. One-dimensional arrays are called vectors.

2. Strings are vectors of characters. Characters are objects in their own right.

3. Sequences include lists and vectors. Many sequence functions take keyword arguments from a standard set.

4. Parsing is easy in Lisp because it has so many functions that work on strings.

5. Calling defstruct defines a structure with named fields. It is a good example of a program that writes programs.

6. Binary search trees are useful for maintaining a sorted collection of objects.

7. Hash tables provide a more efficient way to represent sets and mappings.

Exercises

1. Define a function to take a square array (an array whose dimensions are $(n\ n)$) and rotate it 90° clockwise:

```
> (quarter-turn #2A((a b) (c d)))
#2A((C A) (D B))
```

You'll need array-dimensions (page 361).

2. Read the description of `reduce` on page 368, then use it to define:

    (a) `copy-list`

    (b) `reverse` (for lists)

3. Define a structure to represent a tree where each node contains some data and has up to three children. Define

    (a) a function to copy such a tree (so that no node in the copy is `eql` to a node in the original)

    (b) a function that takes an object and such a tree, and returns true if the object is `eql` to the data field of one of the nodes

4. Define a function that takes a BST and returns a list of its elements ordered from greatest to least.

5. Define `bst-adjoin`. This function should take the same arguments as `bst-insert`, but should only insert the object if there is nothing `eql` to it in the tree.

6. The contents of any hash table can be described by an assoc-list whose elements are $(k \ . \ v)$, for each key-value pair in the hash table. Define a function that

    (a) takes an assoc-list and returns a corresponding hash table

    (b) takes a hash table and returns a corresponding assoc-list

5

Control

Section 2.2 introduced the Common Lisp evaluation rule, which by now should be familiar from long experience. What the operators in this chapter have in common is that they all violate the evaluation rule. They let you direct the course that evaluation will take through the text of a program. If ordinary function calls are the leaves of a Lisp program, these operators are used to build the branches.

5.1 Blocks

Common Lisp has three basic operators for creating blocks of code: `progn`, `block`, and `tagbody`. We have seen `progn` already. The expressions within its body are evaluated in order, and the value of the last is returned:°

```
> (progn
    (format t "a")
    (format t "b")
    (+ 11 12))
ab
23
```

Since only the value of the last expression is returned, the use of `progn` (or any block) implies side-effects.

A `block` is like a `progn` with a name and an emergency exit. The first argument should be a symbol. This becomes the name of the block. At any point within the body, you can halt evaluation and return a value immediately by using `return-from` with the block's name:

```
> (block head
    (format t "Here we go.")
    (return-from head 'idea)
    (format t "We'll never see this."))
Here we go.
IDEA
```

Calling `return-from` allows your code to make a sudden but graceful exit from anywhere in a body of code. The second argument to `return-from` is returned as the value of the block named by the first. Expressions after the `return-from` are not evaluated.

There is also a `return` macro, which returns its argument as the value of an enclosing block named `nil`:

```
> (block nil
    (return 27))
27
```

Many Common Lisp operators that take a body of expressions implicitly enclose the body in a `block` named `nil`. All iteration constructs do, for example:

```
> (dolist (x '(a b c d e))
    (format t "~A " x)
    (if (eql x 'c)
        (return 'done)))
A B C
DONE
```

The body of a function defined with `defun` is implicitly enclosed in a `block` with the same name as the function, so you can say:

```
(defun foo ()
  (return-from foo 27))
```

Outside of an explicit or implicit `block`, neither `return-from` nor `return` will work.

Using `return-from` we can write a better version of `read-integer`:

```
(defun read-integer (str)
  (let ((accum 0))
    (dotimes (pos (length str))
      (let ((i (digit-char-p (char str pos))))
        (if i
            (setf accum (+ (* accum 10) i))
            (return-from read-integer nil))))
    accum))
```

The version on page 68 had to check all the characters before building the integer. Now the two steps can be combined, because we can abandon the calculation if we encounter a character that's not a digit.

The third basic block construct is `tagbody`, within which you can use gotos. Atoms appearing in the body are interpreted as labels; giving such a label to go sends control to the expression following it. Here is an exceedingly ugly piece of code for printing out the numbers from 1 to 10:

```
> (tagbody
    (setf x 0)
    top
    (setf x (+ x 1))
    (format t "~A " x)
    (if (< x 10) (go top)))
1 2 3 4 5 6 7 8 9 10
NIL
```

This operator is mainly something that other operators are built upon, not something you would use yourself. Most iteration operators have an implicit `tagbody`, so it's possible (though rarely desirable) to use labels and go within their bodies.

How do you decide which block construct to use? Nearly all the time you'll use `progn`. If you want to allow for sudden exits, use `block` instead. Most programmers will never use `tagbody` explicitly.

5.2   Context

Another operator we've used to group expressions is `let`. It takes a body of code, but also allows us to establish new variables for use within the body:

```
> (let ((x 7)
        (y 2))
    (format t "Number")
    (+ x y))
Number
9
```

An operator like `let` creates a new *lexical context*. Within this context there are two new variables, and variables from outer contexts may have thereby become invisible.

Conceptually, a `let` expression is like a function call. Section 2.14 showed that, as well as referring to a function by name, we could refer to it literally by using a lambda expression. Since a lambda expression is like the name of a function, we can use one, as we would a function name, as the first element in a function call:

```
> ((lambda (x) (+ x 1)) 3)
4
```

The preceding `let` expression is exactly equivalent to:

```
((lambda (x y)
   (format t "Number")
   (+ x y))
 7
 2)
```

Any questions you have about `let` should be dealt with by passing the buck to `lambda`, because entering a `let` is conceptually equivalent to doing a function call.°

One of the things this model makes clear is that the value of one `let`-created variable can't depend on other variables created by the same `let`. For example, if we tried to say

```
(let ((x 2)
      (y (+ x 1)))
  (+ x y))
```

then the x in (+ x 1) would *not* be the x established in the previous line, because the whole expression is equivalent to

```
((lambda (x y) (+ x y)) 2
                        (+ x 1))
```

Here it's obvious that the (+ x 1) passed as an argument to the function cannot refer to the parameter x within the function.

So what if you do want the value of one new variable to depend on the value of another variable established by the same expression? In that case you would use a variant called `let*`:

```
> (let* ((x 1)
         (y (+ x 1)))
    (+ x y))
3
```

A `let*` is functionally equivalent to a series of nested `let`s. This particular example is equivalent to:

```
(let ((x 1))
  (let ((y (+ x 1)))
    (+ x y)))
```

In both `let` and `let*`, initial values default to `nil`. Such variables need not be enclosed within lists:

```
> (let (x y)
    (list x y))
(NIL NIL)
```

The `destructuring-bind` macro is a generalization of `let`. Instead of single variables, it takes a *pattern*—one or more variables arranged in the form of a tree—and binds them to the corresponding parts of some actual tree. For example:

```
> (destructuring-bind (w (x y) . z) '(a (b c) d e)
    (list w x y z))
(A B C (D E))
```

It causes an error if the tree given as the second argument doesn't match the pattern given as the first.

5.3　Conditionals

The simplest conditional is `if`; all the others are built upon it. The simplest after `if` is `when`, which takes an expression and a body of code. The body will be evaluated if the test expression returns true. So

```
(when (oddp that)
  (format t "Hmm, that's odd.")
  (+ that 1))
```

is equivalent to

```
(if (oddp that)
    (progn
      (format t "Hmm, that's odd.")
      (+ that 1)))
```

The opposite of `when` is `unless`; it takes the same arguments, but the body will be evaluated only if the test expression returns false.

The mother of all conditionals (in both senses) is `cond`, which brings two new advantages: it allows multiple conditions, and the code associated with each has an implicit `progn`. It's intended for use in situations where we would otherwise have to make the third argument of an `if` another `if`. For example, this pseudo-member

```
(defun our-member (obj lst)
  (if (atom lst)
      nil
      (if (eql (car lst) obj)
          lst
          (our-member obj (cdr lst))))))
```

could also be defined as

```
(defun our-member (obj lst)
  (cond ((atom lst) nil)
        ((eql (car lst) obj) lst)
        (t (our-member obj (cdr lst))))))
```

In fact, a Common Lisp implementation will probably implement cond by translating the latter into the former.

In general, cond takes zero or more arguments. Each one must be a list consisting of a condition followed by zero or more expressions. When the cond expression is evaluated, the conditions are evaluated in order until one of them returns true. When it does, the expressions associated with it are evaluated in order, and the value of the last is returned as the value of the cond. If there are no expressions after the successful condition

```
> (cond (99))
99
```

the value of the condition itself is returned.

Since a cond clause with a condition of t will always succeed, it is conventional to make the final, default clause have t as the condition. If no clause succeeds, the cond returns nil, but it is usually bad style to take advantage of this return value. (For an example of the kind of problem that can occur, see page 292.)

When you want to compare a value against a series of constants, there is case. We might use case to define a function to return the number of days in a month:

```
(defun month-length (mon)
  (case mon
    ((jan mar may jul aug oct dec) 31)
    ((apr jun sept nov) 30)
    (feb (if (leap-year) 29 28))
    (otherwise "unknown month")))
```

A case expression begins with an argument whose value will be compared against the keys in each clause. Then come zero or more clauses, each one beginning with either a key, or a list of keys, followed by zero or more expressions. The keys are treated as constants; they will not be evaluated. The value of the first argument is compared (using eql) to the key/s at the head of each clause. If there is a match, the expressions in the rest of that clause are evaluated, and the value of the last is returned as the value of the case.

The default clause may have the key t or otherwise. If no clause succeeds, or the successful clause contains only keys,

```
> (case 99 (99))
NIL
```

then the case returns nil.

The typecase macro is similar to case, except that the keys in each clause should be type specifiers, and the value of the first argument is compared to the keys using typep instead of eql. (An example of typecase appears on page 107.)

5.4   Iteration

The basic iteration operator is do, which was introduced in Section 2.13. Since do contains both an implicit block and an implicit tagbody, we now know that it's possible to use return, return-from, and go within the body of a do.

Section 2.13 mentioned that the first argument to do had to be a list of specifications for variables, each possibly of the form

$$(variable\ initial\ update)$$

The *initial* and *update* forms are optional. If the *update* form is omitted, the variable won't be updated on successive iterations. If the *initial* form is also omitted, the variable will be initially nil.

In the example on page 23,

```
(defun show-squares (start end)
  (do ((i start (+ i 1)))
      ((> i end) 'done)
    (format t "~A ~A~%" i (* i i))))
```

the *update* form refers to the variable created by the do. This is commonplace. It would be rare to find a do whose *update* forms didn't refer to at least one of its own variables.

When more than one variable is to be updated, the question arises, if an *update* form refers to a variable that has its own *update* form, does it get the updated value or the value from the previous iteration? With do, it gets the latter:

```
> (let ((x 'a))
    (do ((x 1 (+ x 1))
         (y x x))
        ((> x 5))
      (format t "(~A ~A)  " x y)))
(1 A)  (2 1)  (3 2)  (4 3)  (5 4)
NIL
```

On each iteration, x gets its previous value plus 1; y also gets the *previous* value of x.

But there is also a do*, which has the same relation to do as let* does to let. Any *initial* or *update* form can refer to a variable from a previous clause, and it will get the current value:

```
> (do* ((x 1 (+ x 1))
        (y x x))
       ((> x 5))
     (format t "(~A ~A)  " x y))
(1 1)  (2 2)  (3 3)  (4 4)  (5 5)
NIL
```

Besides do and do* there are several special-purpose iteration operators. To iterate over the elements of a list, we can use dolist:

```
> (dolist (x '(a b c d) 'done)
    (format t "~A " x))
A B C D
DONE
```

The third expression within the initial list will be evaluated and returned as the value of the dolist when iteration terminates. It defaults to nil.

Similar in spirit is dotimes, which for some *n* iterates over the integers from 0 to $n-1$:

```
> (dotimes (x 5 x)
    (format t "~A " x))
0 1 2 3 4
5
```

As with dolist, the third expression in the initial list is optional and defaults to nil. Notice that it can refer to the iteration variable.

The function mapc is like mapcar but does not cons up a new list as a return value, so the only reason to use it is for side-effects. It is more flexible than dolist, because it can traverse multiple lists in parallel:

THE POINT OF do

In "The Evolution of Lisp," Steele and Gabriel express the point of do *so well that the passage is worth quoting in its entirety:*

Arguments over syntax aside, there is something to be said for recognizing that a loop that steps only one variable is pretty useless, in *any* programming language. It is almost always the case that one variable is used to generate successive values while another is used to accumulate a result. If the loop syntax steps only the generating variable, then the accumulating variable must be stepped "manually" by using assignment statements. . .or some other side effect. The multiple-variable do loop reflects an essential symmetry between generation and accumulation, allowing iteration to be expressed without explicit side effects:

```
(defun factorial (n)
  (do ((j n (- j 1))
       (f 1 (* j f)))
      ((= j 0) f)))
```

It is indeed not unusual for a do loop of this form to have an empty body, performing all its real work in the *step* forms.°

```
> (mapc #'(lambda (x y)
            (format t "~A ~A  " x y))
         '(hip flip slip)
         '(hop flop slop))
HIP HOP  FLIP FLOP  SLIP SLOP
(HIP FLIP SLIP)
```

It always returns its second argument.

5.5 Multiple Values

One used to say, in order to emphasize the importance of functional programming, that every Lisp expression returned a value. Now things are not so simple; in Common Lisp, an expression can return zero or more values. The maximum number of return values is implementation-dependent, but it will be at least 19.

Multiple values allow a function that calculates several things to return them without having to build a structure to contain them all. For example, the built-in get-decoded-time returns the current time in nine values: second, minute, hour, date, month, day, and two others.

Multiple values also make it possible to have lookup functions that can distinguish between finding `nil` and failing to find something. This is why `gethash` returns two values. Because it uses the *second* value to indicate success or failure, we can store `nil` in a hash table just like any other value.

The `values` function returns multiple values. It returns exactly the values you give it as arguments:

```
> (values 'a nil (+ 2 4))
A
NIL
6
```

If a `values` expression is the last thing to be evaluated in the body of a function, its return values become those of the function. Multiple values are passed on intact through any number of returns:

```
> ((lambda () ((lambda () (values 1 2)))))
1
2
```

However, if something is expecting only one value, all but the first will be discarded:

```
> (let ((x (values 1 2)))
    x)
1
```

By using `values` with no arguments, it's possible to return no values. In that case, something expecting one will get `nil`:

```
> (values)
> (let ((x (values)))
    x)
NIL
```

To receive multiple values, we use `multiple-value-bind`:

```
> (multiple-value-bind (x y z) (values 1 2 3)
    (list x y z))
(1 2 3)
> (multiple-value-bind (x y z) (values 1 2)
    (list x y z))
(1 2 NIL)
```

If there are more variables than values, the leftover ones will be nil. If there are more values than variables, the extra values will be discarded. So to print just the time we might write:°

```
> (multiple-value-bind (s m h) (get-decoded-time)
    (format nil "~A:~A:~A" h m s))
"4:32:13"
```

You can pass on multiple values as the arguments to a second function using multiple-value-call:

```
> (multiple-value-call #'+ (values 1 2 3))
6
```

There is also a function multiple-value-list:

```
> (multiple-value-list (values 'a 'b 'c))
(A B C)
```

which is like using multiple-value-call with #'list as the first argument.

5.6   Aborts

You can use return to exit from a block at any point. Sometimes we want to do something even more drastic, and transfer control back through several function calls. To do this we use catch and throw. A catch expression takes a tag, which can be any kind of object, followed by a body of expressions.

```
(defun super ()
  (catch 'abort
    (sub)
    (format t "We'll never see this.")))

(defun sub ()
  (throw 'abort 99))
```

The expressions are evaluated in order, as if in a progn. At any point within this code or code called by it, a throw with the corresponding tag will cause the catch expression to return immediately:

```
> (super)
99
```

A throw with a given tag will pass control through (and thereby kill) any catches with other tags in order to reach the one with the matching tag. If there is no pending catch with the right tag, the throw causes an error.

Calling error also interrupts execution, but instead of transferring control to another point higher up in the calling tree, it transfers control to the Lisp error handler. Usually the result will be to invoke a break loop. Here is what might happen in a hypothetical Common Lisp implementation:

```
> (progn
    (error "Oops!")
    (format t "After the error."))
Error: Oops!
      Options: :abort, :backtrace
>>
```

For more on errors and conditions, see Section 14.6 and Appendix A.

Sometimes you want code to be proof against interruptions like throws and errors. By using an unwind-protect, you can ensure that such interruptions won't leave your program in an inconsistent state. An unwind-protect takes any number of arguments and returns the value of the first. However, the remaining expressions will be evaluated even if the evaluation of the first is interrupted.

```
> (setf x 1)
1
> (catch 'abort
    (unwind-protect
        (throw 'abort 99)
        (setf x 2)))
99
> x
2
```

Here, even though the throw sends control back to the waiting catch, unwind-protect ensures that the second expression gets evaluated on the way out. Whenever certain actions have to be followed by some kind of cleanup or reset, unwind-protect may be useful. One example is mentioned on page 121.

5.7   Example: Date Arithmetic

In some applications it's useful to be able to add and subtract dates—to be able to calculate, for example, that the date 60 days after December 17, 1997 is February 15, 1998. In this section we will write a utility for date arithmetic. We will convert dates to integers, with zero fixed at January 1, 2000. We will be able to manipulate such integers using the built-in + and − functions, and when we're finished, convert the result back to a date.

To convert a date to an integer, we will add together the number of days represented by each of its components. For example, the integer value of November 13, 2004 is the sum of the number of days up to 2004, plus the number of days up to November, plus 13.

One thing we'll need here is a table listing the number of days up to the start of each month in a non-leap year. We can use Lisp to derive the contents of this table. We start by making a list of the lengths of each of the months:

```
> (setf mon '(31 28 31 30 31 30 31 31 30 31 30 31))
(31 28 31 30 31 30 31 31 30 31 30 31)
```

We can test that the lengths add up properly by applying + to the list:

```
> (apply #'+ mon)
365
```

Now if we reverse the list and use `maplist` to apply + to successive cdrs, we can get the number of days up to the beginning of each month:

```
> (setf nom (reverse mon))
(31 30 31 30 31 31 30 31 30 31 28 31)
> (setf sums (maplist #'(lambda (x)
                          (apply #'+ x))
                      nom))
(365 334 304 273 243 212 181 151 120 90 59 31)
> (reverse sums)
(31 59 90 120 151 181 212 243 273 304 334 365)
```

These numbers indicate that there are 31 days up to the start of February, 59 up to the start of March, and so on.

The list we just created is transformed into a vector in Figure 5.1, which contains the code for converting dates to integers.

There are four stages in the life of a typical Lisp program: it is written, then read, then compiled, then run. One of the distinctive things about Lisp is that it's there at every stage. You can invoke Lisp when your program is running, of course, but you can also invoke it when your program is compiled (Section 10.2) and when it is read (Section 14.3). The way we derived month shows how you can use Lisp even as you're writing a program.

Efficiency usually only matters in the last of the four stages, run-time. In the first three stages you can feel free to take advantage of the power and flexibility of lists without worrying about the cost.

```
(defconstant month
  #(0 31 59 90 120 151 181 212 243 273 304 334 365))

(defconstant yzero 2000)

(defun leap? (y)
  (and (zerop (mod y 4))
       (or (zerop (mod y 400))
           (not (zerop (mod y 100)))))))

(defun date->num (d m y)
  (+ (- d 1) (month-num m y) (year-num y)))

(defun month-num (m y)
  (+ (svref month (- m 1))
     (if (and (> m 2) (leap? y)) 1 0)))

(defun year-num (y)
  (let ((d 0))
    (if (>= y yzero)
        (dotimes (i (- y yzero) d)
          (incf d (year-days (+ yzero i))))
        (dotimes (i (- yzero y) (- d))
          (incf d (year-days (+ y i)))))))

(defun year-days (y) (if (leap? y) 366 365))
```

Figure 5.1: Date arithmetic: Converting dates to integers.

If you used the code in Figure 5.1 to drive a time machine, people would probably disagree with you about the date when you arrived. European dates have shifted, even in comparatively recent times, as people got a more precise idea of the length of a year. In English-speaking countries, the last such discontinuity was in 1752, when the date went straight from September 2 to September 14.°

The number of days in a year depends on whether it is a leap year. A year is a leap year if it is divisible by 4, unless it is divisible by 100, in which case it isn't—unless it is divisible by 400, in which case it is. So 1904 was a leap year, 1900 wasn't, and 1600 was.

To determine whether one number is divisible by another we use the function mod, which returns the remainder after division:

```
> (mod 23 5)
3
> (mod 25 5)
0
```

The first argument is divisible by the second if the remainder is zero. The function `leap?` uses this technique to determine whether its argument is a leap year:

```
> (mapcar #'leap? '(1904 1900 1600))
(T NIL T)
```

The function we'll use to convert dates to integers is `date->num`. It returns the sum of the values for each component of a date. To find the number of days up to the start of the month, it calls `month-num`, which looks in `month`, then adds 1 if the month is after February in a leap year.

To find the number of days up to the start of the year, `date->num` calls `year-num`, which returns the integer representing January 1 of that year. This function works by counting up or down from the year y given as an argument toward year zero (2000).

Figure 5.2 shows the second half of the code. The function `num->date` converts integers back to dates. It calls `num-year`, which returns the year in the date, and the number of days left over. It passes the latter to `num-month`, which extracts the month and day.

Like `year-num`, `num-year` counts up or down from year zero, one year at a time. It accumulates days until it has a number whose absolute value is greater than or equal to that of n. If it was counting down, then it can return the values from the current iteration. Otherwise it will overshoot the year, and must return the values from the previous iteration. This is the point of `prev`, which on each iteration will be given the value that `days` had on the previous iteration.

The function `num-month` and its subroutine `nmon` behave like `month-num` in reverse. They go from value to position in the constant vector `month`, while `month-num` goes from position to value.

The first two functions in Figure 5.2 could have been combined in one. Instead of returning values to another function, `num-year` could invoke `num-month` directly. The code is easier to test interactively when it's broken up like this, but now that it works, the next step might be to combine them.

With `date->num` and `num->date`, date arithmetic is easy.° We use them as in `date+`, which can add or subtract days from a date. If we ask `date+` for the date 60 days from December 17, 1997,

```
> (multiple-value-list (date+ 17 12 1997 60))
(15 2 1998)
```

we get February 15, 1998.

```
(defun num->date (n)
  (multiple-value-bind (y left) (num-year n)
    (multiple-value-bind (m d) (num-month left y)
      (values d m y))))

(defun num-year (n)
  (if (< n 0)
      (do* ((y (- yzero 1) (- y 1))
            (d (- (year-days y)) (- d (year-days y))))
           ((<= d n) (values y (- n d))))
      (do* ((y yzero (+ y 1))
            (prev 0 d)
            (d (year-days y) (+ d (year-days y))))
           ((> d n) (values y (- n prev))))))

(defun num-month (n y)
  (if (leap? y)
      (cond ((= n 59) (values 2 29))
            ((> n 59) (nmon (- n 1)))
            (t        (nmon n)))
      (nmon n)))

(defun nmon (n)
  (let ((m (position n month :test #'<)))
    (values m (+ 1 (- n (svref month (- m 1)))))))

(defun date+ (d m y n)
  (num->date (+ (date->num d m y) n)))
```

Figure 5.2: Date arithmetic: Converting integers to dates.

Summary

1. Common Lisp has three basic block constructs: progn; block, which allows returns; and tagbody, which allows gotos. Many built-in operators have implicit blocks.

2. Entering a new lexical context is conceptually equivalent to a function call.

3. Common Lisp provides conditionals suited to various situations. All can be defined in terms of if.

4. There is a similar variety of operators for iteration.

5. Expressions can return multiple values.

6. Computations can be interrupted, and protected against the consequences of interruption.

Exercises

1. Translate the following expressions into equivalent expressions that don't use `let` or `let*`, and don't cause the same expression to be evaluated twice.

   (a) `(let ((x (car y)))`
       `  (cons x x))`
   (b) `(let* ((w (car x))`
            `   (y (+ w z)))`
       `  (cons w y))`

2. Rewrite `mystery` (page 29) to use `cond`.

3. Define a function that returns the square of its argument, and which does not compute the square if the argument is a positive integer less than or equal to 5.

4. Rewrite `num-month` (Figure 5.1) to use `case` instead of `svref`.

5. Define iterative and recursive versions of a function that takes an object *x* and vector *v*, and returns a list of all the objects that immediately precede *x* in *v*:

   ```
   > (precedes #\a "abracadabra")
   (#\c #\d #\r)
   ```

6. Define iterative and recursive versions of a function that takes an object and a list, and returns a new list in which the object appears between each pair of elements in the original list:

   ```
   > (intersperse '- '(a b c d))
   (A - B - C - D)
   ```

7. Define a function that takes a list of numbers and returns true iff the difference between each successive pair of them is 1, using

   (a) recursion

   (b) do

   (c) mapc and return

8. Define a single recursive function that returns, as two values, the maximum and minimum elements of a vector.

9. The program in Figure 3.12 continues to search as the first complete path works its way through the queue. In broad searches this would be a problem.

   (a) Using catch and throw, modify the program to return the first complete path as soon as it is discovered.

   (b) Rewrite the program to do the same thing without using catch and throw.

6

Functions

Understanding functions is one of the keys to understanding Lisp. Conceptually, functions are at the core of Lisp. Practically, they are one of the most useful tools at your disposal.

6.1 Global Functions

The predicate `fboundp` tells whether there is a function with a given symbol as its name. If a symbol is the name of a function, `symbol-function` will return it:

```
> (fboundp '+)
T
> (symbol-function '+)
#<Compiled-Function + 17BA4E>
```

By setting the `symbol-function` of some name to a function,

```
(setf (symbol-function 'add2)
      #'(lambda (x) (+ x 2)))
```

we thereby define a new global function, which we can use just as if we had defined it with `defun`:

```
> (add2 1)
3
```

In fact, defun does little more than translate something like

```
(defun add2 (x) (+ x 2))
```

into the setf expression above. Using defun makes programs look nicer, and may help the compiler, but strictly speaking you don't need it to write programs.

By making the first argument to defun a list of the form (setf f), you define what happens when the first argument to setf is a call to f.° The following pair of functions defines primo as a synonym for car:

```
(defun primo (lst) (car lst))
```

```
(defun (setf primo) (val lst)
  (setf (car lst) val))
```

In the definition of a function whose name is of the form (setf f), the first parameter represents the new value, and the remaining parameters represent arguments to f.°

Now any setf of primo will be a call to the latter function above:

```
> (let ((x (list 'a 'b 'c)))
    (setf (primo x) 480)
    x)
(480 B C)
```

It's not necessary to define primo in order to define (setf primo), but such definitions usually come in pairs.

Since strings are Lisp expressions, there is no reason they can't appear within bodies of code. A string by itself does not have side-effects, and so doesn't make any difference unless it's the last expression. If you make a string the first expression in the body of a function defined with defun,

```
(defun foo (x)
  "Implements an enhanced paradigm of diversity."
  x)
```

then that string will become the function's documentation string. The documentation for a globally defined function can be retrieved by calling documentation:

```
> (documentation 'foo 'function)
"Implements an enhanced paradigm of diversity."
```

6.2   Local Functions

Functions defined via defun or setf of symbol-function are *global* functions. Like global variables you have access to them anywhere. It is also possible to define *local* functions, which, like local variables, are only accessible within a certain context.

Local functions can be defined with labels, which is a kind of let for functions. Its first argument, instead of being a list of specifications for new local variables, is a list of definitions of new local functions. Each element of the list is of the form

$$(name \; parameters \; . \; body)$$

Within the remainder of the labels expression, calling *name* is equivalent to calling (lambda *parameters . body*).

```
> (labels ((add10 (x) (+ x 10))
           (consa (x) (cons 'a x)))
    (consa (add10 3)))
(A . 13)
```

The analogy to let breaks down in one respect. Local functions defined by a labels expression can refer to any other functions defined there, including themselves. So it's possible to define recursive local functions this way:

```
> (labels ((len (lst)
             (if (null lst)
                 0
                 (+ (len (cdr lst)) 1))))
    (len '(a b c)))
3
```

Section 5.2 showed how a let expression could be understood as a function call. A do expression can be similarly explained as a call to a recursive function. A do of the form

```
(do ((x a (b x))
     (y c (d y)))
    ((test x y) (z x y))
  (f x y))
```

is equivalent to

```
(labels ((rec (x y)
            (cond ((test x y)
                   (z x y))
                  (t
                   (f x y)
                   (rec (b x) (d y)))))))
   (rec a c))
```

This model can be used to resolve any questions you might still have about
the behavior of do.

6.3   Parameter Lists

Section 2.1 showed that with prefix notation + could take any number of
arguments. Since then we have seen several functions that could take varying
numbers of arguments. To write such functions ourselves, we need to use
something called a *rest* parameter.

   If we insert the token &rest before the last variable in the parameter list
of a function, then when the function is called, this variable will be set to a
list of all the remaining arguments. Now we can see how funcall would be
written in terms of apply. It might be defined as:

```
(defun our-funcall (fn &rest args)
  (apply fn args))
```

   We have also seen operators in which arguments could be omitted, and
would default to certain values. Such parameters are called *optional* parameters. (By contrast, ordinary parameters are sometimes called *required*
parameters.) If the symbol &optional occurs in the parameter list of a
function,

```
(defun philosoph (thing &optional property)
  (list thing 'is property))
```

then all the arguments after it are optional, and default to nil:

```
> (philosoph 'death)
(DEATH IS NIL)
```

We give an explicit default by enclosing it in a list with the parameter. This
version of philosoph

```
(defun philosoph (thing &optional (property 'fun))
  (list thing 'is property))
```

has a more cheerful default:

```
> (philosoph 'death)
(DEATH IS FUN)
```

The default for an optional parameter need not be a constant. It can be any Lisp expression. If this expression isn't a constant, it will be evaluated anew each time a default is needed.

A *keyword parameter* is a more flexible kind of optional parameter. If you put the symbol &key in a parameter list, then all the parameters after it are optional. Moreover, when the function is called, these parameters will be identified not by their position, but by symbolic tags that precede them:

```
> (defun keylist (a &key x y z)
    (list a x y z))
KEYLIST
> (keylist 1 :y 2)
(1 NIL 2 NIL)
> (keylist 1 :y 3 :x 2)
(1 2 3 NIL)
```

Like ordinary optional parameters, keyword parameters default to nil, but explicit defaults may be specified in the parameter list.

Keywords and their associated arguments can be collected in rest parameters and passed on to other functions that are expecting them. For example, we could define adjoin as:

```
(defun our-adjoin (obj lst &rest args)
  (if (apply #'member obj lst args)
      lst
      (cons obj lst)))
```

Since adjoin takes the same keyword arguments as member, we just collect them in a rest argument and pass them on to member.

Section 5.2 introduced the destructuring-bind macro. In the general case, each subtree in the pattern given as the first argument may be as complex as the parameter list of a function:

```
> (destructuring-bind ((&key w x) &rest y) '((:w 3) a)
    (list w x y))
(3 NIL (A))
```

6.4   Example: Utilities

Section 2.6 mentioned that Lisp consists mostly of Lisp functions, just like the
ones you can define yourself. This is a useful feature to have in a programming
language: you don't have to modify your ideas to suit the language, because
you can modify the language to suit your ideas. If you find yourself wishing
that Common Lisp included a certain function, you can write it yourself, and
it will be just as much a part of the language as + or eql.

Experienced Lisp programmers work bottom-up as well as top-down.
While they're writing their program down toward the language, they also
build the language up toward their program. This way, language and program
meet sooner, and more neatly.

Operators written to augment Lisp are called *utilities*. As you write more
Lisp programs, you will find that you develop a collection of them, and that
many of the utilities you write during one project will turn out to be useful in
the next one.

Professional programmers often find that the program they're working
on now has a great deal in common with some program they wrote in the
past. It is this feeling that makes the idea of software reuse so attractive.
Somehow reuse has become associated with object-oriented programming.
But software does not have to be object-oriented to be reusable—this is
obvious when we look at programming languages (that is, compilers), which
are the most reusable software of all.

The way to get reusable software is to write programs bottom-up, and
programs don't have to be object-oriented to be written bottom-up. In fact,
the functional style seems even better adapted for writing reusable software.
Consider sort. You are unlikely ever to have to write your own sort routines
in Common Lisp; sort is so fast and so general that it would not be worth
the trouble. *That's* reusable software.

You can do the same thing in your own programs by writing utilities.
Figure 6.1 contains a selection of them. The first two, single? and append1,
are included to show that even very short utilities can be useful. The former
returns true when its argument is a list of one element,

```
> (single? '(a))
T
```

and the latter is like cons, but adds an element to the end of the list instead
of the front:

```
> (append1 '(a b c) 'd)
(A B C D)
```

The next utility, map-int, takes a function and an integer n, and returns
a list of the results of calling the function on the integers from 0 to n-1.

```
(defun single? (lst)
  (and (consp lst) (null (cdr lst))))

(defun append1 (lst obj)
  (append lst (list obj)))

(defun map-int (fn n)
  (let ((acc nil))
    (dotimes (i n)
      (push (funcall fn i) acc))
    (nreverse acc)))

(defun filter (fn lst)
  (let ((acc nil))
    (dolist (x lst)
      (let ((val (funcall fn x)))
        (if val (push val acc))))
    (nreverse acc)))

(defun most (fn lst)
  (if (null lst)
      (values nil nil)
      (let* ((wins (car lst))
             (max (funcall fn wins)))
        (dolist (obj (cdr lst))
          (let ((score (funcall fn obj)))
            (when (> score max)
              (setf wins obj
                    max  score))))
        (values wins max))))
```

Figure 6.1: Utility functions.

This turns out to be especially useful when one is testing code. (One of the advantages of Lisp's interactive environment is that it's easy to write programs to test your programs.) If we just wanted a list of the numbers from 0 to 9, we could say:

```
> (map-int #'identity 10)
(0 1 2 3 4 5 6 7 8 9)
```

And if we wanted a list of 10 random numbers between 0 and 99 (inclusive), we could ignore the parameter and just say:

```
> (map-int #'(lambda (x) (random 100))
            10)
(85 40 73 64 28 21 40 67 5 32)
```

The definition of map-int illustrates one of the standard Lisp idioms for building a list. We create an accumulator acc, initially nil, and push successive objects onto it. When we're finished, we reverse the accumulator.[1]

We see the same idiom in filter. This function takes a function and a list, and returns all the non-nil values returned by the function as it is applied to the elements of the list:

```
> (filter #'(lambda (x)
              (and (evenp x) (+ x 10)))
           '(1 2 3 4 5 6 7))
(12 14 16)
```

Another way to think of filter is as a generalized version of remove-if.

The last function in Figure 6.1, most, returns the element of a list with the highest score, according to some scoring function. It returns two values, the winning element, and its score:

```
> (most #'length '((a b) (a b c) (a)))
(A B C)
3
```

If there is a tie, the element occurring first is returned.

Notice that the last three functions in Figure 6.1 all take functions as arguments. Lisp makes it convenient to pass functions as arguments, and that's one of the reasons it is so well suited to bottom-up programming.° A successful utility must be general, and it's easier to abstract out the general when you can pass the specific as a functional argument.

The functions given in this section were general-purpose utilities. They could be used in almost any kind of program. But you can write utilities for specific classes of programs as well. Indeed, as we'll see when we get to macros, you can write your own specialized languages on top of Lisp, if you want to. If you are trying to write reusable software, this would seem the surest way to do it.

---

[1] In this context, nreverse (described on page 222) does the same thing as reverse, but is more efficient.

6.5   Closures

A function can be returned as the value of an expression just like any other kind of object. Here is a function that takes one argument, and returns a function to combine arguments of that type:

```
(defun combiner (x)
  (typecase x
    (number #'+)
    (list   #'append)
    (t      #'list)))
```

On top of this we can build a general combination function

```
(defun combine (&rest args)
  (apply (combiner (car args))
         args))
```

which takes arguments of any type and combines them in a way appropriate to their type. (To simplify the example, we assume that the arguments will all be of the same type.)

```
> (combine 2 3)
5
> (combine '(a b) '(c d))
(A B C D)
```

Section 2.10 mentioned that lexical variables are only valid within the context where they are defined. Along with this restriction comes the promise that they will *continue* to be valid for as long as something is using the context.

If a function is defined within the scope of a lexical variable, it can continue to refer to that variable, even if it is returned as a value outside the context where the variable was created. Here we create a function that adds 3 to its argument:

```
> (setf fn (let ((i 3))
              #'(lambda (x) (+ x i))))
#<Interpreted-Function C0A51E>
> (funcall fn 2)
5
```

When a function refers to a variable defined outside it, it's called a *free* variable. A function that refers to a free lexical variable is called a *closure*.[2] The variable must persist as long as the function does.

---

[2]The name "closure" is left over from earlier Lisp dialects. It derives from the way closures have to be implemented under dynamic scope.

A closure is a combination of a function and an environment. Closures are created implicitly whenever a function refers to something from the surrounding lexical environment. This happens quietly in a function like the following one, but it is the same idea.

```
(defun add-to-list (num lst)
  (mapcar #'(lambda (x)
              (+ x num))
          lst))
```

This function takes a number and a list, and returns a list of the sum of each element and the number. The variable num within the lambda expression is free, so in cases like this we're passing a closure to mapcar.

A more conspicuous example would be a function that returned a different closure each time it was called. The following function returns an adder:

```
(defun make-adder (n)
  #'(lambda (x)
      (+ x n)))
```

It takes a number, and returns a function that adds that number to *its* argument:

```
> (setf add3 (make-adder 3))
#<Interpreted-Function C0EBF6>
> (funcall add3 2)
5
> (setf add27 (make-adder 27))
#<Interpreted-Function C0EE4E>
> (funcall add27 2)
29
```

We can even make several closures share variables. Here we define two functions that share a counter.

```
(let ((counter 0))
  (defun reset ()
    (setf counter 0))
  (defun stamp ()
    (setf counter (+ counter 1))))
```

Such a pair of functions might be used to create time-stamps. Each time we call stamp we get a number one higher than the previous, and by calling reset we can set the counter back to zero:

```
> (list (stamp) (stamp) (reset) (stamp))
(1 2 0 1)
```

You could do the same thing with a global counter, but this way the counter is protected from unintended references.

Common Lisp has a built-in function `complement` that takes a predicate and returns the opposite predicate. For example:

```
> (mapcar (complement #'oddp)
          '(1 2 3 4 5 6))
(NIL T NIL T NIL T)
```

With closures such a function is easy to write:

```
(defun our-complement (f)
  #'(lambda (&rest args)
     (not (apply f args))))
```

If you stop to think about it, this is a remarkable little example; yet it is just the tip of the iceberg. Closures are one of the uniquely wonderful things about Lisp. They open the door to programming techniques that would be inconceivable in other languages.°

6.6   Example: Function Builders

Dylan is a hybrid of Scheme and Common Lisp, with a syntax like Pascal.° It has a large number of functions that return functions: besides `complement`, which we saw in the previous section, Dylan includes `compose`, `disjoin`, `conjoin`, `curry`, `rcurry`, and `always`. Figure 6.2 contains Common Lisp implementations of these functions, and Figure 6.3 shows some equivalences that follow from their definitions.

The first, `compose`, takes one or more functions and returns a new function in which all of them are applied in succession. That is,

```
(compose #'a #'b #'c)
```

returns a function equivalent to

```
#'(lambda (&rest args) (a (b (apply #'c args))))
```

This means that the last argument to `compose` can take any number of arguments, but the other functions all have to take exactly one argument.

Here we build a function that takes the square root of its argument, then rounds it, then returns a list containing it:

```
> (mapcar (compose #'list #'round #'sqrt)
          '(4 9 16 25))
((2) (3) (4) (5))
```

```
(defun compose (&rest fns)
  (destructuring-bind (fn1 . rest) (reverse fns)
    #'(lambda (&rest args)
        (reduce #'(lambda (v f) (funcall f v))
                rest
                :initial-value (apply fn1 args)))))

(defun disjoin (fn &rest fns)
  (if (null fns)
      fn
      (let ((disj (apply #'disjoin fns)))
        #'(lambda (&rest args)
            (or (apply fn args) (apply disj args))))))

(defun conjoin (fn &rest fns)
  (if (null fns)
      fn
      (let ((conj (apply #'conjoin fns)))
        #'(lambda (&rest args)
            (and (apply fn args) (apply conj args))))))

(defun curry (fn &rest args)
  #'(lambda (&rest args2)
      (apply fn (append args args2))))

(defun rcurry (fn &rest args)
  #'(lambda (&rest args2)
      (apply fn (append args2 args))))

(defun always (x) #'(lambda (&rest args) x))
```

Figure 6.2: Dylan function builders.

The next two functions, disjoin and conjoin, both take one or more predicates as arguments: disjoin returns a predicate that returns true when any of the predicates return true, and conjoin returns a predicate that returns true when all of the predicates return true.

```
> (mapcar (disjoin #'integerp #'symbolp)
          '(a "a" 2 3))
(T NIL T T)
```

```
        cddr = (compose #'cdr #'cdr)
         nth = (compose #'car #'nthcdr)
        atom = (compose #'not #'consp)
             = (rcurry #'typep 'atom)
          <= = (disjoin #'< #'=)
       listp = (disjoin #'null #'consp)
             = (rcurry #'typep 'list)
          1+ = (curry #'+ 1)
             = (rcurry #'+ 1)
          1- = (rcurry #'- 1)
      mapcan = (compose (curry #'apply #'nconc) #'mapcar)
  complement = (curry #'compose #'not)
```

Figure 6.3: Some equivalences.

```
> (mapcar (conjoin #'integerp #'oddp)
          '(a "a" 2 3))
(NIL NIL NIL T)
```

If predicates are considered as defining sets, disjoin returns the union of its arguments, and conjoin returns the intersection.

The functions curry and rcurry ("right curry") are similar in spirit to make-adder in the previous section. Both take a function and some of the arguments to it, and return a new function that expects the rest of the arguments. Either of the following is equivalent to (make-adder 3):

```
(curry #'+ 3)
(rcurry #'+ 3)
```

The difference between curry and rcurry becomes evident when the function is one for which the order of arguments matters. If we curry -, we get a function that subtracts its argument from a certain number,

```
> (funcall (curry #'- 3) 2)
1
```

while if we rcurry -, we get a function that subtracts a certain number from its argument:

```
> (funcall (rcurry #'- 3) 2)
-1
```

Finally, always is the Common Lisp function constantly. It takes an argument and returns a function that returns it. Like identity, it is useful mainly in situations where functional arguments are required.

6.7   Dynamic Scope

Section 2.11 distinguished between local and global variables. The real
distinction here is between lexical variables, which have lexical scope, and
special variables, which have dynamic scope. But it's almost the same
distinction, because local variables are nearly always lexical variables, and
global variables are always special variables.

Under lexical scope, a symbol refers to the variable that has that name in
the context where the symbol appears. Local variables have lexical scope by
default. So if we define a function in an environment where there is a variable
called x,

```
(let ((x 10))
  (defun foo ()
    x))
```

then the x in the body will refer to that variable, regardless of any x that might
exist where foo is called:

```
> (let ((x 20)) (foo))
10
```

With dynamic scope, we look for a variable in the environment where the
function is called, not in the environment where it was defined.° To cause
a variable to have dynamic scope, we must declare it to be special in any
context where it occurs. If we defined foo instead as

```
(let ((x 10))
  (defun foo ()
    (declare (special x))
    x))
```

then the x within the function will no longer refer to the lexical variable
existing where the function was defined, but will refer to whatever special x
exists at the time the function is called:

```
> (let ((x 20))
    (declare (special x))
    (foo))
20
```

A declare can begin any body of code where new variables are created.
The special declaration is unique, in that it can change the way a program
behaves. Chapter 13 discusses other kinds of declarations. All other declarations are simply advice to the compiler; they may make a program run faster,
but they will not change what it does.

Global variables established by calling setf at the toplevel are implicitly special:

```
> (setf x 30)
30
> (foo)
30
```

Within a file of code, it makes a program clearer if you don't rely on the implicit special declaration, and instead use defparameter.

Where is dynamic scope useful? Usually it is used to give some global variable a new value temporarily. For example, there are 11 global variables that control the way objects are printed, including *print-base*, which is 10 by default. If you want to display numbers in hexadecimal (base 16), you can do it by rebinding *print-base*:

```
> (let ((*print-base* 16))
    (princ 32))
20
32
```

Two things are displayed here: the output generated by princ, and the value it returns. They represent the same number, displayed first in hexadecimal because *print-base* was 16 when it was printed, and the second time in decimal because, outside the let expression, *print-base* reverts to its previous value, 10.

6.8   Compilation

Common Lisp functions can be compiled either individually or by the file. If you just type a defun expression into the toplevel,

```
> (defun foo (x) (+ x 1))
FOO
```

many implementations will create an interpreted function. You can check whether a function is compiled by passing it to compiled-function-p:

```
> (compiled-function-p #'foo)
NIL
```

If you give the name of foo to compile

```
> (compile 'foo)
FOO
```

its definition will be compiled, and the interpreted definition will be replaced by the compiled one. Compiled and interpreted functions behave the same, except with respect to `compiled-function-p`.

You can also give lists as arguments to `compile`. This use of `compile` is discussed on page 161.

There is one kind of function you can't give as an argument to `compile`: a function like `stamp` or `reset` that was typed into the toplevel within a distinct lexical context (e.g. a `let`).[3] It would be ok to define these functions within a file, and then compile and load the file. The restriction is imposed on interpreted code for implementation reasons, not because there's anything wrong with defining functions in distinct lexical environments.

The usual way to compile Lisp code is not to compile functions individually, but to compile whole files with `compile-file`. This function takes a filename and creates a compiled version of the source file—typically with the same base name but a different extension. When the compiled file is loaded, `compiled-function-p` should return true for all the functions defined in the file.

When one function occurs within another, and the containing function is compiled, the inner function should also be compiled. So when `make-adder` (page 108) is compiled, it will return compiled functions:

```
> (compile 'make-adder)
MAKE-ADDER
> (compiled-function-p (make-adder 2))
T
```

6.9   Using Recursion

Recursion plays a greater role in Lisp than in most other languages. There seem to be three main reasons why:

1. *Functional programming.* Recursive algorithms are less likely to involve side-effects.

2. *Recursive data structures.* Lisp's implicit use of pointers makes it easy to have recursively defined data structures. The most common is the list: a list is either `nil`, or a cons whose cdr is a list.

3. *Elegance.* Lisp programmers care a great deal about the beauty of their programs, and recursive algorithms are often more elegant than their iterative counterparts.

---

[3] In pre-ANSI Common Lisps, the first argument to `compile` also could not be a function that was already compiled.

Students sometimes find recursion difficult to understand at first. But as Section 3.9 pointed out, you don't have to think about all the invocations of a recursive function if you want to judge whether or not is correct.

The same is true if you want to write a recursive function. If you can describe a recursive solution to a problem, it's usually straightforward to translate your solution into code. To solve a problem using recursion, you have to do two things:

1. You have to show how to solve the problem in the general case by breaking it down into a finite number of similar, but smaller, problems.

2. You have to show how to solve the smallest version of the problem—the base case—by some finite number of operations.

If you can do this, you're done. You know that a finite problem will get solved eventually, because each recursion makes it smaller, and the smallest problem takes a finite number of steps.

For example, in the following recursive algorithm for finding the length of a proper list, we find the length of a smaller list on each recursion:

1. In the general case, the length of a proper list is the length of its cdr plus 1.

2. The length of an empty list is 0.

When this description is translated into code, the base case has to come first; but when formulating recursive algorithms, one usually begins with the general case.

The preceding algorithm is explicitly described as a way of finding the length of a proper list. When you define a recursive function, you have to be sure that the way you break up the problem does in fact lead to smaller subproblems. Taking the cdr of a proper list yields a smaller subproblem for length, but taking the cdr of a circular list would not.

Here are two more examples of recursive algorithms. Again, both assume finite arguments. Notice in the second that we break the problem into *two* smaller problems on each recursion:

| member | Something is a member of a list if it is the first element, or a member of the cdr. Nothing is a member of the empty list. |
| copy-tree | The copy-tree of a cons is a cons made of the copy-tree of its car, and the copy-tree of its cdr. The copy-tree of an atom is itself. |

Once you can describe an algorithm this way, it is a short step to writing a recursive definition.

Some algorithms are most naturally expressed in such terms and some are not. You would have to bend over backwards to define our-copy-tree (page 41) without using recursion. On the other hand, the iterative version of show-squares on page 23 is probably easier to understand than the recursive version on page 24. Sometimes it may not be obvious which form will be more natural until you try to write the code.

If you're concerned with efficiency, there are two more issues to consider. One, tail-recursion, will be discussed in Section 13.2. With a good compiler there should be little or no difference in speed between a tail-recursive function and a loop. However, if you would have to go out of your way to make a function tail-recursive, it may be better just to use iteration.

The other issue to bear in mind is that the obvious recursive algorithm is not always the most efficient. The classic example is the Fibonacci function. It is defined recursively,

1. $\text{Fib}(0) = \text{Fib}(1) = 1$.

2. $\text{Fib}(n) = \text{Fib}(n-1) + \text{Fib}(n-2)$.

but the literal translation of this definition,

```
(defun fib (n)
  (if (<= n 1)
      1
      (+ (fib (- n 1))
         (fib (- n 2)))))
```

is appallingly inefficient. The same computations are done over and over. If you ask for (fib 10), the function computes (fib 9) and (fib 8). But to compute (fib 9), it has to compute (fib 8) again, and so on.

Here is an iterative function that computes the same result:

```
(defun fib (n)
  (do ((i  n (- i 1))
       (f1 1 (+ f1 f2))
       (f2 1 f1))
      ((<= i 1) f1)))
```

The iterative version is not as clear, but it is far more efficient. How often does this kind of thing happen in practice? Very rarely—that's why all textbooks use the same example—but it is something one should be aware of.

Summary

1. A named function is a function stored as the `symbol-function` of a symbol. The `defun` macro hides such details. It also allows you to define documentation strings, and specify how `setf` should treat calls.

2. It is possible to define local functions, similar in spirit to local variables.

3. Functions can have optional, rest, and keyword parameters.

4. Utilities are additions to Lisp. They are an example of bottom-up programming on a small scale.

5. Lexical variables persist as long as something refers to them. Closures are functions that refer to free variables. You can write functions that return closures.

6. Dylan provides functions for building functions. Using closures, it's easy to implement them in Common Lisp.

7. Special variables have dynamic scope.

8. Lisp functions can be compiled individually, or (more usually) by the file.

9. A recursive algorithm solves a problem by dividing it into a finite number of similar, but smaller, problems.

Exercises

1. Define a version of `tokens` (page 67) that takes `:test` and `:start` arguments defaulting to `#'constituent` and 0 respectively.

2. Define a version of `bin-search` (page 60) that takes `:key`, `:test`, `:start`, and `:end` arguments with the usual meanings and defaults.

3. Define a function that takes any number of arguments and returns the number of arguments passed to it.

4. Modify `most` (page 105) to return, as two values, the two highest-scoring elements of a list.

5. Define `remove-if` (no keywords) in terms of `filter` (page 105).

6. Define a function that takes one argument, a number, and returns the greatest argument passed to it so far.

7. Define a function that takes one argument, a number, and returns true if it is greater than the argument passed to the function the last time it was called. The function should return `nil` the first time it is called.

8. Suppose `expensive` is a function of one argument, an integer between 0 and 100 inclusive, that returns the result of a time-consuming computation. Define a function `frugal` that returns the same answer, but only calls `expensive` when given an argument it has not seen before.

9. Define a function like `apply`, but where any number printed out before it returns will be printed, by default, in octal (base 8).

7

Input and Output

Common Lisp has powerful I/O facilities. For input, along with the usual functions for reading characters, we get `read`, which includes a complete parser. For output, along with the usual functions for writing characters, we get `format`, which is almost a language in its own right. This chapter introduces all the basic concepts.

There are two kinds of streams, character streams and binary streams. This chapter describes operations on character streams; binary streams are covered in Section 14.2.

7.1 Streams

Streams are Lisp objects representing sources and/or destinations of characters. To read from or write to a file, you open it as a stream. But streams are not identical with files. When you read or print at the toplevel, you also use a stream. You can even create streams that read from or write to strings.

By default, input is read from the stream `*standard-input*`. The default place for output is `*standard-output*`. Initially they will probably be the same place: a stream representing the toplevel.

Already we have seen `read` and `format` used to read from and print to the toplevel. The former takes an optional argument, which should be a stream, and defaults to `*standard-input*`. The first argument to `format` can also be a stream, but when it is `t`, the output is sent to `*standard-output*`. So what we have been doing so far is using the defaults. We could do the same I/O operations on any stream.

A *pathname* is a portable way of specifying a file. A pathname has six components: host, device, directory, name, type, and version. You can make one by calling `make-pathname` with one or more of the corresponding keyword arguments. In the simplest case, you could just specify the name and let the rest of the pathname default:

```
> (setf path (make-pathname :name "myfile"))
#P"myfile"
```

The basic function for opening a file is `open`. It takes a pathname[1] and a large number of optional keyword arguments, and if successful, returns a stream that points to the file.

You specify how you intend to use a stream when you create it. The `:direction` argument signals whether you are going to write to the stream, read from it, or both. The three corresponding values are `:input`, `:output`, and `:io`. If the stream is used for output, the `:if-exists` argument says what to do if the destination file already exists; usually it should be `:supersede`. So to create a stream on which you can write to the file `"myfile"`, you might say:

```
> (setf str (open path :direction :output
                       :if-exists :supersede))
#<Stream C017E6>
```

The printed representation of streams is implementation-dependent.

Now if we give this stream as the first argument to `format`, it will print to the stream instead of the toplevel:

```
> (format str "Something~%")
NIL
```

If we look at the file at this point, the output may or may not be there. Some implementations save up output to write in chunks. It may not all appear until we close the stream:

```
> (close str)
NIL
```

Always close a file when you are finished using it; nothing is guaranteed about its contents until you do. Now if we look in the file `"myfile"`, there should be single line:

```
Something
```

---

[1] You can give a string instead of a pathname, but this is not portable.

If we just want to read from a file, we open a stream with `:direction`
`:input`:

```
> (setf str (open path :direction :input))
#<Stream C01C86>
```

We can use any input function on a file. Section 7.2 describes input in more
detail. Here as an example we will use `read-line` to read a line of text from
the file:

```
> (read-line str)
"Something"
NIL
> (close str)
NIL
```

Remember to close a file when you're finished reading from it.

Much of the time one does not use `open` and `close` directly to do file I/O.
The `with-open-file` macro is often more convenient. Its first argument
should be a list containing a variable name followed by arguments you might
give to `open`. After this it takes a body of code, which is evaluated with
the variable bound to a stream created by passing the remaining arguments to
`open`. Afterward the stream is automatically closed. So our entire file-writing
operation could be expressed:

```
(with-open-file (str path :direction :output
                          :if-exists :supersede)
   (format str "Something~%"))
```

The `with-open-file` macro puts the `close` within an `unwind-protect`
(page 92), so the file is guaranteed to get closed, even if an error interrupts
the evaluation of the body.

7.2 Input

The two most popular input functions are `read-line` and `read`. The former
reads all the characters up to a newline, returning them in a string. It takes
an optional stream argument; if the stream is omitted, it will default to
`*standard-input*`:

```
> (progn
    (format t "Please enter your name: ")
    (read-line))
Please enter your name: Rodrigo de Bivar
"Rodrigo de Bivar"
NIL
```

This is the function to use if you want verbatim input. (The second return value is true only if `read-line` ran out of input before encountering a newline.)

In the general case, `read-line` takes four optional arguments: a stream; an argument to tell whether or not to cause an error on encountering end-of-file; what to return instead if the previous argument is `nil`; and a fourth argument (discussed on page 235) that can usually be ignored.

So to display the contents of a file at the toplevel, we might use the following function:

```
(defun pseudo-cat (file)
  (with-open-file (str file :direction :input)
    (do ((line (read-line str nil 'eof)
               (read-line str nil 'eof)))
        ((eql line 'eof))
      (format t "~A~%" line))))
```

If you want input parsed into Lisp objects, use `read`. This function reads exactly one expression, and stops at the end of it. So it could read less than a line or more than a line. And of course what it reads has to be valid Lisp syntax.

If we use `read` at the toplevel, it will let us use as many newlines as we want within an expression:

```
> (read)
(a
b
c)
(A B C)
```

On the other hand, if we type several expressions on a single line, `read` will stop processing characters after the first, leaving the remaining characters to be picked up by whatever reads next from this stream. So if in response to the prompt printed by `ask-number` (page 20) we type several expressions on a line, the following will happen:

```
> (ask-number)
Please enter a number. a b
Please enter a number. Please enter a number. 43
43
```

Two successive prompts are printed on the second line. The first call to `read` returns a, which is not a number, so the function asks again for a number. But the first `read` only read up to the end of a. So the next call to `read` returns b, causing another prompt.

You may want to avoid using read directly to process user input. The preceding function would be better off if it used read-line to get what the user typed, then called read-from-string on the resulting string.° This function takes a string and returns the first expression read from it:

```
> (read-from-string "a b c")
A
2
```

It also returns a second value, a number indicating the position in the string at which it stopped reading.

In the general case, read-from-string can take two optional and three keyword arguments. The two optional arguments are the third and fourth arguments to read: whether an end-of-file (or in this case string) should cause an error, and if not, what to return instead. The keyword parameters :start and :end can be used to delimit the portion of the string read.

All these input functions are defined in terms of the primitive read-char, which reads a single character. It takes the same four optional arguments as read and read-line. Common Lisp also defines a function called peek-char, which is like read-char but does not remove the character from the stream.

7.3 Output

The three simplest output functions are prin1, princ, and terpri. For all three the last argument is an optional stream argument, which defaults to *standard-output*.

The difference between prin1 and princ is roughly that prin1 generates output for programs, and princ generates output for people. So, for example, prin1 prints the double-quotes around a string, and princ doesn't:

```
> (prin1 "Hello")
"Hello"
"Hello"
> (princ "Hello")
Hello
"Hello"
```

Both return their first argument—which, incidentally, is displayed by prin1. The function terpri just prints a newline.

It is useful to have these functions as background when explaining the behavior of the more general format. This function can be used for almost all output. It takes a stream (or t or nil), a format string, and zero or more additional arguments. The format string may contain *format directives*, which are preceded by a ~ (tilde). Some format directives act as placeholders in the string. Their places will be taken by the representations of the arguments given after the format string.

If we give t as the first argument, output is sent to *standard-output*. If we give nil, format returns as a string what it would have printed. For the sake of brevity we'll do this in all the examples here.

Depending on one's point of view, format is either amazingly powerful or horribly complex. There are a large number of format directives, only a few of which most programmers will ever use. Two of the most commonly used format directives are ~A and ~%. (It doesn't matter whether you say ~a or ~A, but the latter form is more common because it makes the format directive stand out.) A ~A is a placeholder for a value, which will be printed as if by princ. A ~% represents a newline.

```
> (format nil "Dear ~A,~%  Our records indicate..."
          "Mr. Malatesta")
"Dear Mr. Malatesta,
  Our records indicate..."
```

Here format has returned a single value, consisting of a string containing a newline.

The ~S format directive is just like ~A, but prints objects as if by print, rather than princ:

```
> (format t "~S  ~A" "z" "z")
"z"  z
NIL
```

Format directives can take arguments. ~F, which is used for printing right-justified floating-point numbers, can take up to five:

1. The total number of characters to be printed. Defaults to the exact length of the number.

2. The number of digits to print after the decimal. Defaults to all of them.

3. The number of digits to shift the decimal point to the left (thereby effectively multiplying the number by 10). Defaults to none.

4. The character to print instead of the number if it is too long to fit in the space allowed by the first argument. If no character is specified, an over-long number will be printed using as much space as it needs.

5. The character to print to the left before the digits start. Defaults to a blank.

Here is a rare example with all five arguments:

```
> (format nil "~10,2,0,'*,' F" 26.21875)
"    26.22"
```

This is the original number rounded to 2 decimal places, (with the decimal point shifted left 0 places), right-justified in a field of 10 characters, padded on the left by blanks. Notice that a character given as an argument is written as '*, not the usual #*. Since the number fit in 10 characters, the fourth argument didn't have to be used.

All these arguments are optional. To use the default you can simply omit the corresponding argument. If all we want to do is print a number rounded to two decimal places, we can say:

```
> (format nil "~,2,,,F" 26.21875)
"26.22"
```

You can also omit a series of trailing commas, so the more usual way to write the preceding directive would be:

```
> (format nil "~,2F" 26.21875)
"26.22"
```

Warning: When format rounds, it does not guarantee to round up or to round down. That is, (format nil "~,1F" 1.25) could yield either "1.2" or "1.3". So if you are using format to display information that the user expects to see rounded in one particular way (e.g. dollar amounts), you should round the number explicitly before printing it.

7.4 Example: String Substitution

As an example of I/O, this section shows how to write a simple program to do string substitution in text files. We're going to write a function that can replace each instance of a string *old* in a file with some other string *new.* The simplest way to do this is to look at each character in the input file and compare it to the first character of *old.* If they don't match, we can just print the input character straight to the output file. If they do match, we compare the next input character against the *second* character of *old,* and so on. If the characters are the same all the way to the end of *old,* we have a successful match, and we print *new* to the output file.°

What happens, though, if we get part of the way through *old* and the match fails? For example, suppose we are looking for the pattern "abac", and the input file contains "ababac". The input will seem to match the pattern until we get to the fourth character, which is c in the pattern and b in the input. At this point we can write the initial a to the output file, because we know that no match begins there. But some of the characters that we have read from input file we still need: for example, the third character, a, does begin a successful match. So before we can implement this algorithm, we need a place to store characters that we've read from the input file but might still need.

A queue for storing input temporarily is called a *buffer*. In this case, because we know we'll never need to store more than a predetermined number of characters, we can use a data structure called a *ring buffer*. A ring buffer is a vector underneath. What makes it a ring is the way it's used: we store incoming values in successive elements, and when we get to the end of the vector, we start over at the beginning. If we never need to store more than n values, and we have a vector of length n or greater, then we never have to overwrite a live value.

The code in Figure 7.1 implements operations on ring buffers. The buf structure has five fields: a vector that will contain the objects stored in the buffer, and four other fields that will contain indices into the vector. Two of these indices, start and end, we would need for any use of ring buffers: start points to the first value in the buffer, and will be incremented when we pop a value; end points to the last value in the buffer, and is incremented when we insert a new one.

The other two indices, used and new, are something we need to add to the basic ring buffer for this application. They will range between start and end. In fact, it will always be true that

$$\text{start} \leq \text{used} \leq \text{new} \leq \text{end}$$

You can think of used and new as being like start and end for the current match. When we start a match, used will be equal to start and new will be equal to end. We will increment used as we match successive characters from the buffer. When used reaches new, we have read all the characters that were in the buffer at the time the match started. We don't want to use more than the characters that were in the buffer when the match started, or we would end up using the same characters multiple times. Hence the distinct new index, which starts out equal to end, but is not incremented as new characters are inserted into the buffer during a match.

The function bref takes a buffer and an index, and returns the element stored at that index. By using the index mod the length of the vector, we can pretend that we have an arbitrarily long buffer. Calling (new-buf n) yields a new buffer able to hold up to n objects.

To insert new values into a buffer, we will use buf-insert. It simply increments the end and puts the new value at that location. The converse is buf-pop, which returns the first value in a buffer, then increments its start. These two functions would come with any ring buffer.

```
(defstruct buf
  vec (start -1) (used -1) (new -1) (end -1))

(defun bref (buf n)
  (svref (buf-vec buf)
         (mod n (length (buf-vec buf)))))

(defun (setf bref) (val buf n)
  (setf (svref (buf-vec buf)
               (mod n (length (buf-vec buf))))
        val))

(defun new-buf (len)
  (make-buf :vec (make-array len)))

(defun buf-insert (x b)
  (setf (bref b (incf (buf-end b))) x))

(defun buf-pop (b)
  (prog1
    (bref b (incf (buf-start b)))
    (setf (buf-used b) (buf-start b)
          (buf-new  b) (buf-end   b))))

(defun buf-next (b)
  (when (< (buf-used b) (buf-new b))
    (bref b (incf (buf-used b)))))

(defun buf-reset (b)
  (setf (buf-used b) (buf-start b)
        (buf-new  b) (buf-end   b)))

(defun buf-clear (b)
  (setf (buf-start b) -1 (buf-used  b) -1
        (buf-new   b) -1 (buf-end    b) -1))

(defun buf-flush (b str)
  (do ((i (1+ (buf-used b)) (1+ i)))
      ((> i (buf-end b)))
    (princ (bref b i) str)))
```

Figure 7.1: Operations on ring buffers.

The next two functions are ones that we need specifically for this application: buf-next reads a value from a buffer without popping it, and buf-reset resets the used and new indices to their initial values, start and end. If we have already read all the values up to new, buf-next returns nil. It won't be a problem distinguishing this from a real value because we're only going to store characters in the buffer.

Finally, buf-flush flushes a buffer by writing all the live elements to a stream given as the second argument, and buf-clear empties a buffer by resetting all the indices to -1.

The functions defined in Figure 7.1 are used in Figure 7.2, which contains the code for string substitution. The function file-subst takes four arguments; a string to look for, a string to replace it, an input file, and an output file. It creates streams representing each of the files, then calls stream-subst to do the real work.

The second function, stream-subst, uses the algorithm sketched at the beginning of this section. It reads from the input stream one character at a time. Until the input character matches the first element of the sought-for string, it is written immediately to the output stream (1). When a match begins, the characters involved are queued in the buffer buf (2).

The variable pos points to the position of the character we are trying to match in the sought-for string. When and if pos is equal to the length of this string, we have a complete match, and we write the replacement string to the output stream, also clearing the buffer (3). If the match fails before this point, we can pop the first character in the buffer and write it to the output stream, after which we reset the buffer and start over with pos equal to zero (4).

The following table shows what happens when we substitute "baric" for "baro" in a file containing just the word barbarous:

CHAR	SOURCE	MATCH	CASE	OUTPUT	BUFFER
b	file	b	2		b
a	file	a	2		b a
r	file	r	2		b a r
b	file	o	4	b	b.a r b.
a	buffer	b	1	a	a.r b.
r	buffer	b	1	r	r.b.
b	buffer	b	1		r b:
a	file	a	2		r b:a
r	file	r	2		r b:a r
o	file	o	3	baric	
u	file	b	1	u	
s	file	b	1	s	

```
(defun file-subst (old new file1 file2)
  (with-open-file (in file1 :direction :input)
    (with-open-file (out file2 :direction :output
                                :if-exists :supersede)
      (stream-subst old new in out))))

(defun stream-subst (old new in out)
  (let* ((pos 0)
         (len (length old))
         (buf (new-buf len))
         (from-buf nil))
    (do ((c (read-char in nil :eof)
            (or (setf from-buf (buf-next buf))
                (read-char in nil :eof))))
        ((eql c :eof))
      (cond ((char= c (char old pos))
             (incf pos)
             (cond ((= pos len)                ; 3
                    (princ new out)
                    (setf pos 0)
                    (buf-clear buf))
                   ((not from-buf)             ; 2
                    (buf-insert c buf))))
            ((zerop pos)                       ; 1
             (princ c out)
             (when from-buf
               (buf-pop buf)
               (buf-reset buf)))
            (t                                 ; 4
             (unless from-buf
               (buf-insert c buf))
             (princ (buf-pop buf) out)
             (buf-reset buf)
             (setf pos 0))))
    (buf-flush buf out)))
```

Figure 7.2: String substitution.

The first column is the current character—the value of c; the second shows whether it was read from the buffer or directly from the input stream; the third shows the character it has to match—the posth element of old; the fourth shows which case is evaluated as a result; the fifth shows what is thereby written to the output stream; and the last column shows the contents of the buffer afterwards. In the last column, the positions of used and new are shown by a period after the character they point to; when both point to the same position, it is indicated by a colon.

If the file "test1" contained the following text

```
The struggle between Liberty and Authority is the most
conspicuous feature in the portions of history with which
we are earliest familiar, particularly in that of Greece,
Rome, and England.
```

then after evaluating (file-subst " th" " z" "test1" "test2"), the file "test2" would read:

```
The struggle between Liberty and Authority is ze most
conspicuous feature in ze portions of history with which
we are earliest familiar, particularly in zat of Greece,
Rome, and England.
```

To keep this example as simple as possible, the code shown in Figure 7.2 just replaces one string with another. It would be easy to generalize it to search for a pattern instead of a literal string. All you would have to do is replace the call to char= with a call to whatever more general matching function you wanted to write.

7.5 Macro Characters

A *macro character* is a character that gets special treatment from read. A lowercase a, for example, is ordinarily handled just like a lowercase b, but a left parenthesis is something different: it tells Lisp to begin reading a list.

A macro character or combination of macro characters is also known as a *read-macro*. Many of Common Lisp's predefined read-macros are abbreviations. Quote, for example: as an expression like 'a is read, it is expanded by the reader into a list, (quote a). When you type quoted expressions into the toplevel, they are evaluated as soon as they are read, so ordinarily you never see this transformation. You can make it visible by invoking read explicitly:

```
> (car (read-from-string "'a"))
QUOTE
```

Quote is unusual for a read-macro in that it's expressed as a single character. With a limited character set, you can only have so many one-character read-macros; most of the read-macros in Common Lisp are expressed using two or more characters.

Such read-macros are called *dispatching* read-macros, and the first character is called the dispatching character. All the predefined dispatching read-macros use the sharp sign, #, as the dispatching character. We have seen quite a few of them already. For example, #' is an abbreviation for (function ...) in the same way that ' is an abbreviation for (quote ...).

Other dispatching read-macros we've seen include #(...), which yields a vector; #nA(...) which yields an array; #\, which yields a character; and #S(n ...), which yields a structure. When objects of each of these types are displayed by prin1 (or format with ~S), they are displayed using the corresponding read-macros.[2] This means that you can write such objects out and read them back in:

```
> (let ((*print-array* t))
    (vectorp (read-from-string (format nil "~S"
                                       (vector 1 2)))))
T
```

Of course, what we get back is not the same vector, but a new one with the same elements.

Not all objects are displayed in a distinct, readable form. Both functions and hash tables, for example, tend to be displayed as #<...>. In fact, #< is also a read-macro, but one that exists specifically to cause an error if it is encountered by read. Functions and hash tables can't be written out and read back in, and this read-macro ensures that users will have no illusions on this point.[3]

When you're defining your own representations for things (the print-functions of structures, for example), you should keep this principle in mind. Either use a representation that can be read back in, or use #<...>.

Summary

1. Streams are sources of input or destinations of output. In character streams, the input and output consists of characters.

2. The default stream points to the toplevel. New streams can be made by opening files.

---

[2]To get vectors and arrays displayed this way, set *print-array* to t.

[3]Lisp couldn't just use sharp-quote to represent functions, because sharp-quote by itself offers no way to represent a closure.

3. You can get input as parsed objects, as strings of characters, or as individual characters.

4. The format function provides elaborate control over output.

5. To substitute one string for another in a text file, you have to read characters into a buffer.

6. When read encounters a macro character like ' , it calls the associated function.

Exercises

1. Define a function that takes a filename and returns a list of strings representing each line in the file.

2. Define a function that takes a filename and returns a list of the expressions in the file.

3. Suppose that in some format for text files, comments are indicated by a % character. Everything from this character to the end of the line is ignored. Define a function that takes two filenames, and writes to the second file a copy of the first, minus comments.

4. Define a function that takes a two-dimensional array of floats and displays it in neat columns. Each element should be printed with two digits after the decimal point, in a field 10 characters wide. (Assume all will fit.) You will need array-dimensions (page 361).

5. Modify stream-subst to allow wildcards in the pattern. If the character + occurs in old, it should match any input character.

6. Modify stream-subst so that the pattern can include an element that matches any digit character, an element that matches any alphanumeric character, or an element that matches any character. The pattern must also be able to match any specific input character. (Hint: old can no longer be a string.)

8

Symbols

We've used symbols quite a bit already. There is more to them than meets the eye. It may be best not to bother about the underlying mechanism at first. You can use symbols as data objects and as names for things without understanding how the two roles are related. But at a certain point, it's useful to stop and consider what's really going on. This chapter explains the details.

8.1 Symbol Names

Chapter 2 described symbols as variable names existing as objects in their own right. But the range of possible Lisp symbols is broader than the range of variable names allowed in most languages. In fact, a symbol can have any string as its name. You can get the name of a symbol by calling `symbol-name`:

```
> (symbol-name 'abc)
"ABC"
```

Notice that the name of this symbol is all uppercase letters. By default Common Lisp converts all alphabetic characters in a symbol's name into uppercase as they are read. This means that, by default, Common Lisp is not case-sensitive:

```
> (eql 'aBc 'Abc)
T
> (CaR '(a b c))
A
```

There is a special syntax for referring to symbols whose names contain whitespace or other things that might otherwise be significant to the reader. Any sequence of characters between vertical bars is treated as a symbol. You can put anything in the name of a symbol this way:

```
> (list '|Lisp 1.5| '|| '|abc| '|ABC|)
(|Lisp 1.5| || |abc| ABC)
```

When the name of such a symbol is read, there is no case conversion, and macro characters are treated just like other characters.

So which symbols can you refer to without using vertical bars? Essentially, any symbol whose name is neither a number nor contains characters significant to the reader. A quick way to find out if you could refer to a symbol without using vertical bars is to see how Lisp prints it. If Lisp represents a symbol without vertical bars, as it did the last symbol in the list above, then you can too.

Remember that the vertical bars are a special syntax for denoting symbols. They are not part of the symbol's name:

```
> (symbol-name '|a b c|)
"a b c"
```

(If you want to use a vertical bar in the name of a symbol, you can do it by putting a backslash before the bar.)

8.2   Property Lists

In Common Lisp every symbol has a *property-list*, or *plist*. The function get takes a symbol and a key of any type, and returns the value associated with that key in the symbol's property list:

```
> (get 'alizarin 'color)
NIL
```

It uses eql to compare keys. If the specified property isn't found, get returns nil.

To associate a value with a key you can use setf with get:

```
> (setf (get 'alizarin 'color) 'red)
RED
> (get 'alizarin 'color)
RED
```

Now the color property of alizarin is red.

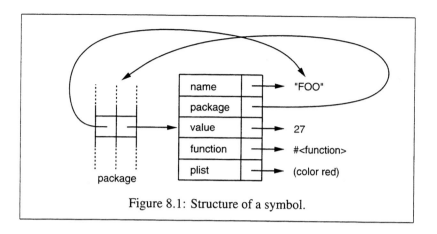

Figure 8.1: Structure of a symbol.

The function `symbol-plist` returns the property list of a symbol:

```
> (setf (get 'alizarin 'transparency) 'high)
HIGH
> (symbol-plist 'alizarin)
(TRANSPARENCY HIGH COLOR RED)
```

Notice that property lists are not represented as assoc-lists, though they are used the same way.

In Common Lisp, property lists aren't used very much. They have largely been superseded by hash tables (Section 4.8).

8.3   Symbols Are Big

Symbols are created implicitly when we type their names, and when they are displayed the name is all we see. Under the circumstances it's easy to think that the symbol is what we see, and nothing more. But there is more to symbols than meets they eye.

From the way we use them and the way they look, it might seem that symbols would be small objects, like integers. In fact a symbol is a substantial object, more like the kind of structure that might be defined by `defstruct`. A symbol can have a name, a home package, a value as a variable, a value as a function, and a property list. Figure 8.1 shows how symbols are represented internally.

Few programs use so many symbols that it would be worth using something else to save space. But it is worth bearing in mind that symbols are real objects, and not just names. When two variables are set to the same symbol, it's the same as when two variables are set to the same list: both variables have pointers to the same object.

8.4 Creating Symbols

Section 8.1 showed how to get from symbols to their names. It's also possible
to go in the other direction, from strings to symbols. This gets a little more
complicated, because we have to introduce the topic of packages.

Conceptually, packages are symbol-tables, mapping names to symbols.
Every ordinary symbol belongs to a particular package. A symbol that belongs
to a package is said to be *interned* in that package. Functions and variables
have symbols as their names. Packages enforce modularity by restricting
which symbols are accessible, and thus, which functions and variables one
can refer to.

Most symbols are interned when they are read. The first time you type the
name of a new symbol, Lisp will create a new symbol object and intern it in
the current package (which by default will be common-lisp-user). But you
can also intern a symbol by giving a string and an optional package argument
to intern:

```
> (intern "RANDOM-SYMBOL")
RANDOM-SYMBOL
NIL
```

The package argument defaults to the current package, so the preceding
expression returns the symbol in the current package whose name is the
string "RANDOM-SYMBOL", creating such a symbol if it doesn't already exist.
The second return value shows whether the symbol already existed; in this
case, it didn't.

Not all symbols are interned. It can sometimes be useful to have an
uninterned symbol, for the same reason that it can be useful to have an
unlisted phone number. Uninterned symbols are called *gensyms*. We'll see
the point of gensyms when we come to macros in Chapter 10.

8.5 Multiple Packages

Larger programs are often divided up into multiple packages. If each part of
a program is in its own package, then someone working on one part of the
program will be able to use a symbol as the name of a function or variable
without worrying that the name is already used elsewhere.

In languages that don't provide a way to define multiple namespaces, the
programmers working on a big project usually work out some convention to
ensure that they don't use the same names. For example, the programmer
writing the display code might only use names beginning with disp_, while
the programmer writing the math code only used names beginning with

math_. So if the math code included a function to do fast Fourier transforms, it might be called math_fft.

Packages just provide a way to do this automatically. If you define your functions in a separate package, you can use whatever names you like. Only symbols that you explicitly *export* will be visible in other packages, and there they will usually have to be preceded (or *qualified*) by the name of the package that owns them.

For example, suppose a program is divided into two packages, math and disp. If the symbol fft is exported by the math package, then code in the disp package will be able to refer to it as math:fft. Within the math package, it will be possible to refer to it as simply fft.

Here is what you might put at the top of a file containing a distinct package of code:

```
(defpackage "MY-APPLICATION"
            (:use "COMMON-LISP" "MY-UTILITIES")
            (:nicknames "APP")
            (:export "WIN" "LOSE" "DRAW"))

(in-package my-application)
```

The defpackage defines a new package called my-application.[1] It *uses* two other packages, common-lisp and my-utilities, which means that symbols exported by these packages will be accessible *without* package qualifiers. Most packages will use common-lisp—you don't want to have to qualify the names of the built-in Lisp operators and variables.

The my-application package itself exports just three symbols: win, lose, and draw. Since the call to defpackage gave my-application the nickname app, code in other packages will be able to refer to them as e.g. app:win.

The defpackage is followed by an in-package that makes the current package be my-application. All the unqualified symbols in the rest of the file will be interned in my-application—unless there is another in-package later on. When a file has been loaded, the current package is always reset to the value it had before the load began.

8.6 Keywords

Symbols in the keyword package (known as *keywords*) have two unique properties: they always evaluate to themselves, and you can refer to them

---

[1] The names in the call to defpackage are all uppercase because, as mentioned in Section 8.1, symbol names are converted to uppercase by default.

anywhere simply as :x, instead of keyword:x. When keyword parameters were first introduced on page 44, it might have seemed more natural for the call to read (member '(a) '((a) (z)) test: #'equal) rather than (member '(a) '((a) (z)) :test #'equal). Now we see why the unnatural-looking second form is actually the correct one. The colon prefixed to test is just to identify it as a keyword.

Why use keywords instead of ordinary symbols? Because they are accessible anywhere. A function that takes symbols as arguments should usually be written to expect keywords. For example, this function could safely be called from any package:

```
(defun noise (animal)
  (case animal
    (:dog :woof)
    (:cat :meow)
    (:pig :oink)))
```

If it had been written to use ordinary symbols, it would only work when called from the package in which it was defined, unless the keys were exported as well.

8.7   Symbols and Variables

One potentially confusing thing about Lisp is that symbols are related to variables in two very different ways. When a symbol is the name of a special variable, the value of the variable is stored in a field within the symbol (Figure 8.1). The symbol-value function refers to that field, so we have a direct connection between a symbol and the value of the special variable it represents.

With lexical variables, things are completely different. A symbol used as a lexical variable is just a placeholder. The compiler will translate it into a reference to a register or a location in memory. In the eventual compiled code, there will be no trace of the symbol (unless it is retained somewhere for use by the debugger). So of course there is no connection between symbols and the values of the lexical variables they represent; by the time there is a value, the symbol is gone.

8.8   Example: Random Text

If you're going to write programs that operate on words, it's often a good idea to use symbols instead of strings, because symbols are conceptually atomic. Symbols can be compared in one step with eql, while strings have to be compared character-by-character with string-equal or string=. As an example, this section shows how to write a program to generate random text. The first part of the program will read a sample text (the larger the better), accumulating information about the likelihood of any given word following another. The second part will take random walks through the network of words built in the first, after each word making a weighted random choice among the words that followed it in the original sample.

The resulting text will always be locally plausible, because any two words that occur together will be two words that occurred together in the input text. What's surprising is how often you can get entire sentences—sometimes entire paragraphs—that seem to make sense.

Figure 8.2 contains the first half of the program, the code for reading the sample text. The data derived from it will be stored in the hash table *words*. The keys in this hash table will be symbols representing words, and the values will be assoc-lists like the following:

```
(((|sin| . 1) (|wide| . 2) (|sights| . 1))
```

This is the value associated with the key |discover| when Milton's *Paradise Lost* is used as the sample text. It indicates that "discover" was used four times in the poem, being twice followed by "wide" and once each by "sin" and "sights".

The function read-text accumulates this information. It takes a pathname, and builds an assoc-list like the one shown above for each word encountered in the file. It works by reading the file one character at a time, accumulating words in the string buffer. With maxword = 100, the program will be able to read words of up to 100 letters, which is sufficient for English.

As long as the next character is a letter (as determined by alpha-char-p) or an apostrophe, we keep accumulating characters. Any other character ends the word, whereupon the corresponding symbol is sent to see. Several kinds of punctuation are also recognized as if they were words; the function punc returns the pseudo-word corresponding to a punctuation character.

The function see registers each word seen. It needs to know the previous word as well as the one just recognized—hence the variable prev. Initially this variable is set to the period pseudo-word; after see has been called, it will always contain the last word sent to the function.

After read-text returns, *words* will contain an entry for each word in the input file. By calling hash-table-count you can see how many distinct words there were. Few English texts have over 10,000.

Now comes the fun part. Figure 8.3 contains the code that generates text from the data accumulated by the code in Figure 8.2. The recursive function generate-text drives the process. It takes a number indicating the number of words to be generated, and an optional previous word. Using the default will make the generated text start at the beginning of a sentence.

```
(defparameter *words* (make-hash-table :size 10000))

(defconstant maxword 100)

(defun read-text (pathname)
  (with-open-file (s pathname :direction :input)
    (let ((buffer (make-string maxword))
          (pos 0))
      (do ((c (read-char s nil :eof)
              (read-char s nil :eof)))
          ((eql c :eof))
        (if (or (alpha-char-p c) (char= c #\'))
            (progn
              (setf (aref buffer pos) c)
              (incf pos))
            (progn
              (unless (zerop pos)
                (see (intern (string-downcase
                               (subseq buffer 0 pos)))))
              (setf pos 0))
            (let ((p (punc c)))
              (if p (see p)))))))))

(defun punc (c)
  (case c
    (#\. '|.|) (#\, '|,|) (#\; '|;|)
    (#\! '|!|) (#\? '|?|) ))

(let ((prev '|.|))
  (defun see (symb)
    (let ((pair (assoc symb (gethash prev *words*))))
      (if (null pair)
          (push (cons symb 1) (gethash prev *words*))
          (incf (cdr pair))))
    (setf prev symb)))
```

Figure 8.2: Reading sample text.

```
(defun generate-text (n &optional (prev '|.|))
  (if (zerop n)
      (terpri)
      (let ((next (random-next prev)))
        (format t "~A " next)
        (generate-text (1- n) next))))

(defun random-next (prev)
  (let* ((choices (gethash prev *words*))
         (i (random (reduce #'+ choices
                            :key #'cdr))))
    (dolist (pair choices)
      (if (minusp (decf i (cdr pair)))
          (return (car pair))))))
```

Figure 8.3: Generating text.

To get a new word, generate-text calls random-next with the previous word. This function makes a random choice among the words that followed prev in the input text, weighted according to the frequency of each.°

At this point it would be time to give the program a test run. But in fact you have already seen an example of what it produces: the stanza at the beginning of this book, which was generated by using Milton's *Paradise Lost* as the input text.°

Summary

1. Any string can be the name of a symbol, but symbols created by read are transformed into uppercase by default.

2. Symbols have associated property lists, which behave like assoc-lists, though they don't have the same form.

3. Symbols are substantial objects, more like structures than mere names.

4. Packages map strings to symbols. To create an entry for a symbol in a package is to intern it. Symbols do not have to be interned.

5. Packages enforce modularity by restricting which names you can refer to. By default your programs will be in the user package, but larger programs are often divided into several packages defined for that purpose.

6. Symbols can be made accessible in other packages. Keywords are self-evaluating and accessible in any package.

7. When a program operates on words, it's convenient to represent the words as symbols.

Exercises

1. Is it possible for two symbols to have the same name but not be `eql`?

2. Estimate the difference between the amount of memory used to represent the string `"FOO"` and the amount used to represent the symbol `foo`.

3. The call to `defpackage` on page 137 used only strings as arguments. We could have used symbols instead. Why might this have been dangerous?

4. Add the code necessary to make the code in Figure 7.1 be in a package named `"RING"`, and that in Figure 7.2 be in a package named `"FILE"`. The existing code should remain unchanged.

5. Write a program that can verify whether or not a quote was produced by Henley (Section 8.8).

6. Write a version of Henley that can take a word and generate a sentence with that word in the middle of it.

9

Numbers

Number-crunching is one of Common Lisp's strengths. It has a rich set of numeric types, and its features for manipulating numbers compare favorably with any language.

9.1 Types

Common Lisp provides four distinct types of numbers: integers, floating-point numbers, ratios, and complex numbers. Most of the functions described in this chapter work on numbers of any type. A few, explicitly noted, accept all but complex numbers.

An integer is written as a string of digits: 2001. A floating-point number can be written as a string of digits containing a decimal point, 253.72, or in scientific notation, 2.5372e2. A ratio is written as a fraction of integers: 2/3. And the complex number $a+bi$ is written as #c(a b), where a and b are any two real numbers of the same type.

The predicates integerp, floatp, and complexp return true for numbers of the corresponding types. Figure 9.1 shows the hierarchy of numeric types.

Here are some general rules of thumb for determining what kind of number a computation will return:

1. If a numeric function receives one or more floating-point numbers as arguments, the return value will be a floating-point number (or a complex number with floating-point components). So (+ 1.0 2) evaluates to 3.0, and (+ #c(0 1.0) 2) evaluates to #c(2.0 1.0).

143

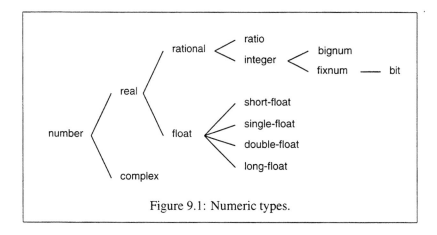

Figure 9.1: Numeric types.

2. Ratios that divide evenly will be converted into integers. So (/ 10 2) will return 5.

3. Complex numbers whose imaginary part would be zero will be converted into reals. So (+ #c(1 -1) #c(2 1)) evaluates to 3.

Rules 2 and 3 apply to arguments as soon as they are read, so:

```
> (list (ratiop 2/2) (complexp #c(1 0)))
(NIL NIL)
```

9.2   Conversion and Extraction

Lisp provides functions for converting, and extracting components of, the four kinds of numbers. The function float converts any real number to a floating-point number:

```
> (mapcar #'float '(1 2/3 .5))
(1.0 0.6666667 0.5)
```

Reducing numbers to integers is not necessarily *conversion*, because it can involve some loss of information. The function truncate returns the integer component of any real number:

```
> (truncate 1.3)
1
0.29999995
```

The second return value is the original argument minus the first return value. (The difference of .00000005 is due to the inherent inexactitude of floating-point computation.)

The functions floor, ceiling, and round also derive integers from their arguments. Using floor, which returns the greatest integer less than or equal to its argument, and ceiling, which returns the least integer greater than or equal to its argument, we can generalize mirror? (page 46) to recognize all palindromes:

```
(defun palindrome? (x)
  (let ((mid (/ (length x) 2)))
    (equal (subseq x 0 (floor mid))
           (reverse (subseq x (ceiling mid))))))
```

Like truncate, floor and ceiling also return as a second value the difference between the argument and the first return value:

```
> (floor 1.5)
1
0.5
```

In fact, we could think of truncate as being defined:

```
(defun our-truncate (n)
  (if (> n 0)
      (floor n)
      (ceiling n)))
```

The function round returns the nearest integer to its argument. When the argument is equidistant from two integers, Common Lisp, like many programming languages, does *not* round up. Instead it rounds to the nearest even digit:

```
> (mapcar #'round '(-2.5 -1.5 1.5 2.5))
(-2 -2 2 2)
```

In some numerical applications this is a good thing, because rounding errors tend to cancel one another out. However, if end-users are expecting your program to round certain values up, you must provide for this yourself.[1] Like its cousins, round returns as its second value the difference between the argument and the first return value.

The function mod returns just the second value that floor would return; and rem returns just the second value that truncate would return. We used

---

[1] When format rounds for display, it doesn't even guarantee to round to an even or odd digit. See page 125.

mod on page 94 to determine if one number was divisible by another, and on page 127 to find the actual position of an element in a ring buffer.

For reals, the function signum returns either 1, 0, or -1, depending on whether its argument is positive, zero, or negative. The function abs returns the absolute value of its argument. Thus (* (abs *x*) (signum *x*)) = *x*.

```
> (mapcar #'signum '(-2 -0.0 0.0 0 .5 3))
(-1 -0.0 0.0 0 1.0 1)
```

In some implementations -0.0 may exist in its own right, as above. Functionally it makes little difference whether it does or not, because in numeric code -0.0 behaves exactly like 0.0.

Ratios and complex numbers are conceptually two-part structures. The functions numerator and denominator return the corresponding components of a ratio or integer. (If the number is an integer, the former returns the number itself and the latter returns 1.) The functions realpart and imagpart return the real and imaginary components of any number. (If the number isn't complex, the former returns the number itself and the latter returns zero.)

The function random takes an integer or floating-point number. An expression of the form (random *n*) returns a number greater than or equal to zero and less than *n*, and of the same type as *n*.

9.3   Comparison

The predicate = returns true when its arguments are numerically equal—when the difference between them is zero.

```
> (= 1 1.0)
T
> (eql 1 1.0)
NIL
```

It is less strict than eql, which also requires its arguments to be of the same type.

The predicates for comparing numbers are < (less than) , <= (less than or equal), = (equal), >= (greater than or equal), > (greater than), and /= (different). All of them take one or more arguments. With one argument they all return t. For all except /=, a call with three or more arguments,

```
(<= w x y z)
```

is equivalent to the conjunction of a binary operator applied to successive pairs of arguments:

```
(and (<= w x) (<= x y) (<= y z))
```

Since /= returns true if *no two* of its arguments are =, the expression

```
(/= w x y z)
```

is equivalent to

```
(and (/= w x) (/= w y) (/= w z)
     (/= x y) (/= x z) (/= y z))
```

The specialized predicates zerop, plusp, and minusp take one argument and return true if it is =, >, and < zero, respectively. These functions do not overlap. Although -0.0 (if an implementation uses it) is preceded by a negative sign, it is = to 0,

```
> (list (minusp -0.0) (zerop -0.0))
(NIL T)
```

and therefore zerop, not minusp.

The predicates oddp and evenp apply only to integers. The former is true only of odd integers, and the latter only of even ones.

Of the predicates described in this section, only =, /=, and zerop apply to complex numbers.

The functions max and min return, respectively, the maximum and minimum of their arguments. Both require at least one:

```
> (list (max 1 2 3 4 5) (min 1 2 3 4 5))
(5 1)
```

If the arguments to either include floating-point numbers, the type of the result is implementation-dependent.

9.4 Arithmetic

The functions for addition and subtraction are + and -. Both can take any number of arguments, including none, in which case they return 0. An expression of the form (- *n*) returns −*n*. An expression of the form

```
(- x y z)
```

is equivalent to

```
(- (- x y) z)
```

There are also two functions 1+ and 1-, which return their argument plus 1 and minus 1 respectively. The name 1- is a bit misleading, because (1- x) returns $x - 1$, not $1 - x$.

The macros `incf` and `decf` increment and decrement their argument, respectively. An expression of the form (`incf` x n) is similar in effect to (`setf` x (+ x n)), and (`decf` x n) to (`setf` x (- x n)). In both cases the second argument is optional and defaults to 1.

The function for multiplication is *. It takes any number of arguments. When given no arguments it returns 1. Otherwise it returns the product of its arguments.

The division function, /, expects at least one argument. A call of the form (/ n) is equivalent to (/ 1 n),

```
> (/ 3)
1/3
```

while a call of the form

```
(/ x y z)
```

is equivalent to

```
(/ (/ x y) z)
```

Notice the similarity between - and / in this respect.

When given two integers, / will return a ratio if the first is not a multiple of the second:

```
> (/ 365 12)
365/12
```

If what you're trying to do is find out how long an average month is, for example, this may give the impression that the toplevel is playing games with you. In such cases, what you really need is to call `float` on a ratio, not / on two integers:

```
> (float 365/12)
30.416666
```

9.5 Exponentiation

To find x^n we call (`expt` x n),

```
> (expt 2 5)
32
```

and to find $\log_n x$ we call (`log` x n):

```
> (log 32 2)
5.0
```

This will ordinarily return a floating-point number.

To find e^x there is a distinct function `exp`,

```
> (exp 2)
7.389056
```

and to find a natural logarithm you can just use `log`, because the second argument defaults to e:

```
> (log 7.389056)
2.0
```

To find roots you can call `expt` with a ratio as the second argument,

```
> (expt 27 1/3)
3.0
```

but for finding square roots the function `sqrt` should be faster:

```
> (sqrt 4)
2.0
```

9.6 Trigonometric Functions

The constant `pi` is a floating-point representation of π. Its precision is implementation-dependent. The functions `sin`, `cos`, and `tan` find the sine, cosine, and tangent, respectively, of angles expressed in radians:

```
> (let ((x (/ pi 4)))
    (list (sin x) (cos x) (tan x)))
(0.7071067811865475d0 0.7071067811865476d0 1.0d0)
```

These functions all take negative and complex arguments.

The functions `asin`, `acos`, and `atan` implement the inverse of sine, cosine, and tangent. For arguments between -1 and 1 inclusive, `asin` and `acos` return real numbers.

Hyperbolic sine, cosine, and tangent are implemented by `sinh`, `cosh`, and `tanh`, respectively. Their inverses are likewise `asinh`, `acosh`, and `atanh`.

9.7   Representation

Common Lisp imposes no limit on the size of integers. Small integers fit in
one word of memory and are called *fixnums*. When a computation produces an
integer too large to fit in one memory word, Lisp switches to a representation
(a *bignum*) that uses multiple words of memory. So the effective limit on the
size of an integer is imposed by physical memory, not by the language.

The constants `most-positive-fixnum` and `most-negative-fixnum`
indicate the largest magnitudes an implementation can represent without
having to use bignums. In many implementations they are:

```
> (values most-positive-fixnum most-negative-fixnum)
536870911
-536870912
```

The predicate `typep` takes an argument and a type name and returns true if
the argument is of the specified type. So,

```
> (typep 1 'fixnum)
T
> (typep (1+ most-positive-fixnum) 'bignum)
T
```

The limits on the values of floating-point numbers are implementation-
dependent. Common Lisp provides for up to four types of floating-point numbers: `short-float`, `single-float`, `double-float`, and `long-float`.
Implementations are not required to use distinct formats for all four types
(and few do).

The general idea is that a short float is supposed to fit in a single word,
that single and double floats are supposed to provide the usual idea of single-
and double-precision floating-point numbers, and that long floats can be
something really big, if desired. But an implementation could perfectly well
implement all four the same way.

You can specify what format you want a floating-point number to be by
substituting the letters s, f, d, or l for the e when a number is represented
in scientific notation. (You can use uppercase too, and this is a good idea
for long floats, because l looks so much like 1.) So to make the largest
representation of 1.0 you would write 1L0.

Sixteen global constants mark the limits of each format in a given implementation. Their names are of the form m-s-f, where m is most or least, s
is positive or negative, and f is one of the four types of float.°

Floating-point underflow and overflow are signalled as errors by Common
Lisp:

```
> (* most-positive-long-float 10)
Error: floating-point-overflow.
```

9.8   Example: Ray-Tracing

As an example of a mostly numerical application, this section shows how to write a ray-tracer. Ray-tracing is the rendering algorithm deluxe: it yields the most realistic images, but takes the most time.

To generate a 3D image, we need to define at least four things: an eye, one or more light sources, a simulated world consisting of one or more surfaces, and a plane (the *image plane*) that serves as a window onto this world. The image we generate is the projection of the world onto a region of the image plane.

What makes ray-tracing unusual is the way we find this projection: we go pixel-by-pixel along the image plane, tracing the light back into the simulated world. This approach brings three main advantages: it makes it easy to get real-world optical effects like transparency, reflected light, and cast shadows; it allows us to define the simulated world directly in terms of whatever geometric objects we want, instead of having to construct them out of polygons; and it is straightforward to implement.

Figure 9.2 contains some math utilities we are going to need in our ray-tracer. The first, `sq`, just returns the square of its argument. The next, `mag`, returns the length of a vector given its x, y, and z components. This function is used in the next two. We use it in `unit-vector`, which returns three values representing the components of a unit vector with the same direction as the vector whose components are x, y, and z:

```
> (multiple-value-call #'mag (unit-vector 23 12 47))
1.0
```

And we use mag in `distance`, which returns the distance between two points in 3-space. (Defining the `point` structure to have a `:conc-name` of `nil` means that the access functions for the fields will have the same names as the fields: x instead of `point-x`, for example.)

Finally, `minroot` takes three reals a, b, and c, and returns the smallest real x for which $ax^2 + bx + c = 0$. When a is nonzero, the roots of this equation are yielded by the familiar formula:

$$x = \frac{-b \pm \sqrt{b^2 - 4ac}}{2a}$$

Figure 9.3 contains code defining a minimal ray-tracer. It generates black and white images illuminated by a single light source, at the same position as the eye. (The results thus tend to look like flash photographs.)

The `surface` structure will be used to represent the objects in the simulated world. More precisely, it will be `included` in the structures defined to represent specific kinds of objects, like spheres. The `surface` structure itself contains only a single field: a color ranging from 0 (black) to 1 (white).

```
(defun sq (x) (* x x))

(defun mag (x y z)
  (sqrt (+ (sq x) (sq y) (sq z))))

(defun unit-vector (x y z)
  (let ((d (mag x y z)))
    (values (/ x d) (/ y d) (/ z d))))

(defstruct (point (:conc-name nil))
  x y z)

(defun distance (p1 p2)
  (mag (- (x p1) (x p2))
       (- (y p1) (y p2))
       (- (z p1) (z p2))))

(defun minroot (a b c)
  (if (zerop a)
      (/ (- c) b)
      (let ((disc (- (sq b) (* 4 a c))))
        (unless (minusp disc)
          (let ((discrt (sqrt disc)))
            (min (/ (+ (- b) discrt) (* 2 a))
                 (/ (- (- b) discrt) (* 2 a))))))))
```

Figure 9.2: Math utilities.

The image plane will be the plane defined by the x- and y-axes. The eye will be on the z-axis, 200 units from the origin. So to be visible through the image plane, the surfaces that get inserted into *world* (initially nil) will have to have negative z coordinates. Figure 9.4 illustrates a ray passing through a point on the image plane and hitting a sphere.

The function tracer takes a pathname and writes an image to the corresponding file. Image files will be written in a simple ASCII format called PGM. By default, images will be 100×100. The header in our PGM files will consist of the tag P2, followed by integers indicating the breadth (100) and height (100) of the image in pixels, and the highest possible value (255). The remainder of the file will consist of 10,000 integers between 0 (black) and 255 (white), representing 100 horizontal stripes of 100 pixels.

```
(defstruct surface  color)

(defparameter *world* nil)
(defconstant eye (make-point :x 0 :y 0 :z 200))

(defun tracer (pathname &optional (res 1))
  (with-open-file (p pathname :direction :output)
    (format p "P2 ~A ~A 255" (* res 100) (* res 100))
    (let ((inc (/ res)))
      (do ((y -50 (+ y inc)))
          ((< (- 50 y) inc))
        (do ((x -50 (+ x inc)))
            ((< (- 50 x) inc))
          (print (color-at x y) p))))))

(defun color-at (x y)
  (multiple-value-bind (xr yr zr)
                       (unit-vector (- x (x eye))
                                    (- y (y eye))
                                    (- 0 (z eye)))
    (round (* (sendray eye xr yr zr) 255))))

(defun sendray (pt xr yr zr)
  (multiple-value-bind (s int) (first-hit pt xr yr zr)
    (if s
        (* (lambert s int xr yr zr) (surface-color s))
        0)))

(defun first-hit (pt xr yr zr)
  (let (surface hit dist)
    (dolist (s *world*)
      (let ((h (intersect s pt xr yr zr)))
        (when h
          (let ((d (distance h pt)))
            (when (or (null dist) (< d dist))
              (setf surface s hit h dist d))))))
    (values surface hit)))

(defun lambert (s int xr yr zr)
  (multiple-value-bind (xn yn zn) (normal s int)
    (max 0 (+ (* xr xn) (* yr yn) (* zr zn)))))
```

Figure 9.3: Ray-tracing.

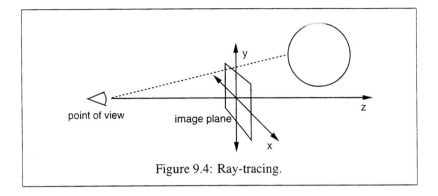

Figure 9.4: Ray-tracing.

The resolution of the image can be adjusted by giving an explicit `res`. If `res` is 2, for example, then the same image will be rendered with 200×200 pixels.

The image is a 100×100 square on the image plane. Each pixel represents the amount of light that passes through the image plane at that point on the way to the eye. To find the amount of light at each pixel, `tracer` calls `color-at`. This function finds the vector from the eye to that point, then calls `sendray` to trace the course of this vector back into the simulated world; `sendray` will return an intensity value between 0 and 1, which is then scaled to an integer between 0 and 255 for display.

To determine the intensity of a ray, `sendray` has to find the object that it was reflected from. To do this it calls `first-hit`, which considers all the surfaces in `*world*`, and returns the surface (if any) that the ray hits first. If the ray doesn't hit anything, `sendray` just returns the background color, which by convention is 0 (black). If the ray does hit something, we have to find out the amount of light shining on the surface at the point where the ray hits it.

Lambert's law says that the intensity of light reflected by a point on a surface is proportional to the dot-product of the unit normal vector N at that point (the vector of length 1 that is perpendicular to the surface there), and the unit vector L from the point to the light source:

$$i = N \cdot L$$

If the light is shining right at the point, N and L will be coincident, and the dot-product will be 1, the maximum value. If the surface is turned 90° to the light at that point, then N and L will be perpendicular, and their dot-product will be 0. If the light is behind the surface, the dot-product will be negative.

In our program, we are assuming that the light source is at the eye, so `lambert`, which uses this rule to find the illumination at some point on a surface, returns the dot-product of the normal with the ray we were tracing.

In sendray this value is multiplied by the color of the surface (a dark surface is dark even when well-illuminated) to determine the overall intensity at that point.

For simplicity, we will have only one kind of object in our simulated world, spheres. Figure 9.5 contains the code involving spheres. The sphere structure includes surface, so a sphere will have a color as well as a center and radius. Calling defsphere adds a new one to the world.

The function intersect considers the type of surface involved and calls the corresponding intersect function. At the moment there is only one, sphere-intersect, but intersect is written so that it can easily be extended to deal with other kinds of objects.

How do we find the intersection of a ray with a sphere? The ray is represented as a point $p = \langle x_0, y_0, z_0 \rangle$, and a unit vector $v = \langle x_r, y_r, z_r \rangle$. Every point on the ray can be expressed as $p + nv$, for some n—that is, as $\langle x_0 + nx_r, y_0 + ny_r, z_0 + nz_r \rangle$. Where the ray hits the sphere, the distance from that point to the center $\langle x_c, y_c, z_c \rangle$ will be equal to the sphere's radius r. So at the intersection the following equation will hold:

$$r = \sqrt{(x_0 + nx_r - x_c)^2 + (y_0 + ny_r - y_c)^2 + (z_0 + nz_r - z_c)^2}$$

This yields

$$an^2 + bn + c = 0$$

where

$$a = x_r^2 + y_r^2 + z_r^2$$

$$b = 2((x_0 - x_c)x_r + (y_0 - y_c)y_r + (z_0 - z_c)z_r)$$

$$c = (x_0 - x_c)^2 + (y_0 - y_c)^2 + (z_0 - z_c)^2 - r^2$$

To find the intersection we just find the roots of this quadratic equation. It might have zero, one, or two real roots. No roots means that the ray misses the sphere; one root means that it intersects the sphere at one point (a grazing hit); and two roots means that it intersects the sphere at two points (in one side and out the other). In the latter case, we want the smaller of the two roots; n increases as the ray travels away from the eye, so the first hit is the smaller n. Hence the call to minroot. If there is a root, sphere-intersect returns the point representing $\langle x_0 + nx_r, y_0 + ny_r, z_0 + nz_r \rangle$.

The other two functions in Figure 9.5, normal and sphere-normal, are analogous to intersect and sphere-intersect. Finding the normal to a sphere is easy—it's just the vector from the point to the center of the sphere.

Figure 9.6 shows how we would generate an image; ray-test defines 38 spheres (not all of which will be visible) and then generates an image

```
(defstruct (sphere (:include surface))
  radius center)

(defun defsphere (x y z r c)
  (let ((s (make-sphere
             :radius r
             :center (make-point :x x :y y :z z)
             :color  c)))
    (push s *world*)
    s))

(defun intersect (s pt xr yr zr)
  (funcall (typecase s (sphere #'sphere-intersect))
           s pt xr yr zr))

(defun sphere-intersect (s pt xr yr zr)
  (let* ((c (sphere-center s))
         (n (minroot (+ (sq xr) (sq yr) (sq zr))
                     (* 2 (+ (* (- (x pt) (x c)) xr)
                             (* (- (y pt) (y c)) yr)
                             (* (- (z pt) (z c)) zr)))
                     (+ (sq (- (x pt) (x c)))
                        (sq (- (y pt) (y c)))
                        (sq (- (z pt) (z c)))
                        (- (sq (sphere-radius s)))))))
    (if n
        (make-point :x  (+ (x pt) (* n xr))
                    :y  (+ (y pt) (* n yr))
                    :z  (+ (z pt) (* n zr)))))))

(defun normal (s pt)
  (funcall (typecase s (sphere #'sphere-normal))
           s pt))

(defun sphere-normal (s pt)
  (let ((c (sphere-center s)))
    (unit-vector (- (x c) (x pt))
                 (- (y c) (y pt))
                 (- (z c) (z pt)))))
```

Figure 9.5: Spheres.

```
(defun ray-test (&optional (res 1))
  (setf *world* nil)
  (defsphere 0 -300 -1200 200 .8)
  (defsphere -80 -150 -1200 200 .7)
  (defsphere 70 -100 -1200 200 .9)
  (do ((x -2 (1+ x)))
      ((> x 2))
    (do ((z 2 (1+ z)))
        ((> z 7))
      (defsphere (* x 200) 300 (* z -400) 40 .75)))
  (tracer (make-pathname :name "spheres.pgm") res))
```

Figure 9.6: Using the ray-tracer.

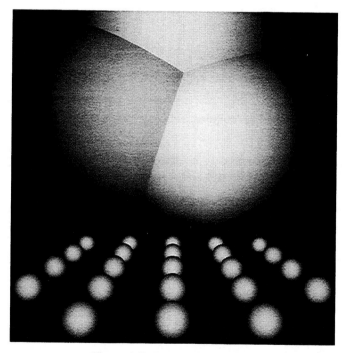

Figure 9.7: Ray-traced image.

file called "spheres.pgm". Figure 9.7 shows the resulting image, generated with a res of 10.

A real ray-tracer could generate much more sophisticated images, because it would consider more than just the contribution of a single light source to a point on a surface. There might be multiple light sources, each of different intensities. They would not ordinarily be at the eye, in which case the program would have to check to see whether the vector to a light source intersected another surface, which would then be casting its shadow onto the first. Putting the light source at the eye saves us from having to consider this complication, because we can't see any of the points that are in shadow.

A real ray-tracer would also follow the ray beyond the first surface it hit, adding in some amount of light reflected by other surfaces. It would do color, of course, and would also be able to model surfaces that were transparent or shiny. But the basic algorithm would remain much as shown in Figure 9.3, and many of the refinements would just involve recursive uses of the same ingredients.

A real ray-tracer would probably also be highly optimized. The program given here is written for brevity, and is not even optimized as a Lisp program, let alone as a ray-tracer. Merely adding type and inline declarations (Section 13.3) could make it more than twice as fast.

Summary

1. Common Lisp provides integers, ratios, floating-point numbers, and complex numbers.

2. Numbers can be simplified and converted, and their components can be extracted.

3. Predicates for comparing numbers take any number of arguments, and compare successive pairs—except /=, which compares all pairs.

4. Common Lisp provides roughly the numerical functions you might see on a low-end scientific calculator. The same functions generally apply to numbers of several types.

5. Fixnums are integers small enough to fit in one word. They are quietly but expensively converted to bignums when necessary. Common Lisp provides for up to four types of floating-point number. The limits of each representation are implementation-dependent constants.

6. A ray-tracer generates an image by tracing the light that makes each pixel back into a simulated world.

Exercises

1. Define a function that takes a list of reals and returns true iff they are in nondecreasing order.

2. Define a function that takes an integer number of cents and returns four values showing how to make that number out of 25-, 10-, 5- and 1-cent pieces, using the smallest total number of coins.

3. A faraway planet is inhabited by two kinds of beings, wigglies and wobblies. Wigglies and wobblies are equally good at singing. Every year there is a great competition to chooses the ten best singers. Here are the results for the past ten years:

YEAR	1	2	3	4	5	6	7	8	9	10
WIGGLIES	6	5	6	4	5	5	4	5	6	5
WOBBLIES	4	5	4	6	5	5	6	5	4	5

Write a program to simulate such a contest. Do your results suggest that the committee is, in fact, choosing the ten best singers each year?

4. Define a function that takes 8 reals representing the endpoints of two segments in 2-space, and returns either nil if the segments do not intersect, or two values representing the x- and y-coordinates of the intersection if they do.

5. Suppose f is a function of one (real) argument, and that min and max are nonzero reals with different signs such that f has a root (returns zero) for one argument i such that min $< i <$ max. Define a function that takes four arguments, f, min, max, and epsilon, and returns an approximation of i accurate to within plus or minus epsilon.

6. *Horner's method* is a trick for evaluating polynomials efficiently. To find $ax^3 + bx^2 + cx + d$ you evaluate $x(x(ax+b)+c)+d$. Define a function that takes one or more arguments—the value of x followed by n reals representing the coefficients of an $(n-1)$th-degree polynomial—and calculates the value of the polynomial by Horner's method.

7. How many bits would you estimate your implementation uses to represent fixnums?

8. How many distinct types of float does your implementation provide?

10

Macros

Lisp code is expressed as lists, which are Lisp objects. Section 2.3 claimed that this made it possible to write programs that would write programs. This chapter shows how to cross the line from expressions to code.

10.1 Eval

It's obvious how to generate expressions: just call `list`. What we haven't considered is how to make Lisp treat them as code. The missing link is the function `eval`, which takes an expression, evaluates it, and returns its value:

```
> (eval '(+ 1 2 3))
6
> (eval '(format t "Hello"))
Hello
NIL
```

If this looks familiar, it should. It's `eval` we have been talking to all this time. The following function implements something very like the toplevel:

```
(defun our-toplevel ()
  (do ()
      (nil)
    (format t "~%> ")
    (print (eval (read)))))
```

For this reason the toplevel is also known as a read-eval-print loop.

Calling eval is one way to cross the line between lists and code. However, it is not a very good way:

1. It's inefficient: eval is handed a raw list, and either has to compile it on the spot, or evaluate it in an interpreter. Either way is much slower than running compiled code.

2. The expression is evaluated with no lexical context. If you call eval within a let, for example, the expressions passed to eval cannot refer to variables established by the let.

There are much better ways (described in the next section) to take advantage of the possibility of generating code. Indeed, one of the only places where it is legitimate to use eval is in something like a toplevel loop.

For programmers the main value of eval is probably as a conceptual model for Lisp. We can imagine it defined as a big cond expression:

```
(defun eval (expr env)
  (cond ...
        ((eql (car expr) 'quote) (cadr expr))
        ...
        (t (apply (symbol-function (car expr))
                  (mapcar #'(lambda (x)
                              (eval x env))
                          (cdr expr))))))
```

Most expressions are handled by the default clause, which says to get the function referred to in the car, evaluate all the arguments in the cdr, and return the result of applying the former to the latter.[1]

However, we can't do this for an expression like (quote x), since the whole point of quote is to preserve its argument from evaluation. So we have to have a distinct clause just for quote. That's what a special operator is, essentially: an operator that has to be implemented as a special case in eval.

The functions coerce and compile provide a similar bridge from lists to code. You can coerce a lambda expression into a function,

```
> (coerce '(lambda (x) x) 'function)
#<Interpreted-Function BF9D96>
```

and if you give nil as the first argument to compile, it will compile a lambda expression given as the second argument.

---

[1]To really duplicate Lisp, eval would have to take a second argument (here env) to represent the lexical environment. This model of eval is inaccurate in that it retrieves the function before evaluating the arguments, whereas in Common Lisp the order of these two operations is deliberately unspecified.

```
> (compile nil '(lambda (x) (+ x 2)))
#<Compiled-Function BF55BE>
NIL
NIL
```

Since coerce and compile can take lists as arguments, a program could build new functions on the fly. However, this is a drastic measure, comparable to calling eval, and should be viewed with the same suspicion.

The trouble with eval, coerce, and compile is not that they cross the line between lists and code, but that they do it at run-time. Crossing the line is expensive. Doing it at compile-time is good enough in most cases, and costs nothing when your program runs. The next section shows how to do this.

10.2   Macros

The most common way to write programs that write programs is by defining macros. *Macros* are operators that are implemented by transformation. You define a macro by saying how a call to it should be translated. This translation, called *macro-expansion*, is done automatically by the compiler. So the code generated by your macros becomes an integral part of your program, just as if you had typed it in yourself.

Macros are usually defined by calling defmacro. A defmacro looks a lot like a defun, but instead of defining the value a call should produce, it defines how a call should be translated. For example, a macro to set its argument to nil might be defined as follows:

```
(defmacro nil! (x)
  (list 'setf x nil))
```

This defines a new operator called nil!, which will take one argument. A call of the form (nil! *a*) will be translated into (setf *a* nil) before being compiled or evaluated. So if we type (nil! x) into the toplevel,

```
> (nil! x)
NIL
> x
NIL
```

it is exactly equivalent to typing the expansion, (setf x nil).

To test a function, we call it, but to test a macro, we look at its expansion. The function macroexpand-1 takes a macro call and generates its expansion:

```
> (macroexpand-1 '(nil! x))
(SETF X NIL)
T
```

A macro call can expand into another macro call. When the compiler (or the toplevel) encounters a macro call, it simply keeps expanding it until it is no longer one.

The secret to understanding macros is to understand how they are implemented. Underneath, they're just functions that transform expressions. For example, if you pass an expression of the form (nil! *a*) to this function

```
(lambda (expr)
  (apply #'(lambda (x) (list 'setf x nil))
         (cdr expr)))
```

it will return (setf *a* nil). When you use defmacro, you're defining a function much like this one. All macroexpand-1 does, when it sees an expression whose car is known to be the name of a macro, is pass the expression to the corresponding function.

10.3   Backquote

The backquote read-macro makes it possible to build lists from templates. Backquote is used extensively in macro definitions. While a regular quote is a close-quote (apostrophe) on the keyboard, a backquote is an open-quote. It's called "backquote" because it looks like a normal quote tilted backwards.

Used by itself, a backquote is equivalent to a regular quote:

```
> '(a b c)
(A B C)
```

Like a regular quote, a backquote alone protects its argument from evaluation.

The advantage of backquote is that, within a backquoted expression, you can use , (comma) and ,@ (comma-at) to turn evaluation back on. If you prefix a comma to something within a backquoted expression, it will be evaluated. Thus we can use backquote and comma together to build list templates:

```
> (setf a 1 b 2)
2
> '(a is ,a and b is ,b)
(A IS 1 AND B IS 2)
```

By using backquote instead of a call to list, we can write macro definitions that look like the expansions they will produce. For example, nil! could be defined as:

```
(defmacro nil! (x)
  '(setf ,x nil))
```

Comma-at is like comma, but splices its argument (which should be a list). Instead of the list itself, its elements are inserted in the template:

```
> (setf lst '(a b c))
(A B C)
> '(lst is ,lst)
(LST IS (A B C))
> '(its elements are ,@lst)
(ITS ELEMENTS ARE A B C)
```

Comma-at is useful in macros that have rest parameters representing for example, a body of code. Suppose we want a while macro that will evaluate its body so long as an initial test expression remains true:

```
> (let ((x 0))
    (while (< x 10)
      (princ x)
      (incf x)))
0123456789
NIL
```

We can define such a macro by using a rest parameter to collect a list of the expressions in the body, then using comma-at to splice this list into the expansion:

```
(defmacro while (test &rest body)
  '(do ()
      ((not ,test))
     ,@body))
```

10.4 Example: Quicksort

Figure 10.1 contains an example of a function that relies heavily on macros—a function to sort vectors using the Quicksort algorithm.° The algorithm works as follows:

1. You begin by choosing some element as the *pivot*. Many implementations choose an element in the middle of the sequence to be sorted.

2. Then you *partition* the vector, swapping elements until all the elements less than the pivot are to the left of all those greater than or equal to the pivot.

```
(defun quicksort (vec l r)
  (let ((i l)
        (j r)
        (p (svref vec (round (+ l r) 2))))    ; 1
    (while (<= i j)                            ; 2
      (while (< (svref vec i) p) (incf i))
      (while (> (svref vec j) p) (decf j))
      (when (<= i j)
        (rotatef (svref vec i) (svref vec j))
        (incf i)
        (decf j)))
    (if (> (- j l) 1) (quicksort vec l j))     ; 3
    (if (> (- r i) 1) (quicksort vec i r)))
  vec)
```

Figure 10.1: Quicksort.

3. Finally, if either of the partitions has two or more elements, you apply the algorithm recursively to those segments of the vector.

With each recursion the partitions get smaller, till finally the vector is completely sorted.

The implementation in Figure 10.1 takes a vector and two integers that mark the range to be sorted. The element currently in the middle of this range is chosen as the pivot (p). Then the partition is done by working inward from either end of the range, and swapping elements that are either too big to be on the left side or too small to be on the right. (Giving two arguments to rotatef swaps their values.) Finally, if either partition contains multiple elements, they are sorted by the same process.

As well as the while macro we defined in the previous section, the implementation in Figure 10.1 uses the built-in when, incf, decf, and rotatef macros. Using these macros makes the code substantially shorter and clearer.

10.5   Macro Design

Writing macros is a distinct kind of programming, with its own unique aims and problems. Being able to change what the compiler sees is almost like being able to rewrite it. So when you start writing macros, you have to start thinking like a language designer.

This section gives a quick overview of the problems involved, and the techniques used to solve them. As an example, we will define a macro called ntimes, which takes a number *n* and evaluates its body *n* times:

```
> (ntimes 10
    (princ "."))
. . . . . . . . . .
NIL
```

Here is an incorrect definition of ntimes that illustrates some issues in macro design:

```
(defmacro ntimes (n &rest body)              ; wrong
  '(do ((x 0 (+ x 1)))
       ((>= x ,n))
     ,@body))
```

This definition may look ok at first sight. In the case above it would work as intended. But in fact it is broken in two ways.

One of the problems that macro designers have to think about is inadvertent *variable capture*. This happens when a variable used in a macro expansion happens to have the same name as a variable existing in the context where the expansion is inserted. The incorrect definition of ntimes creates a variable x. So if the macro is called in a place where there is already a variable with that name, it may not do what we expect:

```
> (let ((x 10))
    (ntimes 5
      (setf x (+ x 1)))
    x)
10
```

If ntimes did what it was supposed to, this expression should increment x five times, and finally return 15. But because the macro expansion happens to use x as its iteration variable, the setf expression increments the value of *that* x, not the one that we meant to increment. Once the macro call is expanded, the preceding expression becomes:

```
(let ((x 10))
  (do ((x 0 (+ x 1)))
      ((>= x 5))
    (setf x (+ x 1)))
  x)
```

The most general solution is not to use ordinary symbols anywhere they might be captured. Instead we can use gensyms (Section 8.4). Because read interns every symbol it sees, there is no way a gensym could be eql to any symbol occurring in a program text. If we rewrite the definition of ntimes to use a gensym instead of x, it will at least be safe from variable capture:

```
(defmacro ntimes (n &rest body)                        ; wrong
  (let ((g (gensym)))
    '(do ((,g 0 (+ ,g 1)))
         ((>= ,g ,n))
      ,@body)))
```

However, this macro is still susceptible to another problem: multiple evaluation. Because the first argument is inserted directly into the do, it will be evaluated on each iteration. This mistake shows most clearly when the first argument is an expression with side-effects:

```
> (let ((v 10))
    (ntimes (setf v (- v 1))
      (princ ".")))
. . . . .
NIL
```

Since v is initially 10 and setf returns the value of its second argument, this should print nine periods. In fact it prints only five.

We see why if we look at the expression with the macro call expanded:

```
(let ((v 10))
  (do ((#:g1 0 (+ #:g1 1)))
      ((>= #:g1 (setf v (- v 1))))
    (princ ".")))
```

On each iteration we compare the iteration variable (gensyms usually print as symbols preceded by #:) not against 9, but against an expression that decreases each time it is evaluated. It is as if the horizon gets closer each time we look at it.

The way to avoid unintended multiple evaluations is to set a variable to the value of the expression in question before any iteration. This usually involves another gensym:

```
(defmacro ntimes (n &rest body)
  (let ((g (gensym))
        (h (gensym)))
    '(let ((,h ,n))
       (do ((,g 0 (+ ,g 1)))
           ((>= ,g ,h))
         ,@body))))
```

Here, finally, is a correct definition of ntimes.

Unintended variable capture and multiple evaluation are the major problems that can afflict macros, but they are not the only ones. With experience it is no more difficult to avoid such errors than it is to avoid more familiar errors, like dividing by zero. But because macros give us a new kind of power, the kind of problems we have to worry about are also new.

Your Common Lisp implementation is a good place to learn more about macro design. By expanding calls to the built-in macros, you can usually understand how they were written. Here is the expansion most implementations will generate for a cond expression:

```
> (pprint (macroexpand-1 '(cond (a b)
                                 (c d e)
                                 (t f))))

(IF A
    B
    (IF C
        (PROGN D E)
        F))
```

The function pprint, which prints expressions indented like code, is especially useful when looking at macro expansions.

10.6   Generalized Reference

Since a macro call is expanded right into the code where it appears, any macro call whose expansion could be the first argument to setf can itself be the first argument to setf. For example, if we defined a synonym for car,

```
(defmacro cah (lst) '(car ,lst))
```

then because a call to car can be the first argument to setf, so could a call to cah:

```
> (let ((x (list 'a 'b 'c)))
    (setf (cah x) 44)
    x)
(44 B C)
```

Writing a macro that expands into a setf is another question, and a more difficult one than it might seem at first. It might seem that you could implement incf, say, simply as

```
(defmacro incf (x &optional (y 1))          ; wrong
  '(setf ,x (+ ,x ,y)))
```

But this would not work. These two expressions are not equivalent:

```
(setf (car (push 1 lst)) (1+ (car (push 1 lst))))
```

```
(incf (car (push 1 lst)))
```

If lst is initially nil, then the second expression will set it to (2), but the first expression would set it to (1 2).

Common Lisp provides define-modify-macro as a way of writing a restricted class of macros on setf. It takes three arguments: the name of the macro, its additional parameters (the place is implicitly the first), and the name of a function that yields the new value of the place. So we could define incf as

```
(define-modify-macro our-incf (&optional (y 1)) +)
```

and a version of push for the end of a list as

```
(define-modify-macro append1f (val)
  (lambda (lst val) (append lst (list val))))
```

The latter would work as follows:

```
> (let ((lst '(a b c)))
    (append1f lst 'd)
    lst)
(A B C D)
```

Incidentally, neither push nor pop can be defined as modify-macros, the former because the place is not its first argument, and the latter because its return value is not the modified object.

10.7   Example: Macro Utilities

Section 6.4 introduced the concept of a utility, a general-purpose operator like those that make up Lisp itself. We can use macros to define utilities that could not be written as functions. We've seen several examples already: nil!, ntimes, and while all have to be written as macros, because all have to control the way in which their arguments are evaluated. This section gives some more examples of the kinds of utilities you can write with macros. Figure 10.2 contains a selection that have proven their worth in practice.

The first, for, is similar in design to while (page 164). It is for loops whose bodies are evaluated with a new variable bound to a range of values:

```
> (for x 1 8
    (princ x))
12345678
NIL
```

```
(defmacro for (var start stop &body body)
  (let ((gstop (gensym)))
    `(do ((,var ,start (1+ ,var))
          (,gstop ,stop))
         ((> ,var ,gstop))
       ,@body)))

(defmacro in (obj &rest choices)
  (let ((insym (gensym)))
    `(let ((,insym ,obj))
       (or ,@(mapcar #'(lambda (c) `(eql ,insym ,c))
                     choices)))))

(defmacro random-choice (&rest exprs)
  `(case (random ,(length exprs))
     ,@(let ((key -1))
         (mapcar #'(lambda (expr)
                     `(,(incf key) ,expr))
                 exprs))))

(defmacro avg (&rest args)
  `(/ (+ ,@args) ,(length args)))

(defmacro with-gensyms (syms &body body)
  `(let ,(mapcar #'(lambda (s)
                     `(,s (gensym)))
                 syms)
     ,@body))

(defmacro aif (test then &optional else)
  `(let ((it ,test))
     (if it ,then ,else)))
```

Figure 10.2: Macro utilities.

This is less work to write than the equivalent do,

```
(do ((x 1 (1+ x)))
    ((> x 8))
  (princ x))
```

which is very close to the actual expansion:

```
(do ((x 1 (1+ x))
     (#:g1 8))
    ((> x #:g1))
  (princ x))
```

The macro has to introduce an additional variable to hold the value that marks the end of the range. The 8 in the example above might have been a call, and we would not want to evaluate it multiple times. The additional variable has to be a gensym, in order to avoid inadvertent variable capture.

The second macro in Figure 10.2, in, returns true if its first argument is eql to any of the other arguments. The expression that we can write as

```
(in (car expr) '+ '- '*)
```

we would otherwise have to write as

```
(let ((op (car expr)))
  (or (eql op '+)
      (eql op '-)
      (eql op '*)))
```

Indeed, the first expression expands into one like the second, except that the variable op is replaced by a gensym.

The next example, random-choice, randomly chooses an argument to evaluate. We had to choose randomly between two alternatives on page 74. The random-choice macro implements the general solution. A call like

```
(random-choice (turn-left) (turn-right))
```

gets expanded into:

```
(case (random 2)
  (0 (turn-left))
  (1 (turn-right)))
```

The next macro, with-gensyms is intended to be used mainly within macro bodies. It's not unusual, especially in macros for specific applications, to have to gensym several variables. With this macro, instead of

```
(let ((x (gensym)) (y (gensym)) (z (gensym)))
  ...)
```

we can write

```
(with-gensyms (x y z)
  ...)
```

So far, none of the macros defined in Figure 10.2 could have been defined as functions. As a rule, the only reason to write something as a macro is because you can't write it as a function. But there are a few exceptions to this rule. Sometimes you may want to define an operator as a macro in order to make it do some of its work at compile-time. The macro avg, which returns the average of its arguments,

```
> (avg 2 4 8)
14/3
```

is an example of such a macro. We could write avg as a function,

```
(defun avg (&rest args)
  (/ (apply #'+ args) (length args)))
```

but then it would have to find the number of arguments at run-time. As long as we are willing to forgo applying avg, why not make this call to length at compile-time?

The last macro in Figure 10.2 is aif, which is included as an example of intentional variable capture. It allows us to use the variable it to refer to the value returned by the test argument in a conditional. That is, instead of

```
(let ((val (calculate-something)))
  (if val
      (1+ val)
      0))
```

we can write

```
(aif (calculate-something)
     (1+ it)
     0)
```

Used judiciously, intentional variable capture can be a valuable technique. Common Lisp itself uses it in several places: both next-method-p and call-next-method rely on variable capture, for example.

Macros like these show clearly what it means to write programs that write your programs for you. Once you have defined for, you don't have to write out the whole do expression. Is it worth writing a macro just to save typing? Very much so. Saving typing is what programming languages are all about; the purpose of a compiler is to save you from typing your program in machine language. And macros allow you to bring to your specific applications the same kinds of advantages that high-level languages bring to programming in general. By the careful use of macros, you may be able to make your programs significantly shorter than they would be otherwise, and proportionately easier to read, write, and maintain.

If you doubt this, consider what your programs would look like if you didn't use any of the built-in macros. All the expansions those macros generate, you would have to generate by hand. You can use this question in the other direction as well. As you're writing a program, ask yourself, am I writing macroexpansions? If so, the macros that generate those expansions are the ones you need to write.

10.8 On Lisp

Now that macros have been introduced, we see that even more of Lisp is written in Lisp than we might have expected. Most of the Common Lisp operators that aren't functions are macros, and they are all written in Lisp. Only 25 of Common Lisp's built-in operators are special operators.

John Foderaro has called Lisp "a programmable programming language."° By writing your own functions and macros, you can turn Lisp into just about any language you want. (We'll see a graphic demonstration of this possibility in Chapter 17.) Whatever turns out to be the right form for your program, you can be assured that you will be able to shape Lisp to suit it.

Macros are one of the key ingredients in this flexibility. They allow you to transform Lisp almost beyond recognition, and yet to do so in a principled, efficient way. Within the Lisp community, macros are a topic of increasing interest. It's clear already that one can do amazing things with them, but more certainly remain to be discovered. By you, if you want. Lisp has always put its evolution in the hands of the programmer. That's why it survives.

Summary

1. Calling eval is one way to make Lisp treat lists as code, but it's inefficient and unnecessary.

2. You define a macro by saying what a call should expand into. Underneath, macros are just functions that return expressions.

3. A macro body defined with backquote resembles the expansion it will produce.

4. The macro designer must be aware of variable capture and multiple evaluation. Macros can be tested by pretty-printing their expansions.

5. Multiple evaluation is a problem for most macros that expand into setfs.

6. Macros are more flexible than functions, and can be used to define a broader range of utilities. You can even use variable capture to advantage.

7. Lisp has survived because it puts its evolution in the hands of the programmer. Macros are part of what makes this possible.

Exercises

1. If x is a, y is b, and z is (c d), write backquoted expressions containing only variables that yield each of the following:

    (a) ((C D) A Z)

    (b) (X B C D)

    (c) ((C D A) Z)

2. Define `if` in terms of `cond`.

3. Define a macro that takes a number *n* followed by one or more expressions, and returns the value of the *n*th expression:

```
> (let ((n 2))
    (nth-expr n (/ 1 0) (+ 1 2) (/ 1 0)))
3
```

4. Define `ntimes` (page 167) to expand into a (local) recursive function instead of a `do`.

5. Define a macro `n-of` that takes a number *n* and an expression, and returns a list of *n* successive values returned by the expression:

```
> (let ((i 0) (n 4))
    (n-of n (incf i)))
(1 2 3 4)
```

6. Define a macro that takes a list of variables and a body of code, and ensures that the variables revert to their original values after the body of code is evaluated.

7. What's wrong with the following definition of push?

```
(defmacro push (obj lst)
  '(setf ,lst (cons ,obj ,lst)))
```

Give an example of a call where it would not do the same thing as the real push.

8. Define a macro that doubles its argument:

```
> (let ((x 1))
    (double x)
    x)
2
```

11

CLOS

The Common Lisp Object System, or CLOS, is a set of operators for doing object-oriented programming. Because of their common history it is conventional to treat these operators as a group.° Technically, they are in no way distinguished from the rest of Common Lisp: defmethod is just as much (and just as little) an integral part of the language as defun.

11.1 Object-Oriented Programming

Object-oriented programming means a change in the way programs are organized. This change is analogous to the one that has taken place in the distribution of processor power. In 1970, a multi-user computer system meant one or two big mainframes connected to a large number of dumb terminals. Now it is more likely to mean a large number of workstations connected to one another by a network. The processing power of the system is now distributed among individual users instead of centralized in one big computer.

Object-oriented programming breaks up traditional programs in much the same way. Instead of having a single program that operates on an inert mass of data, the data itself is told how to behave, and the program is implicit in the interactions of these new data "objects."

For example, suppose we want to write a program to find the areas of two-dimensional shapes. One way to do this would be to write a single function that looked at the type of its argument and behaved accordingly, as in Figure 11.1.

```
(defstruct rectangle
  height width)

(defstruct circle
  radius)

(defun area (x)
  (cond ((rectangle-p x)
         (* (rectangle-height x) (rectangle-width x)))
        ((circle-p x)
         (* pi (expt (circle-radius x) 2)))))
> (let ((r (make-rectangle)))
    (setf (rectangle-height r) 2
          (rectangle-width r)  3)
    (area r))
6
```

Figure 11.1: Area with structures and a function.

Using CLOS we might write an equivalent program as in Figure 11.2. In the object-oriented model, our program gets broken up into several distinct *methods*, each one intended for certain kinds of arguments. The two methods in Figure 11.2 implicitly define an area function that works just like the one in Figure 11.1. When we call area, Lisp looks at the type of the argument and invokes the corresponding method.

Together with this way of breaking up functions into distinct methods, object-oriented programming implies *inheritance*—both of slots and methods. The empty list given as the second argument in the two defclasses in Figure 11.2 is a list of superclasses. Suppose we define a new class of colored objects, and then a class of colored circles that has both colored and circle as superclasses:

```
(defclass colored ()
  (color))

(defclass colored-circle (circle colored)
  ())
```

When we make instances of colored-circle, we will see two kinds of inheritance:

```
(defclass rectangle ()
  (height width))

(defclass circle ()
  (radius))

(defmethod area ((x rectangle))
  (* (slot-value x 'height) (slot-value x 'width)))

(defmethod area ((x circle))
  (* pi (expt (slot-value x 'radius) 2)))

> (let ((r (make-instance 'rectangle)))
    (setf (slot-value r 'height) 2
          (slot-value r 'width)  3)
    (area r))
6
```

Figure 11.2: Area with classes and methods.

1. Instances of colored-circle will have two slots: radius, which is inherited from the circle class, and color, which is inherited from the colored class.

2. Because there is no area method defined explicitly for instances of colored-circle, if we call area on an instance of colored-circle, we will get the method defined for the circle class.

In practical terms, object-oriented programming means organizing a program in terms of methods, classes, instances, and inheritance. Why would you want to organize programs this way? One of the claims of the object-oriented approach is that it makes programs easier to change. If we want to change the way objects of class ob are displayed, we just change the display method of the ob class. If we want to make a new class of objects like obs but different in a few respects, we can create a subclass of ob; in the subclass, we change the properties we want, and all the rest will be inherited by default from the ob class. And if we just want to make a single ob that behaves differently from the rest, we can create a new child of ob and modify the child's properties directly. If the program was written carefully to begin with, we can make all these types of modifications without even looking at the rest of the code.°

11.2   Classes and Instances

In Section 4.6 we went through two steps to create structures: we called defstruct to lay out the form of a structure, and a specific function like make-point to make them. Creating instances requires two analogous steps. First we define a *class*, using defclass:

```
(defclass circle ()
  (radius center))
```

This definition says that instances of the circle class will have two *slots* (like fields in a structure), named radius and center respectively.

To make instances of this class, instead of calling a specific function, we call the general make-instance with the class name as the first argument:

```
> (setf c (make-instance 'circle))
#<Circle #XC27496>
```

To set the slots in this instance, we can use setf with slot-value:

```
> (setf (slot-value c 'radius) 1)
1
```

Like structure fields, the values of uninitialized slots are undefined.

11.3   Slot Properties

The third argument to defclass must be a list of slot definitions. The simplest slot definition, as in the example above, is a symbol representing its name. In the general case, a slot definition can be a list of a name followed by one or more properties. Properties are specified like keyword arguments.

By defining an :accessor for a slot, we implicitly define a function that refers to the slot, making it unnecessary to call slot-value. If we update our definition of the circle class as follows,

```
(defclass circle ()
  ((radius :accessor circle-radius)
   (center :accessor circle-center)))
```

then we will be able to refer to the slots as circle-radius and circle-center respectively:

```
> (setf c (make-instance 'circle))
#<Circle #XC5C726>
```

```
> (setf (circle-radius c) 1)
1
> (circle-radius c)
1
```

By specifying a :writer or a :reader instead of an :accessor, we could get just the first half of this behavior, or just the second.

To specify a default value for a slot, we have to give an :initform argument. If we want to be able to initialize the slot in the call to make-instance, we define a parameter name as an :initarg.[1] With both added, our class definition might become:

```
(defclass circle ()
  ((radius :accessor circle-radius
           :initarg :radius
           :initform 1)
   (center :accessor circle-center
           :initarg :center
           :initform (cons 0 0)))))
```

Now when we make an instance of a circle we can either pass a value for a slot using the keyword parameter defined as the slot's :initarg, or let the value default to that of the slot's :initform.

```
> (setf c (make-instance 'circle :radius 3))
#<Circle #XC2DE0E>
> (circle-radius c)
3
> (circle-center c)
(0 . 0)
```

Note that :initargs take precedence over :initforms.

We can specify that some slots are to be *shared*—that is, their value is the same for every instance. We do this by declaring the slot to have :allocation :class. (The alternative is for a slot to have :allocation :instance, but since this is the default there is no need to say so explicitly.) When we change the value of such a slot in one instance, that slot will get the same value in every other instance. So we would want to use shared slots to contain properties that all the instances would have in common.

For example, suppose we wanted to simulate the behavior of a flock of tabloids. In our simulation we want to be able to represent the fact that when one tabloid takes up a subject, they all do. We can do this by making all the instances share a slot. If the tabloid class is defined as follows,

---

[1] Initarg names are usually keywords, but they don't have to be.

```
(defclass tabloid ()
  ((top-story :accessor tabloid-story
              :allocation :class)))
```

then if we make two instances of tabloids, whatever becomes front-page news to one instantly becomes front-page news to the other:

```
> (setf daily-blab      (make-instance 'tabloid)
        unsolicited-mail (make-instance 'tabloid))
#<Tabloid #XC2AB16>
> (setf (tabloid-story daily-blab) 'adultery-of-senator)
ADULTERY-OF-SENATOR
> (tabloid-story unsolicited-mail)
ADULTERY-OF-SENATOR
```

The :documentation property, if given, should be a string to serve as the slot's documentation. By specifying a :type, you are promising that the slot will only contain elements of that type. Type declarations are explained in Section 13.3.

11.4 Superclasses

The second argument to defclass is a list of *superclasses*. A class inherits the union of the slots of its superclasses. So if we define the class screen-circle to be a subclass of both circle and graphic,

```
(defclass graphic ()
  ((color   :accessor graphic-color   :initarg :color)
   (visible :accessor graphic-visible :initarg :visible
            :initform t)))

(defclass screen-circle (circle graphic)
  ())
```

then instances of screen-circle will have four slots, two inherited from each superclass. A class does not have to create any new slots of its own; screen-circle exists just to provide something instantiable that inherits from both circle and graphic.

The accessors and initargs work for instances of screen-circle just as they would for instances of circle or graphic:

```
> (graphic-color (make-instance 'screen-circle
                                :color 'red :radius 3))
RED
```

We can cause every `screen-circle` to have some default initial `color` by specifying an initform for this slot in the `defclass`:

```
(defclass screen-circle (circle graphic)
  ((color :initform 'purple)))
```

Now instances of `screen-circle` will be purple by default:

```
> (graphic-color (make-instance 'screen-circle))
PURPLE
```

11.5   Precedence

We've seen how classes can have multiple superclasses. When there are methods defined for several of the classes to which an instance belongs, Lisp needs some way to decide which one to use. The point of *precedence* is to ensure that this happens in an intuitive way.

For every class there is a *precedence list*: an ordering of itself and its superclasses from most specific to least specific. In the examples so far, precedence has not been an issue, but it can become one in bigger programs. Here's a more complex class hierarchy:

```
(defclass sculpture () (height width depth))

(defclass statue (sculpture) (subject))

(defclass metalwork () (metal-type))

(defclass casting (metalwork) ())

(defclass cast-statue (statue casting) ())
```

Figure 11.3 contains a network representing `cast-statue` and its superclasses.

To build such a network for a class, start at the bottom with a node representing that class. Draw links upward to nodes representing each of its immediate superclasses, laid out from left to right as they appeared in the calls to `defclass`. Repeat the process for each of those nodes, and so on, until you reach classes whose only immediate superclass is `standard-object`—that is, classes for which the second argument to `defclass` was (). Create links from those classes up to a node representing `standard-object`, and one from that node up to another node representing the class `t`. The result will be a network that comes to a point at both top and bottom, as in Figure 11.3.

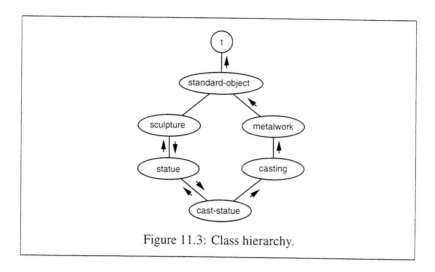

Figure 11.3: Class hierarchy.

The precedence list for a class can be computed by traversing the corresponding network as follows:

1. Start at the bottom of the network.

2. Walk upward, always taking the leftmost unexplored branch.

3. If you are about to enter a node and you notice another path entering the same node from the right, then instead of entering the node, retrace your steps until you get to a node with an unexplored path leading upward. Go back to step 2.

4. When you get to the node representing t, you're done. The order in which you first entered each node determines its place in the precedence list.

One of the consequences of this definition (in fact, of rule 3) is that no class appears in the precedence list before one of its subclasses.

The arrows in Figure 11.3 show how it would be traversed. The precedence list determined by this graph is: `cast-statue`, `statue`, `sculpture`, `casting`, `metalwork`, `standard-object`, `t`. Sometimes the word *specific* is used as shorthand to refer to the position of a class in a given precedence list. The preceding list runs from most specific to least specific.

The main point of precedence is to decide what method gets used when a generic function is invoked. This process is described in the next section. The other time precedence matters is when a slot with a given name is inherited from several superclasses. The note on page 408 explains the rules that apply when this happens.°

11.6 Generic Functions

A generic function is a function made up of one or more methods. Methods
are defined with defmethod, which is similar in form to defun:

```
(defmethod combine (x y)
  (list x y))
```

Now combine has one method. If we call combine at this point, we will get
the two arguments in a list:

```
> (combine 'a 'b)
(A B)
```

So far we haven't done anything we could not have done with a normal
function. The unusual thing about a generic function is that we can continue
to add new methods for it.

First, we define some classes for the new methods to refer to:

```
(defclass stuff () ((name :accessor name :initarg :name)))
(defclass ice-cream (stuff) ())
(defclass topping (stuff) ())
```

This defines three classes: stuff, which is just something with a name, and
ice-cream and topping, which are subclasses of stuff.

Now here is a second method for combine:

```
(defmethod combine ((ic ice-cream) (top topping))
  (format nil "~A ice-cream with ~A topping."
          (name ic)
          (name top)))
```

In this call to defmethod the parameters are *specialized*: each one appears
in a list with the name of a class. The specializations of a method indicate
the kinds of arguments to which it applies. The method we just defined will
only be used if the arguments to combine are instances of ice-cream and
topping respectively.

How does Lisp decide which method to use when a generic function is
called? It will use the most specific method for which the classes of the
arguments match the specializations of the parameters. Which means that if
we call combine with an instance of ice-cream and an instance of topping,
we'll get the method we just defined:

```
> (combine (make-instance 'ice-cream :name 'fig)
           (make-instance 'topping :name 'treacle))
"FIG ice-cream with TREACLE topping."
```

But with any other arguments, we'll get the first method we defined:

```
> (combine 23 'skiddoo)
(23 SKIDDOO)
```

Because neither of the parameters of the first method is specialized, it will always get last priority, yet will always get called if no other method does. An unspecialized method acts as a safety net, like an `otherwise` clause in a case expression.

Any combination of the parameters in a method can be specialized. In this method only the first argument is:

```
(defmethod combine ((ic ice-cream) x)
  (format nil "~A ice-cream with ~A."
              (name ic)
              x))
```

If we call `combine` with an instance of `ice-cream` and an instance of `topping`, we'll still get the method that's looking for both, because it's more specific:

```
> (combine (make-instance 'ice-cream :name 'grape)
           (make-instance 'topping :name 'marshmallow))
"GRAPE ice-cream with MARSHMALLOW topping."
```

However, if the first argument is `ice-cream` and the second argument is anything but `topping`, we'll get the method we just defined above:

```
> (combine (make-instance 'ice-cream :name 'clam)
           'reluctance)
"CLAM ice-cream with RELUCTANCE."
```

When a generic function is called, the arguments determine a set of one or more *applicable* methods. A method is applicable if the arguments in the call come within the specializations of all its parameters.

If there are no applicable methods we get an error. If there is just one, it is called. If there is more than one, the most specific gets called. The most specific applicable method is determined based on the class precedence for the arguments in the call. The arguments are examined left to right. If the first parameter of one of the applicable methods is specialized on a more specific class than the first parameters of the other methods, then it is the most specific method. Ties are broken by looking at the second argument, and so on.[2]

---

[2] We can't go through all the arguments and still have a tie, because then we would have two methods with exactly the same specializations. That's impossible because the definition of the second would overwrite the first.

In the preceding examples, it is easy to see what the most specific applicable method would be, because all the objects have a single line of descent. An instance of ice-cream is, in order, itself, ice-cream, stuff, a standard-object, and a member of the class t.

Methods don't have to be specialized on classes defined by defclass. They can also be specialized on types (or more precisely, the classes that mirror types). Here is a method for combine that's specialized on numbers:

```
(defmethod combine ((x number) (y number))
  (+ x y))
```

Methods can even be specialized on individual objects, as determined by eql:

```
(defmethod combine ((x (eql 'powder)) (y (eql 'spark)))
  'boom)
```

Specializations on individual objects take precedence over class specializations.

Methods can have parameter lists as complex as ordinary Common Lisp functions, but the parameter lists of all the methods that compose a generic function must be *congruent*. They must have the same number of required parameters, the same number of optional parameters (if any), and must either all use &rest or &key, or all not use them. The following pairs of parameter lists are all congruent,

```
(x)              (a)
(x &optional y)  (a &optional b)
(x y &rest z)    (a b &key c)
(x y &key z)     (a b &key c d)
```

and the following pairs are not:

```
(x)              (a b)
(x &optional y)  (a &optional b c)
(x &optional y)  (a &rest b)
(x &key x y)     (a)
```

Only required parameters can be specialized. Thus each method is uniquely identified by its name and the specializations of its required parameters. If we define another method with the same qualifiers and specializations, it overwrites the original one. So by saying

```
(defmethod combine ((x (eql 'powder)) (y (eql 'spark)))
  'kaboom)
```

we redefine what combine does when its arguments are powder and spark.

11.7 Auxiliary Methods

Methods can be augmented by *auxiliary methods,* including before-, after-, and around-methods. Before-methods allow us to say, "But first, do this." They are called, most specific first, as a prelude to the rest of the method call. After-methods allow us to say, "P.S. Do this too." They are called, most specific last, as an epilogue to the method call. Between them, we run what has till now been considered just the method, but is more precisely known as the *primary method.* The value of this call is the one returned, even if after-methods are called later.

Before- and after-methods allow us to wrap new behavior around the call to the primary method. Around-methods provide a more drastic way of doing the same thing. If an around-method exists, it will be called *instead* of the primary method. Then, at its own discretion, the around-method may itself invoke the primary method (via the function `call-next-method`, which is provided just for this purpose).

This is called *standard method combination.* In standard method combination, calling a generic function invokes

1. The most specific around-method, if there is one.

2. Otherwise, in order,

    (a) All before-methods, from most specific to least specific.

    (b) The most specific primary method.

    (c) All after-methods, from least specific to most specific.

The value returned is the value of the around-method (in case 1) or the value of the most specific primary method (in case 2).

Auxiliary methods are defined by putting a qualifying keyword after the method name in the call to defmethod. If we define a primary speak method for the speaker class as

```
(defclass speaker () ())

(defmethod speak ((s speaker) string)
  (format t "~A" string))
```

then calling speak with an instance of speaker just prints the second argument:

```
> (speak (make-instance 'speaker)
         "I'm hungry")
I'm hungry
NIL
```

By defining a subclass intellectual, which wraps before- and after-methods around the primary speak method,

```
(defclass intellectual (speaker) ())

(defmethod speak :before ((i intellectual) string)
  (princ "Perhaps "))

(defmethod speak :after ((i intellectual) string)
  (princ " in some sense"))
```

we can create a subclass of speakers that always have the last (and the first) word:

```
> (speak (make-instance 'intellectual)
         "I'm hungry")
Perhaps I'm hungry in some sense
NIL
```

As the preceding outline of standard method combination noted, all before- and after-methods get called. So if we define before- or after-methods for the speaker superclass,

```
(defmethod speak :before ((s speaker) string)
  (princ "I think "))
```

they will get called in the middle of the sandwich:

```
> (speak (make-instance 'intellectual)
         "I'm hungry")
Perhaps I think I'm hungry in some sense
NIL
```

Regardless of what before- or after-methods get called, the value returned by the generic function is the value of the most specific primary method—in this case, the nil returned by format.

This changes if there are around-methods. If there is an around-method specialized for the arguments passed to the generic function, the around-method will get called first, and the rest of the methods will only run if the around-method decides to let them. An around- or primary method can invoke the next method by calling call-next-method. Before doing so, it can use next-method-p to test whether there is a next method to call.

With around-methods we can define another, more cautious, subclass of speaker:

```
(defclass courtier (speaker) ())

(defmethod speak :around ((c courtier) string)
  (format t "Does the King believe that ~A? " string)
  (if (eql (read) 'yes)
      (if (next-method-p) (call-next-method))
      (format t "Indeed, it is a preposterous idea.~%"))
  'bow)
```

When the first argument to speak is an instance of the courtier class, the courtier's tongue is now guarded by the around-method:

```
> (speak (make-instance 'courtier) "kings will last")
Does the King believe that kings will last? yes
I think kings will last
BOW
> (speak (make-instance 'courtier) "the world is round")
Does the King believe that the world is round? no
Indeed, it is a preposterous idea.
BOW
```

Note that, unlike before- and after-methods, the value returned by the around-method is returned as the value of the generic function.

11.8 Method Combination

In standard method combination the only primary method that gets called is the most specific (though it can call others via call-next-method). Instead we might like to be able to combine the results of all applicable primary methods.

It's possible to define methods that are combined in other ways—for example, for a generic function to return the sum of all the applicable primary methods. *Operator* method combination can be understood as if it resulted in the evaluation of a Lisp expression whose first element was some operator, and whose arguments were calls to the applicable primary methods, in order of specificity. If we defined the price generic function to combine values with +, and there were no applicable around-methods, it would behave as though it were defined:

```
(defun price (&rest args)
  (+ (apply ⟨most specific primary method⟩ args)
     ⋮
     (apply ⟨least specific primary method⟩ args)))
```

If there are applicable around-methods, they take precedence, just as in standard method combination. Under operator method combination, an around-method can still call the next method via `call-next-method`. However, primary methods can no longer use `call-next-method`.

We can specify the type of method combination to be used by a generic function with a `:method-combination` clause in a call to `defgeneric`:

```
(defgeneric price (x)
  (:method-combination +))
```

Now the `price` method will use + method combination; any `defmethod`s for `price` must have + as the second argument. If we define some classes with prices,

```
(defclass jacket () ())
(defclass trousers () ())
(defclass suit (jacket trousers) ())

(defmethod price + ((jk jacket)) 350)
(defmethod price + ((tr trousers)) 200)
```

then when we ask for the price of an instance of `suit`, we get the sum of the applicable `price` methods:

```
> (price (make-instance 'suit))
550
```

The following symbols can be used as the second argument to `defmethod` or in the `:method-combination` option to `defgeneric`:

```
+    and    append    list    max    min    nconc    or    progn
```

You can also use `standard`, which yields standard method combination.

Once you specify the method combination a generic function should use, all methods for that function must use the same kind. Now it would cause an error if we tried to use another operator (or `:before` or `:after`) as the second argument in a `defmethod` for `price`. If we want to change the method combination of `price`, we must remove the whole generic function by calling `fmakunbound`.

11.9   Encapsulation

Object-oriented languages often provide some way of distinguishing between the actual representation of objects and the interface they present to the world. Hiding implementation details brings two advantages: you can change the implementation without affecting the object's outward appearance, and you prevent objects from being modified in potentially dangerous ways. Hidden details are sometimes said to be *encapsulated*.

Although encapsulation is often associated with object-oriented programming, the two ideas are really separate. You can have either one without the other. We saw an example of encapsulation on a small scale on page 108. The functions `stamp` and `reset` work by sharing a counter, but calling code does not need to know about this counter, nor can it modify it directly.

In Common Lisp, packages are the standard way to distinguish between public and private information. To restrict access to something, we put it in a separate package, and only export the names that are part of the external interface.

We can encapsulate a slot by exporting the names of the methods that can modify it, but not the name of the slot itself. For example, we could define a `counter` class and associated `increment` and `clear` methods as follows:

```
(defpackage "CTR"
           (:use "COMMON-LISP")
           (:export "COUNTER" "INCREMENT" "CLEAR"))

(in-package ctr)

(defclass counter () ((state :initform 0)))

(defmethod increment ((c counter))
  (incf (slot-value c 'state)))

(defmethod clear ((c counter))
  (setf (slot-value c 'state) 0))
```

Under this definition, code outside the package would be able to make instances of `counter` and call `increment` and `clear`, but would not have legitimate access to the name `state`.

If you want to do more than just distinguish between the internal and external interface to a class, and actually make it *impossible* to reach the value stored in a slot, you can do that too. Simply unintern its name after you've defined the code that needs to refer to it:

```
(unintern 'state)
```

Then there is no way, legitimate or otherwise, to refer to the slot from any package.°

11.10   Two Models

Object-oriented programming is a confusing topic partly because there are
two models of how to do it: the message-passing model and the generic
function model. The message-passing model came first. Generic functions
are a generalization of message-passing.

In the message-passing model, methods belong to objects, and are inherited in the same sense that slots are. To find the area of an object, we send it
an area message,

```
tell obj area
```

and this invokes whatever area method obj has or inherits.

Sometimes we have to pass additional arguments. For example, a move
method might take an argument specifying how far to move. If we wanted to
tell obj to move 10, we might send it the following message:

```
tell obj move 10
```

If we put this another way,

```
(move obj 10)
```

the limitation of the message-passing model becomes clearer. In message-
passing, we only specialize the first parameter. There is no provision for
methods involving multiple objects—indeed, the model of objects responding
to messages makes this hard even to conceive of.

In the message-passing model, methods are *of* objects, while in the generic
function model, they are specialized *for* objects. If we only specialize the first
parameter, they amount to exactly the same thing. But in the generic function
model, we can go further and specialize as many parameters as we need to.
This means that, functionally, the message-passing model is a subset of the
generic function model. If you have generic functions, you can simulate
message-passing by only specializing the first parameter.

Summary

1. In object-oriented programming, the function f is defined implicitly via
   the f methods of the objects that have them. Objects inherit methods
   from their parents.

2. Defining a class is like defining a structure, but more verbose. A shared
   slot belongs to a whole class.

3. A class inherits the slots of its superclasses.

4. The ancestors of a class are ordered into a precedence list. The precedence algorithm is best understood visually.

5. A generic function consists of all the methods with a given name. A method is identified by its name and the specializations of its parameters. Argument precedence determines the method used when a generic function is called.

6. Methods can be augmented by auxiliary methods. Standard method combination means calling the around-method, if there is one; otherwise the before-, most specific primary, and after-methods.

7. In operator method combination, all the primary methods are treated as arguments to some operator.

8. Encapsulation can be done via packages.

9. There are two models of object-oriented programming. The generic function model is a generalization of the message-passing model.

Exercises

1. Define accessors, initforms, and initargs for the classes defined in Figure 11.2. Rewrite the associated code so that it no longer calls slot-value.

2. Rewrite the code in Figure 9.5 so that spheres and points are classes, and intersect and normal are generic functions.

3. Suppose that a number of classes are defined as follows:

```
(defclass a (c d) ...)        (defclass e () ...)
(defclass b (d c) ...)        (defclass f (h) ...)
(defclass c () ..)            (defclass g (h) ...)
(defclass d (e f g) ...)      (defclass h () ...)
```

   (a) Draw the network representing the ancestors of a, and list the classes an instance of a belongs to, from most to least specific.

   (b) Do the same for b.

4. Suppose that you already have the following functions:

   precedence: takes an object and returns its precedence list, a list of classes ordered from most specific to least specific.

methods: takes a generic function and returns a list of all its methods.

specializations: takes a method and returns a list of the specializations of the parameters. Each element of the returned list will be either a class, or a list of the form (eql *x*), or t (indicating that the parameter is unspecialized).

Using these functions (and not compute-applicable-methods or find-method), define a function most-spec-app-meth that takes a generic function and a list of the arguments with which it has been called, and returns the most specific applicable method, if any.

5. Without changing the behavior of the generic function area (Figure 11.2) in any other respect, arrange it so that a global counter gets incremented each time area is called.

6. Give an example of a problem that would be difficult to solve if only the first argument to a generic function could be specialized.

12

Structure

Section 3.3 explained how Lisp's use of pointers allows us to put any value anywhere. This statement is full of possibilities, not all of them good. For example, an object can be an element of itself. Whether this is good or bad depends on whether it's done on purpose or by accident.

12.1 Shared Structure

Lists can share conses in common. In the simplest case, one list might be part of another. After

```
> (setf part (list 'b 'c))
(B C)
> (setf whole (cons 'a part))
(A B C)
```

the first cons is part of (in fact, is the cdr of) the second. In situations like this, we say that the two lists *share structure*. The underlying structure of the two lists is represented in Figure 12.1.

The predicate `tailp` detects this situation. It takes two lists and returns true if the first would be encountered on traversing the second:

```
> (tailp part whole)
T
```

We could imagine it written as:

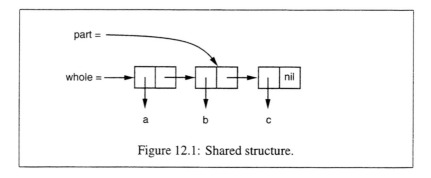

Figure 12.1: Shared structure.

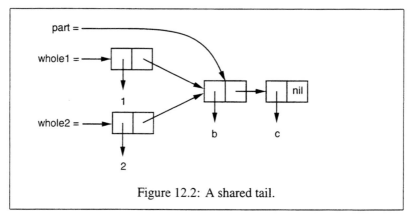

Figure 12.2: A shared tail.

```
(defun our-tailp (x y)
  (or (eql x y)
      (and (consp y)
           (our-tailp x (cdr y)))))
```

As the definition suggests, every list is a tail of itself, and nil is a tail of every proper list.

In the more complex case, two lists can share structure without either one being a tail of the other. This happens when they share a tail in common, as in Figure 12.2. We can create this situation as follows:

```
(setf part  (list 'b 'c)
      whole1 (cons 1 part)
      whole2 (cons 2 part))
```

Now whole1 and whole2 share structure without either list being part of the other.

When we have nested lists, it's important to distinguish between the lists sharing structure, and their elements sharing structure. *Top-level list structure*

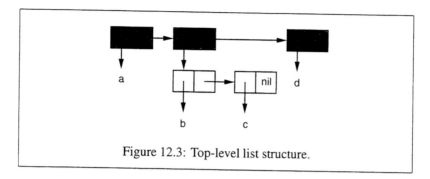

Figure 12.3: Top-level list structure.

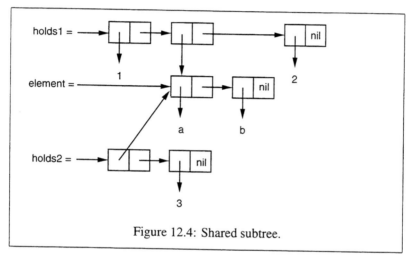

Figure 12.4: Shared subtree.

refers to the conses that make up a list, not including any conses that make up its elements. Figure 12.3 shows the top-level list structure of a nested list.

Whether two conses share structure depends on whether we are considering them as lists or as trees. Two nested lists may share structure as trees, without sharing structure as lists. The following code creates the situation shown in Figure 12.4, in which two lists contain the same list as an element:

```
(setf element (list 'a 'b)
      holds1  (list 1 element 2)
      holds2  (list element 3))
```

Although the second element of holds1 shares structure with (in fact, is identical to) the first element of holds2, holds1 and holds2 do not share structure as lists. Two lists only share structure *as lists* if they share top-level list structure, which holds1 and holds2 do not.

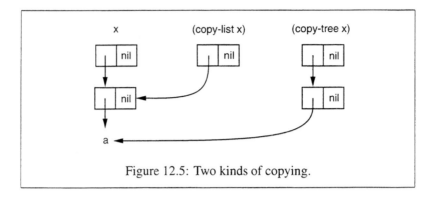

Figure 12.5: Two kinds of copying.

If we want to avoid sharing structure, we can do it by copying. The function copy-list, which could be defined as

```
(defun our-copy-list (lst)
  (if (null lst)
      nil
      (cons (car lst) (our-copy-list (cdr lst)))))
```

will return a list that doesn't share top-level list structure with the original list. The function copy-tree, which might be defined as

```
(defun our-copy-tree (tr)
  (if (atom tr)
      tr
      (cons (our-copy-tree (car tr))
            (our-copy-tree (cdr tr)))))
```

will return a list that doesn't even share tree structure with the original list. Figure 12.5 shows the difference between calling copy-list and copy-tree on a nested list.

12.2   Modification

Why would we want to avoid sharing structure? Up to this point, the issue of shared structure has been just an intellectual exercise. It would not have made any difference to any program we've written so far. It is when we modify objects that shared structure becomes an issue. If two lists share structure, and we modify one, then we may inadvertently be modifying the other.

In the previous section, we saw how to make one list a tail of another:

```
(setf whole (list 'a 'b 'c)
      tail (cdr whole))
```

Since this will make `tail` identical with the cdr of `whole`. if we modify either `tail` or the cdr of `whole`, we are modifying the same cons:

```
> (setf (second tail) 'e)
E
> tail
(B E)
> whole
(A B E)
```

The same thing can also happen, of course, if two lists share the same tail.

It's not always an error to modify two things at once. Sometimes it might be what you want. But when it happens inadvertently, modifying shared structure can cause some very subtle bugs. Lisp programmers learn to be aware of shared structure, and to suspect it immediately in certain kinds of errors. When a list mysteriously changes for no apparent reason, it is probably because you changed something else that shared structure with it.

It is not the shared structure that's dangerous, but the changing. To be on the safe side, simply avoid using `setf` (or related operators like `pop`, `rplaca`, etc.) on list structure, and you won't run into any problems. If some application absolutely requires you to modify list structure, find out where the lists come from to make sure that they don't share structure with anything that shouldn't be changed. If they do, or if you can't predict where the lists will come from, make the changes to a copy.

You have to be doubly careful when you are calling a function written by someone else. Until you know otherwise, consider the possibility that anything you pass to the function

1. could have destructive operations done to it, and/or

2. could be saved somewhere, so that if you later modified the object, you would also be modifying part of something that the other code was maintaining for its own use.[1]

In both cases, the solution is to pass a copy.

In Common Lisp, a function called in the course of traversing list structure (e.g. an argument to `mapcar` or `remove-if`) is not allowed to modify the structure being traversed. The consequences of evaluating such code are undefined.

---

[1]For example, in Common Lisp it's an error to modify a string being used as a symbol name, and since the definition of `intern` doesn't say that it copies its argument, we must assume that it's an error to modify any string that has been passed to `intern` to create a new symbol.

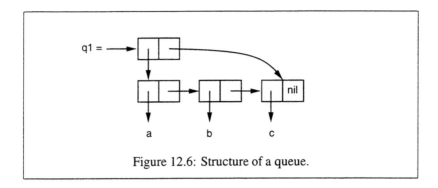

Figure 12.6: Structure of a queue.

12.3 Example: Queues

Shared structure is not just something to worry about. It's also something you can put to use. This section shows how to use shared structure to represent queues. A queue is a repository from which objects can be retrieved, one at a time, in the order in which they were inserted. This principle is known as FIFO, from "first in, first out."

It's easy to represent stacks using lists, because in a stack you insert and retrieve from the same end. Representing queues is more difficult, because insertion and retrieval happen at different ends. To implement queues efficiently, we need somehow to get hold of both ends of a list.

Figure 12.6 suggests a strategy we could use. It shows how we might represent a queue of a, b, and c. A queue is a pair of a list, and the last cons in that same list. Call these *front* and *back*. To retrieve an element from the queue we just pop *front*. To add an element, we create a new cons, make it the cdr of *back*, and then set *back* to it.

The code in Figure 12.7 implements this strategy. It's used as below:

```
> (setf q1 (make-queue))
(NIL)
> (progn (enqueue 'a q1)
         (enqueue 'b q1)
         (enqueue 'c q1))
(A B C)
```

At this point, q1 is the structure shown in Figure 12.6:

```
> q1
((A B C) C)
```

Now we can try dequeueing some elements:

```
(defun make-queue () (cons nil nil))

(defun enqueue (obj q)
  (if (null (car q))
      (setf (cdr q) (setf (car q) (list obj)))
      (setf (cdr (cdr q)) (list obj)
            (cdr q) (cdr (cdr q))))
  (car q))

(defun dequeue (q)
  (pop (car q)))
```

Figure 12.7: Implementing queues.

```
> (dequeue q1)
A
> (dequeue q1)
B
> (enqueue 'd q1)
(C D)
```

12.4 Destructive Functions

Common Lisp includes several functions that are allowed to modify list
structure. These functions are destructive for reasons of efficiency. Though
they may recycle conses passed to them as arguments, they are not meant to
be called for their side-effects.

For example, delete is a destructive version of remove. While it is
allowed to trash the list passed to it as an argument, it doesn't promise to do
anything. This is what happens in most implementations:

```
> (setf lst '(a r a b i a))
(A R A B I A)
> (delete 'a lst)
(R B I)
> lst
(A R B I)
```

As with remove, if you want side-effects, you should use setf with the return
value:

```
(setf lst (delete 'a lst))
```

As an example of how destructive functions recycle the lists passed to them, consider nconc, the destructive version of append.[2] This two-argument version shows clearly how two existing lists are sewn together:

```
(defun nconc2 (x y)
  (if (consp x)
      (progn
        (setf (cdr (last x)) y)
        x)
      y))
```

We go to the last cons cell in the first list, and set its cdr to point to the second list. A proper multi-argument nconc could be defined as in Appendix B.

The function mapcan is like mapcar, but splices together the values returned by the function (which must be lists) using nconc:

```
> (mapcan #'list
          '(a b c)
          '(1 2 3 4))
(A 1 B 2 C 3)
```

This function might be defined as follows:

```
(defun our-mapcan (fn &rest lsts)
  (apply #'nconc (apply #'mapcar fn lsts)))
```

Use mapcan with caution, because it is destructive. It splices together the returned lists with nconc, so they had better not be needed elsewhere.

This kind of function is particularly useful in problems that can be understood as collecting all the nodes at one level of some tree. For example, if children returns a list of someone's children, then we could define a function to return a list of someone's grandchildren as follows:

```
(defun grandchildren (x)
  (mapcan #'(lambda (c)
              (copy-list (children c)))
          (children x)))
```

This function calls copy-list on the assumption that children returns a list that's stored somewhere, instead of making a fresh one.

A nondestructive variant of mapcan might be defined:

```
(defun mappend (fn &rest lsts)
  (apply #'append (apply #'mapcar fn lsts)))
```

---

[2]The n originally stood for "non-consing." Several destructive functions have names beginning with n.

```
(defun bst-insert! (obj bst <)
  (if (null bst)
      (make-node :elt obj)
      (progn (bsti obj bst <)
             bst)))

(defun bsti (obj bst <)
  (let ((elt (node-elt bst)))
    (if (eql obj elt)
        bst
        (if (funcall < obj elt)
            (let ((l (node-l bst)))
              (if l
                  (bsti obj l <)
                  (setf (node-l bst)
                        (make-node :elt obj))))
            (let ((r (node-r bst)))
              (if r
                  (bsti obj r <)
                  (setf (node-r bst)
                        (make-node :elt obj))))))))))
```

Figure 12.8: Binary search trees: Destructive insertion.

If we used mappend, we could leave out the copy-list in the definition of grandchildren:

```
(defun grandchildren (x)
  (mappend #'children (children x)))
```

12.5 Example: Binary Search Trees

In some situations it's more natural to use destructive operations than non-destructive ones. Section 4.7 showed how to maintain a sorted collection of objects in a binary search tree, or BST. The functions given in Section 4.7 were all nondestructive, but in the situations where we would actually use BSTs, this is a needless precaution. This section shows how to define destructive insertion and deletion functions that are more likely to be useful in practice.

Figure 12.8 shows how to define a destructive version of bst-insert (page 72). It takes the same arguments and has the same return value. The only difference is that it may modify the BST given as the second argument.

As Section 2.12 warned, being destructive doesn't mean that a function is meant to be called for side-effects. And indeed, if you want to build a BST using `bst-insert!`, you have to call it the same way you would call the original `bst-insert`:

```
> (setf *bst* nil)
NIL
> (dolist (x '(7 2 9 8 4 1 5 12))
    (setf *bst* (bst-insert! x *bst* #'<)))
NIL
```

You *could* define an analogue of push for BSTs, but the techniques for doing so are beyond the scope of this book. (For the curious, this macro is defined on page 409.°)

Figure 12.9 contains a destructive `bst-delete`, which is to `bst-remove` (page 74) as `delete` is to `remove`. And like `delete`, it's not meant to be called for side-effects. You should call `bst-delete` as you would call `bst-remove`:

```
> (setf *bst* (bst-delete 2 *bst* #'<))
#<7>
> (bst-find 2 *bst* #'<)
NIL
```

12.6   Example: Doubly-Linked Lists

Ordinary Lisp lists are singly linked lists, meaning that the pointers go in one direction: you can get to the next element, but not the preceding one. In a *doubly linked* list, the pointers go in both directions, so you can go backward as well as forward. This section shows how to create and manipulate doubly linked lists.

Figure 12.10 shows how to implement doubly linked lists using structures. Considered as a structure, a cons has two fields: the car, which points to the data, and the cdr, which points to the next element. To represent an element in a doubly linked list we will need a third field, to point to the preceding element. The `defstruct` in Figure 12.10 defines a three-part object called a `dl` (for "doubly linked") that we will use to build doubly linked lists. The `data` field of a `dl` corresponds to the car of a cons, and the `rest` field to the cdr. The `prev` field will be like a cdr that goes in the other direction. (Figure 12.11 shows a doubly linked list of three elements.) The empty doubly linked list will be `nil`, just like the empty list.

By this call to `defstruct` we define functions corresponding to car, cdr and consp for doubly linked lists: `dl-data`, `dl-next`, and `dl-p`. The print-

```
(defun bst-delete (obj bst <)
  (if bst (bstd obj bst nil nil <))
  bst)

(defun bstd (obj bst prev dir <)
  (let ((elt (node-elt bst)))
    (if (eql elt obj)
        (let ((rest (percolate! bst)))
          (case dir
            (:l (setf (node-l prev) rest))
            (:r (setf (node-r prev) rest))))
        (if (funcall < obj elt)
            (if (node-l bst)
                (bstd obj (node-l bst) bst :l <))
            (if (node-r bst)
                (bstd obj (node-r bst) bst :r <))))))))

(defun percolate! (bst)
  (cond ((null (node-l bst))
         (if (null (node-r bst))
             nil
             (rperc! bst)))
        ((null (node-r bst)) (lperc! bst))
        (t (if (zerop (random 2))
               (lperc! bst)
               (rperc! bst)))))

(defun lperc! (bst)
  (setf (node-elt bst) (node-elt (node-l bst)))
  (percolate! (node-l bst)))

(defun rperc! (bst)
  (setf (node-elt bst) (node-elt (node-r bst)))
  (percolate! (node-r bst)))
```

Figure 12.9: Binary search trees: Destructive deletion.

function for dls calls dl->list, which returns an ordinary list containing
the elements of a dl.

The function dl-insert is like cons for doubly linked lists. At least,
it's like cons in that it is the basic constructor function. It's unlike cons

```
(defstruct (dl (:print-function print-dl))
  prev data next)

(defun print-dl (dl stream depth)
  (declare (ignore depth))
  (format stream "#<DL ~A>" (dl->list dl)))

(defun dl->list (lst)
  (if (dl-p lst)
      (cons (dl-data lst) (dl->list (dl-next lst)))
      lst))

(defun dl-insert (x lst)
  (let ((elt (make-dl :data x :next lst)))
    (when (dl-p lst)
      (if (dl-prev lst)
          (setf (dl-next (dl-prev lst)) elt
                (dl-prev elt) (dl-prev lst)))
      (setf (dl-prev lst) elt))
    elt))

(defun dl-list (&rest args)
  (reduce #'dl-insert args
          :from-end t :initial-value nil))

(defun dl-remove (lst)
  (if (dl-prev lst)
      (setf (dl-next (dl-prev lst)) (dl-next lst)))
  (if (dl-next lst)
      (setf (dl-prev (dl-next lst)) (dl-prev lst)))
  (dl-next lst))
```

Figure 12.10: Building doubly linked lists.

in that it actually modifies the doubly linked list passed to it as the second argument. In this situation it is the most natural thing to do. You don't have to do anything to the rest of an ordinary list to cons something onto it, but if you want to put something on the front of a doubly linked list, you have to make the prev field of the rest of the list point back to the new element.

To put it another way, several normal lists can share the same tail. But in doubly linked lists the tails have to point back at the structure that precedes

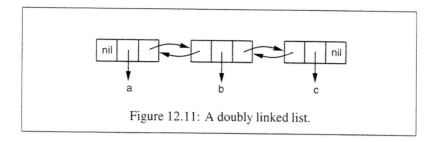

Figure 12.11: A doubly linked list.

them, so no two doubly linked lists can have the same tail. If dl-insert weren't destructive, it would always have to copy its second argument.

Another interesting difference between singly and doubly linked lists is how you hold them. You hold a singly linked list by the front; when you set a variable to a list, it has a pointer to the first cons. But since a doubly linked list is connected in both directions, you can hold it at any point. So dl-insert is also unlike cons in that it can put a new element anywhere in a doubly linked list, not just on the front.

The function dl-list is the dl analogue of list. You give it any number of arguments and it returns a dl containing them:

```
> (dl-list 'a 'b 'c)
#<DL (A B C)>
```

It uses reduce, which, with :from-end true and an :initial-value of nil, makes the preceding call equivalent to

```
(dl-insert 'a (dl-insert 'b (dl-insert 'c nil)))
```

If you replaced #'dl-insert in the definition of dl-list with #'cons, it would behave like list. Here is the new code in use:

```
> (setf dl (dl-list 'a 'b))
#<DL (A B)>
> (setf dl (dl-insert 'c dl))
#<DL (C A B)>
> (dl-insert 'r (dl-next dl))
#<DL (R A B)>
> dl
#<DL (C R A B)>
```

Finally, dl-remove is for removing an element from a doubly linked list. Like dl-insert, it makes sense for it to be destructive.

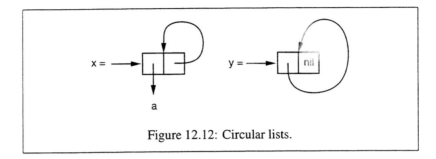

Figure 12.12: Circular lists.

12.7   Circular Structure

By modifying list structure it's possible to create circular lists. There are two kinds of circular lists. The more useful kind are those whose top-level list structure is a loop. Such lists are called *cdr-circular* because the loop passes through the cdr part of a cons.

To make a cdr-circular list with one element, you set the cdr of a list to be the list itself:

```
> (setf x (list 'a))
(A)
> (progn (setf (cdr x) x) nil)
NIL
```

At this point x is a circular list, with the structure shown in Figure 12.12.

If Lisp tried to print the list we just created, it would usually display (a a a a a, *ad infinitum*. But if we set the global *print-circle* to t, objects will be displayed in a way that can represent circular structure:

```
> (setf *print-circle* t)
T
> x
#1=(A . #1#)
```

If you need to, you can use the #*n*= and #*n*# read-macros to represent shared structure yourself.

Cdr-circular lists could be useful—to represent buffers or pools, for example. The following function would take any non-cdr-circular, nonempty list and convert it into a cdr-circular list with the same elements:

```
(defun circular (lst)
  (setf (cdr (last lst)) lst))
```

The other kind of circular lists are *car-circular* lists. A car-circular list is a tree that has itself as a subtree. They are so called because the loop passes through the car of some cons. Here we create a car-circular list whose second element is itself:

```
> (let ((y (list 'a )))
    (setf (car y) y)
    y)
#1=(#1#)
```

Figure 12.12 shows the resulting structure. Though car-circular, this list is a proper list. Cdr-circular lists are never proper lists, but car-circular lists can be, unless they are disqualified for some other reason.

A list could be both car- and cdr-circular. The car and the cdr of this cons will be the cons itself:

```
> (let ((c (cons 1 1)))
    (setf (car c) c
          (cdr c) c)
    c)
#1=(#1# . #1#)
```

It's hard to imagine what the use of such an object would be. Indeed, the main reason to know about circular lists may be to avoid creating them by accident, because most functions that traverse list structure will go into an infinite loop if they are given a list that's circular in the dimension they traverse.

Circular structure can be an issue for other kinds of objects besides lists. For example, an array can contain itself as an element:

```
> (setf *print-array* t)
T
> (let ((a (make-array 1)))
    (setf (aref a 0) a)
    a)
#1=#(#1#)
```

Indeed, just about anything that can have elements can have itself as an element.

It's quite common to have circularities involving structures created by defstruct. For example, a structure *c* representing an element in a tree might have a parent field that contained another structure *p* whose child field in turn contained *c*:

```
> (progn (defstruct elt
            (parent nil) (child nil))
        (let ((c (make-elt))
              (p (make-elt)))
           (setf (elt-parent c) p
                 (elt-child p) c)
           c))
#1=#S(ELT PARENT #S(ELT PARENT NIL CHILD #1#) CHILD NIL)
```

In the print-function of such a structure, you would either want to bind
print-circle to t, or avoid printing the values of the fields through
which cycles might pass.

12.8   Constant Structure

Because constants are effectively part of the code in which they occur, it
is also important not to modify them, or you may inadvertently create self-
rewriting programs. A quoted list is a constant, so you should be careful not
to modify any cons that was ever part of a quoted list in the text of a program.
For example, if we use the following predicate to test whether something is
an arithmetic operator,

```
(defun arith-op (x)
  (member x '(+ - * /)))
```

then its return value, if true, will incorporate at least part of a quoted list. If
we modify the return value,

```
> (nconc (arith-op '*) '(as it were))
(* / AS IT WERE)
```

then we could be modifying the list within arith-op, and thereby changing
what the function does:

```
> (arith-op 'as)
(AS IT WERE)
```

It is not necessarily an error to write a function that returns constant structure. But when you are considering whether it's safe to perform destructive
operations on something, you must certainly take this into account.

There are several ways to write arith-op so that it doesn't return part
of a quoted list. In the general case, you can ensure safety by replacing any
quoted list with a call to list, which returns a new list each time:

```
(defun arith-op (x)
  (member x (list '+ '- '* '/)))
```

In this case, calling list is an inefficient solution. You would be better off using find instead of member:

```
(defun arith-op (x)
  (find x '(+ - * /)))
```

The problem described in this section is most likely to happen with lists, but it could happen with complex objects of any type: arrays, strings, structures, instances, and so on. You shouldn't modify anything that occurs literally in the text of a program.

Even if you want to write self-modifying programs, modifying constants is not the way to do it. The compiler *can* wire constants into the code, and destructive operators *can* modify their arguments, but neither is guaranteed. The way to write self-modifying programs, if that's what you want, is to use closures (Section 6.5).

Summary

1. Two lists can share a tail. Lists can share structure as trees without sharing top-level list structure. Shared structure can be avoided by copying.

2. Shared structure can usually be ignored, but it must be considered if you are going to modify lists. Modifying one list can modify other lists that share structure with it.

3. Queues can be represented as conses in which the car points to the first cons in a list and the cdr to the last.

4. For reasons of efficiency, destructive functions are allowed to modify their arguments.

5. In some applications, destructive implementations are the most natural.

6. Lists can be car- or cdr-circular. Lisp can represent circular and shared structure.

7. Constants occurring in the text of a program should not be modified.

Exercises

1. Draw three different trees that would print as ((A) (A) (A)). Write an expression that generates each.

2. Assuming make-queue, enqueue, and dequeue are defined as in Figure 12.7, draw the queue in box-notation after each step:

```
> (setf q (make-queue))
(NIL)
> (enqueue 'a q)
(A)
> (enqueue 'b q)
(A B)
> (dequeue q)
A
```

3. Define a function copy-queue that returns a copy of a queue.

4. Define a function that takes an object and a queue, and puts the object on the *front* of the queue.

5. Define a function that takes an object and a queue, and (destructively) moves the first (eql) instance of the object to the front of the queue.

6. Define a function that takes an object and a possibly cdr-circular list, and returns true if the object is a member of the list.

7. Define a function that returns true when its argument is a cdr-circular list.

8. Define a function that returns true when its argument is a car-circular list.

13

Speed

Lisp is really two languages: a language for writing fast programs and a language for writing programs fast. In the early stages of a program you can trade speed for convenience. Then once the structure of your program begins to crystallize, you can refine critical portions to make them faster.

It's difficult to give general advice about optimization, because of the variation between Common Lisp implementations. A change that made your program faster in one implementation might make it slower in another. This is something that comes with the territory. The more powerful the language, the further you are from the machine, and the further you are from the machine, the greater the chance that different implementations will take different paths toward it. So while there are some techniques that are almost certain to make your programs faster, the aim of this chapter will be to suggest rather than to prescribe.

13.1 The Bottleneck Rule

Three points can be made about optimization, regardless of the implementation: it should be focused on bottlenecks, it should not begin too early, and it should begin with algorithms.

Probably the most important thing to understand about optimization is that programs tend to have a few bottlenecks that account for a great part of the execution time. According to Knuth, "most of the running time in non-IO-bound programs is concentrated in about 3% of the source text."° Optimizing these parts of the program will make it run noticeably faster; optimizing the rest of the program will be a waste of time in comparison.

So the crucial first step in optimizing any program is to find the bottle-necks. Many Lisp implementations come with *profilers* that can watch a program as it's running and report the amount of time spent in each part. A profiler is a valuable tool—perhaps even a necessity—in producing the most efficient code. If your Lisp implementation provides one, use it to guide optimization. If not, you are reduced to guessing where the bottlenecks are, and you might be surprised how often such guesses turn out to be wrong.

A corollary of the bottleneck rule is that one should not put too much effort into optimization early in a program's life. Knuth puts the point even more strongly: "Premature optimization is the root of all evil (or at least most of it) in programming."° It's hard to see where the real bottlenecks will be when you've just started writing a program, so there's more chance you'll be wasting your time. Optimizations also tend to make a program harder to change, so trying to write a program and optimize it at the same time can be like trying to paint a picture with paint that dries too fast.

You end up with better programs if each task can be emphasized at the appropriate time. One of the benefits of Lisp is that it lets you work at a range of different speeds: you can write slow code fast or fast code slow. In the early stages of a program you tend to work in the former mode, then as optimization takes precedence you switch into the latter. As the bottleneck rule suggests, this is a more effective use of your time. In a very low-level language, like assembler, you are essentially optimizing every line of the program. Most of this effort is wasted, because the bottlenecks only make up a small part of it. A more abstract language allows you to spend a greater proportion of your time on the bottlenecks, and so get most of the gains with a fraction of the effort.

When you do turn to optimization, begin at the top. That is, make sure that you're using the most efficient algorithm before you resort to low-level coding tricks. The potential gains are greater—perhaps great enough that you won't have to resort to coding tricks after all. This rule has to be balanced against the preceding one, though. Sometimes decisions about algorithms have to be made early.

13.2 Compilation

Five parameters control the way your code is compiled: speed refers to the speed of the code produced by the compiler; compilation-speed refers to the speed at which your program will be compiled; safety refers to the amount of error-checking done in the object code; space refers to the size and memory needs of the object code; and debug refers to the amount of information retained for debugging.

INTERACTIVE VS. INTERPRETED

Lisp is an interactive language, but a language does not have to be interpreted to be interactive. Early Lisp implementations were implemented by interpreters, and the idea arose that Lisp's unique qualities depended on its being interpreted. This idea is mistaken: Common Lisp is the same language compiled as it is interpreted.

At least two Common Lisp implementations do not even include interpreters. In these implementations, expressions typed into the toplevel are compiled before being evaluated. So it is not merely old-fashioned to call the toplevel the "interpreter," it can be an error of fact.

The compilation parameters are not real variables. They are assigned weights from 0 (unimportant) to 3 (most important) in declarations. If a major bottleneck occurred in the inner loop of some function, we might add a declaration like the following:

```
(defun bottleneck (...)
  (do (...)
     (...)
   (do (...)
      (...)
    (declare (optimize (speed 3) (safety 0)))
    ...)))
```

Generally you would not want to add such declarations until the code was finished and tested.

To ask globally for the fastest possible code, regardless of the consequences, you could say:

```
(declaim (optimize (speed 3)
                   (compilation-speed 0)
                   (safety 0)
                   (debug 0)))
```

This would be a drastic step, and probably not even necessary, given the bottleneck rule.[1]

One particularly important kind of optimization done by Lisp compilers is the optimization of tail calls. Giving speed the maximum weight will ensure tail call optimization by any compiler capable of it.

---

[1]Older implementations may not provide declaim; instead use proclaim and quote the argument.

A call is a *tail call* if nothing remains to be done after it returns. The following function returns the length of a list:

```
(defun length/r (lst)
  (if (null lst)
      0
      (1+ (length/r (cdr lst)))))
```

The recursive call is not a tail call, because after it returns, its value has to be passed to 1+. However, this version is tail-recursive,

```
(defun length/tr (lst)
  (labels ((len (lst acc)
             (if (null lst)
                 acc
                 (len (cdr lst) (1+ acc)))))
    (len lst 0)))
```

or more precisely, the local function len is, because nothing more has to happen after the recursive call returns. Instead of building its return value on the way back up the recursion, like length/r, it accumulates the return value on the way down. Hence the additional parameter acc, which can simply be returned at the end of the last recursive call.

A good compiler can compile a tail call into a goto, and so can compile a tail-recursive function into a loop.° In typical machine language code, when control arrives for the first time at the segment of instructions representing len, there is information on the stack saying what to do upon returning. Because nothing remains to be done after the recursive call, this information remains valid for the second invocation as well: what we are supposed to do on returning from the second invocation is simply to return from the first invocation. So after setting the parameters to their new values, we can just jump back to the beginning of the function and act as if this *were* the second invocation. There is no need to do a real function call.

Another way to have the abstraction of function calls without the cost is to have functions compiled inline. This is valuable mainly for small functions, where the machinery of calling the function could entail more work than the function itself performs. For example, the following function tells whether something is a list of a single element:

```
(declaim (inline single?))

(defun single? (lst)
  (and (consp lst) (null (cdr lst))))
```

Because this function is globally declared inline, a reference to `single?`
within a compiled function should no longer require a real function call.[2] If
we define a function that calls it,

```
(defun foo (x)
  (single? (bar x)))
```

then when `foo` is compiled, the code for `single?` should be compiled right
into it, just as if we had written

```
(defun foo (x)
  (let ((lst (bar x)))
    (and (consp lst) (null (cdr lst)))))
```

in the first place.

There are two limitations on inline compilation. Recursive functions can't
be inlined. And if an inlined function is redefined, we have to recompile any
function that calls it, or the calling function will still reflect the old definition.

In some earlier dialects of Lisp, one used macros (Section 10.2) to avoid
function calls. In Common Lisp this is no longer supposed to be necessary.

Different Lisp compilers do varying amounts of optimization. If you
want to see the code your compiler produces for a function, try calling
`disassemble`. This function takes a function or function name and displays
its compiled form. Even if what you see is completely incomprehensible,
you can still use `disassemble` to determine whether declarations are being
used: compile two version of the function, one with the declaration and one
without, and see if the code displayed by `disassemble` differs between the
two. You can use a similar technique to see if functions are being compiled
inline. In either case, be sure to set the compilation parameters beforehand
to get the fastest code.°

13.3   Type Declarations

If you're learning Lisp as a second language, you may have been puzzled by
the omission up to this point of something that's *de rigueur* in most other
languages: type declarations.

In most languages, you have to declare the type of each variable, and
the variable can only hold values of that type. Such a language is said to
be *strongly typed*. As well as being a lot of work for the programmer, this
approach imposes restrictions on what you can do. In such a language it's
hard to write functions that work for different kinds of arguments, or to have

---

[2]For inline declarations to have an effect, you may also have to set the compilation parameters
to get fast code.

data structures that contain different kinds of elements.° The advantage of this approach is that whenever the compiler sees an addition, for example, it knows beforehand what kind of addition is involved. If both arguments are integers, it can hard-wire an integer addition in the object code.

As Section 2.15 mentioned, Common Lisp uses a more flexible approach called manifest typing.[3] Values have types, not variables. Variables can hold objects of any type.

If we left it at that, we would have to pay for this flexibility in speed. Because it can take several different types of numbers, + would have to look at the types of each of its arguments, and decide what kind of addition to do at run-time.

If we just want an integer addition after all, this is an inefficient way to get it. So Common Lisp's approach is: tell me as much as you know. If we know ahead of time that both of the arguments in some addition will be fixnums, then we can declare them to be such, and the compiler will hard-wire an integer addition just as in C.

So the difference between the two approaches to typing need not entail any difference in speed. It's just that the first approach makes type declarations mandatory, and the second doesn't. In Common Lisp, type declarations are completely optional. They may make a program faster, but (unless incorrect) they will not change its behavior.

Global declarations are made with `declaim`, which should be followed by one or more declaration forms. A type declaration is a list containing the symbol `type`, followed by a type name and the names of one or more variables. So to declare the type of a global variable, one could say:

```
(declaim (type fixnum *count*))
```

In ANSI Common Lisp you can omit the `type` and say simply:

```
(declaim (fixnum *count*))
```

Local declarations are made with `declare`, which takes the same arguments as `declaim`. Declarations can begin any body of code where variables have just been created: in `defun`, `lambda`, `let`, `do`, and so on. To declare a function's parameters to be `fixnums`, for example, we would say:

```
(defun poly (a b x)
  (declare (fixnum a b x))
  (+ (* a (expt x 2)) (* b x)))
```

---

[3]There are two ways to describe Lisp's approach to typing: by where the type information is kept, and by when it is used. Manifest typing means that the type information is attached to the data objects, and *run-time typing* means that type information is used at run-time. In practice they mean the same thing.

A variable name in a type declaration refers to the variable with that name in the context where the declaration occurs—to the variable whose value would be altered if it were instead an assignment.

You can also declare that the value of an expression will be of a certain type, by using the. If we know beforehand that a, b, and x will not only be fixnums, but that they will be small enough fixnums that all the intermediate results will be fixnums, we can say:

```
(defun poly (a b x)
  (declare (fixnum a b x))
  (the fixnum (+ (the fixnum (* a (the fixnum (expt x 2))))
                 (the fixnum (* b x)))))
```

Looks a bit awkward, doesn't it? Fortunately, there are two reasons that you rarely have to clutter up your numeric code with thes in this way. One is that it's easy to use macros to insert such declarations for you.° The other is that some implementations use special tricks to make fixnum arithmetic fast without declarations.

There are a great many types in Common Lisp—a potentially unlimited number, considering that you can define new types yourself. However, declarations only matter for a few. When does it pay to make type declarations? There are two general rules:

1. It pays to declare the types of arguments to functions that work for arguments of several different types (but not all types). If you knew that the arguments in a call to + would always be fixnums, or that the first argument in a call to aref would always be a particular kind of array, it could pay to make a type declaration.

2. It is usually only worthwhile to make declarations for types near the bottom of the type hierarchy: declaring something to be of type fixnum or simple-array might be useful, but declaring something to be of type integer or sequence probably would not.

Type declarations are particularly important for the contents of complex objects, including arrays, structures, and instances. Such declarations can improve efficiency in two ways: as well as allowing the compiler to determine the types of arguments to functions, they make it possible to represent these objects more efficiently in memory.

If nothing is known about the type of elements an array will contain, it has to be represented in memory as a block of pointers. But if it is known that the array will only contain, say, double-floats, then the array can be represented as a block of actual double-floats. This way the array will take less space, because we no longer need a pointer to point to each of the double-floats, and

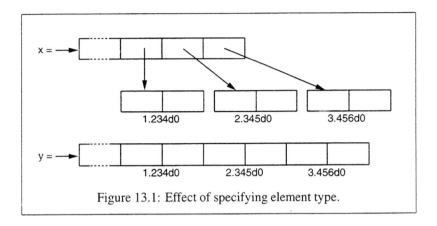

Figure 13.1: Effect of specifying element type.

access will be faster, because we don't have to follow pointers to read and write elements.

You can specify the kind of values that an array will contain by giving the :element-type argument to make-array. Such an an array is called a *specialized* array. Figure 13.1 shows what would happen, in most implementations, as a result of evaluating the following code:

```
(setf x (vector 1.234d0 2.345d0 3.456d0)
      y (make-array 3 :element-type 'double-float)
      (aref y 0) 1.234d0
      (aref y 1) 2.345d0
      (aref y 2) 3.456d0)
```

Each rectangle in Figure 13.1 represents a word of memory. The two arrays each consist of a header of unspecified length, followed by some representation of the three elements. In x, each element is represented by a pointer. All three pointers happen to point to double-floats at the moment, but we could store objects of any type in this vector. In y, each element is an actual double-float. This is faster and takes less space, but it means that the vector can only hold double-floats.

Note that we use aref to refer to the elements of y. A specialized vector is no longer a simple vector, so we can no longer use svref to refer to its elements.

As well as specifying the element type of an array when you create it, you should declare the dimensions and element type of an array in code that uses it. A full vector declaration would look like:

```
(declare (type (vector fixnum 20) v))
```

This declares v to be a vector of length 20, specialized for fixnums.

```
(setf a (make-array '(1000 1000)
                    :element-type 'single-float
                    :initial-element 1.0s0))

(defun sum-elts (a)
  (declare (type (simple-array single-float (1000 1000))
                 a))
  (let ((sum 0.0s0))
    (declare (type single-float sum))
    (dotimes (r 1000)
      (dotimes (c 1000)
        (incf sum (aref a r c))))
    sum))
```

Figure 13.2: Summing an array.

The most general form of array declaration consists of the array type followed by the element type and a list of dimensions:

```
(declare (type (simple-array fixnum (4 4)) ar))
```

This declares that `ar` will be a 4×4 simple array specialized for fixnums.

Figure 13.2 shows how to create a 1000×1000 array of single-floats, and how to write a function to sum the elements of such an array. Arrays are stored in row-major order and should be traversed that way when possible.

We will use `time` to compare the performance of `sum-elts` with and without declarations. The `time` macro displays some (implementation-dependent) measure of how long it takes to evaluate an expression. It's only meaningful to time compiled functions. In one implementation, if we compile `sum-elts` with the compilation parameters set to get the fastest code, it returns in less than half a second:

```
> (time (sum-elts a))
User Run Time = 0.43 seconds
1000000.0
```

If we take the type declarations out of `sum-elts` and recompile it, the same computation takes more than five seconds:

```
> (time (sum-elts a))
User Run Time = 5.17 seconds
1000000.0
```

The importance of type declarations, especially for arrays and numbers, cannot be overemphasized. Here, two lines of code make `sum-elts` twelve times faster.

13.4   Garbage Avoidance

As Lisp allows you to delay thinking about the types of variables, it also allows you to delay thinking about memory allocation. In the early stages of a program it frees your imagination not to have to think about (or deal with bugs involving) memory allocation. As a program matures, it can rely less on dynamic allocation and so become faster.

However, consing less does not always make a program faster. In Lisp implementations with bad garbage collectors, programs that cons a lot tend to run slowly. Until recently, most Lisp implementations have had bad garbage collectors, and so it has become a tradition that efficient programs should cons as little as possible. Recent developments have turned this conventional wisdom on its head. Some implementations now have such sophisticated garbage collectors that it is faster to cons up new objects and throw them away than it is to recycle them.

This section introduces some ways to make programs cons less. Whether consing less will make your programs run faster depends on the implementation. Again, the best advice is to try it and see.

There are a lot of things you can do to reduce consing. Some of them won't affect the shape of your program at all. For example, one of the easiest steps you can take is to use destructive functions. The following table lists some commonly used functions and their destructive counterparts.

SAFE	DESTRUCTIVE
append	nconc
reverse	nreverse
remove	delete
remove-if	delete-if
remove-duplicates	delete-duplicates
subst	nsubst
subst-if	nsubst-if
union	nunion
intersection	nintersection
set-difference	nset-difference

When you know it's safe to modify a list, you can use `delete` instead of `remove`, `nreverse` instead of `reverse`, and so on.

If you want to eliminate consing entirely, you don't have to give up the possibility of creating things on the fly. What you have to avoid is allocating space for them on the fly, and reclaiming it by garbage collection. The general solution is to allocate blocks of memory beforehand, and explicitly recycle used blocks yourself. *Beforehand* could mean at compile-time, or in some initialization routine. When speed begins to matter depends on the application.

For example, when circumstances allow us to impose a limit on the size of a stack, we could have the stack grow and shrink along a pre-allocated vector, instead of building it out of conses. Common Lisp has built-in support for using vectors as stacks. If we give the optional `fill-pointer` argument to `make-array`, we will get a vector that seems to be expandable. The first argument to `make-array` specifies the amount of storage to be allocated for the vector, but the `fill-pointer`, when given, specifies the initial effective length:

```
> (setf *print-array* t)
T
> (setf vec (make-array 10 :fill-pointer 2
                          :initial-element nil))
#(NIL NIL)
```

The vector we just made will seem to sequence functions as if it had only two elements,

```
> (length vec)
2
```

but it will be able to grow until it has up to ten. Because vec has a fill pointer, we can use the functions `vector-push` and `vector-pop` to push and pop elements as if it were a list:

```
> (vector-push 'a vec)
2
> vec
#(NIL NIL A)
> (vector-pop vec)
A
> vec
#(NIL NIL)
```

When we called `vector-push`, it incremented the fill pointer and returned its old value. As long as the fill pointer is less than the initial argument to `make-array`, we can push new elements onto the vector; when it runs out of space, `vector-push` will return nil. We could push up to eight more elements onto vec at this point.

```
(defconstant dict (make-array 25000 :fill-pointer 0))

(defun read-words (from)
  (setf (fill-pointer dict) 0)
  (with-open-file (in from :direction :input)
    (do ((w (read-line in nil :eof)
            (read-line in nil :eof)))
        ((eql w :eof))
      (vector-push w dict))))

(defun xform (fn seq) (map-into seq fn seq))

(defun write-words (to)
  (with-open-file (out to :direction :output
                          :if-exists :supersede)
    (map nil #'(lambda (x)
                 (fresh-line out)
                 (princ x out))
         (xform #'nreverse
                (sort (xform #'nreverse dict)
                      #'string<)))))
```

Figure 13.3: Generating a rhyming dictionary.

One disadvantage of vectors with fill pointers is that they are no longer simple vectors. We have to use aref instead of svref to refer to elements. This cost has to be balanced against the potential gains.

In applications that involve very long sequences, you may want to use map-into instead of map. Instead of a sequence type, map-into takes as its first argument an actual sequence to hold the result. This sequence can be one of those from which the arguments to the function are taken. So, for example, if you want to increment each element of a vector v, you might write:

```
(setf v (map-into v #'1+ v))
```

Figure 13.3 shows an example of an application that uses a large vector: a program to generate a simple rhyming dictionary (or more precisely, a dictionary of sight rhymes). The function read-words reads words from a file containing one per line,° and the function write-words prints them out in reverse alphabetical order. That is, the output might begin with

```
a amoeba alba samba marimba...
```

and end with

```
...megahertz gigahertz jazz buzz fuzz
```

By taking advantage of fill-pointers and map-into, we can write this program in a way that's both simple and efficient.

In numeric applications, be careful of bignums. Bignum arithmetic conses, as well as being inherently slower. But even if your program must return bignums in the end, you may be able to make it more efficient by arranging that intermediate results are usually fixnums.

Another way to avoid garbage collection is to encourage the compiler to allocate objects on the stack instead of the heap. When you know that you will only need something temporarily, you may be able to avoid allocating space for it on the heap by declaring it to have *dynamic extent*.

By giving a dynamic extent declaration for a variable, you're saying that the variable's value need not last any longer than the variable does. When could the value last longer than the variable? Here's an example:

```
(defun our-reverse (lst)
  (let ((rev nil))
    (dolist (x lst)
      (push x rev))
    rev))
```

In our-reverse, the list passed as an argument will be accumulated in reverse order in rev. When the function returns, the variable rev will go away. However, the list that is its value will persist: it is sent back to the calling function, where who knows what fate awaits it.

In contrast, consider the following implementation of adjoin:

```
(defun our-adjoin (obj lst &rest args)
  (if (apply #'member obj lst args)
      lst
      (cons obj lst)))
```

In this case, we can see from the definition of the function that the list in args is going nowhere. It need not last longer than the variable itself. This is the kind of situation where it would make sense to make a dynamic extent declaration. If we add such a declaration,

```
(defun our-adjoin (obj lst &rest args)
  (declare (dynamic-extent args))
  (if (apply #'member obj lst args)
      lst
      (cons obj lst)))
```

```
(defparameter *harbor* nil)

(defstruct ship
  name flag tons)

(defun enter (n f d)
  (push (make-ship :name n :flag f :tons d)
        *harbor*))

(defun find-ship (n)
  (find n *harbor* :key #'ship-name))

(defun leave (n)
  (setf *harbor*
        (delete (find-ship n) *harbor*)))
```

Figure 13.4: Harbor.

then the compiler is free (but not required) to allocate space for args on the stack, where it will be automatically discarded on return from our-adjoin.

13.5   Example: Pools

In applications that involve data structures, you can avoid dynamic allocation by pre-allocating a certain number of them in a *pool*. When you need a structure, you get one from the pool, and when you're finished with one, you send it back to the pool.° To illustrate the use of pools, we'll write a quick prototype of a program to keep track of the ships in a harbor, and then rewrite it to use a pool.

Figure 13.4 contains the first version. The global *harbor* will be a list of ships, each represented by a ship structure. The function enter is called when a ship enters the harbor; find-ship finds a ship with a given name (if there is one); and leave is called when a ship leaves the harbor.

This would be a perfectly good way to write the initial version of a program, but it will generate a lot of garbage. As this program runs it will cons in two ways: new structures will have to be allocated as ships enter the harbor, and new conses will have to be made as *harbor* grows.

We can eliminate both sources of consing by allocating the space at compile-time. Figure 13.5 contains a second version of the program that shouldn't cons at all.

```
(defconstant pool (make-array 1000 :fill-pointer t))

(dotimes (i 1000)
  (setf (aref pool i) (make-ship)))

(defconstant harbor (make-hash-table :size 1100
                                     :test #'eq))

(defun enter (n f d)
  (let ((s (if (plusp (length pool))
               (vector-pop pool)
               (make-ship))))
    (setf (ship-name s)       n
          (ship-flag s)       f
          (ship-tons s)       d
          (gethash n harbor) s)))

(defun find-ship (n) (gethash n harbor))

(defun leave (n)
  (let ((s (gethash n harbor)))
    (remhash n harbor)
    (vector-push s pool)))
```

Figure 13.5: Harbor, version 2.

Strictly speaking, the new version does cons, just not at run-time. In the second version, harbor is a hash table instead of a list, so all the space for it will be allocated at compile-time. A thousand ship structures will also be created at compile-time, and stored in the vector pool. (If the :fill-pointer argument is t, the fill pointer points to the end of the vector.) Now when enter needs a new structure, it gets one from the pool instead of calling make-ship. And when leave removes a ship from harbor, instead of being thrown away, it is sent back to the pool.

What we're doing by using pools is taking over the job of memory management. Whether this actually makes our program run faster depends on how our Lisp implementation manages memory. Generally speaking, it pays to use pools only in implementations with primitive garbage collectors, or in real-time applications where the unpredictability of GC would be a problem.

13.6 Fast Operators

The beginning of this chapter described Lisp as two different languages. In one sense this is literally true. If you look closely at the design of Common Lisp, you can see that some features are intended mainly for speed, and others mainly for convenience.

For example, there are three functions you could use to retrieve the element at a given position in a vector: `elt`, `aref`, and `svref`. Such variety exists to allow you to squeeze as much performance out of a program as possible. So if you can use `svref`, do. Conversely, a part of a program where speed is important probably should not be calling `elt`, which works for both arrays and lists.

Instead of calling `elt` on a list, you can call `nth`, which is specifically for lists. Yet there is only a single function, `length`, for finding the length of any sequence. Why doesn't Common Lisp provide a separate version for lists? Because if your program is finding the lengths of lists, it's already lost, as far as speed is concerned. In this case, as in many others, the design of the language suggests what is fast and what isn't.

Another pair of similar functions are `eql` and `eq`. The former is the default predicate for testing identity, but the latter is faster if you know that the arguments won't be characters or numbers. Two objects are `eq` when they have the same location in memory. Numbers and characters may not be associated with any particular memory location, so `eq` does not apply to them (though in most implementations it does work for fixnums). For arguments of any other kind, `eq` will return the same value as `eql`.

It's always fastest to compare objects using `eq`, because all Lisp has to do is compare the pointers to them. So `eq` hash tables (as in Figure 13.5) should offer the fastest access. In an `eq` hash table, `gethash` can just hash on pointers, without even looking at what they point to. Access is not the only thing to consider, however; `eq` and `eql` hash tables incur extra costs under copying garbage collection algorithms because they have to be rehashed after a GC. If this becomes a problem, the best solution may be to use an `eql` hash table with fixnums as keys.

Calling `reduce` can be a more efficient alternative to `apply` when the function in question has a rest parameter. For example, instead of something like

```
(apply #'+ '(1 2 3))
```

it can be more efficient to say:

```
(reduce #'+ '(1 2 3))
```

Not only does it help to call the right functions, it helps to call them the right way. Rest, optional, and keyword parameters are expensive. With ordinary parameters, the arguments in a function call are simply left by the caller where the callee knows to look for them. But other kinds of parameters involve processing at run-time. Keyword parameters are the worst. For built-in functions, good compilers take special measures to compile calls with keyword arguments into fast code. But in your own functions it is just as well to avoid using them in speed-critical parts of a program. It is also wise not to push large numbers of arguments into rest parameters, if this can be avoided.

Individual compilers sometimes perform their own particular optimizations. For example, some compilers can optimize case statements where the keys are integers in a narrow range. Check your user's manual for hints about such implementation-specific optimizations.

13.7   Two-Phase Development

In applications where speed is paramount, you may want to rewrite part of a Lisp program in a lower-level language like C or assembler. You can use this technique with programs written in any language—critical parts of C programs are often rewritten in assembler—but the more abstract the language, the greater the benefits of developing programs in two phases.

Common Lisp does not prescribe a way of integrating code written in other languages. This is left up to the implementation, but almost all implementations provide some way to do it.

It may seem wasteful to write a program in one language and then to rewrite part of it in another. In fact, experience has shown this to be a good way to develop software. It can be easier to aim for functionality first, and then for speed, than to try to achieve both at the same time.

If programming were an entirely mechanical process—a matter of simply translating specifications into code—it would be reasonable to do everything in a single step. But programming is never like that. No matter how precise the specifications, programming always involves a certain amount of exploration—usually a lot more than anyone had anticipated.

It might seem that if the specifications were *good*, programming *would* simply be a matter of translating them into code. This is a widespread misconception. Programming necessarily involves exploration, because specifications are necessarily vague. If they weren't vague, they wouldn't be specifications.

In other fields, it may be desirable for specifications to be as precise as possible. If you're asking for a piece of metal to be cut to a certain shape, it's probably best to say exactly what you want. But this rule does not extend to software, because programs and specifications are made out of the same thing: text. You *can't* write specifications that say exactly what you want. If the specifications were that precise, then they would be the program.°

In applications that involve a substantial amount of exploration (and again, more do than anyone admits), it can pay to separate implementation into two phases. And the medium you use in the first phase need not be the final one. For example, the standard way to make bronze sculptures is to begin with clay. You build a sculpture out of clay first, and then use that to make a mold in which the bronze sculpture is cast.° No clay remains in the final sculpture, but you can see its effect in the shape of the bronze. Imagine how much more difficult it would be to produce the same thing starting with a lump of bronze and a chisel. For the same reasons, it can be better to write a program in Lisp, and then rewrite it in C, than to try to write it in C from the start.

Summary

1. Optimization should not begin too early, should be focused on bottle-necks, and should begin with algorithms.

2. Five parameters control compilation. They can be set with local or global declarations.

3. A good compiler can optimize tail calls, turning a tail-recursive function into a loop. Inline compilation is another way to avoid function calls.

4. Type declarations are not necessary, but they can make a program more efficient. Type declarations are especially important in numeric code, and code that deals with arrays.

5. Consing less can make a program faster, especially in implementations with primitive garbage collectors. Solutions include using destructive functions, pre-allocating blocks of space, and stack allocation.

6. In some situations, it might pay to draw objects from a pre-allocated pool.

7. Some parts of Common Lisp are designed for speed and others for flexibility.

8. Programming necessarily involves exploration. Exploration and optimization should be separated—sometimes even to the extent of using different languages for each.

Exercises

1. Test whether your compiler observes inline declarations.

2. Rewrite the following function to be tail-recursive. How much faster is it when compiled?

```
(defun foo (x)
  (if (zerop x)
      0
      (+ 1 (foo (1- x))))))
```

Note: you will have to add another parameter.

3. Add declarations to the following programs. How much faster can you make them?

    (a) The date arithmetic code in Section 5.7.

    (b) The ray-tracer in Section 9.8.

4. Rewrite the breadth-first search code in Section 3.15 so that it conses as little as possible.

5. Modify the binary search tree code in Section 4.7 to use pools.

14

Advanced Topics

This chapter is optional. It describes a selection of the more esoteric features of Common Lisp. Common Lisp is like an iceberg: a great part of its functionality is invisible to most users, who never need it. You may never need to define packages or read-macros of your own, but when you do, it is helpful to have examples to work from.

14.1 Type Specifiers

Types are not objects in Common Lisp. There is no object that corresponds to the type `integer`, for example. What we get from a function like `type-of`, and give as an argument to a function like `typep`, is not a type, but a type specifier.

A type specifier is the name of a type. The simplest type specifiers are symbols like `integer`. These form a hierarchy in Common Lisp. At the top of the hierarchy is the type `t`—all objects are of type `t`. The hierarchy is not a tree. There are two paths from `nil` to the top, for example: one through `atom`, and the other through `list` and `sequence`.

A type is really just a set of objects. Which means that there are as many types as there are sets of objects: an infinite number. We can denote some of these sets with atomic type specifiers: `integer` denotes the set of all the integers. But we can also construct compound type specifiers that refer to any set of objects.

For example, if a and b are two type specifiers, then (`or` a b) denotes the union of the type denoted by a and that denoted by b. That is, an object is of type (`or` a b) if it is of type a or type b.

If `circular?` were a function that returned true of cdr-circular lists, then to denote the set of proper sequences you could use:[1]

```
(or vector (and list (not (satisfies circular?))))
```

Some of the atomic type specifiers can also appear in compound type specifiers. To denote the set of integers between 1 and 100 inclusive, we would use:

```
(integer 1 100)
```

Such a type specifier is said to denote a *finite type*.

In a compound type-specifier, you can leave some information unspecified by using * in place of an argument. So

```
(simple-array fixnum (* *))
```

describes the set of two-dimensional simple arrays specialized for fixnums, and

```
(simple-array fixnum *)
```

describes the set (a supertype of the first) of simple arrays specialized for fixnums. Trailing asterisks can be dropped, so in the latter case we could have said:

```
(simple-array fixnum)
```

If no arguments are given to a compound type-specifier, you can use an atom. So `simple-array` describes the set of all simple arrays.

If there is some compound type specifier that you'd like to use repeatedly, you can define an abbreviation for it with `deftype`. This macro is just like `defmacro`, but expands into a type specifier instead of an expression. By saying

```
(deftype proseq ()
  '(or vector (and list (not (satisfies circular?)))))
```

we define `proseq` as a new atomic type specifier:

```
> (typep #(1 2) 'proseq)
T
```

If you define a type-specifier to take arguments, the arguments are treated as forms (that is, not evaluated), just as with `defmacro`. So

---

[1]Though the standard does not seem to mention this, you can assume that the type-specifiers `and` and `or` only consider as many of their arguments as they need to, like the `and` and `or` macros.

```
(deftype multiple-of (n)
  '(and integer (satisfies (lambda (x)
                            (zerop (mod x ,n)))))))
```

defines (multiple-of *n*) as a specifier for all multiples of *n*:

```
> (typep 12 '(multiple-of 4))
T
```

Type specifiers are interpreted, and therefore slow, so you would generally be better off defining a function to make this kind of test.

14.2   Binary Streams

Chapter 7 mentioned that there were binary streams as well as character streams. A binary stream is a source and/or destination not of characters but of *integers*. You create a binary stream by specifying a subtype of integer—most often unsigned-byte—as the :element-type when you open the stream.

There are only two functions for I/O on binary streams, read-byte and write-byte. So here is how you might define a function to copy a file:

```
(defun copy-file (from to)
  (with-open-file (in from :direction :input
                           :element-type 'unsigned-byte)
    (with-open-file (out to :direction :output
                            :element-type 'unsigned-byte)
      (do ((i (read-byte in nil -1)
              (read-byte in nil -1)))
          ((minusp i))
        (declare (fixnum i))
        (write-byte i out)))))
```

By specifying just unsigned-byte as the :element-type, you let the operating system choose the length of a byte. If you specifically wanted to read or write 7-bit integers, for example, you would use

```
(unsigned-byte 7)
```

as the :element-type instead.

14.3 Read-Macros

Section 7.5 introduced the concept of a macro character, a character that has
a special meaning to `read`. Each such character has a function associated
with it that tells `read` what to do when the character is encountered. You can
change the function associated with an existing macro character, or define
new read-macros of your own.

The function `set-macro-character` provides one way to define read-
macros. It takes a character and a function, and thereafter when `read` encounters the character, it returns the result of calling the function.

One of the oldest read-macros in Lisp is `'`, the quote. We could define it
as:

```
(set-macro-character #\'
  #'(lambda (stream char)
      (list (quote quote) (read stream t nil t))))
```

When `read` encounters an instance of `'` in a normal context, it will return the
result of calling this function on the current stream and character. (The function ignores this second parameter, which will always be the quote character.)
So when `read` sees `'a`, it will return `(quote a)`.

Now we see the point of the last argument to `read`. It says whether the
call to `read` occurs within a call to `read`. The arguments to `read` will be the
same in nearly all read-macros: the stream; the second argument, `t`, which
says that `read` should signal an error if the next thing it sees is the end-of-file;
the third argument, which says what to return instead of generating an error
is therefore irrelevant; and the fourth argument, `t`, which says that the call to
`read` is a recursive one.

You can (with `make-dispatch-macro-character`) define your own
dispatching macro characters, but since `#` is already defined as one, you may
as well use it. Six combinations beginning with `#` are explicitly reserved for
your use: `#!`, `#?`, `#[`, `#]`, `#{`, and `#}`.

You can define new dispatching macro character combinations by calling
`set-dispatch-macro-character`, which is like `set-macro-character`
except that it takes two character arguments. This code defines `#?` as a
read-macro that returns a list of integers.

```
(set-dispatch-macro-character #\# #\?
  #'(lambda (stream char1 char2)
      (list 'quote
            (let ((lst nil))
              (dotimes (i (+ (read stream t nil t) 1))
                (push i lst))
              (nreverse lst)))))
```

Now #?*n* will be read as a list of all the integers from 0 to *n*. For example:

```
> #?7
(0 1 2 3 4 5 6 7)
```

After simple macro characters, the most commonly defined macro characters are list delimiters. Another character combination reserved for the user is #{. Here we define it as a more elaborate kind of left parenthesis:

```
(set-macro-character #\} (get-macro-character #\)))

(set-dispatch-macro-character #\# #\{
  #'(lambda (stream char1 char2)
      (let ((accum nil)
            (pair (read-delimited-list #\} stream t)))
        (do ((i (car pair) (+ i 1)))
            ((> i (cadr pair))
             (list 'quote (nreverse accum)))
          (push i accum))))))
```

This defines an expression of the form #{x y} to read as a list of all the integers between x and y, inclusive:

```
> #{2 7}
(2 3 4 5 6 7)
```

The function `read-delimited-list` is provided just for such read-macros. Its first argument is the character to treat as the end of the list. For } to be recognized as a delimiter, it must first be given this role, hence the preliminary call to `set-macro-character`.

If you want to use a read-macro in the file in which it is defined, the definition should be wrapped in an `eval-when` expression, to ensure that it is evaluated at compile time. Otherwise the definition will be compiled, but not evaluated until the compiled file is loaded.

14.4 Packages

A package is a Lisp object that maps names to symbols. The current package is always stored in the global variable *package*. When Common Lisp starts up, the current package will be common-lisp-user, informally known as the user package. The function package-name returns the name of a package, and find-package returns the package with a given name:

```
> (package-name *package*)
"COMMON-LISP-USER"
> (find-package "COMMON-LISP-USER")
#<Package "COMMON-LISP-USER" 4CD15E>
```

Usually a symbol is interned in the package that was current at the time it was read. The function symbol-package takes a symbol and returns the package in which it is interned.

```
> (symbol-package 'sym)
#<Package "COMMON-LISP-USER" 4CD15E>
```

Interestingly, this expression returns the value it does because the expression had to be read before it could be evaluated, and reading the expression caused sym to be interned. For future use, let's give sym a value:

```
> (setf sym 99)
99
```

Now we will create and switch to a new package:

```
> (setf *package* (make-package 'mine
                                :use '(common-lisp)))
#<Package "MINE" 63390E>
```

At this point there should be eerie music, because we are in a different world: sym here is not what it used to be.

```
MINE> sym
Error: SYM has no value.
```

Why did this happen? Because the sym we set to 99 above is a distinct symbol from sym here in mine.[2] To refer to the original sym from outside the user package, we must prefix the package name and two colons:

```
MINE> common-lisp-user::sym
99
```

So different symbols with the same print-name can coexist in different packages. There can be one sym in package common-lisp-user and another sym in package mine, and they will be distinct symbols. That's the point of packages. If you're writing your program in a separate package, you can choose names for your functions and variables without worrying that someone

---

[2]Some implementations of Common Lisp print the package name before the toplevel prompt whenever we are not in the user package.

will use the same name for something else. Even if they use the same name, it won't be the same symbol.

Packages also provide a means of information-hiding. Programs must refer to functions and variables by their names. If you don't make a given name available outside your package, it becomes unlikely that code in another package will be able to use or modify what it refers to.

It's usually bad style to use package prefixes with double colons. By doing so you are violating the modularity that packages are supposed to provide. If you have to use a double colon to refer to a symbol, it's because someone didn't want you to.

Usually one should only refer to symbols that have been *exported*. If we go back to the user package (in-package sets *package*) and export a symbol interned there,

```
MINE> (in-package common-lisp-user)
#<Package "COMMON-LISP-USER" 4CD15E>
> (export 'bar)
T
> (setf bar 5)
5
```

we cause it to be visible to other packages. Now when we return to mine, we can refer to bar with only a single colon, because it is a publicly available name:

```
> (in-package mine)
#<Package "MINE" 63390E>
MINE> common-lisp-user:bar
5
```

By *importing* bar into mine, we can go one step further and make mine actually share the symbol bar with the user package:

```
MINE> (import 'common-lisp-user:bar)
T
MINE> bar
5
```

After importing bar we can refer to it without any package qualifier at all. The two packages now share the same symbol; there can't be a distinct mine:bar.

What if there already was one? In that case, the call to import would have caused an error, as we see if we try to import sym:

```
MINE> (import 'common-lisp-user::sym)
Error: SYM is already present in MINE.
```

Before, when we tried unsuccessfully to evaluate sym in mine, we thereby caused a symbol sym to be interned there. It had no value and therefore generated an error, but the interning happened simply as a consequence of typing its name. So now when we try to import sym into mine, there is already a symbol there with the same name.

Another way to get access to symbols from another package is to *use* it:

```
MINE> (use-package 'common-lisp-user)
T
```

Now *all* symbols exported by the user package can be used without any qualifier in mine. (If sym had been exported by the user package, this call would also have generated an error.)

The package containing the names of built-in operators and variables is called common-lisp. Since we gave the name of this package in the :use argument of the make-package that created mine, all of Common Lisp's names will be visible here:

```
MINE> #'cons
#<Compiled-Function CONS 462A3E>
```

As with compilation, operations on packages are not usually done at the toplevel like this. More often the calls are contained in source files. Generally it will suffice to begin a file with a defpackage and an in-package, as on page 137.

The kind of modularity provided by packages is actually a bit odd. We have modules not of objects, but of names. Every package that uses common-lisp has access to the name cons, because common-lisp includes a function with that name. But in consequence a variable called cons would also be visible in every package that used common-lisp. If packages are confusing, this is the main reason why; they're not based on objects, but on their names.°

14.5   The Loop Facility

The loop macro was originally designed to help inexperienced Lisp users write iterative code. Instead of writing Lisp code, you express your program in a form meant to resemble English, and this is then translated into Lisp. Unfortunately, loop is more like English than its designers ever intended: you can use it in simple cases without quite understanding how it works, but to understand it in the abstract is almost impossible.

If you are one of the many Lisp programmers who have been planning one day to understand what loop does, there is some good news and some bad

news. The good news is that you are not alone: almost no one understands
it. The bad news is that you probably never will, because the ANSI standard
does not really give a formal specification of its behavior.

The only real definition of this macro is its implementation, and the only
way to understand it (so far as one can) is by examples. The chapter of the
ANSI standard dealing with loop consists largely of examples, and we will
use the same approach here to introduce the basic concepts involved.

The first thing one notices about the loop macro is that it has *syntax*. A
loop expression contains not subexpressions but *clauses*. The clauses are
not delimited by parentheses; instead, each kind has a distinct syntax. In that,
loop resembles traditional Algol-like languages. But the other distinctive
feature of loop, which makes it as unlike Algol as Lisp, is that the order in
which things happen is only loosely related to the order in which the clauses
occur.

There are three phases in the evaluation of a loop expression, and a given
clause can contribute code to more than one phase. The phases are as follows:

1. *Prologue.* Evaluated once as a prelude to iteration. Includes setting
   variables to their initial values.

2. *Body.* Evaluated on each iteration. Begins with the termination tests,
   followed by the body proper, then the updating of iteration variables.

3. *Epilogue.* Evaluated once iteration is completed. Concludes with the
   return of the value(s) of the loop expression.

We will look at some examples of loop clauses and consider what kind of
code they might contribute to each phase.

For example, in the simplest kind of loop expression we might see
something like the following:

```
> (loop for x from 0 to 9
        do (princ x))
0123456789
NIL
```

This loop expression prints the integers from 0 to 9 and returns nil. The
first clause,

```
for x from 0 to 9
```

contributes code to the first two phases, causing x to be set to 0 in the prologue,
compared to 9 at the beginning of the body, and incremented at the end. The
second clause,

```
do (princ x)
```

contributes code (the `princ` expression) to the body proper.

A more general kind of `for` clause specifies an initial and update form. Termination can then be controlled by something like a `while` or `until` clause.

```
> (loop for x = 8 then (/ x 2)
        until (< x 1)
        do (princ x))
8421
NIL
```

You can use `and` to create a compound `for` clause in which two variables will be initialized and updated in parallel:

```
> (loop for x from 1 to 4
        and y from 1 to 4
        do (princ (list x y)))
(1 1)(2 2)(3 3)(4 4)
NIL
```

Otherwise, if there are multiple `for` clauses, the variables will be updated sequentially.

Another thing one typically wants to do in iterative code is accumulate some kind of value. For example:

```
> (loop for x in '(1 2 3 4)
        collect (1+ x))
(2 3 4 5)
```

Using `in` instead of `from` in the `for` clauses causes the variable to be set to successive elements of a list instead of successive integers.

In this case the `collect` clause contributes code to all three phases. In the prologue an anonymous accumulator is set to `nil`; in the body `(1+ x)` is appended to this accumulator; and in the epilogue its value is returned.

This is the first example to return a particular value. There are clauses for explicitly specifying the return value, but in the absence of such clauses, a `collect` clause determines the return value. So what we've done here is duplicate `mapcar`.

The most common use of `loop` is probably to collect the results of calling a function a certain number of times:

```
> (loop for x from 1 to 5
        collect (random 10))
(3 8 6 5 0)
```

```
(defun most (fn lst)
  (if (null lst)
      (values nil nil)
      (let* ((wins (car lst))
             (max (funcall fn wins)))
        (dolist (obj (cdr lst))
          (let ((score (funcall fn obj)))
            (when (> score max)
              (setf wins obj
                    max  score))))
        (values wins max))))

(defun num-year (n)
  (if (< n 0)
      (do* ((y (- yzero 1) (- y 1))
            (d (- (year-days y)) (- d (year-days y))))
           ((<= d n) (values y (- n d))))
      (do* ((y yzero (+ y 1))
            (prev 0 d)
            (d (year-days y) (+ d (year-days y))))
           ((> d n) (values y (- n prev))))))
```

Figure 14.1: Iteration without loop.

Here we get a list of five random numbers. It was for cases like this that we
defined map-int (page 105). Why do we need map-int if we have loop?
One can as easily ask, why do we need loop if we have map-int?[°]

A collect clause can also accumulate its value into a named variable.
The following function takes a list of numbers and returns lists of the even
and odd elements:

```
(defun even/odd (ns)
  (loop for n in ns
        if (evenp n)
          collect n into evens
          else collect n into odds
        finally (return (values evens odds))))
```

A finally clause contributes code to the epilogue. In this case it specifies
the return value.

A sum clause is like a collect clause, but accumulates a number instead
of a list. To get the sum of the numbers from 1 to n we could write:

```
(defun most (fn lst)
  (if (null lst)
      (values nil nil)
      (loop with wins = (car lst)
            with max = (funcall fn wins)
            for obj in (cdr lst)
            for score = (funcall fn obj)
            when (> score max)
                 do (setf wins obj
                          max  score)
            finally (return (values wins max)))))

(defun num-year (n)
  (if (< n 0)
      (loop for y downfrom (- yzero 1)
            until (<= d n)
            sum (- (year-days y)) into d
            finally (return (values (+ y 1) (- n d))))
      (loop with prev = 0
            for y from yzero
            until (> d n)
            do (setf prev d)
            sum (year-days y) into d
            finally (return (values (- y 1)
                                    (- n prev)))))))
```

Figure 14.2: Iteration with `loop`.

```
(defun sum (n)
  (loop for x from 1 to n
        sum x))
```

Further details of `loop` are covered in Appendix D, beginning on page 325. As an example, Figure 14.1 contains two iterative functions from preceding chapters, and Figure 14.2 shows the same functions rendered into `loop`s.

One loop clause can refer to variables established by another. In the definition of even/odd, for example, the `finally` clause refers to the variables established by the two `collect` clauses. The relations between such variables are one of the greatest ambiguities in the definition of `loop`. Consider the following two expressions:

```
(loop for y = 0 then z
      for x from 1 to 5
      sum 1 into z
      finally (return (values y z)))

(loop for x from 1 to 5
      for y = 0 then z
      sum 1 into z
      finally (return (values y z)))
```

They seem simple enough—they each have only four clauses. Do they return the same values? What values do they return? You will search the standard in vain for the answers. Each loop clause is simple enough by itself. But the way they *combine* is extremely complicated—and ultimately, not even well-defined.

For such reasons, the use of loop cannot be recommended. The most that can be said for it, in typical examples like those shown in Figure 14.2, is that it makes the code look easier to understand.

14.6 Conditions

In Common Lisp, *conditions* include errors and other situations that can arise at run-time. When a condition is signalled, the corresponding handler is invoked. The default handler for error conditions usually invokes a break-loop. But Common Lisp provides a variety of operators for signalling and handling conditions. It's possible to override the default handlers, or even write new handlers of your own.

Most programmers will not deal with conditions directly. However, there are several layers of more abstract operators that use conditions, and to understand these operators it helps to know about the underlying mechanism.

Common Lisp has several operators for signalling errors. The most basic is error. One way to call it is to give it the same arguments that you might pass to format:

```
> (error "Your report uses ~A as a verb." 'status)
Error: Your report uses STATUS as a verb.
      Options: :abort, :backtrace
>>
```

Unless such a condition is handled, execution will be interrupted, as above.

More abstract operators for signalling errors include ecase, check-type and assert. The former is like case, but signals an error if none of the keys match:

```
> (ecase 1 (2 3) (4 5))
Error: No applicable clause.
        Options: :abort, :backtrace
>>
```

The regular case will return nil if no key matches, but since it's bad style to take advantage of this return value, you might as well use ecase whenever you don't have an otherwise clause.

The check-type macro takes a place, a type name, and an optional string, and signals a *correctable error* if the value of the place is not of the designated type. The handler for a correctable error will give us the option of providing a new value:

```
> (let ((x '(a b c)))
    (check-type (car x) integer "an integer")
    x)
Error: The value of (CAR X), A, should be an integer.
        Options: :abort, :backtrace, :continue
>> :continue
New value of (CAR X)? 99
(99 B C)
>
```

In this example, (car x) was set to the new value that we supplied, and execution resumed, returning what it would have returned if (car x) had originally contained the value we supplied.

This macro is defined in terms of the more general assert, which takes a test expression and a list of one or more places, followed by the arguments you might give to error:

```
> (let ((sandwich '(ham on rye)))
    (assert (eql (car sandwich) 'chicken)
            ((car sandwich))
            "I wanted a ~A sandwich." 'chicken)
    sandwich)
Error: I wanted a CHICKEN sandwich.
        Options: :abort, :backtrace, :continue
>> :continue
New value of (CAR SANDWICH)? 'chicken
(CHICKEN ON RYE)
>
```

It's also possible to establish new handlers, but most programmers will only take advantage of this possibility indirectly, by using macros like

ignore-errors. This macro behaves like progn if none of its arguments
cause an error. But if an error is signalled during the evaluation of one of its
arguments, execution will not be interrupted. Instead the ignore-errors
expression will immediately return two values: nil and the condition that
was signalled.

For example, if at some point you want the user to be able to enter an
expression, but you don't want an error to interrupt execution if the input is
syntactically ill-formed, you could write:

```
(defun user-input (prompt)
  (format t prompt)
  (let ((str (read-line)))
    (or (ignore-errors (read-from-string str))
        nil)))
```

This function just returns nil if the input contains syntax errors:

```
> (user-input "Please type an expression> ")
Please type an expression> #%@#+!!
NIL
```

15

Example: Inference

The next three chapters offer examples of substantial Lisp programs. These examples were chosen to illustrate the form that longer programs take, and also the kinds of problems for which Lisp is especially well-suited.

In this chapter we will write a program that makes inferences based on a collection of if-then rules. This is a classic example—not only in the sense that it often appears in textbooks, but also because it reflects the original idea of Lisp as a language for "symbolic computation." A lot of the earliest Lisp programs had the flavor of the example in this chapter.

15.1 The Aim

In this program, we're going to represent information in a familiar form: a list consisting of a predicate followed by zero or more arguments. To represent the fact that Donald is the parent of Nancy, we might say:

```
(parent donald nancy)
```

As well as facts, our program is going to represent rules that tell what can be inferred from the facts we already have. We will represent such rules as

```
(<- head body)
```

where *head* is the then-part and *body* is the if-part. Within the *head* and *body* we will represent variables as symbols beginning with question marks. So this rule

```
(<- (child ?x ?y) (parent ?y ?x))
```

says that if *y* is the parent of *x*, then *x* is the child of *y*; or more precisely, that we can prove any fact of the form (child *x y*) by proving (parent *y x*).

It will be possible for the body (if-part) of a rule to be a complex expression, containing the logical operators and, or, and not. So if we want to represent the rule that if *x* is the parent of *y*, and *x* is male, then *x* is the father of *y*, we would write:

```
(<- (father ?x ?y) (and (parent ?x ?y) (male ?x)))
```

Rules may depend on facts implied by other rules. For example, the first rule we wrote was for proving facts of the form (child *x y*). If we defined a rule

```
(<- (daughter ?x ?y) (and (child ?x ?y) (female ?x)))
```

then using it to prove (daughter *x y*) might cause the program to use the first rule to prove (child *x y*).

The proof of an expression can continue back through any number of rules, so long as it eventually ends up on the solid ground of known facts. This process is sometimes called *backward chaining*. The *backward* comes from the fact that this kind of inference first considers the then-part, to see if the rule will be useful, before going on to prove the if-part. The *chaining* comes from the way that rules can depend on other rules, forming a chain (though in fact it's more like a tree) that leads from what we want to prove back to what we already know.°

15.2 Matching

In order to write our backward-chaining program, we are going to need a function to do pattern-matching: a function that can compare two lists, possibly containing variables, to see if there is some way of assigning values to the variables which makes the two equal. For example, if ?x and ?y are variables, then the two lists

```
(p ?x ?y c ?x)
(p a  b c  a)
```

match when ?x = a and ?y = b, and the lists

```
(p ?x b ?y a)
(p ?y b  c a)
```

match when ?x = ?y = c.

Figure 15.1 contains a function called match. It takes two trees, and if they can be made to match, it returns an assoc-list showing how:

```
(defun match (x y &optional binds)
  (cond
   ((eql x y) (values binds t))
   ((assoc x binds) (match (binding x binds) y binds))
   ((assoc y binds) (match x (binding y binds) binds))
   ((var? x) (values (cons (cons x y) binds) t))
   ((var? y) (values (cons (cons y x) binds) t))
   (t
    (when (and (consp x) (consp y))
      (multiple-value-bind (b2 yes)
                           (match (car x) (car y) binds)
        (and yes (match (cdr x) (cdr y) b2))))))))

(defun var? (x)
  (and (symbolp x)
       (eql (char (symbol-name x) 0) #\?)))

(defun binding (x binds)
  (let ((b (assoc x binds)))
    (if b
        (or (binding (cdr b) binds)
            (cdr b)))))
```

Figure 15.1: Matching function.

```
> (match '(p a b c a) '(p ?x ?y c ?x))
((?Y . B) (?X . A))
T
> (match '(p ?x b ?y a) '(p ?y b c a))
((?Y . C) (?X . ?Y))
T
> (match '(a b c) '(a a a))
NIL
```

As match compares its arguments element by element, it builds up assignments of values to variables, called *bindings*, in the parameter binds. If the match is successful, match returns the bindings generated; otherwise, it returns nil. Since not all successful matches generate any bindings, match, like gethash, returns a second value to show that the match succeeded:

```
> (match '(p ?x) '(p ?x))
NIL
T
```

When match returns nil and t as above, it indicates a successful match that
yielded no bindings. In English, the match algorithm works as follows:

1. If x and y are eql they match; otherwise,

2. If x is a variable that has a binding, they match if it matches y; otherwise,

3. If y is a variable that has a binding, they match if it matches x; otherwise,

4. If x is a variable (without a binding), they match and thereby establish
   a binding for it; otherwise,

5. If y is a variable (without a binding), they match and thereby establish
   a binding for it; otherwise,

6. They match if they are both conses, and the cars match, and the cdrs
   match with the bindings generated thereby.

Here is an example illustrating, in order, each of the six cases:

```
> (match '(p ?v  b ?x  d (?z ?z))
         '(p  a ?w  c ?y ( e  e))
         '((?v . a) (?w . b)))
((?Z . E) (?Y . D) (?X . C) (?V . A) (?W . B))
T
```

To find the value (if there is one) associated with a variable in a list of
bindings, match calls binding. This function has to be recursive, because
matching can build up binding lists in which a variable is only indirectly
associated with its value: ?x might be bound to a in virtue of the list containing
both (?x . ?y) and (?y . a).

```
> (match '(?x a) '(?y ?y))
((?Y . A) (?X . ?Y))
T
```

By matching ?x with ?y and then ?y with a, we establish indirectly that ?x
must be a.

```
(defvar *rules* (make-hash-table))

(defmacro <- (con &optional ant)
  `(length (push (cons (cdr ',con) ',ant)
                 (gethash (car ',con) *rules*))))
```

Figure 15.2: Defining rules.

15.3   Answering Queries

Now that the concept of bindings has been introduced, we can say more precisely what our program will do: it will take an expression, possibly containing variables, and return all the bindings that make it true given the facts and rules that we have. For example, if we have just the fact

```
(parent donald nancy)
```

and we ask the program to prove

```
(parent ?x ?y)
```

it should return something like

```
(((?x . donald) (?y . nancy)))
```

which says that there is exactly one way for the expression to be true: if ?x is donald and ?y is nancy.

Now that we have a matching function we are already a good part of the way to our destination. Figure 15.2 contains the code for defining rules. The rules are going to be contained in a hash table called *rules*, hashed according to the predicate in the head. This imposes the restriction that we can't use variables in the predicate position. We could eliminate this restriction by keeping all such rules in a separate list, but then to prove something we would have to match it against every one.

We will use the same macro, <-, to define both facts and rules. A fact will be represented as a rule with a head but no body. This is consistent with our definition of rules. A rule says that you can prove the head by proving the body, so a rule with no body means that you don't have to prove anything to prove the head. Here are two familiar examples:

```
> (<- (parent donald nancy))
1
> (<- (child ?x ?y) (parent ?y ?x))
1
```

```
(defun prove (expr &optional binds)
  (case (car expr)
    (and (prove-and (reverse (cdr expr)) binds))
    (or  (prove-or (cdr expr) binds))
    (not (prove-not (cadr expr) binds))
    (t   (prove-simple (car expr) (cdr expr) binds)))))

(defun prove-simple (pred args binds)
  (mapcan #'(lambda (r)
              (multiple-value-bind (b2 yes)
                                   (match args (car r)
                                          binds)
                (when yes
                  (if (cdr r)
                      (prove (cdr r) b2)
                      (list b2)))))
          (mapcar #'change-vars
                  (gethash pred *rules*))))

(defun change-vars (r)
  (sublis (mapcar #'(lambda (v) (cons v (gensym "?")))
                  (vars-in r))
          r))

(defun vars-in (expr)
  (if (atom expr)
      (if (var? expr) (list expr))
      (union (vars-in (car expr))
             (vars-in (cdr expr)))))
```

Figure 15.3: Inference.

Calls to <- return the number of rules now stored under a given predicate; wrapping the push in a call to length saves us from seeing a big return value at the toplevel.

Figure 15.3 contains most of the code we need for inference. The function prove is the pivot on which inference turns. It takes an expression and an optional list of bindings. If the expression doesn't contain logical operators, it calls prove-simple, and it is here that chaining takes place. This function works by looking at all the rules with the right predicate, and trying to match the head of each with the fact it is trying to prove. For each head that matches,

it calls prove on the body, with the new bindings generated by the match.
The lists of bindings returned by each call to prove are then collected by
mapcan and returned:

```
> (prove-simple 'parent '(donald nancy) nil)
(NIL)
> (prove-simple 'child '(?x ?y) nil)
(((#:?6 . NANCY) (#:?5 . DONALD) (?Y . #:?5) (?X . #:?6)))
```

Both of the return values above indicate that there is one way to prove what we
asked about. (A failed proof would return nil.) The first example generated
one empty set of bindings, and the second generated one set of bindings in
which ?x and ?y were (indirectly) bound to nancy and donald.

Incidentally, we see here a good example of the point made on page 23.
Because our program is written in a functional style, we can test each function
interactively.

What about those gensyms in the second return value? If we are going to
use rules containing variables, we need to avoid the possibility of two rules
accidentally containing the same variable. If we define two rules as follows

```
(<- (child ?x ?y) (parent ?y ?x))

(<- (daughter ?y ?x) (and (child ?y ?x) (female ?y)))
```

then we mean that for *any* x and y, x is the child of y if y is the parent of x,
and for *any* x and y, y is the daughter of x if y is the child of x and female.
The relationship of the variables within each rule is significant, but the fact
that the two rules happen to use the same variables is entirely coincidental.

If we used these rules as written, they would not work that way. If we
tried to prove that a was b's daughter, matching against the head of the second
rule would leave ?y bound to a and ?x to b. We could not then match the
head of the first rule with these bindings:

```
> (match '(child ?y ?x)
         '(child ?x ?y)
         '((?y . a) (?x . b)))
NIL
```

To ensure that the variables in a rule imply only something about the relations
of arguments within that rule, we replace all the variables in a rule with
gensyms. This is the purpose of the function change-vars. A gensym
could not possibly turn up as a variable in another rule. But because rules can
be recursive, we also have to guard against the possibility of a rule clashing
with itself, so change-vars has to be called not just when a rule is defined,
but each time it is used.

```
(defun prove-and (clauses binds)
  (if (null clauses)
      (list binds)
      (mapcan #'(lambda (b)
                   (prove (car clauses) b))
              (prove-and (cdr clauses) binds)))))

(defun prove-or (clauses binds)
  (mapcan #'(lambda (c) (prove c binds))
          clauses))

(defun prove-not (clause binds)
  (unless (prove clause binds)
    (list binds)))
```

Figure 15.4: Logical operators.

```
(defmacro with-answer (query &body body)
  (let ((binds (gensym)))
    `(dolist (,binds (prove ',query))
       (let ,(mapcar #'(lambda (v)
                          `(,v (binding ',v ,binds)))
                     (vars-in query))
         ,@body))))
```

Figure 15.5: Interface macro.

Now all that remains is to define the functions that prove complex expressions. These are shown in Figure 15.4. Handling an or or not expression is particularly simple. In the former case we collect all the bindings returned by each of the expressions within the or. In the latter case, we return the current bindings iff the expression within the not yields none.

The function prove-and is only a little more complicated. It works like a filter, proving the first expression for each set of bindings that can be established for the remaining expressions. This would cause the expressions within the and to be considered in reverse order, except that the call to prove-and within prove reverses them to compensate.

Now we have a working program, but it's not very user-friendly. It's a nuisance to have to decipher the lists of bindings returned by prove—and

```
(with-answer (p ?x ?y)
  (f ?x ?y))
```

is macroexpanded into:

```
(dolist (#:g1 (prove '(p ?x ?y)))
  (let ((?x (binding '?x #:g1))
        (?y (binding '?y #:g1)))
    (f ?x ?y)))
```

Figure 15.6: Expansion of a call to with-answer.

they only get longer as the rules get more complex. Figure 15.5 contains a macro that will make our program more pleasant to use: a with-answer expression will take a query (not evaluated) and a body of expressions, and will evaluate its body once for each set of bindings generated by the query, with each pattern variable bound to the value it has in the bindings.

```
> (with-answer (parent ?x ?y)
    (format t "~A is the parent of ~A.~%" ?x ?y))
DONALD is the parent of NANCY.
NIL
```

This macro does the work of deciphering the bindings for us, and gives us a convenient way of using prove in programs. Figure 15.6 shows what an expansion looks like, and Figure 15.7 shows some examples of it in use.

15.4   Analysis

It may seem as if the code we've written in this chapter is simply the natural way to implement such a program. In fact it is grossly inefficient. What we've done here, essentially, is to write an interpreter. We could implement the same program as a compiler.

Here is a sketch of how it would be done. The basic idea would be to pack the whole program into the macros <- and with-answer, and make them do at macro-expansion time most of the work the program now does at run-time. (The germ of this idea is visible in avg, on page 170.) Instead of representing rules as lists, we would represent them as functions, and instead of having functions like prove and prove-and to interpret expressions at run-time, we would have corresponding functions to transform expressions into code. The expressions are available at the time a rule is defined. Why wait until it

If we do a (clrhash *rules*) and then define the following rules and
facts,

```
(<- (parent donald nancy))
(<- (parent donald debbie))
(<- (male donald))
(<- (father ?x ?y) (and (parent ?x ?y) (male ?x)))
(<- (= ?x ?x))
(<- (sibling ?x ?y) (and (parent ?z ?x)
                         (parent ?z ?y)
                         (not (= ?x ?y))))
```

we will be able to make inferences like the following:

```
> (with-answer (father ?x ?y)
    (format t "~A is the father of ~A.~%" ?x ?y))
DONALD is the father of DEBBIE.
DONALD is the father of NANCY.
NIL
> (with-answer (sibling ?x ?y)
    (format t "~A is the sibling of ~A.~%" ?x ?y))
DEBBIE is the sibling of NANCY.
NANCY is the sibling of DEBBIE.
NIL
```

Figure 15.7: The program in use.

is used in order to analyze them? The same goes for with-answer, which
would call the same functions as <- to generate its expansion.

This sounds like it would be a lot more complicated than the program
we wrote in this chapter, but in fact it would probably only be about two or
three times as long. Readers who would like to learn about such techniques
should see *On Lisp* or *Paradigms of Artificial Intelligence Programming*,
which contain several examples of programs written in this style.

16

Example: Generating HTML

In this chapter we will write a simple HTML generator—a program that automatically generates collections of interlinked web pages. As well as illustrating particular Lisp techniques, this chapter offers a characteristic example of bottom-up programming. We begin with general-purpose HTML utilities, and then treat them like a programming language in which to write the generator proper.

16.1 HTML

HTML (HyperText Markup Language) is what web pages are made of. It is a very simple language. But, if there's not much you can do with HTML, it does have the advantage of being easy to learn. This section gives an overview of HTML.

You view web pages using a program called a *web browser*. The browser retrieves HTML files, usually from a remote computer, and displays them on your screen. An HTML file is a text file containing *tags* that act as instructions to the browser.

Figure 16.1 contains an example of a simple HTML file, and Figure 16.2 shows how this page might be displayed by a web browser. Notice that the text between angle brackets is not displayed. These are the tags. HTML has two sorts of tags. One kind appear in pairs of the form

```
<tag> ... </tag>
```

The first tag marks the beginning of some kind of environment, and the second marks the end. One tag of this kind is <h2>. All the text that occurs between

257

```
<center>
<h2>Your Fortune</h2>
</center>
<br><br>
Welcome to the home page of the Fortune Cookie
Institute.  FCI is a non-profit institution
dedicated to the development of more realistic
fortunes.  Here are some examples of fortunes
that fall within our guidelines:
<ol>
<li>Your nostril hairs will grow longer.
<li>You will never learn how to dress properly.
<li>Your car will be stolen.
<li>You will gain weight.
</ol>
Click <a href="research.html">here</a> to learn
more about our ongoing research projects.
```

Figure 16.1: An HTML file.

Your Fortune

Welcome to the home page of the Fortune Cookie Institute. FCI is a non-profit institution dedicated to the development of more realistic fortunes. Here are some examples of fortunes that fall within our guidelines:

1. Your nostril hairs will grow longer.

2. You will never learn how to dress properly.

3. Your car will be stolen.

4. You will gain weight.

Click **here** to learn more about our ongoing research projects.

Figure 16.2: Display of a web page.

an `<h2>` and `</h2>` will be displayed in a larger font. (The largest font is `<h1>`.)

Other tags that come in pairs include `<ol>` ("ordered list"), which creates a numbered list, `<center>`, which causes text to be centered, and `<a...>` ("anchor"), which creates a link.

It's the links that make text into hypertext. Text that comes between `<a...>` and `</a>` will be displayed by most browsers in a distinctive way—usually it will be underlined—and clicking on that text can make the browser jump to another page. The part of the tag that comes after the a tells the browser where to go when someone clicks on the link. A tag like

```
<a href="foo.html">
```

indicates a link to another HTML file in the same directory. So when anyone clicks on the link in Figure 16.2, their browser will retrieve and display the page stored in `"research.html"`.

Links do not have to point to files in the same directory. Our example doesn't show this, but links can refer to files anywhere on the Internet.

The other kind of tag doesn't have an end marker. Tags of this kind in Figure 16.1 include `<br>` ("break"), which indicates a newline, and `<li>` ("list item"), which indicates a new item within a list environment. HTML has more tags than this, but the ones used in Figure 16.1 will be almost all we'll need in this chapter.

16.2   HTML Utilities

In this section we'll define some utilities for generating HTML. Figure 16.3 contains basic utilities for generating tags. All send their output to `*standard-output*`; we will be able to redirect the output to a file by rebinding this variable.

The macros as and with are both for generating expressions between tags. The former takes a string and prints it between tags,

```
> (as center "The Missing Lambda")
<center>The Missing Lambda</center>
NIL
```

while the latter takes a body of code and puts it between calls that print tags:

```
> (with center
    (princ "The Unbalanced Parenthesis"))
<center>
The Unbalanced Parenthesis
</center>
NIL
```

```
(defmacro as (tag content)
  '(format t "<~(~A~)>~A</~(~A~)>"
              ',tag ,content ',tag))

(defmacro with (tag &rest body)
  '(progn
     (format t "~&<~(~A~)>~%" ',tag)
     ,@body
     (format t "~&</~(~A~)>~%" ',tag)))

(defun brs (&optional (n 1))
  (fresh-line)
  (dotimes (i n)
    (princ "<br>"))
  (terpri))
```

Figure 16.3: Utilities for generating tags.

Both use the ~(...~) format directive to generate lowercase tags. Case is not significant in tags, but HTML files that contain a lot of tags are easier to read if the tags are lowercase.

While as tends to put its output all on one line, with puts the tags on separate lines. (The ~& format directive ensures that output begins on a new line.) This is done only to make the HTML files more readable. Whitespace around tags has no effect when the pages are displayed.

The last utility in Figure 16.3, brs, just generates multiple line breaks. In many browsers these can be used to control vertical spacing.

Figure 16.4 contains utilities for use in generating HTML files. The first returns the name of the file corresponding to a symbol. In a real application, this function might return a path to a designated directory. Here it simply appends ".html" to the symbol's name.

The macro page is for generating a whole web page. It is similar in spirit to with-open-file, on which it's built. The expressions in the body will be evaluated with *standard-output* bound to a stream made by opening the HTML file corresponding to name.

Section 6.7 showed how we could bind a special variable temporarily. In the example on page 113, we bound *print-base* to 16 for the duration of a let. The expansion of page similarly binds *standard-output* to a stream that points to an HTML file. If we call as or princ within the body of a page, the output gets sent to the corresponding file.

```
(defun html-file (base)
  (format nil "~(~A~).html" base))

(defmacro page (name title &rest body)
  (let ((ti (gensym)))
    `(with-open-file (*standard-output*
                        (html-file ,name)
                        :direction :output
                        :if-exists :supersede)
       (let ((,ti ,title))
         (as title ,ti)
         (with center
           (as h2 (string-upcase ,ti)))
         (brs 3)
         ,@body))))
```

Figure 16.4: HTML file utilities.

The `title` will be printed at the top of the page, followed by whatever output is generated by the body. So the call

```
(page 'paren "The Unbalanced Parenthesis"
  (princ "Something in his expression told her..."))
```

will cause the file "paren.html" (as html-file is currently defined) to contain:

```
<title>The Unbalanced Parenthesis</title>
<center>
<h2>THE UNBALANCED PARENTHESIS</h2>
</center>
<br><br><br>
Something in his expression told her...
```

All the tags here are ones we've seen before, except `<title>`. The text given as the `<title>` in an HTML file does not appear on the page itself; it is usually the title of the window containing the page.

Figure 16.5 contains utilities for generating links. The `with-link` macro is similar in spirit to `with`. It takes a body of code, which will be evaluated between expressions that generate a link to the HTML file whose base name is given as the second argument:

```
(defmacro with-link (dest &rest body)
  `(progn
     (format t "<a href=\"~A\">" (html-file ,dest))
     ,@body
     (princ "</a>")))

(defun link-item (dest text)
  (princ "<li>")
  (with-link dest
    (princ text)))

(defun button (dest text)
  (princ "[ ")
  (with-link dest
    (princ text))
  (format t " ]~%"))
```

Figure 16.5: Utilities for generating links.

```
> (with-link 'capture
    (princ "The Captured Variable"))
<a href="capture.html">The Captured Variable</a>
"</a>"
```

It is used in link-item, which takes a string and generates a list item that is also a link,

```
> (link-item 'bq "Backquote!")
<li><a href="bq.html">Backquote!</a>
"</a>"
```

and in button, which generates a link between square brackets,

```
> (button 'help "Help")
[ <a href="help.html">Help</a> ]
NIL
```

so that it resembles a button.

16.3   An Iteration Utility

In this section we pause to define a general-purpose utility that we are going to need in the program proper. How do we know beforehand that we are

```
(defun map3 (fn lst)
  (labels ((rec (curr prev next left)
             (funcall fn curr prev next)
             (when left
               (rec (car left)
                    curr
                    (cadr left)
                    (cdr left)))))
    (when lst
      (rec (car lst) nil (cadr lst) (cdr lst)))))
```

Figure 16.6: Iteration by threes.

going to need a new utility? We don't. What usually happens is that you start writing a program, discover the need for the new utility, stop to write it, then continue writing the original program. But it would be confusing to represent here all the stops and starts of real programming. Instead we consider just the final results, with the caveat that writing such programs is never so straightforward as it might seem. It takes a lot of rewriting to make a program simple.

Our new utility will be a variant of mapc. It is defined in Figure 16.6. It takes a function and a list, and for each element of the list, calls the function with three arguments: that element, the previous element, and the next element. (It uses nil when there is no previous or next element.)

```
> (map3 #'(lambda (&rest args) (princ args))
        '(a b c d))
(A NIL B)(B A C)(C B D)(D C NIL)
NIL
```

Like mapc it always returns nil. Situations that call for this kind of utility arise often. We will see one in the next section, where we want to make each page have a link to the previous page and the next one.

A subset of the general problem happens when you want to do something between each pair of elements in a list:

```
> (map3 #'(lambda (c p n)
            (princ c)
            (if n (princ " | ")))
        '(a b c d))
A | B | C | D
NIL
```

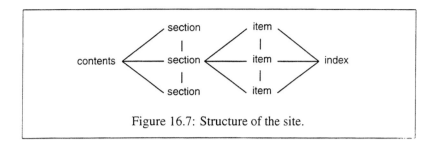

Figure 16.7: Structure of the site.

Programmers frequently encounter this kind of problem—not often enough
for a language to have a built-in operator for it, perhaps, but often enough
that it is very convenient to be able to define such an operator oneself.

16.4   Generating Pages

Like books and magazines, collections of web pages are often organized in
the form of a tree. A book can contain chapters, which contain sections,
which contain subsections, and so on. Collections of web pages typically
have the same shape, even if they don't use the same names.

In this section we'll build a program that can generate collections of web
pages. They will be structured as follows. The first page will be a table of
contents, with links to pages representing one or more *sections*. Each section
will be a page of links to *items* contained in that section. An item will be a
page containing ordinary text.

As well as these links, which follow the lines of the tree, each page will
have links leading backward, up, and forward. The backward and forward
links will lead to the preceding or succeeding sibling page. For example, the
forward link on an item's page will lead to the next item in the same section,
if there is one. The up links will lead back up the tree—from item to section,
and from section to table of contents. There will also be an index: this will be
another page of links, listing all the items in alphabetical order. Figure 16.7
shows the structure of the links between the pages our program will generate.

Figure 16.8 contains the data structures that we'll need and the operators
for defining pages. Our program will deal with two kinds of objects: items
and sections. They have similar structures, but where a section will contain a
list of items, an item will contain a block of text.

Both sections and items have an `id` field. Ids will be symbols, and serve
two purposes. One we see in the definitions of `defitem` and `defsection`:
the id will be *set* to the item or section we create, which gives us a way of
referring to it. The ids will also serve as the base names of the corresponding
files, so the page representing an item `foo`, for example, will be written to
`"foo.html"`.

```
(defparameter *sections* nil)

(defstruct item
  id title text)

(defstruct section
  id title items)

(defmacro defitem (id title text)
  `(setf ,id
         (make-item :id      ',id
                    :title ,title
                    :text  ,text)))

(defmacro defsection (id title &rest items)
  `(setf ,id
         (make-section :id      ',id
                       :title ,title
                       :items (list ,@items))))

(defun defsite (&rest sections)
  (setf *sections* sections))
```

Figure 16.8: Defining a site.

Sections and items also both have `title` fields. These should be strings, and will be used as the titles of the corresponding pages.

The order of items within a section will be that of the arguments to `defsection`. The order of the sections in the table of contents is similarly determined by the arguments to `defsite`.

Figure 16.9 contains the functions that generate the index and the table of contents. The constants `contents` and `index` are strings that will serve as both the titles of those pages and the base names of the files containing them.

The functions `gen-contents` and `gen-index` are similar in outline. Both open an HTML file, generate a title, and then generate a list of links. They differ in that the list of items in the index has to be sorted first. This list is built by `all-items`, which looks at each item and merges it into a list of items seen so far, using `title<` as the ordering function. It's important that the titles are compared using `string-lessp`, which ignores case, rather than `string<`, which doesn't.

```
(defconstant contents "contents")
(defconstant index    "index")

(defun gen-contents (&optional (sections *sections*))
  (page contents contents
    (with ol
      (dolist (s sections)
        (link-item (section-id s) (section-title s))
        (brs 2))
      (link-item index (string-capitalize index)))))

(defun gen-index (&optional (sections *sections*))
  (page index index
    (with ol
      (dolist (i (all-items sections))
        (link-item (item-id i) (item-title i))
        (brs 2)))))

(defun all-items (sections)
  (let ((is nil))
    (dolist (s sections)
      (dolist (i (section-items s))
        (setf is (merge 'list (list i) is #'title<))))
    is))

(defun title< (x y)
  (string-lessp (item-title x) (item-title y)))
```

Figure 16.9: Generating index and table of contents.

In a real application, the comparison would have to be more sophisticated. It would at least have to ignore initial articles like "a" and "the", for example.

Figure 16.10 contains the remainder of the code: gen-site, which generates the whole collection of web pages, along with the functions it calls to generate sections and items.

The whole collection of pages means the table of contents, the index, the pages representing each section, and the pages representing each item. The table of contents and the index are generated by the functions in Figure 16.9. The sections and items are generated by gen-section, which generates the page for the section, and calls gen-item to generate a page for each item in that section.

```
(defun gen-site ()
  (map3 #'gen-section *sections*)
  (gen-contents)
  (gen-index))

(defun gen-section (sect <sect sect>)
  (page (section-id sect) (section-title sect)
    (with ol
      (map3 #'(lambda (item <item item>)
                (link-item (item-id item)
                           (item-title item))
                (brs 2)
                (gen-item sect item <item item>))
            (section-items sect)))
    (brs 3)
    (gen-move-buttons (if <sect (section-id <sect))
                      contents
                      (if sect> (section-id sect>)))))

(defun gen-item (sect item <item item>)
  (page (item-id item) (item-title item)
    (princ (item-text item))
    (brs 3)
    (gen-move-buttons (if <item (item-id <item))
                      (section-id sect)
                      (if item> (item-id item>)))))

(defun gen-move-buttons (back up forward)
  (if back (button back "Back"))
  (if up (button up "Up"))
  (if forward (button forward "Forward")))
```

Figure 16.10: Generating site, sections, and items.

The two functions begin and end similarly. Both take arguments representing an object, its left sibling, and its right sibling; both begin with a title taken from the title field of the object; both end by calling gen-move-buttons to generate buttons that lead back to the left sibling, up to the parent object, and forward to the right sibling. It's in the middle that gen-section and gen-item differ. While the former generates an ordered list of links to the items it contains, the latter just dumps its text to the output file.

```
(defitem des "Fortune Cookies: Dessert or Fraud?" "...")

(defitem case "The Case for Pessimism" "...")

(defsection position "Position Papers" des case)

(defitem luck "Distribution of Bad Luck" "...")

(defitem haz "Health Hazards of Optimism" "...")

(defsection abstract "Research Abstracts" luck haz)

(defsite position abstract)
```

Figure 16.11: A small site.

What the text of an item contains is entirely up to the user. It's perfectly
ok for it to contain HTML tags, for example. The text could well be generated
by another program.

Figure 16.11 shows how one might define a small collection of pages by
hand. In this example, the items are recent publications of the Fortune Cookie
Institute.

17

Example: Objects

In this chapter we're going to implement our own object-oriented language within Lisp. Such a program is called an *embedded language*. Embedding an object-oriented language in Lisp makes an ideal example. As well as being a characteristic use of Lisp, it shows how naturally the abstractions of object-oriented programming map onto the fundamental abstractions of Lisp.

17.1 Inheritance

Section 11.10 explained how generic functions differ from message-passing. In the message-passing model,

1. objects have properties,

2. and respond to messages,

3. and inherit properties and methods from their parents.

CLOS, of course, uses the generic function model. But in this chapter we are interested in writing a minimal object system, not a rival to CLOS, so we will use the older model.

In Lisp, there are already several ways to store collections of properties. One way would be to represent objects as hash tables, and store their properties as entries within them. We then have access to individual properties through gethash:

```
(gethash 'color obj)
```

```
(defun rget (prop obj)
  (multiple-value-bind (val in) (gethash prop obj)
    (if in
        (values val in)
        (let ((par (gethash :parent obj)))
          (and par (rget prop par))))))

(defun tell (obj message &rest args)
  (apply (rget message obj) obj args))
```

Figure 17.1: Inheritance.

Since functions are data objects, we can store them as properties too. This means that we can also have methods; to invoke a given method of an object is to funcall the property of that name:

```
(funcall (gethash 'move obj) obj 10)
```

We can define a Smalltalk style message-passing syntax upon this idea,

```
(defun tell (obj message &rest args)
  (apply (gethash message obj) obj args))
```

so that to tell obj to move 10, we can say

```
(tell obj 'move 10)
```

In fact, the only ingredient plain Lisp lacks is inheritance. We can implement a simple version of that by defining a recursive version of gethash, as in Figure 17.1. (The name rget stands for "recursive get.") Now with a total of eight lines of code we have all three of the minimal elements of object-oriented programming.

Let's try out this code on our original example. We create two objects, one a child of the other:

```
> (setf circle-class        (make-hash-table)
        our-circle          (make-hash-table)
        (gethash :parent our-circle) circle-class
        (gethash 'radius our-circle) 2)
2
```

The object circle-class will hold the area method for all circles. It will be a function of one argument, the object to which the message is originally sent:

```
> (setf (gethash 'area circle-class)
        #'(lambda (x)
            (* pi (expt (rget 'radius x) 2))))
#<Interpreted-Function BF1EF6>
```

Now we can ask for the area of our-circle, and its value will be calculated according to the method defined for the class. We use rget to read a property, and tell to invoke a method:

```
> (rget 'radius our-circle)
2
T
> (tell our-circle 'area)
12.566370614359173
```

Before going on to improve this program, it's worth pausing to consider what we have done. With eight lines of code we have made plain old pre-CLOS Lisp into an object-oriented language. How did we manage to achieve such a feat? There must be some sort of trick involved, to implement object-oriented programming in eight lines of code.

There is a trick, but it is not a programming trick. The trick is, Lisp already was an object-oriented language, or rather, something more general. All we had to do was put a new facade on the abstractions that were already there.

17.2 Multiple Inheritance

So far we have only single inheritance—an object can only have one parent. But we can have multiple inheritance by making the parent property a list, and defining rget as in Figure 17.2.

With single inheritance, when we wanted to retrieve some property of an object, we just searched recursively up its ancestors. If the object itself had no information about the property we wanted, we looked at its parent, and so on. With multiple inheritance we want to perform the same kind of search, but our job is complicated by the fact that an object's ancestors can form a graph instead of a simple tree. We can't just search this graph depth-first. With multiple parents we can have the hierarchy shown in Figure 17.3: a is descended from b and c, which are both descended from d. A depth-first (or rather, height-first) traversal would go a, b, d, c, d. If the desired property were present in both d and c, we would get the value stored in d, not the one stored in c. This would violate the principle that subclasses override the default values provided by their parents.

If we want to implement the usual idea of inheritance, we should never examine an object before one of its descendants. In this case, the proper

```
(defun rget (prop obj)
  (dolist (c (precedence obj))
    (multiple-value-bind (val in) (gethash prop c)
      (if in (return (values val in))))))

(defun precedence (obj)
  (labels ((traverse (x)
             (cons x
                   (mapcan #'traverse
                           (gethash :parents x)))))
    (delete-duplicates (traverse obj))))
```

Figure 17.2: Multiple inheritance.

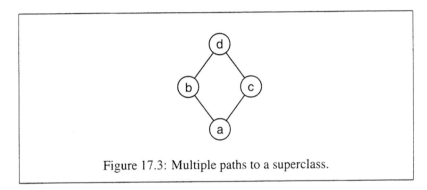

Figure 17.3: Multiple paths to a superclass.

search order would be a, b, c, d. How can we ensure that the search always tries descendants first? The simplest way is to assemble a list of an object and all its ancestors in the proper precedence order, then look at each one in turn.

The function precedence returns a list of an object and all its ancestors in the correct order. It begins by calling traverse to build a list representing the objects encountered in a depth-first traversal. If any of the objects share parents, there will be duplicates in this list. If we preserve only the last of each set of duplicates, we will get a precedence list in the natural order defined by CLOS. (Deleting all but the last duplicate corresponds to rule 3 in the algorithm described on page 183.) The Common Lisp function delete-duplicates is defined to behave this way, so if we just call it on the result of the depth-first traversal, we will get the correct precedence list. Once the precedence list is created, rget searches for the first object with the desired property.

By taking advantage of precedence we can say, for example, that a patriotic scoundrel is a scoundrel first and a patriot second:

```
> (setf scoundrel             (make-hash-table)
        patriot               (make-hash-table)
        patriotic-scoundrel   (make-hash-table)
        (gethash 'serves scoundrel) 'self
        (gethash 'serves patriot)   'country
        (gethash :parents patriotic-scoundrel)
               (list scoundrel patriot))
(#<Hash-Table C41C7E> #<Hash-Table C41F0E>)
> (rget 'serves patriotic-scoundrel)
SELF
T
```

At this point we have a program that's powerful, but ugly and inefficient. In the second stage of the life of a Lisp program, we refine this sketch into something usable.

17.3 Defining Objects

Among the first improvements we need is a function to create objects. The way our program represents objects and their parents need not be visible to the user. If we define a function to build objects, users will be able to make an object and specify its parents in one step. And we can build an object's precedence list at the time it is created, instead of expensively reconstructing it every time we need to find a property or a method.

If we are going to maintain precedence lists instead of constructing them as we need them, we have to deal with the possibility of the lists becoming outdated. Our strategy will be to keep a list of all existing objects, and whenever something's parents are modified, to remake the precedence list of every object affected. This is expensive, but since queries are likely to be much more common than the redefinition of objects' parents, we will get a net saving. Our program will not become any less flexible by this change; we just shift costs from a frequent operation to an infrequent one.

Figure 17.4 contains the new code.° The global *objs* will be a list of all current objects. The function parents retrieves an object's parents; its converse (setf parents) not only sets an object's parents, but calls make-precedence to rebuild any precedence list that might thereby have changed. The lists are built by precedence, as before.

Now instead of calling make-hash-table to make objects, users will call obj, which creates a new object and defines its parents in one step. We also redefine rget to take advantage of stored precedence lists.

```
(defvar *objs* nil)

(defun parents (obj) (gethash :parents obj))

(defun (setf parents) (val obj)
  (prog1 (setf (gethash :parents obj) val)
         (make-precedence obj)))

(defun make-precedence (obj)
  (setf (gethash :preclist obj) (precedence obj))
  (dolist (x *objs*)
    (if (member obj (gethash :preclist x))
        (setf (gethash :preclist x) (precedence x)))))

(defun obj (&rest parents)
  (let ((obj (make-hash-table)))
    (push obj *objs*)
    (setf (parents obj) parents)
    obj))

(defun rget (prop obj)
  (dolist (c (gethash :preclist obj))
    (multiple-value-bind (val in) (gethash prop c)
      (if in (return (values val in))))))
```

Figure 17.4: Creating objects.

17.4   Functional Syntax

Another place for improvement is the syntax of message calls. The `tell` itself is unnecessary clutter, and because it makes verbs come third, it means that our programs can no longer be read like normal Lisp prefix expressions:

```
(tell (tell obj 'find-owner) 'find-owner)
```

We can get rid of the `tell` syntax by defining property names as functions, using the macro `defprop` in Figure 17.5. The optional argument `meth?`, if true, signals that this property should be treated as a method. Otherwise it will be treated as a slot, and the value retrieved by `rget` will simply be returned. Once we have defined the name of either kind of property,

```
(defprop find-owner t)
```

```
(defmacro defprop (name &optional meth?)
  `(progn
     (defun ,name (obj &rest args)
       ,(if meth?
            `(run-methods obj ',name args)
            `(rget ',name obj)))
     (defun (setf ,name) (val obj)
       (setf (gethash ',name obj) val))))

(defun run-methods (obj name args)
  (let ((meth (rget name obj)))
    (if meth
        (apply meth obj args)
        (error "No ~A method for ~A." name obj))))
```

Figure 17.5: Functional syntax.

we can refer to it with a function call, and our code will read like Lisp again:

```
(find-owner (find-owner obj))
```

Our previous example now becomes somewhat more readable:

```
> (progn
    (setf scoundrel           (obj)
          patriot             (obj)
          patriotic-scoundrel (obj scoundrel patriot))
    (defprop serves)
    (setf (serves scoundrel) 'self
          (serves patriot)   'country)
    (serves patriotic-scoundrel))
SELF
T
```

17.5   Defining Methods

So far we define a method by saying something like:

```
(defprop area t)
```

```
(setf circle-class (obj))
```

```
(defmacro defmeth (name obj parms &rest body)
  (let ((gobj (gensym)))
    `(let ((,gobj ,obj))
       (setf (gethash ',name ,gobj)
             (labels ((next () (get-next ,gobj ',name)))
               #'(lambda ,parms ,@body))))))

(defun get-next (obj name)
  (some #'(lambda (x) (gethash name x))
        (cdr (gethash :preclist obj))))
```

Figure 17.6: Defining methods.

```
(setf (area circle-class)
      #'(lambda (c) (* pi (expt (radius c) 2))))
```

Within a method we can get the effect of the built-in call-next-method by calling the first thing we can find under the same name in the cdr of the object's :preclist. So, for example, if we want to define a special circle that prints something in the process of returning its area, we say:

```
(setf grumpy-circle (obj circle-class))

(setf (area grumpy-circle)
      #'(lambda (c)
          (format t "How dare you stereotype me!~%")
          (funcall (some #'(lambda (x) (gethash 'area x))
                         (cdr (gethash :preclist c)))
                   c)))
```

The funcall here is equivalent to a call-next-method, but it shows more internals than we want to look at.

The macro defmeth in Figure 17.6 provides a convenient way to define methods, and makes it easy to call the next method within them. A call to defmeth expands into a setf, but the setf occurs within a labels expression that defines next as a function to retrieve the next method. This function is like next-method-p (page 188), but returns something we can call, and so serves the purpose of call-next-method as well.° Now the preceding two methods could be defined:

```
(defmeth area circle-class (c)
  (* pi (expt (radius c) 2)))
```

```
(defmeth area grumpy-circle (c)
  (format t "How dare you stereotype me!~%")
  (funcall (next) c))
```

Incidentally, notice that the definition of defmeth takes advantage of symbol capture. The body of the method is inserted into a context where the function next is locally defined.

17.6 Instances

So far we have not distinguished between classes and instances. We have used a single term, *object*, to cover both. It is elegant and flexible to treat all objects the same, but grossly inefficient. In most object-oriented applications the inheritance graph will be bottom-heavy. In a simulation of traffic, for example, we might have less than ten objects representing classes of vehicles, and hundreds of objects representing particular vehicles. Since the latter will all share a few precedence lists, it is a waste of time to create them, and a waste of space to store them.

Figure 17.7 defines a macro inst, for making instances. Instances are like other objects (which now may as well be called classes), but have only one parent and do not maintain precedence lists. They are also not included in the list *objs*. In the preceding examples, we could have said:

```
(setf grumpy-circle (inst circle-class))
```

Since some objects will no longer have precedence lists, the functions rget and get-next are now redefined to look at the parents of such objects instead. This gain in efficiency has cost us nothing in flexibility. We can do everything with an instance that we can do with any other kind of object, including make instances of it and redefine its parents. In the latter case, (setf parents) will effectively convert the object to a "class."

17.7 New Implementation

None of the improvements we've made so far have been made at the expense of flexibility. In the latter stages of its development, a Lisp program can usually benefit from some sacrifice of flexibility, and this case is no exception. So far we have been representing all objects as hash tables. This gives us more flexibility than we need, at greater cost than we want. In this section we will rewrite our program to represent objects as simple vectors.

```
(defun inst (parent)
  (let ((obj (make-hash-table)))
    (setf (gethash :parents obj) parent)
    obj))

(defun rget (prop obj)
  (let ((prec (gethash :preclist obj)))
    (if prec
        (dolist (c prec)
          (multiple-value-bind (val in) (gethash prop c)
            (if in (return (values val in)))))
        (multiple-value-bind (val in) (gethash prop obj)
          (if in
              (values val in)
              (rget prop (gethash :parents obj)))))))

(defun get-next (obj name)
  (let ((prec (gethash :preclist obj)))
    (if prec
        (some #'(lambda (x) (gethash name x))
              (cdr prec))
        (get-next (gethash obj :parents) name))))
```

Figure 17.7: Defining instances.

This change will mean giving up the possibility of defining new properties
on the fly. So far we can define a property of any object simply by referring
to it. Now when a class is created, we will have to give a list of the new
properties it has, and when instances are created, they will have exactly the
properties they inherit.

In the previous implementation there was no real division between classes
and instances. An instance was just a class that happened to have one parent.
If we modified the parents of an instance, it would become a class. In the new
implementation there will be a real division between classes and instances; it
will no longer be possible to convert instances to classes.

The code in Figures 17.8–17.10 is a complete new implementation. Figure 17.8 defines the new operators for creating classes and instances. Classes
and instances are represented as vectors. The first three elements of each will
contain information used by the program itself, and the first three macros in
Figure 17.8 are for referring to these elements:

```
(defmacro parents (v) '(svref ,v 0))
(defmacro layout (v) '(the simple-vector (svref ,v 1)))
(defmacro preclist (v) '(svref ,v 2))

(defmacro class (&optional parents &rest props)
  '(class-fn (list ,@parents) ',props))

(defun class-fn (parents props)
  (let* ((all (union (inherit-props parents) props))
         (obj (make-array (+ (length all) 3)
                          :initial-element :nil)))
    (setf (parents obj)  parents
          (layout obj)   (coerce all 'simple-vector)
          (preclist obj) (precedence obj))
    obj))

(defun inherit-props (classes)
  (delete-duplicates
    (mapcan #'(lambda (c)
                (nconc (coerce (layout c) 'list)
                       (inherit-props (parents c))))
            classes)))

(defun precedence (obj)
  (labels ((traverse (x)
             (cons x
                   (mapcan #'traverse (parents x)))))
    (delete-duplicates (traverse obj))))

(defun inst (parent)
  (let ((obj (copy-seq parent)))
    (setf (parents obj)  parent
          (preclist obj) nil)
    (fill obj :nil :start 3)
    obj))
```

Figure 17.8: Vector implementation: Creation.

1. The parents field takes the place of the :parents hash table entry in the old implementation. In a class it will contain a list of parent classes. In an instance it will contain a single parent class.

2. The layout field will contain a vector of property names, indicating the layout of the class or instance from the fourth element on.

3. The preclist field takes the place of the :preclist hash table entry in the old implementation. It will contain the precedence list of a class, or nil in an instance.

Because these operators are macros, they can all be used in the first argument to setf (Section 10.6).

The macro class is for creating classes. It takes an optional list of superclasses, followed by zero or more property names. It returns an object representing a class. The new class will have the union of its local properties (that is, property names) and those inherited from all its superclasses.

```
> (setf *print-array* nil
        geom-class    (class nil area)
        circle-class  (class (geom-class) radius))
#<Simple-Vector T 5 C6205E>
```

Here we create two classes: geom-class has no superclasses, and only one property, area; circle-class is a subclass of geom-class, and adds the property radius.[1] The layout of circle-class

```
> (coerce (layout circle-class) 'list)
(AREA RADIUS)
```

shows the names of the last two of its five fields.[2]

The class macro is just an interface to class-fn, which does the real work. It calls inherit-props to assemble a list of the properties of all the new object's parents, builds a vector of the right length, and sets the first three fields appropriately. (The preclist is built by precedence, which is essentially unchanged.) The remaining fields of the class are set to :nil to indicate that they are uninitialized. To examine the area property of circle-class we could say:

```
> (svref circle-class
         (+ (position 'area (layout circle-class)) 3))
:NIL
```

---

[1] When classes are displayed, *print-array* should be nil. The first element in the preclist of any class is the class itself, so trying to display the internal structure of a class would cause an infinite loop.

[2] The vector is coerced to a list simply to see what's in it. With *print-array* set to nil, the contents of a vector would not be shown.

```
(declaim (inline lookup (setf lookup)))

(defun rget (prop obj next?)
  (let ((prec (preclist obj)))
    (if prec
        (dolist (c (if next? (cdr prec) prec) :nil)
          (let ((val (lookup prop c)))
            (unless (eq val :nil) (return val))))
        (let ((val (lookup prop obj)))
          (if (eq val :nil)
              (rget prop (parents obj) nil)
              val)))))

(defun lookup (prop obj)
  (let ((off (position prop (layout obj) :test #'eq)))
    (if off (svref obj (+ off 3)) :nil)))

(defun (setf lookup) (val prop obj)
  (let ((off (position prop (layout obj) :test #'eq)))
    (if off
        (setf (svref obj (+ off 3)) val)
        (error "Can't set ~A of ~A." val obj))))
```

Figure 17.9: Vector implementation: Access.

Later we will define access functions that do this automatically.

Finally, the function inst is used for making instances. It does not have to be a macro, because it takes just one argument:

```
> (setf our-circle (inst circle-class))
#<Simple-Vector T 5 C6464E>
```

It's instructive to compare inst to class-fn, which does something similar. Because instances have only one parent, there is no need to determine what properties are inherited. The instance can just copy the layout of its parent class. Nor is there any need to build a precedence list, because instances don't have them. Building instances will thus be much faster than building classes—which is as it should be, because creating instances is more common than creating classes in most applications.

Now that we can build a hierarchy of classes and instances we need functions to read and write their properties. The first function in Figure 17.9 is the

new definition of rget. It is similar in shape to the rget in Figure 17.7. The
two branches of the conditional deal with classes and instances respectively.

1. If the object is a class, we traverse its precedence list until we find an
   object in which the value of the desired property is not :nil. If we
   don't find one we return :nil.

2. If the object is an instance, we look for the property locally, and make
   a recursive call to rget if it isn't there.

The new third argument to rget, next?, will be explained later. For now
suffice it to say that if it is nil, rget will behave as usual.

The function lookup and its inverse play the role that gethash did in the
old rget. They use an object's layout to retrieve or set a property with a
given name. This query duplicates the one we made earlier:

```
> (lookup 'area circle-class)
:NIL
```

Since the setf of lookup is also defined, we could define an area method
for circle-class by saying:

```
(setf (lookup 'area circle-class)
      #'(lambda (c)
          (* pi (expt (rget 'radius c nil) 2))))
```

In this program, as in the earlier version, there is no hard distinction between
slots and methods. A "method" is just a field with a function in it. This will
soon be hidden by a more convenient front-end.

Figure 17.10 contains the last of the new implementation. This code
does not add any power to the program, but makes it easier to use. The
macro defprop is essentially unchanged; now it just calls lookup instead of
gethash. As before, it allows us to refer to properties in a functional syntax:

```
> (defprop radius)
(SETF RADIUS)
> (radius our-circle)
:NIL
> (setf (radius our-circle) 2)
2
```

If the optional second argument to defprop is true, it expands into a call to
run-methods, which is also almost unchanged.

```
(declaim (inline run-methods))

(defmacro defprop (name &optional meth?)
  '(progn
     (defun ,name (obj &rest args)
       ,(if meth?
            '(run-methods obj ',name args)
            '(rget ',name obj nil)))
     (defun (setf ,name) (val obj)
       (setf (lookup ',name obj) val))))

(defun run-methods (obj name args)
  (let ((meth (rget name obj nil)))
    (if (not (eq meth :nil))
        (apply meth obj args)
        (error "No ~A method for ~A." name obj))))

(defmacro defmeth (name obj parms &rest body)
  (let ((gobj (gensym)))
    '(let ((,gobj ,obj))
       (defprop ,name t)
       (setf (lookup ',name ,gobj)
             (labels ((next () (rget ,gobj ',name t)))
               #'(lambda ,parms ,@body))))))
```

Figure 17.10: Vector implementation: Interface macros.

Finally, the function defmeth provides a convenient way to define methods. There are three things new about this version: it does an implicit defprop, it calls lookup instead of gethash, and it calls rget instead of get-next (page 278) to get the next method. Now we see the reason for the additional argument to rget. It is so similar to get-next that we can implement both in one function by adding an extra argument. If this extra argument is true, rget takes the place of get-next.

Now we can achieve the same effect as the preceding method definition with something a lot cleaner:

```
(defmeth area circle-class (c)
  (* pi (expt (radius c) 2)))
```

Notice that instead of calling `rget` we can simply call `radius`, because we defined it as a function with `defprop`. Because of the implicit `defprop` done by `defmeth`, we can likewise call `area` to get the area of `our-circle`:

```
> (area our-circle)
12.566370614359173
```

17.8 Analysis

We now have an embedded language suitable for writing real object-oriented programs. It is simple, but for its size quite powerful. And in typical applications it will also be fast. In a typical application, operations on instances should be more common than operations on classes. The central point of our redesign was to make operations on instances cheap.

In our program, building classes is slow and generates a lot of garbage. But this will be acceptable if classes are not built at times when speed is critical. The things that have to be fast are access and instance creation. Access in this program will be about as fast as we can expect without compile-time optimizations.° So will instance creation. And neither operation causes consing. Except, that is, for the vector that represents the instance itself. It seems natural enough that this should be dynamically allocated. But we could avoid dynamically allocating even instances, if we used a strategy like the one presented in Section 13.4.

Our embedded language is a characteristic example of Lisp programming. The mere fact of being an embedded language makes it one. But also characteristic of Lisp is the way in which it evolved from a small, limited version, through a powerful but inefficient version, to a fast but slightly restrictive version.

Lisp's reputation for slowness comes not so much from its own nature (Lisp compilers have been able to generate code as fast as compiled C since the 1980s) as from the fact that so many programmers stop at the second stage. As Richard Gabriel wrote,

> In Lisp, writing programs that perform very poorly is quite easy;
> in C it is almost impossible.°

This is simply a true statement, but it can be read as either a point for Lisp or a point against it:

1. By trading speed for flexibility, you can write programs very easily in Lisp ; in C you don't have this option.

2. Unless you optimize your Lisp code, it is all too easy to end up with slow software.

Which interpretation applies to your programs depends entirely on you. But at least in Lisp you have the option of trading execution speed for your time, in the early stages.

One thing our example program is *not* good for is as a model of CLOS (except possibly for elucidating the mystery of how `call-next-method` works). How much similarity could there be between the elephantine CLOS and this 70-line mosquito? Indeed, the contrasts between the two programs are more instructive than the similarities. First of all, we see what a wide latitude the term "object-oriented" has. Our program is more powerful than a lot of things that have been called object-oriented, and yet it has only a fraction of the power of CLOS.

Our program differs from CLOS in that methods are methods *of* some object. This concept of methods makes them equivalent to functions that dispatch on their first argument. And when we use the functional syntax to invoke them, that's just what our methods look like. A CLOS generic function, in contrast, can dispatch on any of its arguments. The components of a generic function are called methods, and if you define them so that they specialize only their first argument, you can maintain the illusion that they are methods *of* some class or instance. But thinking of CLOS in terms of the message-passing model of object-oriented programming will only confuse you in the end, because CLOS transcends it.

One of the disadvantages of CLOS is that it is so large and elaborate that it conceals the extent to which object-oriented programming is a paraphrase of Lisp. The example in this chapter does at least make that clear. If we were content to implement the old message-passing model, we could do it in a little over a page of code. Object-oriented programming is one thing Lisp can do. A more interesting question is, what else can it do?

A: Debugging

This appendix shows how to debug Lisp programs, and gives examples of some of the more common errors you might encounter.

Break Loops

If you ask Lisp to do something it can't, evaluation will be interrupted by an error message, and you will find yourself in something called a break loop. The way a break loop behaves is implementation-dependent, but usually it will display at least three things: an error message, a list of options, and a distinctive prompt.

You can evaluate expressions within a break loop just as you can within the toplevel. From within the break loop you may be able to discover the cause of the error, or even correct it and continue the evaluation of your program. However, the most common thing you will want to do in a break loop is to get out of it. Most errors are caused by typos or minor oversights, so usually you will just abort the program and return to the toplevel. In this hypothetical implementation, we type :abort to return to the toplevel:

```
> (/ 1 0)
Error: Division by zero.
       Options: :abort, :backtrace
>> :abort
>
```

What you actually type in these situations depends on the implementation.

If an error occurs while you are in a break loop, you end up in another break loop. Most Lisps indicate the level of break loop you're in, either by printing multiple prompts, or by printing a number before the prompt:

```
>> (/ 2 0)
Error: Division by zero.
        Options: :abort, :backtrace, :previous
>>>
```

Now we are two break loops deep. At this point we have a choice of returning to the previous break loop or all the way to the toplevel.

Traces and Backtraces

When your program isn't doing what you expect, sometimes the first thing to settle is, what *is* it doing? If you type (trace foo), then Lisp will display a message each time foo is called or returns, showing the arguments passed to it or the values it returned. You can trace any user-defined function.

A trace is usually indented to show the depth in the calling tree. In a function that does a traversal, like this function which adds 1 to each non-nil element of a tree,

```
(defun tree1+ (tr)
  (cond ((null tr) nil)
        ((atom tr) (1+ tr))
        (t (cons (tree1+ (car tr))
                 (tree1+ (cdr tr))))))
```

the shape of a trace will therefore mirror the shape of the data structure being traversed:

```
> (trace tree1+)
(tree1+)
> (tree1+ '((1 . 3) 5 . 7))
1 Enter TREE1+ ((1 . 3) 5 . 7)
  2 Enter TREE1+ (1 . 3)
    3 Enter TREE1+ 1
    3 Exit TREE1+ 2
    3 Enter TREE1+ 3
    3 Exit TREE1+ 4
  2 Exit TREE1+ (2 . 4)
  2 Enter TREE1+ (5 . 7)
    3 Enter TREE1+ 5
    3 Exit TREE1+ 6
    3 Enter TREE1+ 7
    3 Exit TREE1+ 8
  2 Exit TREE1+ (6 . 8)
1 Exit TREE1+ ((2 . 4) 6 . 8)
((2 . 4) 6 . 8)
```

To turn off tracing for foo, type (untrace foo); to turn off all tracing, type just (untrace).

A more flexible alternative to tracing is to insert diagnostic print statements in your code. If the truth were known, this classic technique would probably turn out to be used ten times as often as sophisticated debugging tools. Which is yet another reason it's so useful to be able to redefine functions interactively.

A *backtrace* is a list of all the calls currently on the stack, made from a break loop when an error has interrupted evaluation. If a trace is like saying, "Show me what you're doing," a backtrace is like asking, "How did we get here?" In a way, traces and backtraces are complementary. A trace will show calls to selected functions everywhere in the calling tree of a program. A backtrace will show every function call in a selected part of the calling tree (the path from the toplevel call to the place where the error occurs).

In a typical implementation, we might get a backtrace by entering :backtrace in a break loop, and it might look as follows:

```
> (tree1+ '((1 . 3) 5 . A))
Error: A is not a valid argument to 1+.
      Options: :abort, :backtrace
>> :backtrace
(1+ A)
(TREE1+ A)
(TREE1+ (5 . A))
(TREE1+ ((1 . 3) 5 . A))
```

Bugs that show up in a backtrace are easier to find. You just look back along the chain of calls until you find the first one that should not have happened. Another advantage of functional programming (Section 2.12) is that all bugs show up in the backtrace. In purely functional code, everything that could have contributed to an error must still be on the stack when the error occurs.

The amount of information in a backtrace varies from implementation to implementation. Some will display a complete history of all pending calls, with the arguments; others will display next to nothing. Generally traces and backtraces of interpreted code contain more information, which is one reason to delay compiling your program until you're sure it works.

Traditionally one debugged code in the interpreter, and compiled it only once it seemed to be working. But this view may be changing: at least two Common Lisp implementations don't include interpreters.

When Nothing Happens

Not all bugs cause evaluation to be interrupted. Another common and possibly more alarming situation is when Lisp seems to be ignoring you. Usually this is a sign that your program is in an infinite loop.

If the loop occurs in iterative code, Lisp will happily continue forever. If it occurs in recursive code (compiled without tail-recursion optimization), you will eventually get an error message saying that Lisp has run out of stack space:

```
> (defun blow-stack () (1+ (blow-stack)))
BLOW-STACK
> (blow-stack)
Error: Stack overflow.
```

In either case, if you suspect an infinite loop, the solution is to interrupt execution, then abort out of the resulting break loop.

Sometimes a program working on a very big problem will run out of stack space without being in an infinite loop. This is rare though. Usually running out of stack is a sign of a programming error.

In recursive functions it is a common error to forget the base case. In English descriptions of recursion, we often omit it. Informally, we might say "obj is a member of lst if it is either the first element, or a member of the rest of lst." Strictly speaking, we should also add that "obj is not a member of lst if it is empty." Otherwise what we're describing is an infinite recursion.

In Common Lisp, car and cdr both return nil if they are given nil as an argument:

```
> (car nil)
NIL
> (cdr nil)
NIL
```

So if we skipped the base case in the definition of member,

```
(defun our-member (obj lst)                               ; wrong
  (if (eql (car lst) obj)
      lst
      (our-member obj (cdr lst))))
```

then it would recurse infinitely if the object we sought wasn't in the list. When we reached the end of the list without finding it, the recursive call would be equivalent to:

```
(our-member obj nil)
```

In a correct definition (page 16), the base case would stop the recursion at this point, returning nil. But in the mistaken definition, the function dutifully finds the car of nil, which is nil, and compares that to the object we're looking for. Unless that happens to be nil, the function then continues looking in the cdr of nil, which is also nil—and the whole process starts over again.

If the cause of an infinite loop isn't obvious, you may be able to diagnose it by looking at a trace or backtrace. Infinite loops fall into two categories. The easy ones to find are ones that depend on program structure. A trace or backtrace would show you immediately what was wrong with our-member.

The more difficult kind of infinite loops are the kind that happen because your data structures are flawed. If you inadvertently create circular structure (page 199), code that traverses it may get caught in an infinite loop. These bugs are difficult to find because problems do not arise till later, in code that's not at fault. The best solution is prevention, as described on page 199: avoid destructive operations until your program is already working, and you are ready to tune it for efficiency.

If Lisp seems to be ignoring you, it could also be that it is waiting for you to finish typing something. In most systems, hitting return has no effect until you have typed a complete expression. The good thing about this approach is that it allows you to type expressions that take up several lines. The bad thing is that if you inadvertently miss a right parenthesis or a close-quote, Lisp will be waiting for you to finish typing an expression that you think you have already finished:

```
> (format t "for example ~A~% 'this)
```

Here we have omitted the close-quote at the end of the format string. Hitting return at this point has no effect, because Lisp thinks we are still in the middle of typing a string.

In some implementations, you can go back to the previous line and insert the close-quote. In systems that don't allow you to edit previous lines, the best solution will usually be to interrupt execution, then abort from the resulting break loop back to the toplevel.

No Value/Unbound

One of the most common complaints you'll hear from Lisp is that a symbol has no value or is unbound. Several distinct problems show themselves in this way.

Local variables, like those established by `let` and `defun`, are valid only within the body of the expression where they are created. So if we try to refer to such a variable outside the `let` that creates it,

```
> (progn
    (let ((x 10))
      (format t "Here x = ~A.~%" x))
    (format t "But now it's gone...~%")
    x)
Here x = 10.
But now it's gone...
Error: X has no value.
```

we get an error. When Lisp complains that something has no value or is unbound, it usually means that you inadvertently referred to a variable that didn't exist. Because there was no local variable called x, Lisp assumed that we were referring to a global variable or constant with that name. The error arose when Lisp tried to look up its value and found that it hadn't been given one. Mistyping the name of a variable will usually have the same result.

A similar problem happens if we inadvertently refer to a function as if it were a variable. For example:

```
> defun foo (x) (+ x 1))
Error: DEFUN has no value.
```

This can seem puzzling the first time it happens: how can `defun` have no value? The cause of the problem is that we have omitted the initial left parenthesis, causing Lisp to interpret the symbol `defun`, which is all it will read, as a reference to a global variable.

It may be that you really have forgotten to initialize some global variable. If you don't give a second argument to `defvar`, your global variable will be declared but not initialized; that may be the root of the problem.

Unexpected Nils

When functions complain about being passed `nil` as an argument, it is usually a sign that something went wrong earlier in the program. Several built-in operators return `nil` to indicate failure. But since `nil` is also a legitimate Lisp object, problems may not arise till later, when some other part of your program tries to put this supposed return value to use.

For example, this function to return the number of days in a month has a bug in it; we have forgotten October:

```
(defun month-length (mon)
  (case mon
    ((jan mar may jul aug dec) 31)
    ((apr jun sept nov) 30)
    (feb (if (leap-year) 29 28)))))
```

If we have another function intended to calculate the number of weeks in a month,

```
(defun month-weeks (mon) (/ (month-length mon) 7.0))
```

then the following can happen:

```
> (month-weeks 'oct)
Error: NIL is not a valid argument to /.
```

The problem arises because none of the `case` clauses in `month-length` applies. When this happens, `case` returns `nil`. Then `month-weeks`, which thinks it is getting a number, passes this value on to `/`, which complains.

Here at least the bug and its manifestation occur close together. Such bugs are harder to find when they are far apart. To avoid this possibility, some dialects of Lisp make it an error for control to run off the end of a `case` or `cond`. In Common Lisp, the thing to do in a situation like this would be to use `ecase`, as described in Section 14.6.

Renaming

A particularly insidious kind of bug comes from renaming a function or variable in some, but not all, of the places where it's used. For example, suppose we define the following (inefficient) function to find the depth of nesting in a nested list:

```
(defun depth (x)
  (if (atom x)
      1
      (1+ (apply #'max (mapcar #'depth x)))))
```

On testing the function, we find that it gives us an answer 1 too big:

```
> (depth '((a)))
3
```

The initial 1 should have been a 0. So we fix this, and while we're at it, give the function a less ambiguous name:

```
(defun nesting-depth (x)
  (if (atom x)
      0
      (1+ (apply #'max (mapcar #'depth x)))))
```

Yet when we test this function on the case above, it returns the *same result:*

```
> (nesting-depth '((a)))
3
```

Didn't we just fix this function? We did, but the answer is not coming from the code we fixed. We forgot to change the name in the recursive call. In the recursive case, our new function still calls `depth`, which of course is still broken.

Keywords as Optional Parameters

If a function takes both keyword and optional parameters, it is a common error unintentionally to supply a keyword as the optional parameter. For example, the function `read-from-string` has the following parameter list:

(read-from-string *string* &optional *eof-error eof-value*
                                    &key *start end preserve-whitespace*)

With such a function you have to supply values for all the optional parameters in order to pass keyword arguments. If you forget about the optional parameters, as in this example,

```
> (read-from-string "abcd" :start 2)
ABCD
4
```

then `:start` and 2 will be the values of the first two optional parameters. If we want `read` to start after the second character, we should say instead:

```
> (read-from-string "abcd" nil nil :start 2)
CD
4
```

Misdeclarations

Chapter 13 explained how to make type declarations for variables and data structures. By making a type declaration for a variable, you are promising that the variable will only contain values of that type. The Lisp compiler will rely on this assumption when generating code. For example, both arguments to this function are declared to be double-floats,

```
(defun df* (a b)
  (declare (double-float a b))
  (* a b))
```

and the compiler is thereby entitled to hard-wire a floating-point multiply in the code it generates for this function.

If df* is called with arguments that are not of the declared type, it might signal an error, or simply return garbage. In one implementation, if we pass two fixnums we get a hardware interrupt:

```
> (df* 2 3)
Error: Interrupt.
```

If you get a serious error like this, it is very likely to have been caused by a value that was not of the declared type.

Warnings

Sometimes Lisp will complain about something without interrupting evaluation. Many such warnings are false alarms. The most common kind may be those generated by the compiler about undeclared or unused variables. For example, in the second call to map-int (page 106), the variable x is not used. If you want the compiler to stop informing you of this fact every time you compile your program, use an ignore declaration:

```
(map-int #'(lambda (x)
             (declare (ignore x))
             (random 100))
         10)
```

B: Lisp in Lisp

This appendix contains Lisp definitions of 58 of the most frequently used Common Lisp operators. Because so much of Lisp is (or can be) written in Lisp, and because Lisp programs are (or can be) quite short, this is a convenient way of explaining the language.

This exercise also shows that, conceptually, Common Lisp not such a large language as it seems. Most Common Lisp operators are effectively library routines; the set of operators that you need to write all the rest is quite small. Those defined in this appendix require only:

```
apply aref backquote block car cdr ceiling char= cons defmacro
documentation eq error expt fdefinition function floor gensym
get-setf-expansion if imagpart labels length multiple-value-bind
nth-value quote realpart symbol-function tagbody type-of typep
= + - / < >
```

The code given here is presented as a way of explaining Common Lisp, not as a way of implementing it. In a real implementation, these operators would be much more efficient, and would do more error-checking. The operators themselves are defined in alphabetic order, for easy reference. If you actually wanted to define a Lisp this way, each macro definition would have to appear before any code that calls it.

```
(defun -abs (n)
  (if (typep n 'complex)
      (sqrt (+ (expt (realpart n) 2) (expt (imagpart n) 2)))
      (if (< n 0) (- n) n)))

(defun -adjoin (obj lst &rest args)
  (if (apply #'member obj lst args) lst (cons obj lst)))
```

```
(defmacro -and (&rest args)
  (cond ((null args) t)
        ((cdr args)  '(if ,(car args) (-and ,@(cdr args))))
        (t           (car args))))

(defun -append (&optional first &rest rest)
  (if (null rest)
      first
      (nconc (copy-list first) (apply #'-append rest))))

(defun -atom (x) (not (consp x)))

(defun -butlast (lst &optional (n 1))
  (nreverse (nthcdr n (reverse lst))))

(defun -cadr (x) (car (cdr x)))

(defmacro -case (arg &rest clauses)
  (let ((g (gensym)))
    '(let ((,g ,arg))
       (cond ,@(mapcar #'(lambda (cl)
                           (let ((k (car cl)))
                             '(,(cond ((member k '(t otherwise))
                                       t)
                                      ((consp k)
                                       '(member ,g ',k))
                                      (t '(eql ,g ',k)))
                               (progn ,@(cdr cl)))))
                       clauses)))))

(defun -cddr (x) (cdr (cdr x)))

(defun -complement (fn)
  #'(lambda (&rest args) (not (apply fn args))))

(defmacro -cond (&rest args)
  (if (null args)
      nil
      (let ((clause (car args)))
        (if (cdr clause)
            '(if ,(car clause)
                 (progn ,@(cdr clause))
                 (-cond ,@(cdr args)))
            '(or ,(car clause)
                 (-cond ,@(cdr args)))))))
```

```lisp
(defun -consp (x) (typep x 'cons))

(defun -constantly (x) #'(lambda (&rest args) x))

(defun -copy-list (lst)
  (labels ((cl (x)
             (if (atom x)
                 x
                 (cons (car x)
                       (cl (cdr x)))))))
    (cons (car lst)
          (cl (cdr lst)))))

(defun -copy-tree (tr)
  (if (atom tr)
      tr
      (cons (-copy-tree (car tr))
            (-copy-tree (cdr tr)))))

(defmacro -defun (name parms &rest body)
  (multiple-value-bind (dec doc bod) (analyze-body body)
    `(progn
       (setf (fdefinition ',name)
             #'(lambda ,parms
                 ,@dec
                 (block ,(if (atom name) name (second name))
                   ,@bod))
             (documentation ',name 'function)
             ,doc)
       ',name)))

(defun analyze-body (body &optional dec doc)
  (let ((expr (car body)))
    (cond ((and (consp expr) (eq (car expr) 'declare))
           (analyze-body (cdr body) (cons expr dec) doc))
          ((and (stringp expr) (not doc) (cdr body))
           (if dec
               (values dec expr (cdr body))
               (analyze-body (cdr body) dec expr)))
          (t (values dec doc body)))))
```

```lisp
; This definition is not strictly correct; see let.

(defmacro -do (binds (test &rest result) &rest body)
  (let ((fn (gensym)))
    `(block nil
       (labels ((,fn ,(mapcar #'car binds)
                  (cond (,test ,@result)
                        (t (tagbody ,@body)
                           (,fn ,@(mapcar #'third binds))))))
         (,fn ,@(mapcar #'second binds))))))

(defmacro -dolist ((var lst &optional result) &rest body)
  (let ((g (gensym)))
    `(do ((,g ,lst (cdr ,g)))
         ((atom ,g) (let ((,var nil)) ,result))
       (let ((,var (car ,g)))
         ,@body))))

(defun -eql (x y)
  (typecase x
    (character (and (typep y 'character) (char= x y)))
    (number    (and (eq (type-of x) (type-of y))
                    (= x y)))
    (t         (eq x y))))

(defun -evenp (x)
  (typecase x
    (integer (= 0 (mod x 2)))
    (t       (error "non-integer argument"))))

(defun -funcall (fn &rest args) (apply fn args))

(defun -identity (x) x)

; This definition is not strictly correct: the expression
; (let ((&key 1) (&optional 2))) is legal, but its expansion
; is not.

(defmacro -let (parms &rest body)
  `((lambda ,(mapcar #'(lambda (x)
                         (if (atom x) x (car x)))
                     parms)
      ,@body)
    ,@(mapcar #'(lambda (x)
                  (if (atom x) nil (cadr x)))
              parms)))
```

```
(defun -list (&rest elts) (copy-list elts))

(defun -listp (x) (or (consp x) (null x)))

(defun -mapcan (fn &rest lsts)
  (apply #'nconc (apply #'mapcar fn lsts)))

(defun -mapcar (fn &rest lsts)
  (cond ((member nil lsts) nil)
        ((null (cdr lsts))
         (let ((lst (car lsts)))
           (cons (funcall fn (car lst))
                 (-mapcar fn (cdr lst)))))
        (t
         (cons (apply fn (-mapcar #'car lsts))
               (apply #'-mapcar fn
                      (-mapcar #'cdr lsts))))))

(defun -member (x lst &key test test-not key)
  (let ((fn (or test
                (if test-not
                    (complement test-not))
                    #'eql)))
    (member-if #'(lambda (y)
                   (funcall fn x y))
               lst
               :key key)))

(defun -member-if (fn lst &key (key #'identity))
  (cond ((atom lst) nil)
        ((funcall fn (funcall key (car lst))) lst)
        (t (-member-if fn (cdr lst) :key key))))

(defun -mod (n m)
  (nth-value 1 (floor n m)))

(defun -nconc (&optional lst &rest rest)
  (if rest
      (let ((rest-conc (apply #'-nconc rest)))
        (if (consp lst)
            (progn (setf (cdr (last lst)) rest-conc)
                   lst)
            rest-conc))
      lst))

(defun -not (x) (eq x nil))
```

```lisp
(defun -nreverse (seq)
  (labels ((nrl (lst)
              (let ((prev nil))
                 (do ()
                    ((null lst) prev)
                   (psetf (cdr lst) prev
                          prev      lst
                          lst       (cdr lst)))))
           (nrv (vec)
              (let* ((len (length vec))
                     (ilimit (truncate (/ len 2))))
                 (do ((i 0 (1+ i))
                      (j (1- len) (1- j)))
                    ((>= i ilimit) vec)
                   (rotatef (aref vec i) (aref vec j))))))
    (if (typep seq 'vector)
        (nrv seq)
        (nrl seq)))))

(defun -null (x) (eq x nil))

(defmacro -or (&optional first &rest rest)
  (if (null rest)
      first
      (let ((g (gensym)))
        `(let ((,g ,first))
           (if ,g
               ,g
               (-or ,@rest))))))

; Not in CL, but needed in several definitions here.

(defun pair (lst)
  (if (null lst)
      nil
      (cons (cons (car lst) (cadr lst))
            (pair (cddr lst)))))

(defun -pairlis (keys vals &optional alist)
  (unless (= (length keys) (length vals))
    (error "mismatched lengths"))
  (nconc (mapcar #'cons keys vals) alist))
```

```
(defmacro -pop (place)
  (multiple-value-bind (vars forms var set access)
                       (get-setf-expansion place)
    (let ((g (gensym)))
      '(let* (,@(mapcar #'list vars forms)
              (,g ,access)
              (,(car var) (cdr ,g)))
         (prog1 (car ,g)
                ,set)))))

(defmacro -prog1 (arg1 &rest args)
  (let ((g (gensym)))
    '(let ((,g ,arg1))
       ,@args
       ,g)))

(defmacro -prog2 (arg1 arg2 &rest args)
  (let ((g (gensym)))
    '(let ((,g (progn ,arg1 ,arg2)))
       ,@args
       ,g)))

(defmacro -progn (&rest args) '(let nil ,@args))

(defmacro -psetf (&rest args)
  (unless (evenp (length args))
    (error "odd number of arguments"))
  (let* ((pairs (pair args))
         (syms (mapcar #'(lambda (x) (gensym))
                       pairs)))
    '(let ,(mapcar #'list
                   syms
                   (mapcar #'cdr pairs))
       (setf ,@(mapcan #'list
                       (mapcar #'car pairs)
                       syms)))))

(defmacro -push (obj place)
  (multiple-value-bind (vars forms var set access)
                       (get-setf-expansion place)
    (let ((g (gensym)))
      '(let* ((,g ,obj)
              ,@(mapcar #'list vars forms)
              (,(car var) (cons ,g ,access)))
         ,set))))
```

```
(defun -rem (n m)
  (nth-value 1 (truncate n m)))

(defmacro -rotatef (&rest args)
  '(psetf ,@(mapcan #'list
                    args
                    (append (cdr args)
                            (list (car args)))))))

(defun -second (x) (cadr x))

(defmacro -setf (&rest args)
  (if (null args)
      nil
    '(setf2 ,@args)))

(defmacro setf2 (place val &rest args)
  (multiple-value-bind (vars forms var set)
                       (get-setf-expansion place)
    '(progn
       (let* (,@(mapcar #'list vars forms)
              (,(car var) ,val))
         ,set)
       ,@(if args '((setf2 ,@args)) nil))))

(defun -signum (n)
  (if (zerop n) 0 (/ n (abs n))))

(defun -stringp (x) (typep x 'string))

(defun -tailp (x y)
  (or (eql x y)
      (and (consp y) (-tailp x (cdr y)))))

(defun -third (x) (car (cdr (cdr x))))

(defun -truncate (n &optional (d 1))
  (if (> n 0) (floor n d) (ceiling n d)))

(defmacro -typecase (arg &rest clauses)
  (let ((g (gensym)))
    '(let ((,g ,arg))
       (cond ,@(mapcar #'(lambda (cl)
                           '((typep ,g ',(car cl))
                             (progn ,@(cdr cl))))
                       clauses)))))
```

```
(defmacro -unless (arg &rest body)
  '(if (not ,arg)
       (progn ,@body)))

(defmacro -when (arg &rest body)
  '(if ,arg (progn ,@body)))

(defun -1+ (x) (+ x 1))

(defun -1- (x) (- x 1))

(defun ->= (first &rest rest)
  (or (null rest)
      (and (or (> first (car rest)) (= first (car rest)))
           (apply #'->= rest))))
```

C: Changes to Common Lisp

ANSI Common Lisp differs substantially from the Common Lisp defined in 1984 by the first edition of Guy Steele's *Common Lisp: the Language*. It also differs, though less so, from the language described in the second (1990) edition. This appendix summarizes some of the more significant changes. Changes since 1990 are listed separately in the last section.

Major Additions

1. The Common Lisp Object System, or CLOS, has become part of the language.

2. The loop macro now implements an embedded language with infix syntax.

3. Common Lisp now includes a group of new operators, collectively called the condition system, for signalling and handling errors and other conditions.

4. Common Lisp now provides explicit support for, and control over, pretty-printing.

Individual Additions

1. The following individual operators have been added:

```
complement                 nth-value
declaim                    print-unreadable-object
defpackage                 readtable-case
delete-package             row-major-aref
destructuring-bind         stream-external-format
fdefinition                with-compilation-unit
file-string-length         with-hash-table-iterator
function-lambda-expression with-package-iterator
```

```
load-time-value              with-standard-io-syntax
map-into
```

2. along with the following individual global variables:

```
*debugger-hook*     *read-eval*     *print-readably*
```

Functions

1. The idea of a function name has been generalized to include expressions of the form (setf *f*). Such expressions are now accepted by any operator or declaration that expects a function name. The new function fdefinition is like symbol-function, but takes a function name in the more general sense.

2. The type function no longer includes fboundp symbols and lambda expressions. Symbols (but not lambda expressions) can still be used where functional arguments are expected. Lambda expressions can now be coerced to functions.

3. Symbols used as names of keyword parameters no longer have to be keywords. (Note that symbols not in the keyword package have to be quoted when used to identify arguments in calls.)

4. Rest parameters are not guaranteed to be freshly consed. Thus it is not safe to modify them destructively.

5. A local function defined with flet or labels, or an expansion function defined by defmacro, macrolet, or defsetf, is implicitly enclosed in a block whose name is the name of whatever is being defined.

6. A function that has an interpreted definition in a non-null lexical environment (e.g. one defined at the toplevel by a defun within a let) cannot be compiled.

Macros

1. Compiler macros and symbol macros have been introduced, along with associated operators.

2. The expansion functions of macros are now specified to be defined in the environment where the call to defmacro occurs. Thus in ANSI Common Lisp it is possible for the code that generates macro expansions to refer to local variables:

```
(let ((op 'car))
  (defmacro pseudocar (lst)
    `(,op ,lst)))
```

In 1984, expansion functions were supposed to be defined in the null environment (i.e. the toplevel).

3. Macro calls are guaranteed not to be re-expanded in compiled code.

4. Macro calls can now be dotted lists.

5. Macros can no longer expand into declares.

Evaluation and Compilation

1. The `eval-when` special operator has been redefined, and all the original keywords are now deprecated.

2. The function `compile-file` now takes `:print` and `:verbose` arguments. New variables `*compile-print*` and `*compile-verbose*` hold the defaults.

3. The new variables `*compile-file-pathname*` and `*compile-file-truename*` are bound during the evaluation of a call to `compile-file`. Likewise `*load-pathname*` and `*load-truename*` during a load.

4. The `dynamic-extent` declaration has been added.

5. The `debug` compilation parameter has been added.

6. The `compiler-let` special operator has been deleted.

7. The `#,` read-macro has been deleted.

8. The global `*break-on-warnings*` has been deleted; its replacement is the more general `*break-on-signals*`.

Side-effects

1. A `setf` method can now have multiple store variables.

2. The ways in which many destructive functions modify their arguments are now more explicitly specified. For example, most operators that could modify lists are not merely allowed to do so, but specified to do so. Such functions *could* now be called for effects rather than values.

3. It is now explicitly forbidden to use mapping functions (and macros like `dolist`) to modify the sequences they are traversing.

Symbols

1. The new global variable `*gensym-counter*` holds an integer used to make the print-names of gensyms. In 1984, the gensym counter could be reset implicitly by giving an integer as the argument to `gensym`; this practice is now deprecated.

2. It is now an error to modify a string used as the name of symbol.

3. The function `documentation` has become a generic function.

Lists

1. The functions `assoc-if`, `assoc-if-not`, `rassoc-if`, and `rassoc-if-not`, and `reduce` now take a `:key` argument.

2. The function `last` now takes an optional second argument indicating the length of the tail to return.

3. With the addition of `complement`, use of `-if-not` functions and `:test-not` keyword arguments is now deprecated.

Arrays

1. New functions have been added to allow programs to ask about type-upgrading of elements of arrays and complex numbers.
2. Array indices are now specified to be fixnums.

Strings and Characters

1. The type `string-char` has been deleted. The type `string` is no longer identical to (`vector string-char`). The type `character` is divided into two new subtypes, `base-char` and `extended-char`. The type `string` has a new subtype `base-string`, which in turn has a new subtype `simple-base-string`.
2. Several functions that create strings now take an `:element-type` argument.
3. The font and bits attributes of characters have been discarded, along with all the associated functions and constants. The only remaining character attribute defined by Common Lisp is the code.
4. Most string functions can coerce the same kinds of arguments as `string`. So (`string= 'x 'x`) now should return `t`.

Structures

1. It is no longer necessary to specify any slots in a call to `defstruct`.
2. The consequences of redefining a structure—that is, calling `defstruct` twice with the same structure name—are undefined.

Hash Tables

1. The function `equalp` now applies to hash tables.
2. New accessors have been added to allow programs to refer to the properties of hash tables: `hash-table-rehash-size`, `hash-table-rehash-threshold`, `hash-table-size`, and `hash-table-test`.

I/O

1. The concept of logical pathnames was introduced, along with associated operators.
2. Several new types of stream have been introduced, with associated predicates and accessors.
3. The `~_`, `~W`, and `~I` format directives have been added. The format directives `~D`, `~B`, `~O`, `~X`, and `~R` all take an extra argument.
4. The functions `write` and `write-to-string` take five new keyword arguments.
5. There is a new read-macro, `#P`, for pathnames.
6. The new variable `*print-readably*` can be used to insist that output be readable.

Numbers

1. Fixnums are now at least 16 bits.
2. There are eight new constants marking the limits of normalized floats.
3. The type `real` has been added; it is a subtype of `number` and a supertype of `rational` and `float`.

Packages

1. The conventional way to define packages in source files has been changed. Toplevel calls to package-related functions are no longer evaluated by the compiler. Users are supposed to use the new `defpackage` macro instead. The old `in-package` function has been replaced by a macro with the same name. The new macro does not evaluate its argument, or take a `:use` argument, or implicitly create packages.
2. The packages `lisp` and `user` have been renamed `common-lisp` and `common-lisp-user`. New packages do not implicitly `use` `common-lisp` as they did `lisp`.
3. The names of all built-in variables, functions, macros, and special operators must be owned by `common-lisp`. It is an error to redefine, rebind, trace, or make declarations for any built-in operator.

Types

1. The `eql` type specifier has been added.
2. The type `common` has been deleted, with the function `commonp`.

Changes Since 1990

1. The following operators have been added:

```
allocate-instance          ensure-directories-exist
array-displacement         lambda
constantly                 read-sequence
define-symbol-macro        write-sequence
```

2. The following operators and variables have been deleted:

```
applyhook                  function-information
*applyhook*                get-setf-method
augment-environment        generic-flet
declare                    generic-function
enclose                    generic-labels
evalhook                   parse-macro
*evalhook*                 variable-information
declaration-information    with-added-methods
define-declaration
```

Instead of `get-setf-method`, use `get-setf-expansion`, the replacement for `get-setf-method-multiple-value`. Also, `declare` is still used—it is just no longer considered to be an operator.

3. The following four operators have been renamed

    `define-setf-[method → expander]`
    `get-setf-[method-multiple-value → expansion]`
    `special-[form → operator]-p`
    `simple-condition-format-[string → control]`

    along with the following two types (new in 1990):

    `base-[character → char]`
    `extended-[character → char]`

4. The module facility, which was deleted in 1990, has been reinstated, but its use is now deprecated.

5. It is possible to use a `values` expression as the first argument to `setf`.

6. The ANSI standard is more specific about which functions accept dotted lists. For example, it is now specified that the arguments to `nconc` can be dotted lists. (Strangely, the arguments to `append` must be proper lists, so `nconc` and `append` no longer take the same arguments.)

7. It's definitely no longer possible to coerce an integer to a character. It is now possible to coerce (setf f) to a function.

8. The restriction that an argument to `compile` had to be defined in the null lexical environment has been relaxed; its environment may include local macro or symbol-macro definitions, or declarations. The first argument may now be a compiled function.

9. The functions `gentemp` and `set` are now deprecated.

10. The symbol `type` can always be omitted in a type declaration. It is thus an error to define a type whose name is that of a declaration, or vice versa.

11. The new `ignorable` declaration can be used to declare that no warning should be issued, whether a variable is used or not.

12. The constant `array-total-size-limit` is now specified to be a fixnum. Thus an argument to `row-major-aref` can always be declared a fixnum.

13. Instead of a `:print-function`, a structure defined with `defstruct` can now have a `:print-object`, which takes only the first two arguments.

14. There is a new type, `boolean`, whose two members are `nil` and `t`.

D: Language Reference

This appendix describes every operator in ANSI Common Lisp. The descriptions follow several conventions:

Entries for functions are lists beginning with the function name, followed by an indication of the parameter list. Entries for special operators and macros are regular expressions indicating the form of a valid call.

In a regular expression, something followed by an asterisk[1] indicates zero or more of them: (a*) could be (), or (a), or (a a), and so on. Something in square brackets indicates zero or one of them: (a [b] c) could be (a c) or (a b c). Curly brackets are sometimes used for grouping: ({a b}*) could be () or (a b), or (a b a b), and so on. A vertical bar indicates a choice between several alternatives: (a {1 | 2} b) could be (a 1 b) or (a 2 b).

PARAMETER NAMES

The parameter names correspond to restrictions on the arguments. If a parameter has the name of a type, then the corresponding argument must be of that type. Additional implications of parameter names are listed in the following table.

Arguments to macros and special operators are not evaluated unless the description says so explicitly. If such an argument is not evaluated, type restrictions implied by its name apply to the argument itself; if it is evaluated, they apply to its value. If a macro argument is evaluated, it is evaluated in the environment where the macro call appears, unless the description explicitly says otherwise.

---

[1]An asterisk, *, is not to be confused with a star, ⋆.

alist   must be an assoc-list, which is a proper list whose elements, if any, are of the form (*key* . *value*).

body   indicates the arguments that could come after the parameter list in a defun expression: either *declaration** [*string*] *expression**, or [*string*] *declaration** *expression**. So an entry like (defun *fname parameters* . *body*) indicates that the syntax of a defun expression could be (defun *fname parameters declaration** [*string*] *expression**), or (defun *fname parameters* [*string*] *declaration** *expression**). If the *string* is followed by at least one *expression*, it is interpreted as a documentation string.

c   must be a complex number.

declaration   must be a list whose car is declare.

environment   indicates an object representing a lexical environment. (You can't create such objects directly, but Lisp uses them internally.) The symbol nil always represents the global environment.

f   must be a float.

fname   must be a function name: either a symbol or a list (setf *s*), where *s* is a symbol.

format   can be either a string that could be the second argument to format, or a function that takes a stream and some optional arguments and (presumably) writes something to the stream.

i   must be an integer.

list   can be a list of any type. Whether or not a *list* can be circular depends on the context. Functions that take lists as arguments can take cdr-circular lists if and only if their purpose never requires them to find the end of the list. So nth can take cdr-circular lists, but find cannot. A parameter called *list* can always be car-circular.

n   must be a non-negative integer.

object   can be of any type.

package   must be a package, a string that is the name of a package, or a symbol whose name is the name of a package.

path   can be a pathname, a stream associated with a file (in which case it indicates the pathname used to open the stream), or a string.

place   must be an expression that could be the first argument to setf.

plist   must be a property list, which is a proper list with an even number of elements.

pprint-dispatch   must be a pprint dispatch table (or possibly nil).

predicate   must be a function.

prolist   must be a proper list.

proseq   must be a proper sequence—that is, a vector or a proper list.

r   must be a real.

tree   imposes no type restriction—everything is a tree. But cannot be a car- or cdr-circular list.

type   must be a type designator.

DEFAULTS

Certain optional parameters always have the same default. An optional *stream* parameter always defaults to `*standard-input*` or `*standard-output*`, depending on whether the operator in question is for use on input or output streams. An optional parameter called *package* always defaults to `*package*`; one called *readtable* always defaults to `*readtable*`; and one called *pprint-dispatch* always defaults to `*print-pprint-dispatch*`.

COMPARISON

Many functions that compare sequence elements take the keyword arguments `key`, `test`, `test-not`, `from-end`, `start`, or `end`. Their use is the same in every case; see page 64. The `key`, `test` and `test-not` arguments must be functions, and the `start` and `end` arguments must be non-negative integers. In the descriptions of functions that take such keyword arguments, words like "match", "member", and "element" are to be understood as modified by the presence of such arguments.

In any function that does comparisons on sequence elements, it is also to be assumed that the default test for equality is `eql`, unless stated otherwise.

STRUCTURE

If an operator returns structure (e.g. lists), it should be understood that the return value can share structure with objects passed as arguments, unless the description says that the return value is newly created. However, only parameters shown in angle brackets (⟨*list*⟩) can actually be modified by the call. If two functions are listed together, the second is a destructive version of the first.

Evaluation and Compilation

(compile *fname* &optional *function*)   Function
> If *function* is not provided and *fname* is the name of an uncompiled function or macro, then replaces that function or macro with a compiled version, returning *fname*. (The lexical environment in which the function or macro is defined should not differ from the global environment except by having local macro or symbol-macro definitions, or declarations.) If *function* (which may be a function or lambda expression) is provided, then coerces it to a function, compiles it, and names it *fname*, returning *fname*. The *fname* may also be nil, in which case the compiled function is returned. Returns two additional values: a second true iff compilation generated errors or warnings; and a third true iff compilation generated errors or warnings other than style warnings.

(compiler-macro-function *fname* &optional *environment*)   Function
> Returns the compiler macro function whose name is *fname* in *environment*, or nil if there isn't one. A compiler macro function is a function of two arguments: the entire call, and the environment in which it occurs. Settable.

(constantp *expression* &optional *environment*)   Function
> Returns true if *expression* is the name of a constant, or a list whose car is quote, or an object that is neither a symbol nor a cons. May also return true for other expressions that the implementation is able to determine are constant.

(declaim *declaration-spec*)   Macro
> Like proclaim, but top-level calls are processed by the compiler, and the *declaration-spec* is not evaluated.

(declare *declaration-spec**)
> Not an operator, but resembles one in that an expression whose car is declare may appear at the beginning of a body of code. Such an expression makes the declarations described by the *declaration-spec*s (not evaluated) apply to all the code in the environment in which the declare appears. The following declarations are allowed: dynamic-extent, ftype, ignorable, ignore, inline, notinline, optimize, special, type.

(define-compiler-macro *fname* *parameters* . *body*)   Macro
> Like defmacro, but defines a compiler macro. Compiler macros are like normal macros, but are expanded only by the compiler, and are expanded before normal macros. Usually, *fname* will be the name of an existing function or macro, and the compiler macro will be defined to optimize certain calls and return the rest unchanged. (It would cause an error if a normal macro returned the original expression.) The documentation string becomes the compiler-macro documentation of *fname*.

(define-symbol-macro *symbol* *expression*)   Macro
> Causes *symbol* to be treated as a macro call, so long as there is not already a special variable called *symbol*. Its expansion will be *expression*. If *symbol* occurs as if it were a variable in a call to setq, the setq will behave like a setf; likewise for multiple-value-setq, which will behave like a setf of values.

(defmacro *symbol parameters* . *body*)   Macro
>   Globally defines a macro named *symbol*. In most cases, calls of the form
>   (*symbol* $a_1 \ldots a_n$) can be understood as being replaced by the value returned
>   by ((lambda *parameters* . *body*) $a_1 \ldots a_n$) before being evaluated. In the
>   general case, the *parameters* are associated with the arguments in the macro call
>   as if by destructuring-bind; and they may contain an &whole parameter,
>   which will be bound to the entire macro call, and an &environment parameter,
>   which will be bound to the environment in which the macro call occurs. The
>   documentation string becomes the function documentation of *symbol*.

(eval *expression*)   Function
>   Evaluates *expression* in the global environment and returns its value(s).

(eval-when (*case**) *expression**)   Special Operator
>   If one of the *cases* applies, the *expressions* are evaluated in order and the value(s)
>   of the last are returned; otherwise returns nil. The *case* :compile-toplevel
>   applies when the eval-when expression is a top-level form in a file being com-
>   piled. The *case* :load-toplevel applies when the eval-when expression
>   is a top-level form in a compiled file being loaded. The *case* :execute
>   applies when the eval-when expression would be evaluated anyway (so us-
>   ing only :execute makes eval-when equivalent to progn). The symbols
>   compile, load, and eval are deprecated synonyms for :compile-toplevel,
>   :load-toplevel, and :execute.

(lambda *parameters* . *body*)   Macro
>   Equivalent to (function (lambda *parameters* . *body*)).

(load-time-value *expression* &optional *constant*)   Special Operator
>   Equivalent to (quote *val*), where *val* is the value returned by *expression* when
>   a file of compiled code containing the load-time-value expression is loaded.
>   If *constant* (not evaluated) is t, indicates that the value is never going to be
>   modified.

(locally *declaration** *expression**)   Special Operator
>   An expression of the form (locally $e_1 \ldots e_n$) is equivalent to (let ()
> $e_1 \ldots e_n$), except that if the call to locally is a top-level form, so are the
>   *expressions*.

(macroexpand *expression* &optional *environment*)   Function
>   Returns the expansion returned by calling macroexpand-1 repeatedly, starting
>   with *expression*, until the result is no longer a macro call. Returns a second
>   value true iff the return value differs from *expression*.

(macroexpand-1 *expression* &optional *environment*)   Function
>   If *expression* is a macro call, does one round of expansion, otherwise returns
>   *expression*. Works by calling *macroexpand-hook*, whose initial value is
>   funcall, on three arguments: the corresponding macro function, *expression*,
>   and *environment*. So ordinarily the expansion is generated by calling the macro
>   function on the arguments passed to macroexpand-1. Returns a second value
>   true iff the return value differs from *expression*.

(macro-function *symbol* &optional *environment*)   Function
    Returns the macro function whose name is *fname* in *environment*, or nil if
    there isn't one. A macro function is a function of two arguments: the entire
    call, and the environment in which it occurs. Settable.

(proclaim *declaration-spec*)   Function
    Globally makes the declaration described by *declaration-spec*. The follow-
    ing declarations are allowed: declaration, ftype, inline, notinline,
    optimize, special, type.

(special-operator-p *symbol*)   Function
    Returns true iff *symbol* is the name of a special operator.

(symbol-macrolet ((*symbol* *expression*)*)   Special Operator
                 *declaration** *expression**)
    Evaluates its body with each *symbol* defined locally to be the corresponding
    symbol-macro, as if by define-symbol-macro.

(the *type* *expression*)   Special Operator
    Returns the value(s) of *expression*, and declares that the value(s) will be of type
    type. (See the values type specifier, page 398.) The number of declarations
    and the number of values can differ: leftover declarations have to be true of
    nil; leftover values have no type declared for them.

(quote *object*)   Special Operator
    Returns its argument without evaluating it.

Types and Classes

(coerce *object* *type*)   Function
    Returns an equivalent object of type *type*. If the *object* is already of that type,
    just returns it. Otherwise, if *object* is a sequence and *type* denotes a type of
    sequence that can contain the elements of *object*, then the result is a sequence of
    that type with the same elements as *object*. If *object* is a string of one character
    or a symbol whose name is a string of one character, and *type* is character,
    returns that character. If *object* is a real and *type* denotes a type of floating-point
    number, the result will be a floating-point approximation of *object*. If *object*
    is a function name (a symbol, or (setf *f*), or a lambda expression), and *type*
    is function, then the result is the function it denotes; in the latter case, the
    function will be defined in the global environment, not the environment where
    the call to coerce occurs.

(deftype *name* *parameters* . *body*)   Macro
    Just like defmacro, except that a "call" to *name* is used as a type designator
    (e.g. within a declare) rather than an expression. The documentation string
    becomes the type documentation of *name*.

(subtypep *type1* *type2* &optional *environment*)   Function
    Returns two values; the first is true iff *type1* can be proved to be a subtype of
    type2, the second iff the relation between the two types is known with certainty.

(type-error-datum *condition*)   Function
  Returns the object that caused the type-error *condition*.

(type-error-expected-type *condition*)   Function
  Returns the type that the offending object was supposed to have had in the
  type-error *condition*.

(type-of *object*)   Function
  Returns a type specifier for a type of which *object* is a member.

(typep *object type* &optional *environment*)   Function
  Returns true iff *object* is of type *type*.

Control and Data Flow

(and *expression**)   Macro
  Evaluates the *expression*s in order, returning nil immediately if one evaluates
  to nil, or if they all return true, the value(s) of the last. Returns t if given no
  arguments.

(apply *function* &rest *args*)   Function
  Calls *function* on *args*, of which there must be at least one. The last *arg* must
  be a list. The arguments to the function consist of each *arg* up to the last, plus
  each element of the last; that is, the argument list is composed as if by list*.
  The *function* can also be a symbol, in which case its global function definition
  is used.

(block *symbol expression**)   Special Operator
  Evaluates its body within a block whose name is *symbol* (not evaluated). Used
  with return-from.

(case *object* (*key expression**)*   Macro
    [({t | otherwise} *expression**)])
  Evaluates *object*, then looks at the remaining clauses in order; if the *object* is
  eql to or a member of the *key* (not evaluated) of some clause, or the clause
  begins with t or otherwise, then evaluates the following *expression*s and
  returns the value(s) of the last. Returns nil if no *key* matches, or the matching
  key has no *expression*s. The symbols t and otherwise may not appear as
  keys, but you can get the same effect by using (t) and (otherwise).

(catch *tag expression**)   Special Operator
  Evaluates its body with a pending catch tag whose name is the value of *tag*.
  Used with throw.

(ccase *object* (*key expression**)*)   Macro
  Evaluates *object*, then looks at the remaining clauses in order; if the *object* is
  eql to or a member of the *key* (not evaluated) of some clause, then evaluates
  the following *expression*s and returns the value(s) of the last. Returns nil if
  the matching *key* has no *expression*s. If no *key* matches, signals a correctable
  type-error. The symbols t and otherwise may not appear as keys, but you
  can get the same effect by using (t) and (otherwise).

(compiled-function-p *object*)   Function
> Returns true iff *object* is a compiled function.

(complement *predicate*)   Function
> Returns a function of one argument that returns true where *predicate* (which should also take one argument) returns false, and false where *predicate* returns true.

(cond ((*test expression**)*))   Macro
> Evaluates *test*s until one returns true. If that *test* has no corresponding *expression*s, returns the value of the *test*. Otherwise evaluates the *expression*s in order, returning the value(s) of the last. If no *test* returns true, returns nil.

(constantly *object*)   Function
> Returns a function that takes any number of arguments and returns *object*.

(ctypecase *object* (*type expression**)*)   Macro
> Evaluates *object*, then looks at the remaining clauses in order; if the *object* is of some *type* (not evaluated), then evaluates the following *expression*s and returns the value(s) of the last. Returns nil if the matching *type* has no *expression*s. If no *type* matches, signals a correctable type-error.

(defconstant *symbol expression* [*string*])   Macro
> Defines *symbol* to be a global constant with the value of *expression*. No local or global variable may have the same name. The *expression* may be evaluated at compile-time. The *string*, if present, becomes the variable documentation of *symbol*. Returns *symbol*.

(define-modify-macro *name parameters symbol* [*string*])   Macro
> An expression of the form (define-modify-macro *m* ($p_1 \ldots p_n$) *f*) defines a new macro *m*, such that a call of the form (*m place* $a_1 \ldots a_n$) will cause *place* to be set to (*f val* $a_1 \ldots a_n$), where *val* represents the value of *place*. The *parameters* may also include rest and optional parameters. The *string*, if present, becomes the documentation of the new macro.

(define-setf-expander *reader parameters . body*)   Macro
> Defines the way calls of the form (setf (*reader* $a_1 \ldots a_n$) *val*) will be expanded; when get-setf-expansion is called on such an expression, it will return the (five) values returned by the *expression*s. The *string*, if present, becomes the setf documentation of *reader*.

(defparameter *symbol expression* [*string*])   Macro
> Gives the global variable *symbol* the value of *expression*. The *string*, if present, becomes the variable documentation of *symbol*. Returns *symbol*.

(defsetf *reader writer* [*string*])   Macro
> Short form: Causes calls of the form (setf (*reader* $a_1 \ldots a_n$) *val*) to be expanded into (*writer* $a_1 \ldots a_n$ *val*). The *reader* and *writer* writer must be symbols, and are not evaluated. The *string*, if present, becomes the setf documentation of *reader*.

(defsetf *reader parameters* (*var**) . *body*)   Macro
    Long form: Causes calls of the form (setf (*reader* $a_1 \ldots a_n$) *val*) to be
    expanded into the expression generated by the evaluation of the body of the
    defsetf, as if it were a defmacro. The *reader* must be a symbol (not evalu-
    ated) that is the name of a function, or a macro that evaluates all its arguments.
    The *parameters* are the parameters of *reader*, and the *vars* will represent the
    value(s) of *val*. The *string*, if present, becomes the setf documentation of
    reader.

    In order to maintain the principle that setf returns the new value of its first
    argument, the expansion generated by a defsetf should return that value.

(defun *fname parameters* . *body*)   Macro
    Globally defines *fname* to be the corresponding function, defined in the lexical
    environment where the defun expression occurs. The body of the function is
    implicitly enclosed in a block named *fname* if *fname* is a symbol, or *f* if *fname*
    is a list of the form (setf *f*). The *string*, if present, becomes the function
    documentation of *fname*.

(defvar *symbol* [*expression* [*string*]])   Macro
    Gives the global variable *symbol* the value of *expression*, if *expression* is
    provided and the variable does not already have a value. The *string*, if present,
    becomes the variable documentation of *symbol*. Returns *symbol*.

(destructuring-bind *variables tree declaration** *expression**)   Macro
    Evaluates its body with variables in *variables* (a tree whose interior nodes are
    parameter lists) bound to the corresponding elements of the value of *tree*. The
    value of *tree* must match the shape of *variables*.

(ecase *object* (*key expression**)*)   Macro
    Like ccase, but signals a non-correctable type-error if no *key* matches.

(eq *object1 object2*)   Function
    Returns true iff *object1* and *object2* are identical.

(eql *object1 object2*)   Function
    Returns true iff *object1* and *object2* are eq, or the same character, or numbers
    that would look the same when printed.

(equal *object1 object2*)   Function
    Returns true iff *object1* and *object2* are eql; or are conses whose cars and
    cdrs are equal; or are strings or bit-vectors of the same length (observing fill
    pointers) whose elements are eql; or are pathnames whose components are
    equivalent. May not terminate for circular arguments.

(equalp *object1 object2*)   Function
    Returns true iff *object1* and *object2* are equal, char-equal, or =; or are conses
    whose cars and cdrs are equalp; or are arrays with the same dimensions whose
    active elements are equalp; or are structures of the same type whose elements
    are equalp; or are hash tables with the same test function and number of
    entries whose keys (as determined by the test function) are all associated with
    equalp values. Reasonable to assume that it may not terminate for circular
    arguments.

(etypecase *object* (*key expression**)*)   Macro
    Like ctypecase, but signals a non-correctable type-error if no *key* matches.

(every *predicate proseq* &rest *proseqs*)   Function
    If the shortest *proseq* has length *n*, returns true iff *predicate*, which must be a
    function of as many arguments as there are *proseqs*, returns true when applied
    to all the first elements, then all the second elements, ... then all the *n*th
    elements. Stops as soon as *predicate* returns nil, returning nil.

(fboundp *fname*)   Function
    Returns true iff *fname* is the name of a global function or macro.

(fdefinition *fname*)   Function
    Returns the global function whose name is *fname*. Settable.

(flet ((*fname parameters . body*)*)   Special Operator
       declaration expression**)
    Evaluates its body with each *fname* defined locally to be the corresponding
    function. Like labels, but the local functions are visible only in the body;
    they may not call one another (and so cannot be recursive).

(fmakunbound *fname*)   Function
    Removes the global function or macro definition for *fname*. Causes an error if
    there isn't one. Returns *fname*.

(funcall *function* &rest *args*)   Function
    Calls *function* on *args*. The *function* can also be a symbol, in which case its
    global function definition is used.

(function *name*)   Special Operator
    Returns the function whose name is *name*, which can be either a symbol, a list
    of the form (setf *f*), or a lambda expression. If *f* is a built-in operator, it is
    implementation-dependent whether or not there is a function called (setf *f*).

(function-lambda-expression *function*)   Function
    Intended to return the lambda expression defining *function*, but can always
    return nil. Returns two additional values: the second, if nil, says that
    function is defined in the null lexical environment; an implementation can use
    the third to express *function*'s name.

(functionp *object*)   Function
    Returns true iff *object* is a function.

(labels ((*fname parameters . body*)*)   Special Operator
       declaration expression**)
    Evaluates its body with each *fname* defined locally to be the corresponding
    function. Like flet, but the local functions are visible within the entire
    labels expression; they may call one another (and so can be recursive).

(get-setf-expansion *place* &optional *environment*)   Function
> Returns five values $v_1 \ldots v_5$ that determine the expansion of (setf *place* *val*) in the *environment*. The five values will be: a list of unique variable names (gensyms); a list of an equal number of values that should be assigned to them; a list of store variables to hold the value(s) of *place*; an expression that will perform the assignment designated by the setf, and can refer to variables from v_1 and v_3; and an expression that will retrieve the original value of *place*, and can refer to variables from v_1.

(go *tag*)   Special Operator
> Within a tagbody expression, transfers control to the point following the nearest lexically enclosing eql *tag*.

(identity *object*)   Function
> Returns *object*.

(if *test* *then* [*else*])   Special Operator
> Evaluates the *test* expression; if it returns true, evaluates and returns the value(s) of the *then* expression; otherwise evaluates and returns the value(s) of the *else* expression, or nil if there is no *else* expression.

(let ({*symbol* | (*symbol* [*value*])}*)   Special Operator
     *declaration** *expression**)
> Evaluates its body with each *symbol* bound to the value of the corresponding *value* expression, or nil if no *value* is given.

(let* ({*symbol* | (*symbol* [*value*])}*)   Special Operator
      *declaration** *expression**)
> Like let, except that *value* expressions may refer to previous *symbol*s.

(macrolet ((*symbol* *parameters* . *body*)*)   Special Operator
          *declaration** *expression**)
> Evaluates its body with each *symbol* defined locally to be the corresponding macro. The expansion functions are defined in the lexical environment where the macrolet expression occurs. Like flet, the local macros may not call one another.

(multiple-value-bind (*symbol**) *expression1*   Macro
                     *declaration** *expression**)
> Evaluates *expression1*, then evaluates its body with each of the *symbol*s (not evaluated) bound to the corresponding return value. If there are too few return values, the leftover variables are bound to nil; if there are too many, the extra values are ignored.

(multiple-value-call *function* *expression**)   Special Operator
> Calls *function* (evaluated) with arguments consisting of all the values returned by all the *expression*s.

(multiple-value-list *expression*)   Macro
> Returns a list of the values returned by *expression*.

(multiple-value-prog1 *expression1* *expression**)   Special Operator
    Evaluates its arguments in order, returning the value(s) of the first.

(multiple-value-setq (*symbol**) *expression*)   Macro
    Assigns the *symbols* (not evaluated) the values returned by *expression*. If there
    are too few return values, the leftover variables are bound to nil; if there are
    too many, the extra values are ignored.

(not *object*)   Function
    Returns true when *object* is nil.

(notany *predicate proseq* &rest *proseqs*)   Function
    An expression of the form (notany *predicate* $s_1 \ldots s_n$) is equivalent to (not
    (some *predicate* $s_1 \ldots s_n$)).

(notevery *predicate proseq* &rest *proseqs*)   Function
    An expression of the form (notevery *predicate* $s_1 \ldots s_n$) is equivalent to
    (not (every *predicate* $s_1 \ldots s_n$)).

(nth-value *n expression*)   Macro
    Returns the *n*th (evaluated) value returned by *expression*. Numbering starts at
    0. Returns nil if *expression* returns less than *n*+1 values.

(or *expression**)   Macro
    Evaluates the *expressions* in order; as soon as one returns true, returns its value.
    Can return multiple values from the last *expression*, but only the last. Returns
    nil if no *expression* returns true.

(prog ({*symbol* | (*symbol* [*value*])}*)   Macro
    declaration* {*tag* | *expression*}*)
    Evaluates its body with each *symbol* bound to the value of the corresponding
    value expression, or nil if no *value* is given. The body is enclosed in an
    implicit tagbody and an implicit block named nil, so the *expressions* can
    include calls to go, return, and return-from.

(prog* ({*symbol* | (*symbol* [*value*])}*)   Macro
    declaration* {*tag* | *expression*}*)
    Like prog, except that *value* expressions may refer to previous *symbols*.

(prog1 *expression1* *expression**)   Macro
    Evaluates its arguments in order, returning the value of the first.

(prog2 *expression1* *expression2* *expression**)   Macro
    Evaluates its arguments in order, returning the value of the second.

(progn *expression**)   Special Operator
    Evaluates its arguments in order, returning the value(s) of the last.

(progv *symbols values expression**)   Special Operator
    Evaluates its body with each variable in *symbols* (which must evaluate to a
    list of symbols) dynamically bound to the corresponding element of values
    (which must evaluate to a list). If there are too many variables, it will cause an
    error to refer to one of the leftover ones in the *expressions*; if there are too few,
    the extra values are ignored.

(psetf *{place value}**)   Macro
> Like setf, but if a *value* expression refers to one of the preceding *place*s, it
> will get the previous value. That is, (psetf x y y x) would exchange the
> values of x and y.

(psetq *{symbol value}**)   Macro
> Like setq, but if a *value* expression refers to a variable that was one of the
> preceding *symbol*s, it will get the previous value. That is, (psetq x y y x)
> would exchange the values of x and y.

(return *expression*)   Macro
> Equivalent to (return-from nil *expression*). Many macros (e.g. do) im-
> plicitly enclose their bodies in blocks named nil.

(return-from *symbol expression*)   Special Operator
> Returns the value(s) of *expression* from the nearest lexically enclosing block
> whose name is *symbol* (not evaluated). Causes an error if the return-from
> expression is not within such a block.

(rotatef *place**)   Macro
> Shifts the values of its arguments left by one place, as if in a circular buffer.
> Evaluates all its arguments in order; then, if the call was of the form (rotatef
> $a_1 \ldots a_n$) puts the value of a_2 in the place referred to by a_1, the value of a_3 in
> the place referred to by a_2, ... and the value of a_1 in the place referred to by
> a_n. Returns nil.

(setf *{place value}**)   Macro
> A generalization of setq: stores in the location associated with each *place* the
> value of the corresponding *value* expression. If a *value* expression refers to
> one of the preceding *place*s, it will get the new value. Returns the value of the
> last *value*.
>
> A valid *place* expression may be: a variable; a call to any function designated
> here as "settable" so long as the relevant argument is a valid place; a call to
> apply whose first argument is #'aref, #'bit, or #'sbit; a call to an accessor
> function defined by defstruct; a the or values expression in which the
> argument(s) are valid *place*s; a call to an operator for which a setf expansion
> has been defined; or a macro call that expands into any of the preceding.

(setq *{symbol value}**)   Special Operator
> Gives each variable *symbol* the value of the corresponding *value* expression. If
> a *value* expression refers to a variable that was one of the preceding *symbol*s,
> it will get the new value. Returns the value of the last *value*.

(shiftf *place1 place* expression*)   Macro
> Shifts the values of its arguments left by one place. Evaluates all its arguments
> in order; then, if the call was of the form (shiftf $a_1 \ldots a_n$ *val*) puts the value
> of a_2 in the place referred to by a_1, the value of a_3 in the place referred to by
> a_2, ... and the value of *val* in the place referred to by a_n. Returns the value of
> a_1.

(some *predicate proseq* &rest *proseqs*) Function

 If the shortest *proseq* has length *n*, returns true iff *predicate*, which must be a function of as many arguments as there are *proseqs*, returns true when applied to all the first elements, or all the second elements, . . . or all the *n*th elements. Stops as soon as *predicate* returns true, returning that value.

(tagbody {*tag* | *expression*}*) Special Operator

 Evaluates the *expressions* in order and returns nil. May contain calls to go, in which case the order in which *expressions* are evaluated (if at all) may be altered. The *tags*, which must be symbols or integers, are not evaluated. Atoms yielded by macro expansions are not treated as tags. All macros whose names begin with do have implicit tagbodies, as do prog and prog*.

(throw *tag expression*) Special Operator

 Returns the value(s) of *expression* from the nearest dynamically enclosing catch expression whose tag is eq to the value of *tag*.

(typecase *object* (*type expression**)* Macro
    [({t | otherwise} *expression**)])

 Evaluates *object*, then looks at the remaining clauses in order; if the *object* is of some *type* (not evaluated), or the clause begins with t or otherwise, then evaluates the following *expressions* and returns the value(s) of the last. Returns nil if no *type* matches, or the matching *type* has no *expressions*.

(unless *test expression**) Macro

 An expression of the form (unless *test* $e_1 \ldots e_n$) is equivalent to (when (not *test*) $e_1 \ldots e_n$).

(unwind-protect *expression1 expression**) Special Operator

 Evaluates its arguments in order, and returns the value(s) of the first. Evaluates the remaining arguments even if the evaluation of the first is interrupted.

(values &rest *objects*) Function

 Returns its arguments.

(values-list *prolist*) Function

 Returns the elements of *prolist*.

(when *test expression**) Macro

 Evaluates the *test* expression; if it returns true, evaluates the *expressions* in order and returns the value(s) of the last; otherwise returns nil. Returns nil if there are no *expressions*.

Iteration

(do ({*var* | (*var* [*init* [*update*]])}*)   Macro
    (*test result**)
    *declaration** {*tag* | *expression*}*)

Evaluates its body first with each *var* bound to the value of the corresponding
init expression (or nil if there isn't one), and on each successive iteration set
to the value of the corresponding *update* expression (or the previous value, if
there isn't one). Each time the body is about to be evaluated, the *test* expression
is evaluated; if it returns false, the body is evaluated, but if it returns true, the
result expressions are evaluated in order and the value of the last is returned.
The body is enclosed in an implicit tagbody, and the whole do expression in
an implicit block named nil.

If an *init* expression refers to a variable with the name of a *var*, it will refer
to the variable with that name in the context where the do expression occurs.
If an *update* expression refers to a *var*, it will get the value from the previous
iteration. That is, variables are established as if by let and updated as if by
psetq.

(do* ({*var* | (*var* [*init* [*update*]])}*)   Macro
     (*test result**)
     *declaration** {*tag* | *expression*}*

Like do, except that variables are established as if by let* and updated as if
by setq.

(dolist (*var list* [*result*])   Macro
         *declaration** {*tag* | *expression*}*)

Evaluates its body with *var* bound to successive elements of the value of *list*.
If the value of *list* is nil, the body is never evaluated. The body is enclosed in
an implicit tagbody, and the whole dolist expression in an implicit block
named nil. Returns the value(s) of the *result* expression, or nil if there isn't
one. The *result* expression may refer to *var*, which will be nil.

(dotimes (*var integer* [*result*])   Macro
          *declaration** {*tag* | *expression*}*)

Evaluates its body with *var* bound to successive integers from 0 to the value of
integer minus 1, inclusive. If the value of *integer* is not positive, the body is
never evaluated. The body is enclosed in an implicit tagbody, and the whole
dotimes expression in an implicit block named nil. Returns the value(s) of
the *result* expression, or nil if there isn't one. The *result* expression may refer
to *var*, which will be the number of times the body was evaluated.

(loop *expression**)   Macro

Short form: If the *expression*s do not include loop keywords, evaluates them in
order, forever. The *expression*s are enclosed in an implicit block named nil.

(loop [*name-clause*] *var-clause* body-clause**) Macro

Long form: The evaluation of a loop expression containing loop keywords proceeds as follows:

1. All the variables created by it are bound, possibly to random values of the proper type.

2. The loop prologue is evaluated.

3. The variables are set to their initial values.

4. End tests are performed.

5. If the end tests all fail, the body of the loop is evaluated; then the variables are updated, and control returns to the previous step.

6. If some end test succeeds, the loop epilogue is evaluated, and a value (see below) is returned.

Individual clauses can contribute code to several different steps. Within steps, expressions are evaluated in the order in which they appear in the source code.

A loop expression is always enclosed in an implicit block. By default its name is nil, but one may be given explicitly in a named clause.

The value returned by a loop expression is the (textually) last accumulated value, or nil if there are none. An accumulated value is the value constructed on successive iterations by a collect, append, nconc, count, sum, maximize, minimize, always, never, or thereis clause.

A *name-clause* is a named clause. A *var-clause* can be a with, initially, finally, or for clause. A *body-clause* can be any kind of clause except a named, with, or for clause. Each of the types of clauses is described below.

CONVENTIONS: Unless a description says so explicitly, elements of loop clauses are not evaluated. A token *type* indicates a type declaration; it must be an ordinary type designator, or a tree of type designators that are matched with corresponding elements of a list as if by destructuring.

SYNONYMS: The loop macro generously assigns synonyms to many keywords. In the following descriptions, the second of each these pairs may be used in place of the first: upfrom, from; downfrom, from; upto, to; downto, to; the, each; of, in; when, if; hash-keys, hash-key; hash-value, hash-values; symbol, symbols; present-symbol, present-symbols; external-symbol, external-symbols; do, doing; collect, collecting; append, appending; nconc, nconcing; count, counting; sum, summing; maximize, maximizing; minimize, minimizing.

named *symbol*

Causes *symbol* to be the name of the implicit block enclosing the loop expression.

with *var1* [*type1*] = *expression1* {and *var* [*type*] = *expression*}*

Binds each *var* to the value of the corresponding *expression*, in parallel as if by a let.

`initially` *expression1 expression**

Causes the *expression*s to be evaluated in order as part of the prologue.

`finally` *expression1 expression**

Causes the *expression*s to be evaluated in order as part of the epilogue.

`for` *var1* [*type1*] *for-rest1* {`and` *var* [*type*] *for-rest*}*

Binds each *var* to the successive values indicated by the corresponding *for-rest* during successive iterations. Multiple `for` clauses linked by ands cause their variables to be initialized and updated in parallel, like do. The possible forms of a *for-rest* are as follows:

[`upfrom` *start*] [{`upto` | `below`} *end*] [`by` *step*]

At least one of the three optional subexpressions must be chosen; if more than one are chosen, they may appear in any order. The variable will initially be bound to the value of *start*, or 0. On successive iterations it will be incremented by the value of *step*, or 1. An `upto` or `below` expression adds an end test; `upto` will stop iteration when the variable is > the value of *end*, `below` when ≥ it. If the synonyms `from` and `to` are used together, or `from` is used without a `to` clause, then the `from` will be interpreted as an `upfrom`.

`downfrom` *start* [{`downto` | `above`} *end*] [`by` *step*]

As above, the subexpressions can appear in any order. The variable will initially be bound to the value of *start*. On successive iterations it will be decremented by *step*, or 1. A `downto` or `above` expression adds an end test; `downto` will stop iteration when the variable is < the value of *end*, `above` when ≤ it.

{`in` | `on`} *list* [`by` *function*]

If the first keyword is `in`, the variable will be bound to successive elements of the value of *list*; if `on`, successive tails. The *function*, if provided, is applied instead of `cdr` to the list after each iteration. Adds an end test: iteration will stop with the end of the list.

= *expression1* [`then` *expression2*]

The variable will initially be bound to the value of *expression1*. On successive iterations its value will be found by evaluating *expression2*, if present, or otherwise *expression1*.

`across` *vector*

The variable will be bound to successive elements of the value of *vector*. Adds an end test: iteration will stop after the last element.

`being the hash-keys of` *hash-table* [`using (hash-value` *v2*)]
`being the hash-values of` *hash-table* [`using (hash-key` *v2*)]

In the first case, the variable will be set on successive iterations to the keys (in no particular order) of *hash-table*, and the optional *v2* will be set to the corresponding values. In the second case, the variable will be set to the values, and *v2* to the keys. Adds an end test: iteration will stop after the last key or value.

being each {symbol | present-symbol | external-symbol}
[of *package*]

The variable will be set to successive symbols accessible in, present in, or external to a package. The *package* argument is used as an argument to find-package. Uses the current package if none is given. Adds an end test: iteration will stop after the last symbol.

do *expression1 expression**

Causes the *expression*s to be evaluated in order.

return *expression*

Causes the loop expression to return the value of *expression* immediately, without evaluating the epilogue.

{collect | append | nconc} *expression* [into *var*]

Accumulates a list, initially nil, during iteration. If the keyword is collect, the list will be a list of all the values returned by *expression*; if append, the values it returned appended together; if nconc, the values it returned nconced together. If a *var* is provided, it will be bound to the list being accumulated, and the list will not be a default return value for the loop.

Within a loop, collect, append and nconc clauses can accumulate into the same variable. If such clauses don't have distinct *var*s, they will be interpreted as doing so.

{count | sum | maximize | minimize} *expression* [into *var*] [*type*]

Accumulates a number during iteration. If the keyword is count, the number will reflect the number of times the *expression* returned true; if sum, the sum of all the values it returned; if maximize, the maximum value it returned; if minimize, the minimum value it returned. With count and sum the number will initially be zero; with maximize and minimize its initial value is unspecified. If a *var* is provided, it will be bound to the number being accumulated, and the number will not be a default return value for the loop. The *type*, if given, declares the type of the accumulated number.

Within a loop, sum and count clauses can accumulate into the same variable. If such clauses don't have distinct *var*s, they will be interpreted as doing so. Ditto for maximize and minimize.

when *test then-clause1* {and *then-clause*}*
[else *else-clause1* {and *else-clause*}*] [end]

Evaluates *test*. If it returns true, the *then-clause*s are evaluated in order; otherwise the *else-clause*s are evaluated in order. The *then-clause*s and *else-clause*s can be do, return, when, unless, collect, append, nconc, count, sum, maximize, or minimize clauses.

The *expression* in *then-clause1* or *else-clause1* can be the it, in which case it will refer to the value of *test*.

unless *test then-clause1* {and *then-clause*}*
      [else *else-clause1* {and *else-clause*}*] [end]

A clause of the form unless *test* $e_1 \ldots e_n$ is equivalent to when (not *test*) $e_1 \ldots e_n$.

repeat *integer*

Adds an end test: iteration will stop after *integer* iterations.

while *expression*

Adds an end test: iteration will stop if *expression* returns false.

until *expression*

Equivalent to while (not *expression*).

always *expression*

Like while, but also provides a return value for the loop: nil if the *expression* returned false, t otherwise.

never *expression*

Equivalent to always (not *expression*).

thereis *expression*

Like until, but also provides a return value for the loop: the value of *expression* if it returned true, nil otherwise.

(loop-finish)   Macro

Can only be used within a loop expression, where it ends iteration and transfers control to the loop epilogue, after which the loop returns normally.

Objects

(add-method *generic-function method*)   Generic Function

Makes *method* a method of *generic-function*, returning *generic-function*. Overwrites any existing method with matching qualifiers and specializations. The *method* may not be a method of another generic function.

(allocate-instance *class* &rest *initargs* &key)   Generic Function

Returns an instance of *class* with uninitialized slots. Allows other keys.

(call-method *method* &optional *next-methods*)   Macro

When called within a method, invokes *method*, returning whatever value(s) it returns. The *next-methods*, if provided, should be a list of methods; they will be the next methods of *method*. The *method* may also be (and the *next-methods* may include) a list of the form (make-method *expression*), which corresponds to a method whose body is *expression*. If such a method is invoked, the *expression* will be evaluated in the global environment, except that there will be a local macro definition of call-method.

`(call-next-method &rest `*args*`)`   Function

   When called within a method, invokes the next method on *args*, returning whatever value(s) it returns. If no *args* are given, uses the arguments passed to the current method (ignoring any assignments done to the parameters). Under standard method combination, `call-next-method` can be called within primary and around methods. If there isn't a next method, calls `no-next-method`, which signals an error by default.

`(change-class `*instance class* `&rest `*initargs* `&key)`   Generic Function

   Changes the class of *instance* to *class*, returning *instance*. An existing slot that has the same name as a local slot in *class* remains intact, otherwise it is discarded. New local slots required by *class* are initialized by calling `update-instance-for-redefined-class`. Allows other keys.

`(class-name `*class*`)`   Generic Function

   Returns the name of *class*. Settable.

`(class-of `*object*`)`   Function

   Returns the class of which *object* is an instance.

`(compute-applicable-methods `*generic-function args*`)`   Generic Function

   Returns a list, sorted from most to least specific, of the methods of *generic-function* that would be applicable if it were invoked on the elements of the list *args*.

`(defclass `*name* `(`*superclass**`) (`*slot-spec**`) `*class-spec**`)`   Macro

   Defines and returns a new class named *name*. If *name* was already a class name, existing instances are updated to conform to the new class. The *superclasses* are the names, in order, of its superclasses. (They need not exist until we want to make instances of the new class.) The slots of the new class are a combination of those inherited from the superclasses, and local slots specified in the *slot-specs*. For an explanation of how conflicts ar resolved, see page 408.

   Each *slot-spec* must be either a *symbol* or a list $(symbol\ k_1\ v_1^*\ldots k_n\ v_n^*)$, where no k is used twice. The *symbol* is the name of the slot. The ks may be:

   `:reader `*fname**

      Defines an unqualified method for each *fname* that returns the value of the corresponding slot.

   `:writer `*fname**

      Defines an unqualified method for each *fname* that refers to the value of the corresponding slot, and is settable but cannot be called directly.

   `:accessor `*fname**

      Defines an unqualified method for each *fname* that refers to the corresponding slot, and is settable.

   `:allocation `*where*

      If *where* is `:instance` (the default), each instance will have its own slot; if `:class`, a single will be shared by all instances.

:initform *expression*

>   When instances are created and there are no explicit or default initargs, the slot will be set to the value of *expression*.

:initarg *symbol**

>   Each *symbol* can be used like a keyword parameter to specify the value of the slot when instances are made by make-instance. The *symbol*s do not have to be actual keywords. The same *symbol* can be used as an initarg for more than one slot in a class.

:type *type*

>   Declares that the slot will contain values of type *type*.

:documentation *string*

>   Provides a documentation string for the slot.

The *class-specs* may be any combination of: (:documentation *string*), (:metaclass *symbol*), or (:default-initargs $k_1 e_1 \ldots k_n e_n$). The latter are used when instances are initialized; see make-instance. If the *e*s are evaluated, they will be evaluated in the expression (In any call to make-instance, every *e* associated with a *k* that does not appear in the call gets evaluated.) The :documentation becomes the documentation of the class. The :metaclass can be used to give the new class a metaclass other than standard-class.

(defgeneric *fname parameters entry**)   Macro

Defines, or augments the definition of, a generic function named *fname*. Returns this function. Causes an error if *fname* is the name of a normal function or a macro.

The *parameters* are a specialized lambda-list; see defmethod. All methods for the generic function must have parameter lists congruent with one another and with *parameters*.

The *entry*s may include one or more of the following:

(:argument-precedence-order *parameter**)

>   Overrides the precedence order implied by the second argument to defgeneric. The *parameter*s must include each of the parameters of the generic function.

(declare (optimize *property**))

>   Declares how the compilation of the generic function itself (e.g. the code that handles dispatch) should be optimized. Does not apply to individual methods. See declare.

(:documentation *string*)

>   Provides function documentation for *fname*.

(`:method-combination` *symbol argument**)

> Specifies that the generic function should use the kind of method combination named by *symbol*. Built-in combination types don't take any arguments, but combination types that do can be defined by using the long form of `define-method-combination`.

(`:generic-function-class` *symbol*)

> Specifies that the generic function should be of the class named *symbol*. This can be used to change the class of an existing generic function. The default is `standard-generic-function`.

(`:method-class` *symbol*)

> Specifies that all methods of the generic function should be of the class named *symbol*. May change the class of existing methods. The default is `standard-method`.

(`:method` *qualifier** *parameters* . *body*)

> Equivalent to (`defmethod` *fname qualifier** *parameters* . *body*) The *entry*s may include more than one expression of this type.

(`define-method-combination` *symbol property**)   Macro
Short form: Defines a new type of method combination. The short form is used for straightforward operator method combination. If $c_1 \ldots c_n$ represent calls to the applicable methods, from most to least specific, of a generic function that uses *symbol* method combination, then the generic function call will be equivalent to (*symbol* $c_1 \ldots c_n$). A *property* can be:

`:documentation` *string*

> Makes *string* the `method-combination` documentation of *symbol*, and also the documentation string of the method combination object.

`:identity-with-one-argument` *bool*

> Makes it possible to optimize generic function calls where there is only one applicable method. If *bool* is true, the value(s) returned by that method will simply be returned by the generic function. Used in `and` and `progn` method combination, for example.

`:operator` *opname*

> Specifies the actual operator (possibly different from *symbol*) to use in the generic function. The *opname* can be a symbol or a lambda expression.

`(define-method-combination` *symbol parameters*   Macro
                            (group-spec*)
                            `[(:arguments` . *parameters2*`)]`
                            `[(:generic-function` *var*`)]`
                            . *body*`)`

Long form: Defines a new form of method combination by specifying how the expansion of a call to the generic function should be computed. A call to a generic function that uses *symbol* method combination will be equivalent to the expression returned by *body*; when this expression is evaluated the only local binding will be a macro definition for `call-method`.

The forms preceding the *body* bind variables that can be used in generating the expansion. The *parameters* get whatever arguments are given after *symbol* in the `:method-combination` argument to `defgeneric`. The *parameters2* (if present) get the *forms* that appear in the call to the generic function; leftover optional parameters get the corresponding initforms; there can also be an `&whole` parameter, which gets a list of all the argument forms. The *var* (if present) will be bound to the generic function object itself.

The *group-spec*s can be used to associate variables with disjoint lists of the applicable methods. Each *group-spec* can be of the form (*var {pattern* | predname} option**). Each *var* will be bound to a list of methods whose qualifiers match some associated *pattern* or satisfy the predicate whose name is the symbol *predname*. (If no *predname* is given there must be at least one *pattern*.) A *pattern* can be *, which matches any list of qualifiers, or a list of symbols, which matches an `equal` list of qualifiers. (This list may also have *s as elements, or as the cdr.) A method with a given list of qualifiers will be accumulated in the first *var* whose predicate returns true of this list, or one of whose *pattern*s matches it. The *option*s can be:

`:description` *format*

> Some programming tools will use *format* as the second argument in a call to `format`, where the third argument is a list of method qualifiers.

`:order` *order*

> If the value of *order* is `:most-specific-first` (the default), then methods will be accumulated most specific first; if it is `:most-specific-last`, they will be accumulated in the reverse order.

`:required` *bool*

> If the value of *bool* is true, then it will cause an error if no methods are accumulated by this clause.

`(defmethod` *fname qualifier* parameters* . *body*`)`   Macro

Defines a method for the generic function named *fname*, which is created if it doesn't exist. Returns the new method. Causes an error if *fname* is the name of a normal function or a macro.

The *qualifiers* are atoms used by method combination. Standard method combination allows the qualifiers to include either `:before`, `:after`, or `:around`.

The *parameters* are like those of a normal function, except that required parameters may be expressed as a list of the form (*name specialization*), where the *specialization* is either a class, a class name, or a list of the form (eql *expression*). The first kind of specialization requires the corresponding argument to be of the specified class; the second requires it to be eql to the value of *expression*, which is evaluated when the defmethod expression is expanded. Methods are uniquely identified by their qualifiers and specializations, and will overwrite existing methods with the same ones. The *parameters* must be congruent with those of every other method of the generic function, and with any parameter list specified in a call to defgeneric.

When this method is invoked, it is equivalent to calling (lambda *parms . body*), where *parms* is *parameters* without the specializations, on the arguments originally passed to the generic function. As with defun, the body is implicitly enclosed in a block named *fname* if *fname* is a symbol, or *f* if *fname* is a list of the form (setf *f*).

(ensure-generic-function *fname* &key *argument-precedence-order* Function
                                     declare documentation
                                     environment generic-function-class
                                     lambda-list method-class
                                     method-combination)

Makes *fname* (which must not be the name of a normal function, or a macro) the name of a generic function with the corresponding properties. If there was already a generic function with this name, the properties are overwritten, possibly after meeting certain restrictions. The *argument-precedence-order, declare, documentation,* and *method-combination* are always overwritten. The *lambda-list* must be congruent with the parameter lists of all existing methods. The *generic-function-class* must be compatible with the old value, in which case change-class is called to change it. When *method-class* is changed, existing methods are not changed.

(find-class *symbol* &optional *error environment*)   Function
Returns the class whose name is *symbol* in *environment*. If there isn't one, generates an error if error is true (the default), otherwise returns nil. Settable; to detach a name from a class, set its find-class to nil.

(find-method *generic-function qualifiers specializers*   Generic Function
           &optional *error*)

Returns the method of *generic-function* whose qualifiers match *qualifiers* and whose specializations match *specializers*. The *specializers* are a list of classes (not names); the class t matches an unspecialized parameter. If there is no such method, then signals an error if *error* is true (the default), otherwise returns nil.

(function-keywords *method*)   Generic Function
Returns two values: a list of the keyword parameters accepted by *method*, and a second value true iff *method* allows other keys.

(`initialize-instance` *instance* `&rest` *initargs* `&key`)   Generic Function
    The built-in primary method calls `shared-initialize` to set the slots of *instance* as specified by *initargs*. Called by `make-instance`. Allows other keys.

(`make-instance` *class* `&rest` *initargs* `&key`)   Generic Function
    Returns a new instance of *class*. The *initargs* must be alternating symbols and values: $k_1\ v_1\ldots k_n\ v_n$. Each slot in the new instance will be initialized as follows: if some k in the *initargs* is an initarg for that slot, then the slot is set to the v corresponding to the first such k; otherwise if *class* or one of its superclasses has default initargs that include a key for the slot, the slot is set to the value of the expression following the first such key in the most specific class; otherwise if the slot has an initform, it is evaluated and the slot is set to its value; otherwise the slot is unbound. Allows other keys.

(`make-instances-obsolete` *class*)   Generic Function
    Called by `defclass` when it is used to change the definition of a *class*. Updates all the instances of *class* (by calling `update-instance-for-redefined-class`), and returns *class*.

(`make-load-form` *object* `&optional` *environment*)   Generic Function
    If *object* is an instance, structure, condition, or class, returns one or two expressions that would, when evaluated in *environment*, yield a value equivalent to *object* at load time.

(`make-load-form-saving-slots` *instance*   Function
                          `&key` *slot-names* *environment*)
    Returns two expressions that, when evaluated in *environment*, yield a value equivalent to *instance* at load time. If *slot-names* is given, only those slots are preserved.

(`method-qualifiers` *method*)   Generic Function
    Returns a list of the qualifiers of *method*.

(`next-method-p`)   Function
    When called within a method, returns true iff there is a next method.

(`no-applicable-method` *generic-function* `&rest` *args*)   Generic Function
    Called when *generic-function* is invoked in *args*, but no method is applicable. The built-in primary method signals an error.

(`no-next-method` *generic-function* *method* `&rest` *args*)   Generic Function
    Called when *method*, a method of *generic-function*, tries to call the next method, and there isn't one. The *args* are the arguments intended for the nonexistent next method. The built-in primary method signals an error.

(`reinitialize-instance` *instance* `&rest` *initargs*)   Generic Function
    Sets the slots of *instance* as specified by *initargs*. The built-in primary method passes the arguments on to `shared-initialize` (with `nil` as the second argument). Allows other keys.

(remove-method ⟨*generic-function*⟩ *method*)   Generic Function
    Destructively removes the *method* from *generic-function*, returning *generic-function*.

(shared-initialize *instance names* &rest *initargs* &key)   Generic Function
    Sets the slots of *instance* as specified by *initargs*. Any remaining slot is initialized to the value of its initform if its name is listed in *names*, or *names* is t. Allows other keys.

(slot-boundp *instance symbol*)   Function
    Returns true iff the slot named *symbol* in *instance* has been set or initialized. If no such slot, calls slot-missing.

(slot-exists-p *object symbol*)   Function
    Returns true iff *object* has a slot named *symbol*.

(slot-makunbound ⟨*instance*⟩ *symbol*)   Function
    Makes the slot of *instance* named *symbol* unbound.

(slot-missing *class object symbol opname*   Generic Function
              &optional *value*)
    Called when the operator whose name is *opname* failed to find a slot named *symbol* in an *object object* of class *class*. (The *value*, when present, is the value this slot was going to be set to.) The built-in primary method signals an error.

(slot-unbound *class instance symbol*)   Generic Function
    Called when slot-value is asked for the value of a slot named *symbol* in *instance* (whose class is *class*), and that slot is unbound. The built-in primary method signals an error. If a new method returns a value, that value will be returned by slot-value.

(slot-value *instance symbol*)   Function
    Returns the value of the slot in *instance* named *symbol*. Calls slot-missing if no such slot, slot-unbound if it is unbound; both signal an error by default. Settable.

(with-accessors ((*var fname*)*) *instance declaration* expression**)   Macro
    Evaluates its body with each *var* bound to the result of calling the corresponding function on the value of *instance*. Each *fname* must be the name of an accessor for the instance.

(with-slots ({*symbol* | (*var symbol*)}*) *instance*   Macro
              declaration* expression*)
    Evaluates its body with each *symbol* (or *var* if one is given) defined as a local symbol-macro referring to the slot named *symbol* in the value of *instance*.

(unbound-slot-instance *condition*)   Function
    Returns the instance whose slot was unbound in *condition*.

(`update-instance-for-different-class` *old new*   Generic Function
                                        `&rest` *initargs*
                                        `&key`)

Called by `change-class` to set the slots when the class of an instance is changed. The *old* instance is a copy of the original instance with dynamic extent; the *new* instance is the original instance, with whatever additional slots are required. The built-in primary method calls `shared-initialize` with: *new*, a list of the names of the new slots, and the *initargs*. Allows other keys.

(`update-instance-for-redefined-class` *instance added*   Generic Function
                                        deleted plist
                                        `&rest` *initargs*)

Called by `make-instances-obsolete` to set the slots when the class of *instance* is redefined; *added* is a list of slots added in the process; *deleted* of those deleted (including any that went from local to shared); and the *plist* has elements of the form (*name . val*) for each element of *deleted* that had a value *val*. The built-in primary method calls `shared-initialize` with: *instance*, *added*, and the *initargs*.

Structures

(`copy-structure` *structure*)   Function

Returns a new structure of the same type as *structure*, in which the values of the fields are `eql`.

(`defstruct` {*symbol* | (*symbol property**)} [*string*] *field**)   Macro

Defines a new structure type whose name is *symbol*, returning *symbol*. If *symbol* is already a structure name, the consequences are undefined, though in fact it is usually safe to re-evaluate an unchanged `defstruct` expression. If *symbol* is `str`, then by default also defines a function `make-str`, which returns new `strs`; a predicate `str-p` that returns true of `strs`; a function `copy-str` that copies `strs`; functions that refer to each of the fields; and a type named `str`.

If the *string* is present it becomes the `structure` documentation of *symbol*. By default it also becomes the `type` documentation of *symbol*, and the documentation attached to the object representing the class named *symbol*.

A *property* may have any of the following forms:

`:conc-name` | (`:conc-name` [*name*])

> The function for referring to a field named `f` in a structure named `str` will be *name*`f` instead of the default `str-f`. If *name* is `nil` or is not provided, then the function will be just `f`.

`:constructor` | `(:constructor [`*name* `[`*parameters*`]])`

> If a non-nil *name* is given, the function for making new structures will be called *name*. If *name* is `nil` no such function will be defined. If no *name* is given, the default name (`make-str`) will be used. If *parameters* is given it must be a list of field names; it becomes the parameter list of the constructor function, and each field of a new structure will be set to the argument in the corresponding position. Several constructors may be defined for a single structure.

`:copier` | `(:copier [`*name*`])`

> If a non-nil *name* is given, the function for copying structures will be called *name*. If *name* is `nil` no such function will be defined. If no *name* is given, the default name (`copy-str`) will be used.

`(:include` *name* *field**`)`

> Means that `strs` will also include all the fields of the existing structure type whose name is *name*. Field access functions for the included structure will also work on the including one. The *fields* in the `:include` expression have the usual syntax for *fields* (see below); they can be used to specify the initform (or lack of one) for a field, or to make a field read-only, or to specify a type for the field (which must be a subtype of the original). If the including structure has a `:type` (see below), the included structure must be of the same type; otherwise the type of the included structure will be a subtype of that of the including structure.

`(:initial-offset` *i*`)`

> Structures will be allocated with the equivalent of *i* unused fields occurring before the actual fields begin. Used only with `:type`.

`:named`

> Structures will be allocated with the name preceding the fields. Used only with `:type`.

`:predicate` | `(:predicate [`*name*`])`

> If a non-nil *name* is given, the predicate for identifying structures will be called *name*. If *name* is `nil` no such function will be defined. If no *name* is given, the default name (`str-p`) will be used. Cannot be used with `:type`, unless `:named` is also specified.

`(:print-function [`*fname*`])`

> When a `str` has to be printed, the function whose name is *fname* (which can also be a lambda expression) will be called with three arguments: the structure, the stream to print to, and an integer representing the print depth. Implemented by making the function a method of `print-object`. Cannot be used with `:type`.

(:print-object [*fname*])

>Like :print-function, but the function is called with just the first two arguments. Only one of :print-function and :print-object may be used.

(:type {vector | (vector *type*) | list})

>Causes the structure to be implemented as an object of the specified type. Individual strs will then be regular vectors or lists; no new type will be defined for the structure, nor any predicate for detecting the structures (unless :named is specified). If the :type is (vector *type*), then :named can be used only if *type* is a supertype of symbol.

Each *field* may be a single symbol *name*, or (*name* [*initform property**]).

The *name* will be the name of the field, and must not be the same as the name of any other field, local or inherited via :include. The field name will be used to construct the name of a (settable) function that will refer to that field; by default if the structure is called str it will be str-*name*, but see :conc-name. The *name* also becomes a keyword parameter in the default function for creating strs, the value of which will go in the corresponding field in the new structure.

The *initform*, if present, will be evaluated in the environment in which the defstruct expression occurred to produce the value of this field each time a new structure is created; if no *initform* is given, the contents of the field will initially be undefined. A *property* can be either of:

:type *type*

>Declares that the field will contain objects of type *type*.

:read-only-p *bool*

>If *bool* is non-nil, the field will be read-only.

Conditions

(abort &optional *condition*)   Function
>Invokes the restart returned by (find-restart 'abort *condition*).

(assert *test* [(*place**) [*cond arg**]])   Macro
>Evaluates *test*. If it returns nil, signals the correctable error denoted by the values of *cond* and *args*. The *places* should be those on which the value of the *test* depends; continuing from the error will allow the user to assign new values to them. Returns nil if it returns at all.

(break &rest *args*)   Function
>Calls format on *args*, then invokes the debugger. Does not signal a condition.

(cell-error-name *condition*)   Function
>Returns the name of the location in the cell-error *condition*.

(cerror *format cond* &rest *args*)   Function
>   Like `error`, except that is possible to continue from the signalled error, re-
>   turning `nil`. The *format* is given to `format` when the option to continue is
>   displayed.

(check-type *place type* [*string*])   Macro
>   Signals a correctable type-error if the value of *place* is not of type *type*. The
>   *string*, if given, should evaluate to a description of the type of value required.

(compute-restarts &optional *condition*)   Function
>   Returns a list of pending restarts, ordered from newest to oldest. If *condition*
>   is supplied, the list will contain all restarts associated with that condition, or
>   with no condition; otherwise it will contain all pending restarts. The returned
>   list must not be modified.

(continue &optional *condition*)   Function
>   Invokes the restart returned by (`find-restart` '`abort` *condition*) if there
>   is one, otherwise returns `nil`.

(define-condition *name* (*parent**) (*slot-spec**) *class-spec**)   Macro
>   Defines a new condition type, returning its name. Has the same syntax and be-
>   havior as `defclass`, except that the *class-specs* may not include a `:metaclass`
>   clause, and may include a `:report` clause. A `:report` clause specifies how
>   the condition is to be reported. The argument may be a symbol or lambda
>   expression denoting a function of two arguments (condition and stream), or it
>   may be a string.

(error *cond* &rest *args*)   Function
>   Signals the simple-error denoted by *cond* and *args*; unless it is handled, the
>   debugger will be invoked.

(find-restart *r* &optional *condition*)   Function
>   Returns the most recent pending restart whose name is *r*, if *r* is a symbol, or
>   which is eq to *r*, if *r* is a restart. If *condition* is supplied, only restarts associated
>   with that condition, or with no condition, are considered. Returns `nil` if the
>   specified restart isn't found.

(handler-bind ((*type handler*)*) *expression**)   Macro
>   Evaluates the *expressions* with local handlers. If a condition is signalled, it
>   is sent to the function (of one argument) denoted by the first *handler* whose
>   *type* is that of the condition. If the handler declines (by returning), the search
>   continues. After trying the local handlers, the system looks for handlers
>   pending when the `handler-bind` expression was evaluated.

(handler-case *test*   Macro
              (*type* ([*var*]) *declaration** *expression**)*
              [(:no-error *parameters declaration** *expression**)])

Evaluates *test*. If a condition is signalled and it is of one of the *types*, then the
condition is handled and the handler-case expression returns the result(s)
of evaluating the *expressions* associated with the first matching *type*, with *var*
(if present) bound to the condition. If no condition is signalled and there is
no :no-error clause, then the handler-case expression returns the value(s)
returned by *test*. If there is a :no-error clause, the handler-case expression
returns the result(s) of evaluating its *expressions* with the *parameters* bound to
the value(s) returned by *test*. The :no-error clause may come first, as well
as last.

(ignore-errors *expression**)   Macro

Like progn, except that the *expressions* are evaluated with a local handler for
errors. This handler will cause the ignore-errors expression to return two
values: nil, and the condition that was signalled.

(invalid-method-error *method format* &rest *args*)   Function

Used to signal an error when there is an applicable method with invalid qualifiers. The *format* and *args* are passed to format to display the error message.

(invoke-debugger *condition*)   Function

Invokes the debugger with *condition*.

(invoke-restart *restart* &rest *args*)   Function

If *restart* is a restart, invokes its restart function on *args*; if it is a symbol,
invokes the restart function of the most recent pending restart with that name
on *args*.

(invoke-restart-interactively *restart*)   Function

Like invoke-restart, but prompts interactively for the arguments.

(make-condition *type* &rest *initargs*)   Function

Returns a new condition of type *type*. Essentially, a specialized version of
make-instance.

(method-combination-error *format* &rest *args*)   Function

Used to signal an error in method combination. The arguments are passed to
format to display the error message.

(muffle-warning &optional *condition*)   Function

Invokes the restart returned by (find-restart 'muffle-warning *condition*).

(restart-bind ((*symbol function* {*key val*}*)*) *expression**)   Macro

Evaluates the *expressions* with new restarts pending. Each *symbol* becomes
the name of a restart whose restart function is the value of the corresponding
function. (If *symbol* is nil the restart will be anonymous.) A *key* can be:

:interactive-function

> The corresponding *val* must evaluate to a function of no arguments that constructs a list of arguments for invoke-restart. The default is to send no arguments.

:report-function

> The corresponding *val* must evaluate to a function of one argument, a stream, that prints on the stream a description of what the restart does.

:test-function

> The corresponding *val* must evaluate to a function of one argument, a condition, which returns true iff the restart is applicable under that condition. By default the restart is applicable under any condition.

(restart-case *test* (*symbol parameters {key val}**   Macro
                  declaration* expression*)*)

Evaluates *test* with new restarts pending. Each *symbol* becomes the name of a restart whose restart function is (lambda *parameters declaration* expression**). (If *symbol* is nil the restart will be anonymous.) A *key* can be:

:interactive

> The corresponding *val* must be a symbol or lambda expression denoting a function of no arguments that constructs a list of arguments for invoke-restart. The default is to send no arguments.

:report

> The corresponding *val* may be a string describing what the restart does, or a symbol or lambda expression denoting a function of one argument, a stream, that prints on the stream a description of what the restart does.

:test

> The corresponding *val* must be a symbol or lambda expression denoting a function of one argument, a condition, which returns true iff the restart is applicable under that condition. By default the restart is applicable under any condition.

(restart-name *restart*)   Function
Returns the name of *restart* or nil if it is anonymous.

(signal *cond* &rest *args*)   Function
Signals the condition denoted by *cond* and *args*. If it is not handled, returns nil.

(simple-condition-format-arguments *condition*)   Function
Returns the format arguments of a simple-condition.

(simple-condition-format-control *condition*)   Function
Returns the format string (or function) of a simple-condition.

(store-value *object* &optional *condition*)   Function
      Invokes the restart returned by (find-restart 'store-value *condition*),
      if there is one, on *object*. Otherwise returns nil.

(use-value *object* &optional *condition*)   Function
      Invokes the restart returned by (find-restart 'use-value *condition*), if
      there is one, on *object*. Otherwise returns nil.

(warn *cond* &rest *args*)   Function
      Signals the simple-warning denoted by *cond* and *args*. If it is not handled,
      prints a warning to *error-output* and returns nil.

(with-condition-restarts *condition restarts expression**)   Macro
      First *condition* is evaluated to produce a condition and *restarts* to produce a list
      of restarts. Then the *expression*s are evaluated with all the restarts associated
      with the condition.

(with-simple-restart (*symbol format arg**) *expression**)   Macro
      Evaluates the *expression*s with a new restart named *symbol* which, if invoked,
      causes the with-simple-restart expression to return two values: nil and
      t. The *format* and *arg*s are passed to format when the restart is described.

Symbols

(boundp *symbol*)   Function
      Returns true iff *symbol* is the name of a special variable.

(copy-symbol *symbol* &optional *props-too*)   Function
      Returns a new uninterned symbol whose name is string= to that of *symbol*.
      If *props-too* is true, the new symbol will have the same symbol-value and
      symbol-function as *symbol*, and a symbol-plist that is a copy of *symbol*'s.

(gensym &optional *prefix*)   Function
      Returns a new uninterned symbol. By default its name will be "G" plus a
      representation of the incremented value of *gensym-counter*. If *prefix* is
      supplied and is a string, it is used instead of "G".

(gentemp &optional (*prefix* "T") *package*)   [Function]
      Returns a new symbol, internal to *package*, whose name is *prefix* followed by
      the representation of an internal counter, which is incremented until the name
      is unique.

(get *symbol key* &optional *default*)   Function
      If the property list of *symbol* is $(k_1 v_1 \ldots k_n v_n)$, and *key* is eq to some k, returns
      the v corresponding to the first such k. Returns *default* if there is no such k.
      Settable.

(keywordp *object*)   Function
      Returns true iff *object* is a symbol in the keyword package.

(make-symbol *string*)   Function
      Returns a new uninterned symbol whose name is string= to *string*.

(`makunbound` *symbol*)   Function
> Deletes the special variable, if any, whose name is *symbol*; (`boundp` *symbol*) will no longer return true. Returns *symbol*.

(`set` *symbol object*)   [Function]
> Equivalent to (`setf` (`symbol-value` *symbol*) *object*).

(`symbol-function` *symbol*)   Function
> Returns the global function whose name is *symbol*. Signals an error if there isn't one. Settable.

(`symbol-name` *symbol*)   Function
> Returns the string that is *symbol*'s name. This string must not be modified.

(`symbolp` *object*)   Function
> Returns true iff *object* is a symbol.

(`symbol-package` *symbol*)   Function
> Returns the home package of *symbol*.

(`symbol-plist` *symbol*)   Function
> Returns the property list of *symbol*. Settable.

(`symbol-value` *symbol*)   Function
> Returns the value of the special variable whose name is *symbol*. Signals an error if there isn't one. Settable.

(`remprop` ⟨*symbol*⟩ *key*)   Function
> If the property list of *symbol* is $(k_1\ v_1 \ldots k_n\ v_n)$, and *key* is `eq` to some k, destructively removes the first such k and the associated v. Returns true iff the *key* was found.

Packages

(`defpackage` *name property**)   Macro
> Returns a package whose name is *name* (or its name, if it is a symbol) with the properties indicated. If there was not already a package named *name*, one is created; otherwise the properties of the existing package are modified. A *property* can be:

> (`:nicknames` *name**)
>> Sets the package's nicknames to the *name*s (or the names of such of them are symbols).

> (`:documentation` *string*)
>> Makes *string* the documentation string of the package.

> (`:use` *package**)
>> Makes the package use each of the *package*s. See `use-package`.

(:shadow *name**)

> The *name*s can be symbols or strings; the corresponding symbols will be shadowed in the package. See shadow.

(:shadowing-import-from *package name**)

> The *name*s can be symbols or strings; the corresponding symbols from *package* will be imported as by shadowing-import into the package.

(:import-from *package name**)

> The *name*s can be symbols or strings; the corresponding symbols from *package* will be imported as by import into the package.

(:export *name**)

> The *name*s can be symbols or strings; the corresponding symbols will be external to the package. See export.

(:intern *name**)

> The *name*s can be symbols or strings; the corresponding symbols are created in the package if they do not already exist. See intern.

(:size *integer*)

> Declares the estimated number of symbols expected in the package.

Any *property* other than :documentation and :size can be duplicated in the arguments. The properties are assigned in the following order: :shadow and :shadowing-import-from; then :use; then :import-from and :intern; then :export. Works at compile-time, if the call is a top-level form.

(delete-package *package*)   Function
Removes *package* from the active packages, though as an object it remains intact. Returns true iff *package* was an active package.

(do-all-symbols (*var* [*result*])   Macro
    *declaration** {*tag* | *expression*}*)
Like do-symbols, but iterates on the symbols accessible in every active package.

(do-external-symbols (*var* [*package* [*result*]])   Macro
    *declaration** {*tag* | *expression*}*)
Like do-symbols, but iterates on the external symbols of *package*.

(do-symbols (*var* [*package* [*result*]])   Macro
    *declaration** {*tag* | *expression*}*)
Evaluates its body with *var* bound to successive symbols accessible in *package*. Symbols inherited from different packages may be encountered multiple times. The body is enclosed in an implicit tagbody, and the whole do-symbols expression in an implicit block named nil. Returns the value(s) of the *result* expression, or nil if there isn't one. The *result* expression may refer to *var*, which will be nil.

`(export` *symbols* `&optional` *package)*   Function
> Makes each of the *symbols* (which must be either a symbol accessible in *package* or a list of such symbols) an external symbol of *package.* Returns `t`.

`(find-all-symbols` *name)*   Function
> Returns a list of every symbol in an active package whose name is *name* (if it is a string) or the name of *name* (if it is a symbol).

`(find-package` *package)*   Function
> Returns the package denoted by *package,* or `nil` if there isn't one.

`(find-symbol` *string* `&optional` *package)*   Function
> Returns the symbol accessible in *package* whose name is *string,* plus a second value indicating that the symbol is either `:internal`, `:external`, or `:inherited`. If there is no symbol named *string,* both return values are `nil`.

`(import` *symbols* `&optional` *package)*   Function
> Makes each of the *symbols* (which must be either a symbol or a list of symbols) accessible in *package.* Symbols that have no home package get *package* as their home package. Returns `t`.

`(in-package` *name)*   Macro
> Sets the current package to be the package denoted by *name* (a string or symbol). Works at compile-time, if the call is a top-level form.

`(intern` *string* `&optional` *package)*   Function
> Returns the symbol accessible in *package* whose name is `string=` to *string,* creating one if necessary. Returns a second value indicating the accessibility of the symbol; it can be `:internal`, `:external`, `:inherited`, or `nil`, indicating that the symbol was newly created.

`(list-all-packages)`   Function
> Returns a new list of every active package.

`(make-package` *name* `&key` *nicknames use)*   Function
> Returns a new package whose name is *name* (or its name, if *name* is a symbol), whose nicknames are the strings in the list *nicknames* plus the names of any symbols therein, and which uses the packages indicated by *use* (a list of packages and/or strings and symbols denoting them).

`(package-error-package` *condition)*   Function
> Returns the package involved in the package-error *condition.*

`(package-name` *package)*   Function
> Returns the string that is the name of *package,* or `nil` if it is not active.

`(package-nicknames` *package)*   Function
> Returns a list of the strings that are nicknames of *package.*

`(packagep` *object)*   Function
> Returns true iff *object* is a package.

`(package-shadowing-symbols` *package)*   Function
> Returns a list of the shadowed symbols of *package.*

(`package-used-by-list` *package*)   Function
>   Returns a list of the packages that *package* is used by.

(`package-use-list` *package*)   Function
>   Returns a list of the packages that *package* uses.

(`rename-package` *⟨package⟩* *name* &optional *nicknames*)   Function
>   Sets the name of *package* to *name* (if it is a string) or the name of *name* (if it is a symbol), and the nicknames of *package* to the strings in the list *nicknames*, plus the names of the symbols in it. Returns the package.

(`shadow` *names* &optional *package*)   Function
>   For each of the *names* (which can be a string, a symbol, or a list of strings and/or symbols), adds the corresponding symbol to the shadowed symbols of *package*, and if the corresponding symbol is not owned by *package*, creates such a symbol in *package*. Returns t.

(`shadowing-import` *symbols* &optional *package*)   Function
>   Makes each of the *symbols* (which must be either a symbol or a list of symbols) internal to *package*, and adds it to the package's shadowed symbols. If there already was a symbol with the same name accessible in *package*, it is uninterned. Returns t.

(`unexport` *symbols* &optional *package*)   Function
>   Makes each of the *symbols* (which must be either a symbol accessible in *package* or a list of such symbols) an internal symbol of *package*. Returns t.

(`unintern` *symbol* &optional *package*)   Function
>   Removes *symbol* from *package* (and from its shadowed symbols). If *package* was *symbol*'s home package, it will no longer have one. Returns true iff *symbol* was accessible in *package*.

(`unuse-package` *packages* &optional *package*)   Function
>   Undoes the effect of a `use-package` with the same arguments. Returns t.

(`use-package` *packages* &optional *package*)   Function
>   Makes all external symbols of the packages denoted by *packages* (which can be a package, string, or symbol, or a list thereof) accessible in *package*. None of the packages involved may be the keyword package. Returns t.

(`with-package-iterator` (*symbol packages key**)   Macro
                         *declaration** *expression**)
>   Evaluates the *expressions* with *symbol* defined as a local macro that returns successive symbols from the packages indicated by *packages* (which must evaluate to a package, or a string or symbol denoting one, or a list thereof). The *keys* indicate the symbols considered, and can include `:internal`, `:external`, and `:inherited`. The local macro returns four values: a value that is true iff a symbol is returned (so `nil` indicates the stream has run dry); the symbol; a keyword indicating whether the symbol is `:internal`, `:external`, or `:inherited`; and the package from which the symbol was obtained. The local macro may return symbols in any order, and may return the same symbol more than once if it is inherited from multiple packages.

Numbers

(abs *n*)   Function
> Returns a non-negative real with the same magnitude as *n*.

(acos *n*)   Function
> Returns the arc cosine of *n*, in radians.

(acosh *n*)   Function
> Returns the hyperbolic arc cosine of *n*.

(arithmetic-error-operands *condition*)   Function
> Returns a list of the operands in the arithmetic-error *condition*.

(arithmetic-error-operation *condition*)   Function
> Returns the operator (or its name) in the arithmetic-error *condition*.

(ash *i pos*)   Function
> Returns the integer obtained by shifting a two's-complement representation of
> *i pos* positions to the left (or right if *pos* is negative).

(asin *n*)   Function
> Returns the arc sine of *n*, in radians.

(asinh *n*)   Function
> Returns the hyperbolic arc sine of *n*.

(atan *n1* &optional (*n2* 1))   Function
> Returns the arc tangent of *n1/n2*, in radians.

(atanh *n*)   Function
> Returns the hyperbolic arc tangent of *n*.

(boole *op i1 i2*)   Function
> Returns the integer that results from applying the logical operation denoted by
> *op* to two's-complement representations of *i1* and *i2*. Common Lisp defines 16
> constants representing bitwise logical operations. The following table shows
> what boole returns when each is given as the first argument:

op	RESULT
boole-1	*i1*
boole-2	*i2*
boole-andc1	(logandc1 *i1 i2*)
boole-andc2	(logandc2 *i1 i2*)
boole-and	(logand *i1 i2*)
boole-c1	(lognot *i1*)
boole-c2	(lognot *i2*)
boole-clr	all 0
boole-eqv	(logeqv *i1 i2*)
boole-ior	(logior *i1 i2*)
boole-nand	(lognand *i1 i2*)
boole-nor	(lognor *i1 i2*)
boole-orc1	(logorc1 *i1 i2*)
boole-orc2	(logorc2 *i1 i2*)
boole-set	all 1
boole-xor	(logxor *i1 i2*)

(byte *length pos*)   Function
    Returns a byte specifier representing *length* bits, the low-order bit of which
    represents 2^{pos}.

(byte-position *spec*)   Function
    Returns $\log_2$ of the number represented by the low-order bit of the byte specifier
    spec.

(byte-size *spec*)   Function
    Returns the number of bits represented by the byte specifier *spec*.

(ceiling *r* &optional (*d* 1))   Function
    Returns two values: the smallest integer *i* greater than or equal to *r/d*, and
    r − *id*. The *d* must be a nonzero real.

(cis *r*)   Function
    Returns a complex number whose real part is (cos *r*) and whose imaginary
    part is (sin *r*).

(complex *r1* &optional *r2*)   Function
    Returns a complex number whose real part is *r1* and whose imaginary part is
    r2, or zero if no *r2* is given.

(complexp *object*)   Function
    Returns true iff *object* is a complex number.

(conjugate *n*)   Function
    Returns the complex conjugate of *n*: *n* if *n* is a real, and #c(*a* −*b*) if *n* is #c(*a*
    b).

(cos *n*)   Function
    Returns the cosine of *n* radians.

(cosh *n*)   Function
    Returns the hyperbolic cosine of *n*.

(decf *place* [*n*])   Macro
    Decrements *place* by *n*, or 1 if no *n* is given.

(decode-float *f*)   Function
    Returns three values: the significand of *f*; its exponent; and a third value
    indicating the sign of *f*, -1.0 if it is negative and 1.0 otherwise. The first and
    third values are floats in the format of *f*, and the second is an integer.

(denominator *rational*)   Function
    If *rational* is *a/b* in canonical form, returns *b*.

(deposit-field *new spec i*)   Function
    Returns the result of replacing the bits of *i* indicated by the byte specifier *spec*
    with the corresponding bits of *new*.

(dpb *new spec i*)   Function
    Returns the result of replacing the bits of *i* indicated by the byte specifier *spec*,
    of size *s*, with the low *s* bits of *new*.

(evenp *i*)   Function
> Returns true iff *i* is even.

(exp *n*)   Function
> Returns e^n.

(expt *n1* *n2*)   Function
> Returns $n1^{n2}$.

(fceiling *r* &optional (*d* 1))   Function
> Like ceiling, but the first return value is a float.

(ffloor *r* &optional (*d* 1))   Function
> Like floor, but the first return value is a float.

(float *n* &optional *f*)   Function
> Returns a floating-point approximation of *n* in the format of *f*, or a single-float if no *f* is given.

(float-digits *f*)   Function
> Returns an integer representing the number of digits in the internal representation of *f*.

(floatp *object*)   Function
> Returns true iff *object* is a floating-point number.

(float-precision *f*)   Function
> Returns an integer representing the number of significant digits in the internal representation of *f*.

(float-radix *f*)   Function
> Returns the radix of the representation of *f*.

(float-sign *f1* &optional (*f2* (float 1 *f1*)))   Function
> Returns positive or negative *f2*, depending on the sign of *f1*.

(floor *r* &optional (*d* 1))   Function
> Returns two values: the greatest integer *i* less than or equal to *r*/*d*, and $r - id$. The *d* must be a nonzero real.

(fround *r* &optional (*d* 1))   Function
> Like round, but the first return value is a float.

(ftruncate *r* &optional (*d* 1))   Function
> Like truncate, but the first return value is a float.

(gcd &rest *is*)   Function
> Returns the greatest common divisor of its arguments, or 0 if none are given.

(imagpart *n*)   Function
> Returns the imaginary part of *n*.

(incf *place* [*n*])   Macro
> Increments *place* by *n*, or 1 if no *n* is given.

(`integer-decode-float` *f*)   Function
> Returns three integers that have the same relation to one another as the values returned by `decode-float`.

(`integer-length` *i*)   Function
> Returns the number of bits needed to represent *i* in two's-complement.

(`integerp` *object*)   Function
> Returns true iff *object* is an integer.

(`isqrt` *i*)   Function
> Returns the greatest integer less than or equal to the positive square root of *i*, which must be positive.

(`lcm` `&rest` *is*)   Function
> Returns the least common multiple of its arguments, or 1 if none are given.

(`ldb` *spec i*)   Function
> Returns the integer whose representation is the bits of *i* specified by the byte specifier *spec*. Settable.

(`ldb-test` *spec i*)   Function
> Returns true if any of the bits of *i* specified by the byte specifier *spec* are 1.

(`log` *n1* `&optional` *n2*)   Function
> Returns $\log_{n2} n1$, or $\log_e n1$ if no *n2* is given.

(`logand` `&rest` *is*)   Function
> Returns the integer that results from anding the two's-complement representations of its arguments, or 0 if no arguments are given.

(`logandc1` *i1 i2*)   Function
> Returns the integer that results from anding the two's-complement representation of *i2* with the complement of that of *i1*.

(`logandc2` *i1 i2*)   Function
> Returns the integer that results from anding the two's-complement representation of *i1* with the complement of that of *i2*.

(`logbitp` *pos i*)   Function
> Returns true iff the *pos*th bit of the two's-complement representation of *i* is 1. The low-order bit is position zero.

(`logcount` *i*)   Function
> Returns the number of 0s in the two's-complement representation of *i* if *i* is negative; otherwise the number of 1s.

(`logeqv` `&rest` *is*)   Function
> Returns the integer that results from exclusive-noring the two's-complement representations of its arguments, or −1 if no arguments are given.

(`logior` `&rest` *is*)   Function
> Returns the integer that results from inclusive-oring the two's-complement representations of its arguments, or 0 if no arguments are given.

(**lognand** *i1 i2*)   Function
    Returns the complement of the integer that results from anding the two's-complement representations of its arguments.

(**lognor** *i1 i2*)   Function
    Returns the complement of the integer that results from oring the two's-complement representations of its arguments.

(**lognot** *i*)   Function
    Returns the integer whose two's-complement representation is the complement of that of *i*.

(**logorc1** *i1 i2*)   Function
    Returns the integer that results from oring the two's-complement representation of *i2* with the complement of that of *i1*.

(**logorc2** *i1 i2*)   Function
    Returns the integer that results from oring the two's-complement representation of *i1* with the complement of that of *i2*.

(**logtest** *i1 i2*)   Function
    Returns true iff any of the 1s in the two's-complement representation of *i1* appear in that of *i2*.

(**logxor** **&rest** *is*)   Function
    Returns the integer that results from exclusive-oring the two's-complement representations of its arguments, or 0 if no arguments are given.

(**make-random-state** **&optional** *state*)   Function
    Returns a new random state. If *state* is a random state, returns a copy of it; if **nil**, a copy of ***random-state***; if **t**, a randomly-initialized random state.

(**mask-field** *spec i*)   Function
    Returns the integer whose representation has the same bits as *i* in the region specified by the byte specifier *spec*, and 0 elsewhere.

(**max** *r1* **&rest** *rs*)   Function
    Returns the greatest of its arguments.

(**min** *r1* **&rest** *rs*)   Function
    Returns the least of its arguments.

(**minusp** *r*)   Function
    Returns true iff *r* is less than zero.

(**mod** *r1 r2*)   Function
    Returns the second value that **floor** would return with the same arguments.

(**numberp** *object*)   Function
    Returns true iff *object* is a number.

(**numerator** *rational*)   Function
    If *rational* is *a/b* in canonical form, returns *a*.

(oddp *i*)   Function
    Returns true iff *i* is odd.

(parse-integer *string* &key *start end radix junk-allowed*)   Function
    Return two values: the base-*radix* (default 10) integer read from *string*, and
    the position in the string of the first unread character. The *start* and *end*
    delimit the string as in sequence functions. The *string* may contain zero or
    more whitespace characters, an optional + or − sign, and one or more digits,
    followed by zero or more whitespace characters. (That is, read-macros are not
    allowed.) If *junk-allowed* is false (the default), it will cause an error if the
    string is in any other format; if it is true, parse-integer will simply return
    nil if it does not encounter a legal integer.

(phase *n*)   Function
    Returns the angle of *n* when it is represented in polar coordinates.

(plusp *r*)   Function
    Returns true iff *r* is greater than zero.

(random *limit* &optional (*state* *random-state*))   Function
    Returns a random number less than *limit* (which must be a positive integer or
    float) and of the same type. The *state* (which gets modified) is the state of the
    random number generator.

(random-state-p *object*)   Function
    Returns true iff *object* is a random state.

(rational *r*)   Function
    Converts *r* to a rational. If *r* is a float, assumes it is completely accurate.

(rationalize *r*)   Function
    Converts *r* to a rational. If *r* is a float, assumes it is accurate only to the
    precision of the representation.

(rationalp *object*)   Function
    Returns true iff *object* is a rational number.

(realp *object*)   Function
    Returns true iff *object* is a real number.

(realpart *n*)   Function
    Returns the real part of *n*.

(rem *r1 r2*)   Function
    Returns the second value that truncate would return with the same arguments.

(round *r* &optional (*d* 1))   Function
    Returns two values: the integer *i* closest to *r/d*, and $r - id$. If *r/d* is equidistant
    from two integers, the even one is chosen. The *d* must be a nonzero real.

(scale-float *f i*)   Function
    Returns the result of multiplying *f* by r^i, where *r* is the radix of the floating-point
    representation.

(signum *n*) Function
> If *n* is real, returns one, zero, or negative one depending on whether *n* is positive, zero, or negative. If *n* is complex, returns a complex number of magnitude one with the same phase.

(sin *n*) Function
> Returns the sine of *n* radians.

(sinh *n*) Function
> Returns the hyperbolic sine of *n*.

(sqrt *n*) Function
> Returns the principal square root of *n*.

(tan *n*) Function
> Returns the tangent of *n* radians.

(tanh *n*) Function
> Returns the hyperbolic tangent of *n*.

(truncate *r* &optional (*d* 1)) Function
> Returns two values: the integer *i* that would result from removing any digits after the decimal point in a decimal representation of *r/d*, and *r* − *id*. The *d* must be a nonzero real.

(upgraded-complex-part-type *type*) Function
> Returns the type of the parts of the most specialized complex number that can hold parts whose type is *type*.

(zerop *n*) Function
> Returns true iff *n* is zero.

(= *n1* &rest *ns*) Function
> Returns true iff the difference between each pair of arguments is zero.

(/= *n1* &rest *ns*) Function
> Returns true iff no two of its arguments are =.

(> *r1* &rest *rs*) Function
> Returns true iff every argument is greater than the preceding one.

(< *r1* &rest *rs*) Function
> Returns true iff every argument is less than the preceding one.

(<= *r1* &rest *rs*) Function
> Returns true iff no argument is less than the preceding one.

(>= *r1* &rest *rs*) Function
> Returns true iff no argument is greater than the preceding one.

(* &rest *ns*) Function
> Returns the product of its arguments, or 1 if none are given.

(+ &rest *ns*) Function
> Returns the sum of its arguments, or 0 if none are given.

(- *nl* &rest *ns*)   Function
> When called with one argument, returns −*nl*. A call of the form (- $a_1 \ldots a_n$)
> returns $a_1 - \ldots - a_n$.

(/ *nl* &rest *ns*)   Function
> When called with one argument (which must not be zero), returns its reciprocal.
> When called with multiple arguments, returns the value of the first divided by
> the product of the rest (which must not include zero).

(1+ *n*)   Function
> Equivalent to (+ *n* 1).

(1- *n*)   Function
> Equivalent to (- *n* 1).

Characters

(alpha-char-p *char*)   Function
> Returns true iff *char* is an alphabetic character.

(both-case-p *char*)   Function
> Returns true iff *char* has case.

(alphanumericp *char*)   Function
> Returns true iff *char* is an alphabetic character or a digit.

(character *c*)   Function
> Returns the character corresponding to a character, a string of one character, or
> a symbol whose name is such a string.

(characterp *object*)   Function
> Returns true iff *object* is a character.

(char-code *char*)   Function
> Returns code attribute of *char*. This value is implementation-dependent, but in
> most implementations it will be the ASCII number.

(char-downcase *char*)   Function
> If *char* is uppercase, returns the corresponding lowercase character; otherwise
> returns *char*.

(char-greaterp *charl* &rest *chars*)   Function
> Like char> but ignores case.

(char-equal *charl* &rest *chars*)   Function
> Like char= but ignores case.

(char-int *char*)   Function
> Returns a non-negative integer representing *char*. If the character does not
> have implementation-defined attributes, it will be the same as the char-code.

(char-lessp *charl* &rest *chars*)   Function
> Like char< but ignores case.

(char-name *char*)   Function
    Returns the string that is the name of *char*, or `nil` if it doesn't have one.

(char-not-greaterp *char1* &rest *chars*)   Function
    Like char<= but ignores case.

(char-not-equal *char1* &rest *chars*)   Function
    Like char/= but ignores case.

(char-not-lessp *char1* &rest *chars*)   Function
    Like char>= but ignores case.

(char-upcase *char*)   Function
    If *char* is lowercase, returns the corresponding uppercase character; otherwise returns *char*.

(char= *char1* &rest *chars*)   Function
    Returns true iff all its arguments are the same.

(char/= *char1* &rest *chars*)   Function
    Returns true iff no two of its arguments are the same.

(char> *char1* &rest *chars*)   Function
    Returns true iff every argument is greater than the preceding one.

(char< *char1* &rest *chars*)   Function
    Returns true iff every argument is less than the preceding one.

(char<= *char1* &rest *chars*)   Function
    Returns true iff no argument is less than the preceding one.

(char>= *char1* &rest *chars*)   Function
    Returns true iff no argument is greater than the preceding one.

(code-char *code*)   Function
    Returns the *char* that has *code* as its code attribute.

(digit-char *i* &optional (*r* 10))   Function
    Returns the character that represents *i* in base *r*.

(digit-char-p *char* &optional (*r* 10))   Function
    Returns true iff *char* is a digit in base *r*.

(graphic-char-p *char*)   Function
    Returns true iff *char* is a graphic character.

(lower-case-p *char*)   Function
    Returns true iff *char* is a lowercase character.

(name-char *name*)   Function
    Returns the character whose name is *name* (or the name of *name*, if it is a symbol). Not case-sensitive.

(standard-char-p *char*)   Function
    Returns true iff *char* is a standard character.

(upper-case-p *char*)   Function
    Returns true iff *char* is an uppercase character.

Conses

(acons *key value alist*)   Function
    Equivalent to (cons (cons *key value*) *alist*).

(adjoin *object prolist* &key *key test test-not*)   Function
    If member would return true with the same arguments, returns *prolist*, otherwise
    returns (cons *object prolist*).

(append &rest *prolists*)   Function
    Returns a list whose elements are the elements of each *prolist*, in order. The last
    argument, which can be of any type, is not copied, so (cdr (append '(a)
    x)) will be eq to x. Returns nil if given no arguments.

(assoc *key alist* &key *key test test-not*)   Function
    Returns the first element in *alist* whose car matches *key*.

(assoc-if *predicate alist* &key *key*)   Function
    Returns the first element in *alist* for whose car *predicate* returns true.

(assoc-if-not *predicate alist* &key *key*)   [Function]
    Returns the first element in *alist* for whose car *predicate* returns false.

(atom *object*)   Function
    Returns true when *object* is not a cons.

(butlast *list* &optional (*n* 1))   Function
(nbutlast ⟨*list*⟩ &optional (*n* 1))   Function
    Returns a copy of *list* without the last *n* elements, or nil if *list* has less than *n*
    elements. Causes an error if *n* is negative.

(car *list*)   Function
    If *list* is a cons, returns its car. If *list* is nil, returns nil. Settable.

(cdr *list*)   Function
    If *list* is a cons, returns its cdr. If *list* is nil, returns nil. Settable.

(c*x*r *list*)   Functions
    where *x* represents a string of one to four as or ds. Equivalent to the corre-
    sponding composition of car and cdr. For example, (cdaar x) is equivalent
    to (cdr (car (car x))). Settable.

(cons *object1 object2*)   Function
    Returns a new cons whose car is *object1* and whose cdr is *object2*. So if *object2*
    is a list of the form $(e_1 \ldots e_n)$, will return $(object1\ e_1 \ldots e_n)$.

(consp *object*)   Function
    Returns true when *object* is a cons.

(copy-alist *alist*)   Function
    Same as (mapcar #'(lambda (x) (cons (car x) (cdr x))) *alist*).

(copy-list *list*)   Function
    Returns a list equal to *list* in which all the top-level list structure consists of
    new conses. If *list* is nil, returns nil.

(`copy-tree` *tree*)   Function
> Returns a new tree with the same shape and leaves as *tree*, but in which all the tree structure consists of new conses. If *tree* is an atom, returns *tree*.

(`endp` *list*)   Function
> Returns true when *list* is `nil`.

(`first` *list*) ... (`tenth` *list*)   Functions
> Return the first through the tenth elements of *list*, or `nil` if *list* does not have that many elements. Settable.

(`getf` *plist key* `&optional` (*default* `nil`))   Function
> If *plist* is $(p_1\ v_1\ \ldots\ p_n\ v_n)$ and p_i is the first p eq to *key*, returns v_i. If no p is eq to *key*, returns *default*. Settable.

(`get-properties` *plist prolist*)   Function
> If *plist* is $(p_1\ v_1\ \ldots\ p_n\ v_n)$ and p_i is the first p eq to some element of *prolist*, returns p_i, v_i, and $(p_i\ v_i\ \ldots\ p_n\ v_n)$. Otherwise returns three nils.

(`intersection` *prolist1 prolist2* `&key` *key test test-not*)   Function
(`nintersection` ⟨*prolist1*⟩ *prolist2* `&key` *key test test-not*)   Function
> Returns a list of the elements of *prolist1* that are members of *prolist2*. Nothing is guaranteed about the order of the elements in the result.

(`last` *list* `&optional` (*n* 1))   Function
> Returns the last *n* conses in *list*, or *list* if it has less than *n* elements. If *n* is 0, returns the cdr of the last cons in *list*.

(`ldiff` *list object*)   Function
> If *object* is a tail of *list*, returns a new list of the elements up to *object*. Otherwise returns a copy of *list*.

(`list` `&rest` *objects*)   Function
> Returns a new list whose elements are *objects*.

(`list*` *object* `&rest` *objects*)   Function
> If only one argument is provided, returns it. Otherwise, (`list*` *arg₁* ... *argₙ*) is equivalent to (`nconc` (`list` *arg₁* ... *argₙ₋₁*) *argₙ*).

(`list-length` *list*)   Function
> Returns the number of conses in *list*, or `nil` if *list* is circular (in contrast to `length`, which is not defined for circular lists). It is an error if *list* is a dotted list.

(`listp` *object*)   Function
> Returns true when *object* is a list—that is, a cons or `nil`.

(`make-list` *n* `&key` (*initial-element* `nil`))   Function
> Returns a new list of *n* initial-elements.

(`mapc` *function prolist* `&rest` *prolists*)   Function
> If the shortest *prolist* has *n* elements, calls *function* *n* times: first on the first element of each *prolist*, and last on the *n*th element of each *prolist*. Returns *prolist*.

(mapcan *function prolist* &rest *prolists*)   Function
 Equivalent to applying nconc to the result of calling mapcar with the same
 arguments.

(mapcar *function prolist* &rest *prolists*)   Function
 If the shortest *prolist* has *n* elements, calls *function n* times: first on the first
 element of each *prolist*, and last on the *n*th element of each *prolist*. Returns a
 list of the values returned by *function*.

(mapcon *function prolist* &rest *prolists*)   Function
 Equivalent to applying nconc to the result of calling maplist with the same
 arguments.

(mapl *function prolist* &rest *prolists*)   Function
 If the shortest *prolist* has *n* elements, calls *function n* times: first on each *prolist*,
 and last on the $(n-1)$th cdr of each *prolist*. Returns *prolist*.

(maplist *function prolist* &rest *prolists*)   Function
 If the shortest *prolist* has *n* elements, calls *function n* times: first on each *prolist*,
 and last on the $(n-1)$th cdr of each *prolist*. Returns a list of the values returned
 by *function*.

(member *object prolist* &key *key test test-not*)   Function
 Returns the tail of *prolist* starting with the first element matching *object*, or
 nil if no element matches.

(member-if *predicate prolist* &key *key test test-not*)   Function
 Returns the tail of *prolist* starting with the first element for which *predicate*
 returns true, or nil if there is no such element.

(member-if-not *predicate prolist* &key *key test test-not*)   [Function]
 Returns the tail of *prolist* starting with the first element for which *predicate*
 returns false, or nil if there is no such element.

(nconc &rest ⟨*lists*⟩)   Function
 Returns a list whose elements are the elements of each *list*, in order. Works
 by setting the cdr of the last cons in each *list* to the succeeding *list*. The final
 argument can be an object of any type. Returns nil if given no arguments.

(nth *n list*)   Function
 Returns the $(n+1)$th element of *list*. Returns nil if *list* has less than $(n+1)$
 elements. Settable.

(nthcdr *n list*)   Function
 Equivalent to calling cdr *n* times in succession with *list* as the initial argument.

(null *object*)   Function
 Returns true when *object* is nil.

(pairlis *keys values* &optional *alist*)   Function
 Returns the same value as either (nconc (mapcar #'cons *keys values*)
 alist) or (nconc (nreverse (mapcar #'cons *keys values*)) *alist*), with
 the additional requirement that *keys* and *values* must be of the same length.

(pop ⟨*place*⟩)   Macro
> Sets *place*, which must evaluate to a list *list*, to (cdr *list*). Returns (car *list*).

(push *object* ⟨*place*⟩)   Macro
> Sets *place* to (cons *object place*). Returns this value.

(pushnew *object* ⟨*place*⟩ &key *key test test-not*)   Macro
> Sets *place*, which must evaluate to a proper list, to the result of calling adjoin with the same arguments. Returns the new value of *place*.

(rassoc *key alist* &key *key test test-not*)   Function
> Returns the first element in *alist* whose cdr matches *key*.

(rassoc-if *predicate alist* &key *key*)   Function
> Returns the first element in *alist* for whose cdr *predicate* returns true.

(rassoc-if-not *predicate alist* &key *key*)   [Function]
> Returns the first element in *alist* for whose cdr *predicate* returns false.

(remf ⟨*place*⟩ *key*)   Macro
> The first argument, *place*, must evaluate to a property list *plist*. If *plist* is (p_1 v_1 ... p_n v_n) and p_i is the first p eq to *key*, destructively removes p_i and v_i from *plist*, and sets *place* to the result. Returns true if it removed something, false otherwise.

(rest *list*)   Function
> Identical to cdr. Settable.

(revappend *list1 list2*)   Function
(nreconc ⟨*list1*⟩ *list2*)   Function
> Equivalent to (nconc (reverse *list1*) *list2*) and (nconc (nreverse *list1*) *list2*) respectively.

(rplaca ⟨*cons*⟩ *object*)   Function
> Equivalent to (setf (car *cons*) *object*), but returns *cons*.

(rplacd ⟨*cons*⟩ *object*)   Function
> Equivalent to (setf (cdr *cons*) *object*), but returns *cons*.

(set-difference *prolist1 prolist2* &key *key test test-not*)   Function
(nset-difference ⟨*prolist1*⟩ *prolist2* &key *key test test-not*)   Function
> Returns a list of the elements of *prolist1* that are not members of *prolist2*. Nothing is guaranteed about the order of the elements in the result.

(set-exclusive-or *prolist1 prolist2* &key *key test test-not*)   Function
(nset-exclusive-or ⟨*prolist1*⟩ ⟨*prolist2*⟩ &key *key test test-not*) Function
> Returns a list of the elements that are members of either *prolist1* or *prolist2*, but not both. Nothing is guaranteed about the order of the elements in the result.

(sublis *alist tree* &key *key test test-not*)   Function
(nsublis *alist* ⟨*tree*⟩ &key *key test test-not*)   Function
> Returns a tree like *tree*, but with each subtree that matches a key in *alist* replaced by the corresponding value. If no changes are required, returns *tree*.

(subsetp *prolist1 prolist2* &key *key test test-not*)   Function
    Returns true when every element of *prolist1* is a member of *prolist2*.

(subst *new old tree* &key *key test test-not*)   Function
(nsubst *new old ⟨tree⟩* &key *key test test-not*)   Function
    Returns a tree like *tree* but with each subtree that matches *old* replaced by *new*.

(subst-if *new predicate tree* &key *key*)   Function
(nsubst-if *new predicate ⟨tree⟩* &key *key*)   Function
    Returns a tree like *tree* but with each subtree for which *predicate* returns true
    replaced by *new*.

(subst-if-not *new predicate tree* &key *key*)   [Function]
(nsubst-if-not *new predicate ⟨tree⟩* &key *key*)   [Function]
    Returns a tree like *tree* but with each subtree for which *predicate* returns false
    replaced by *new*.

(tailp *object list*)   Function
    Returns true when *object* is a tail of *list*—that is, when *object* is `nil` or one of
    the conses that make up *list*.

(tree-equal *tree1 tree2* &key *test test-not*)   Function
    Returns true when `tree1` and `tree2` have the same shape and matching leaves.

(union *prolist1 prolist2* &key *key test test-not*)   Function
(nunion *⟨prolist1⟩ ⟨prolist2⟩* &key *key test test-not*)   Function
    Returns a list of the elements that are members of *prolist1* or *prolist2*. Nothing
    is guaranteed about the order of the elements in the result. If either *prolist1*
    or *prolist2* contain duplicates, then those elements may be duplicated in the
    result.

Arrays

(adjustable-array-p *array*)   Function
    Returns true iff *array* is adjustable.

(adjust-array *⟨array⟩ dimensions* &key ...)   Function
    Returns an array like *array* (identical to it if *array* is adjustable) with some
    changed properties. If any of the *dimensions* are smaller, the original array is
    cropped in that dimension; if larger, the new elements may be determined by
    the `:initial-element` argument. The keys are as in `make-array`, with the
    following additional stipulations:

    `:element-type` *type*

        The *type* must be compatible with the original type.

    `:initial-element` *object*

        Elements of the array required by larger *dimensions* will be *object*; other
        elements will retain their original values.

:initial-contents *seq*

> As in make-array, which means that the existing elements of *array* will be overwritten.

:fill-pointer *object*

> If *object* is nil, the fill pointer (if any) will remain the same.

:displaced-to *array2*

> If *array* originally was displaced, but *array2* is nil, the corresponding elements of the old target array will be copied to the array to be returned, with the :initial-element (if any) filling in the blanks (if any). If *array* originally was not displaced, and *array2* is an array, then the original contents will be lost and the returned array will be displaced to *array2*. Otherwise, as with make-array.

:displaced-index-offset *i*

> If this argument is not supplied, the offset for a displaced array will be zero.

(aref *array* &rest *is*)   Function

Returns the element of *array* whose indices are the *is* (or if *array* is zero-dimension and no *is* are given, its one element). Ignores fill pointers. Settable.

(array-dimension *array* *i*)   Function

Returns the length of the *i*th dimension of *array*. Zero-indexed.

(array-dimensions *array*)   Function

Returns a list of integers representing the length of each dimension of *array*.

(array-displacement *array*)   Function

Returns two values: the array to which *array* is displaced, and the offset. Returns nil and 0 if *array* is not displaced.

(array-element-type *array*)   Function

Returns the element type of *array*.

(array-has-fill-pointer-p *array*)   Function

Returns true iff *array* has a fill pointer.

(array-in-bounds-p *array* &rest *is*)   Function

Returns true iff the same arguments would be valid in a call to aref.

(arrayp *object*)   Function

Returns true iff *object* is an array.

(array-rank *array*)   Function

Returns the number of dimensions *array* has.

(array-row-major-index *array* &rest *is*)   Function

Returns the number of the element specified by the *is* when the elements of *array* are considered in row-major order. Zero-indexed.

(`array-total-size` *array*)   Function
> Returns the number of locations in *array*.

(`bit` *bit-array* &rest *is*)   Function
> Like `aref`, but the argument must be a bit array. Settable.

(`bit-and` ⟨*bit-array1*⟩ *bit-array2* &optional ⟨*arg*⟩)   Function
> For bit-arrays what `logand` is for integers: ands two bit-arrays of the same
> dimensions, returning the resulting array. If *arg* is `t`, the returned array is a
> new one; if `nil`, *bit-array1* is used for the return value; if *arg* is a bit-array (of
> the same dimensions as the first two), it is used.

(`bit-andc1` ⟨*bit-array1*⟩ *bit-array2* &optional ⟨*arg*⟩)   Function
> Like `bit-and`, but analogous to `logandc1`.

(`bit-andc2` ⟨*bit-array1*⟩ *bit-array2* &optional ⟨*arg*⟩)   Function
> Like `bit-and`, but analogous to `logandc2`.

(`bit-eqv` ⟨*bit-array1*⟩ *bit-array2* &optional ⟨*arg*⟩)   Function
> Like `bit-and`, but analogous to `logeqv`.

(`bit-ior` ⟨*bit-array1*⟩ *bit-array2* &optional ⟨*arg*⟩)   Function
> Like `bit-and`, but analogous to `logior`.

(`bit-nand` ⟨*bit-array1*⟩ *bit-array2* &optional ⟨*arg*⟩)   Function
> Like `bit-and`, but analogous to `lognand`.

(`bit-nor` ⟨*bit-array1*⟩ *bit-array2* &optional ⟨*arg*⟩)   Function
> Like `bit-and`, but analogous to `lognor`.

(`bit-not` ⟨*bit-array*⟩ &optional ⟨*arg*⟩)   Function
> For bit-arrays what `lognot` is for integers: returning the logical complement
> of *bit-array*. If *arg* is `t`, the returned array is a new one; if `nil`, *bit-array* is
> used for the return value; if *arg* is a bit-array (of the same dimensions as the
> first), it is used.

(`bit-orc1` ⟨*bit-array1*⟩ *bit-array2* &optional ⟨*arg*⟩)   Function
> Like `bit-and`, but analogous to `logorc1`.

(`bit-orc2` ⟨*bit-array1*⟩ *bit-array2* &optional ⟨*arg*⟩)   Function
> Like `bit-and`, but analogous to `logorc2`.

(`bit-xor` ⟨*bit-array1*⟩ *bit-array2* &optional ⟨*arg*⟩)   Function
> Like `bit-and`, but analogous to `logxor`.

(`bit-vector-p` *object*)   Function
> Returns true iff *object* is a bit vector.

(`fill-pointer` *vector*)   Function
> Returns the fill pointer of *vector*. Settable, but only if *vector* already has a fill
> pointer.

(make-array *dimensions* &key *element-type initial-element*   Function
                                initial-contents adjustable
                                fill-pointer displaced-to
                                displaced-index-offset)

Returns a new array whose dimensions are the *dimensions*, (or if *dimensions* is a single number, a vector of that length). By default the elements can be of any type, and the value of each element is undefined. The keyword arguments may be:

:element-type *type*

Declares that the array will contain objects of type *type*.

:initial-element *object*

Each element of the array will be *object*. Cannot be used with :initial-contents.

:initial-contents *seq*

The elements of the array will be the corresponding elements of the nested sequence *seq*. The argument can also be a single object, if the array is zero-dimensional. Cannot be used with :initial-element.

:adjustable *object*

If *object* is true, the array is guaranteed to be adjustable; it may be anyway.

:fill-pointer *object*

If *object* is true, the array (it must be a vector) will have a fill pointer. If *object* is an integer between zero and the length of the vector, it will be the initial value of the fill pointer.

:displaced-to *array*

The array will be displaced to *array*. A reference to a given element of the returned array will be translated into a reference to the corresponding element of *array* (the element in the same position if the contents of the two arrays were printed, one element at a time, in row-major order).

:displaced-index-offset *i*

The offset for the mapping onto the target array will be *i*. Can only be given if :displaced-to is.

(row-major-aref *array i*)   Function
Returns the *i*th element of *array* when the elements are considered in row-major order. Zero-indexed. Settable.

(sbit *simple-bit-array* &rest *is*)   Function
Like aref, but the argument must be a simple bit array. Settable.

(simple-bit-vector-p *object*)   Function
Returns true iff *object* is a simple bit vector.

(`simple-vector-p` *object*)   Function
> Returns true iff *object* is a simple vector.

(`svref` *simple-vector i*)   Function
> Returns the *i*th element of *simple-vector*. Zero-indexed. Settable.

(`upgraded-array-element-type` *type* &optional *env*)   Function
> Returns the actual element type that the implementation would give to an array whose `:element-type` was declared to be *type*.

(`vector` &rest *objects*)   Function
> Returns a new simple vector whose elements are the *objects*.

(`vectorp` *object*)   Function
> Returns true iff *object* is a vector.

(`vector-pop` *vector*)   Function
> Decrements the fill pointer of *vector* and returns the element it then points to. Causes an error if *vector* doesn't have a fill pointer, or the fill pointer is already 0.

(`vector-push` *object vector*)   Function
> If the fill pointer is already equal to the length of *vector*, simply returns `nil`. Otherwise, replaces the element of the vector to which its fill pointer points with *object*, then increments the fill pointer and returns its old value. Causes an error if *vector* doesn't have a fill pointer.

(`vector-push-extend` *object vector* &optional *i*)   Function
> Like `vector-push`, but if the fill pointer is already equal to the length of *vector*, the vector is first lengthened by *i* elements (or an implementation-dependent default) by calling `adjust-array`.

Strings

(`char` *string i*)   Function
> Returns the *i*th character of *string*. Zero-indexed. Ignores fill pointers. Settable.

(`make-string` *n* &key *initial-element* (*element-type* `'character`)) Function
> Returns a new string of *n* *initial-element*s (the default values of which is implementation-dependent).

(`schar` *simple-string i*)   Function
> Like `char` but the string must be a simple string. Settable.

(`simple-string-p` *object*)   Function
> Returns true iff *object* is a simple string.

(`string` *arg*)   Function
> If *arg* is a string, returns it; if a symbol, returns its name; if a character, returns a string containing it.

(string-capitalize *string* &key *start end*) Function
(nstring-capitalize 〈*string*〉 &key *start end*) Function
    Returns a string in which the first letter of each word is uppercase, and other characters are lowercase. Each sequence of alphabetic characters is a word. The first argument to string-capitalize may also be a symbol, in which case its name is used.

(string-downcase *string* &key *start end*) Function
(nstring-downcase 〈*string*〉 &key *start end*) Function
    Like string-upcase and nstring-upcase, but characters are converted to lowercase.

(string-equal *string1 string2* &key *start1 end1 start2 end2*) Function
    Like string= but ignores case.

(string-greaterp *string1 string2* &key *start1 end1 start2 end2*) Function
    Like string> but ignores case.

(string-upcase *string* &key *start end*) Function
(nstring-upcase 〈*string*〉 &key *start end*) Function
    Returns a string in which lowercase characters are replaced by the corresponding uppercase ones. The *start* and *end* are used as in sequence functions. The first argument to string-upcase may also be a symbol, in which case its name is used.

(string-left-trim *seq string*) Function
    Like string-trim, but only trims from the front.

(string-lessp *string1 string2* &key *start1 end1 start2 end2*) Function
    Like string< but ignores case.

(string-not-equal *string1 string2* &key *start1 end1 start2 end2*) Function
    Like string/= but ignores case.

(string-not-greaterp *string1 string2*
               &key *start1 end1 start2 end2*) Function
    Like string<= but ignores case.

(string-not-lessp *string1 string2* &key *start1 end1 start2 end2*) Function
    Like string>= but ignores case.

(stringp *object*) Function
    Returns true iff *object* is a string.

(string-right-trim *seq string*) Function
    Like string-trim, but only trims from the back.

(string-trim *seq string*) Function
    Returns a string like *string*, but with any characters that appear in *seq* removed from either end.

(string= *string1 string2* &key *start1 end1 start2 end2*)   Function
    Returns true iff the subsequences of *string1* and *string2* are the same length
    and contain the same characters. The parameters *start1* and *end1*, and *start2*
    and *end2*, work like the usual *start* and *end* parameters for *string1* and *string2*
    respectively.

(string/= *string1 string2* &key *start1 end1 start2 end2*)   Function
    Returns true iff string= would return false.

(string< *string1 string2* &key *start1 end1 start2 end2*)   Function
    Returns true iff the two subsequences contain the same characters up to the end
    of the first, and the second is longer; or if the subsequences contain different
    characters, and where they differ for the first time, the character in the first
    substring is char< the one in the second. The parameters are the same as in
    string=.

(string> *string1 string2* &key *start1 end1 start2 end2*)   Function
    Returns true iff the two subsequences contain the same characters up to the end
    of the second, and the first is longer; or if the subsequences contain different
    characters, and where they differ for the first time, the character in the first
    substring is char> the one in the second. The parameters are the same as in
    string=.

(string<= *string1 string2* &key *start1 end1 start2 end2*)   Function
    True iff the arguments are string< or string=.

(string>= *string1 string2* &key *start1 end1 start2 end2*)   Function
    True iff the arguments are string> or string=.

Sequences

(concatenate *type* &rest *sequences*)   Function
    Returns a new sequence of type *type* whose elements are the elements of
    sequences, in order. Copies every *sequence*, even the last.

(copy-seq *proseq*)   Function
    Returns a new sequence of the same type as *proseq* and with the same elements.

(count *object proseq* &key *key test test-not from-end start end*)   Function
    Returns the number of elements in *proseq* that match *object*.

(count-if *predicate proseq* &key *key from-end start end*)   Function
    Returns the number of elements in *proseq* for which *predicate* returns true.

(count-if-not *predicate proseq* &key *key from-end start end*)   [Function]
    Returns the number of elements in *proseq* for which *predicate* returns false.

(elt *proseq n*)   Function
    Returns the $(n + 1)$th element of *proseq*. It is an error if *proseq* has less than
    $n + 1$ elements. Settable.

(fill ⟨*proseq*⟩ *object* &key *start end*)   Function
    Destructively fills *proseq* with *object*. Returns *proseq*.

(find *object proseq* &key *key test test-not from-end start end*)   Function
    Returns the first element in *proseq* that matches *object*.

(find-if *predicate proseq* &key *key from-end start end*)   Function
    Returns the first element in *proseq* for which *predicate* returns true.

(find-if-not *predicate proseq* &key *key from-end start end*)   [Function]
    Returns the first element in *proseq* for which *predicate* returns false.

(length *proseq*)   Function
    Returns the number of elements in *proseq*. If *proseq* has a fill pointer, returns
    the length up to it.

(make-sequence *type n* &key (*initial-element* nil))   Function
    Returns a new sequence of type *type*, whose elements are *n initial-element*s.

(map *type function proseq* &rest *proseqs*)   Function
    If the shortest *proseq* has *n* elements, calls *function n* times: first on the first
    element of each *proseq*, and last on the *n*th element of each *proseq*. Returns a
    sequence of type *type* whose elements are the values returned by *function*. (If
    type is nil, this is like mapc for sequences.)

(map-into ⟨*result*⟩ *function proseq* &rest *proseqs*)   Function
    If the shorter of *result* (which must be a proper sequence) and the shortest
    proseq has *n* elements, calls *function n* times: first on the first element of each
    proseq, and last on the *n*th element of each *proseq*. Destructively replaces
    the first *n* elements of *result* with the values returned by *function*, and returns
    result.

(merge *type* ⟨*sequence1*⟩ ⟨*sequence2*⟩ *predicate* &key *key*)   Function
    Equivalent to (stable-sort (concatenate *type sequence1 sequence2*)
    predicate :key *key*), but destructive and more efficient.

(mismatch *sequence1 sequence2*   Function
        &key *key test test-not from-end start1 end1 start2 end2*)
    Returns the position (zero-indexed) of the first element of *sequence1* at which
    sequence1 and *sequence2* differ. If *sequence1* and *sequence2* match in every
    element, returns nil. The parameters *start1* and *end1*, and *start2* and *end2*,
    work like the usual *start* and *end* parameters for *sequence1* and *sequence2*
    respectively.

(position *object proseq*   Function
        &key *key test test-not from-end start end*)
    Returns the position (zero-indexed) of the first element in *proseq* that matches
    object.

(position-if *predicate proseq* &key *key from-end start end*)   Function
    Returns the position (zero-indexed) of the first element in *proseq* for which
    predicate returns true.

(`position-if-not` *object proseq* `&key` *key from-end start end*)   [Function]
Returns the position (zero-indexed) of the first element in *proseq* for which *predicate* returns false.

(`reduce` *function proseq* `&key` *key from-end start end initial-value*)   Function
If the *function* is *f* and the elements of *proseq* are *a, b, c*, then the behavior of `reduce` is indicated by the following table:

from-end	*initial-value*	EQUIVALENT TO
false	no	$(f\ (f\ a\ b)\ c)$
false	yes	$(f\ (f\ (f\ initial\text{-}value\ a)\ b)\ c)$
true	no	$(f\ a\ (f\ b\ c))$
true	yes	$(f\ a\ (f\ b\ (f\ c\ initial\text{-}value)))$

If *proseq* contains just one element and no *initial-value* is provided, that element is returned. If *proseq* is empty and an *initial-value* is provided, it is returned, but if no *initial-value* is provided, the return value is the result of calling *function* with no arguments. If both *key* and *initial-value* are provided, the former is not called on the latter.

(`remove` *object proseq*   Function
   `&key` *key test test-not from-end start end count*)
(`delete` *object ⟨proseq⟩*   Function
   `&key` *key test test-not from-end start end count*)
Returns a sequence like *proseq* but without the elements that match *object*. If *count* is supplied, only the first *count* instances are removed.

(`remove-duplicates` *proseq*   Function
   `&key` *key test test-not from-end start end*)
(`delete-duplicates` *⟨proseq⟩*   Function
   `&key` *key test test-not from-end start end*)
Returns a sequence like *proseq* without all but the last instance of any duplicate elements.

(`remove-if` *predicate proseq* `&key` *key from-end start end count*)   Function
(`delete-if` *predicate proseq* `&key` *key from-end start end count*)   Function
Returns a sequence like *proseq* but without the elements for which *predicate* returns true. If *count* is supplied, only the first *count* instances are removed.

(`remove-if-not` *predicate proseq*   [Function]
   `&key` *key from-end start end count*)
(`delete-if-not` *predicate ⟨proseq⟩*   [Function]
   `&key` *key from-end start end count*)
Returns a sequence like *proseq* but without the elements for which *predicate* returns false. If *count* is supplied, only the first *count* instances are removed.

(replace ⟨*sequence1*⟩ *sequence2* &key *start1 end1 start2 end2*)   Function
> Destructively replaces *sequence1* with *sequence2*, and returns *sequence1*. The number of elements replaced will be equal to the length of the shorter subsequence. Works if *sequence1* and *sequence2* are eq, but not if they merely share structure. The parameters *start1* and *end1*, and *start2* and *end2*, work like the usual *start* and *end* parameters for *sequence1* and *sequence2* respectively.

(reverse *proseq*)   Function
(nreverse ⟨*proseq*⟩)   Function
> Returns a sequence of the same type as *proseq*, containing the same elements in the reverse order. The sequence returned by reverse is always a copy. If *proseq* is a vector, reverse returns a simple vector.

(search *sequence1* *sequence2*   Function
>   &key *key test test-not from-end start1 end1 start2 end2*)
> Returns the position (zero-indexed) of the first subsequence of *sequence2* that matches *sequence1*. If no matching subsequence is found, returns nil. The parameters *start1* and *end1*, and *start2* and *end2*, work like the usual *start* and *end* parameters for *sequence1* and *sequence2* respectively.

(sort ⟨*proseq*⟩ *predicate* &key *key*)   Function
> Returns a sequence of the same type as *proseq*, containing the same elements, in an order such that there are no two successive elements *e* and *f* such that (*predicate e f*) is false and (*predicate f e*) is true.

(stable-sort ⟨*proseq*⟩ *predicate* &key *key*)   Function
> Like sort, but preserves as much of the original order of the elements of *proseq* as possible.

(subseq *proseq start* &optional *end*)   Function
> Returns a new sequence which is a subsequence of *proseq*. The parameters *start* and *end* indicate a subsequence in the same way as the corresponding keyword arguments: *start* is the position (zero-indexed) of the first element in the subsequence, and *end*, if given, is the position *after* the last element in the subsequence. Settable, as if by replace.

(substitute   *new old proseq*   Function
>   &key *key test test-not from-end start end count*)
(nsubstitute *new old* ⟨*proseq*⟩   Function
>   &key *key test test-not from-end start end count*)
> Returns a sequence like *proseq* except that elements matching *old* are replaced by *new*. If *count* is supplied, only the first *count* instances are replaced.

(substitute-if   *new predicate proseq*   Function
>   &key *key from-end start end count*)
(nsubstitute-if *new predicate* ⟨*proseq*⟩   Function
>   &key *key from-end start end count*)
> Returns a sequence like *proseq* except that elements for which *predicate* returns true are replaced by *new*. If *count* is supplied, only the first *count* instances are replaced.

(substitute-if-not *new predicate proseq*   [Function]
                    &key *key from-end start end count*)
(nsubstitute-if-not *new predicate ⟨proseq⟩*   [Function]
                    &key *key from-end start end count*)

> Returns a sequence like *proseq* except that elements for which *predicate* returns
> false are replaced by *new*. If *count* is supplied, only the first *count* instances
> are replaced.

Hash Tables

(clrhash *hash-table*)   Function
> Removes all the entries from *hash-table* and returns it.

(gethash *key hash-table* &optional *default*)   Function
> Returns the object indexed under *key* in *hash-table*, or *default* if there isn't one.
> Returns a second value true iff an entry was found. Settable.

(hash-table-count *hash-table*)   Function
> Returns the number of entries in *hash-table*.

(hash-table-p *object*)   Function
> Returns true iff *object* is a hash table.

(hash-table-rehash-size *hash-table*)   Function
> Returns a number, with the same significance as the :rehash-size argument
> to make-hash-table, that indicates how much *hash-table* should grow if it
> has to be expanded.

(hash-table-rehash-threshold *hash-table*)   Function
> Returns a number, with the same significance as the :rehash-threshold
> argument to make-hash-table, that indicates when *hash-table* will be ex-
> panded.

(hash-table-size *hash-table*)   Function
> Returns the number of spaces in *hash-table*.

(hash-table-test *hash-table*)   Function
> Returns the function used to determine key equality in *hash-table*.

(make-hash-table &key *test size rehash-size rehash-threshold*)   Function
> Returns a new hash table that uses *test* (default: eql) to determine the equality
> of keys. The *size* is a suggestion of the number of entries expected. The
> *rehash-size* is a suggestion of how much the table should grow if it has to be
> expanded: if an integer, suggests that many spaces should be added; if a float,
> suggests that the number of spaces should be multiplied by that amount. The
> *rehash-threshold* is a number between zero and one that suggests how full the
> table should be allowed to get before being expanded.

(maphash *function hash-table*)   Function
> Applies *function*, which must be a function of two arguments, to the key and
> value of each entry in *hash-table*.

(remhash *key* ⟨*hash-table*⟩)   Function
> Removes the object indexed under *key* from *hash-table*, returning true iff there was one.

(sxhash *object*)   Function
> Essentially, a hashing function for equal hash tables. Returns a unique non-negative fixnum for each set of equal arguments.

(with-hash-table-iterator (*symbol hash-table*)   Macro
                          declaration* expression*)
> Evaluates the *expressions* with *symbol* defined as a local macro that returns information about successive entries in the value of *hash-table*. The local macro usually returns three values: a value that is true iff more values are returned (so nil indicates the stream has run dry); the key of an entry; and the object indexed under it.

Filenames

(directory-namestring *path*)   Function
> Returns an implementation-dependent string representing the directory component of *path*.

(enough-namestring *path* &optional *path2*)   Function
> Returns an implementation-dependent string representing enough of *path* to identify the file when the default is *path2* (default: *default-pathname-defaults*).

(file-namestring *path*)   Function
> Returns an implementation-dependent string representing the name, type, and version components of *path*.

(host-namestring *path*)   Function
> Returns an implementation-dependent string representing the host component of *path*.

(load-logical-pathname-translations *string*)   Function
> Loads the definition of a logical host whose name is *string*, if it is not already loaded. Returns true iff it loaded something.

(logical-pathname *path*)   Function
> Returns the logical pathname corresponding to *path*.

(logical-pathname-translations *host*)   Function
> Returns the list of the translations of the *host*, which must be a logical host or a string denoting one.

(make-pathname &key *host device directory name type version*   Function
               defaults case)

> Returns a pathname made from its arguments. Unspecified elements are taken from *defaults*; if it is not supplied, the default *host* is that of *default-pathname-defaults*, and the default for the other components is nil.

> The *host* can be a string or list of strings that is recognized as a host name. The *device* can be a string. The *directory* can be a string, a list of strings, or :wild. The *name* and *type* can be strings or :wild. The *version* can be a non-negative integer, :wild, or :newest; in many implementations it can also be :oldest, :previous, or :installed. All the preceding arguments can also be nil, in which case the component may get a default value, or :unspecific, which stands for "not applicable," and is not portable.

> The *defaults* argument can be any valid argument to pathname, and is treated the same way. Components that are nil or not given get their values from this default pathname, if it is given.

> If *case* is :local (the default) then pathname components will be in the local system's case; if :common, all-uppercase components indicate the system's customary case, and mixed-case components are taken literally.

(merge-pathnames *path* &optional *default-path version*)   Function

> Returns the pathname that results from filling in any missing components in *path* with those of *default-path* (default: *default-pathname-defaults*). If *path* includes a name component, then the version can come from *version* (which defaults to :newest); otherwise it comes with the other components from *default-path*.

(namestring *path*)   Function

> Returns an implementation-dependent string representing *path*.

(parse-namestring *path* &optional *host default*   Function
                  &key *start end junk-allowed*)

> If *path* is not a string, returns the corresponding pathname as usual. If it is a string, parses it as a logical pathname, the host of which comes from the *host* argument, or the string itself, or the *default* pathname, in that order of preference. Generates an error if no valid pathname is seen, unless *junk-allowed* is true, in which case it returns nil. The *start* and *end* are used as in sequence functions. Returns as a second value the index at which parsing stopped.

(pathname *path*)   Function

> Returns the pathname corresponding to *path*.

(pathname-host *path* &key *case*)   Function

> Returns the host component of *path*. A :case argument is treated as by make-pathname.

(`pathname-device` *path* &key *case*)   Function
> Returns the device component of *path*. A `:case` argument is treated as by `make-pathname`.

(`pathname-directory` *path* &key *case*)   Function
> Returns the directory component of *path*. A `:case` argument is treated as by `make-pathname`.

(`pathname-match-p` *path* *wild-path*)   Function
> Returns true iff *path* matches *wild-path*; any missing components of *wild-path* will be treated as `:wild`.

(`pathname-name` *path* &key *case*)   Function
> Returns the name component of *path*. A `:case` argument is treated as by `make-pathname`.

(`pathnamep` *object*)   Function
> Returns true iff *object* is a pathname.

(`pathname-type` *path* &key *case*)   Function
> Returns the type component of *path*. A `:case` argument is treated as by `make-pathname`.

(`pathname-version` *path* &key *case*)   Function
> Returns the version component of *path*. A `:case` argument is treated as by `make-pathname`.

(`translate-logical-pathname` *path* &key)   Function
> Returns the physical pathname corresponding to *path*.

(`translate-pathname` *path1* *path2* *path3* &key)   Function
> Translates *path1*, which matches the wild pathname *path2*, into the corresponding pathname that matches the wild pathname *path3*.

(`wild-pathname-p` *path* &optional *component*)   Function
> Returns true iff the component of *path* designated by *component* (which can be `:host`, `:device`, `:directory`, `:name`, `:type`, or `:version`) is wild, or, if *component* is `nil`, if *path* has any wild components.

Files

(`delete-file` *path*)   Function
> Deletes the file denoted by *path*. Returns `t`.

(`directory` *path* &key)   Function
> Creates and returns a list of the pathnames representing real files that match *path* (which may contain wild components).

(`ensure-directories-exist` *path* &key *verbose*)   Function
> If the directories containing the file denoted by *path* do not exist, attempts to create them (possibly announcing this, if *verbose* is true). Returns two values: *path*, and a second value true iff any directories were created.

(file-author *path*)   Function
> Returns a string representing the author of the file denoted by *path*, or nil if it
> can't be determined.

(file-error-pathname *condition*)   Function
> Returns the pathname in the file-error *condition*.

(file-write-date *path*)   Function
> Returns the time, in the same format as get-universal-time, at which the
> file denoted by *path* was last written, or nil if it can't be determined.

(probe-file *path*)   Function
> Returns the actual name of the file denoted by *path*, or nil if this file does not
> exist.

(rename-file *path1 path2*)   Function
> Renames the file denotes by *path1* with the name corresponding to *path2*
> (which may not be a stream). Empty components in *path2* default to those of
> *path1*. Returns three values: the resulting pathname, the old actual file name,
> and the new actual file name.

(truename *path*)   Function
> Returns the actual name of the file denoted by *path*; signals an error if the file
> does not exist.

Streams

(broadcast-stream-streams *broadcast-stream*)   Function
> Returns a list of the streams that compose *broadcast-stream*.

(clear-input &optional *stream*)   Function
> Clears any input waiting in *stream*, returning nil.

(clear-output &optional *stream*)   Function
> Discards any buffered output on *stream*, returning nil.

(close *stream* &key *abort*)   Function
> Closes *stream*, returning t if the stream had been open. If *abort* is true, tries
> to remove any sign of the stream having existed—that is, an associated output
> file will be deleted. A closed stream may not be written to, but may be used as
> an argument to functions on pathnames, including open.

(concatenated-stream-streams *concatenated-stream*)   Function
> Returns a list of the streams of *concatenated-stream* that must still be read
> from.

(echo-stream-input-stream *echo-stream*)   Function
> Returns the input stream of *echo-stream*.

(echo-stream-output-stream *echo-stream*)   Function
> Returns the output stream of *echo-stream*.

(`file-length` *stream*)   Function
     Returns the number of elements in *stream*, or `nil` if it cannot be determined.

(`file-position` *stream* &optional *pos*)   Function
     If no *pos* is given, returns the current position in in *stream*, or `nil` if it cannot
     be determined. If *pos* is given, it can be `:start`, `:end`, or a non-negative
     integer, and the position in *stream* is *set* accordingly

(`file-string-length` *stream object*)   Function
     Returns the difference between the current position in *stream* and what it would
     be if *object* were written to it; or `nil` if this cannot be determined.

(`finish-output` &optional *stream*)   Function
     Forces out any buffered output on *stream*, then returns `nil`.

(`force-output` &optional *stream*)   Function
     Like `finish-output`, but does not wait till the I/O operation is completed
     before returning.

(`fresh-line` &optional *stream*)   Function
     Writes a newline to *stream* if it is not at the start of a line.

(`get-output-stream-string` *stream*)   Function
     Returns a string containing all the characters sent to *stream* (which must be
     open) since it was opened, or since the last time `get-output-stream-string`
     was called on it.

(`input-stream-p` *stream*)   Function
     Returns true iff *stream* is an input stream.

(`interactive-stream-p` *stream*)   Function
     Returns true iff *stream* is an interactive stream.

(`listen` &optional *stream*)   Function
     Returns true iff there is a character waiting to be read from *stream*, which is
     intended to be an interactive stream.

(`make-broadcast-stream` &rest *streams*)   Function
     Returns a new broadcast stream composed of *streams*.

(`make-concatenated-stream` &rest *input-streams*)   Function
     Returns a new concatenated stream composed of *input-streams*.

(`make-echo-stream` *input-stream output-stream*)   Function
     Returns a new echo stream that gets input from *input-stream* and sends output
     to *output-stream*.

(`make-string-input-stream` *string* &optional *start end*)   Function
     Returns an input stream that, when read from, will yield the characters in *string*,
     then the end of file. The *start* and *end* are used as in sequence functions.

(`make-string-output-stream` &key *element-type*)   Function
     Returns an output stream that accepts characters of the type specified by
     element-type. Characters written to this stream are not sent anywhere, but
     can be retrieved via `get-output-stream-string`.

(`make-synonym-stream` *symbol*)   Function

Returns a stream that will be a synonym for whatever stream is the value of the special variable whose name is *symbol*.

(`make-two-way-stream` *input-stream output-stream*)   Function

Returns a new two-way stream that gets input from *input-stream* and sends output to *output-stream*.

(`open` *path* **&key** *direction element-type if-exists if-does-not-exist*   Function
              external-format)

Opens and returns a stream to *path*, or possibly `nil` if such a stream can't be created. The keyword arguments determine the properties of the stream as follows:

`:direction` *symbol*

Tells which way objects will flow. Can be: `:input` (the default) which means that it will be possible to read from the stream; `:output`, which means it will be possible to write to it; `:io`, which means both; or `:probe`, which means that the stream will be returned closed.

`:element-type` *type*

Declares the type of objects to be written to or read from the stream. Yields a character stream if *type* is a subtype of `character`; a binary stream if a finite subtype of of `integer`, or `signed-byte` or `unsigned-byte` (in which case the element size is determined by the operating system). The default is `character`.

`:if-exists` *symbol*

Tells what to do if such a file already exists. The possible values are: `:new-version`, the default if the version component of *path* is `:newest`; `:error`, the default otherwise; `:rename`, which causes the existing file to be renamed; `:rename-and-delete`, which causes the existing file to be renamed and deleted, but not expunged; `:overwrite`, which causes the existing file to be modified, starting at the beginning; `:append`, which causes the existing file to be modified, starting at the end; `:supersede`, which causes a new file with the same name to be created, but the original file (probably) not to be deleted until the stream is closed; or `nil`, in which case no stream is created and open returns `nil`.

`:if-does-not-exist` *symbol*

Tells what to do if no such file exists. Possible values: `:error`, the default if *direction* is `:input` or *if-exists* is `:overwrite` or `:append`; `:create`, the default if *direction* is `:output` or `:io` and *if-exists* is neither `:overwrite` nor `:append`; or `nil`, the default if *direction* is `:probe`, in which case no stream is created and open returns `nil`.

`:external-format` *format*

Designates an external file format. The only predefined *format* is `:default`.

(open-stream-p *stream*)   Function
   Returns true iff *stream* is open.

(output-stream-p *stream*)   Function
   Returns true iff *stream* is an output stream.

(peek-char &optional *kind stream eof-error eof-value recursive*)   Function
   Returns a character from *stream* without removing it from the stream. If *kind*
   is nil, returns the first character seen; if t, consumes whitespace characters
   and returns the first non-whitespace character; if a character, consumes all
   characters up to the first instance of it, then returns it. If the end of file is
   encountered, either signals an error or returns *eof-value*, depending on whether
   eof-error is true (the default) or false. The *recursive* argument will be true if
   peek-char was invoked by another input function.

(read-byte *stream* &optional *eof-error eof-value*)   Function
   Reads a byte from *stream*, which must be a binary input stream. If there
   was a byte to read, returns it; otherwise signals an error or returns *eof-value*
   depending on whether *eof-error* is true (the default) or false.

(read-char &optional *stream eof-error eof-value recursive*)   Function
   Removes and returns the first character in *stream*. If the end of file is encountered, either signals an error or returns *eof-value*, depending on whether
   eof-error is true (the default) or false. The *recursive* argument will be true if
   read-char was invoked by another input function.

(read-char-no-hang &optional *stream eof-error eof-value*   Function
                              recursive)
   Like read-char, but returns nil immediately if there are no characters waiting
   in *stream*.

(read-line &optional *stream eof-error eof-value recursive*)   Function
   Returns a string of all the characters up to the first newline (which is read,
   but not included) in *stream*, or the end of file. If no characters are read
   before encountering the end of file, either signals an error or returns *eof-value*,
   depending on whether *eof-error* is true (the default) or false. Returns a second
   value true iff the end of file was encountered. The *recursive* argument will be
   true if read-line was invoked by another input function.

(read-sequence ⟨*proseq*⟩ &optional *stream* &key *start end*)   Function
   Reads elements from *stream* into *proseq*, returning the position of the first
   unchanged element. The *start* and *end* are used as in sequence functions.

(stream-element-type *stream*)   Function
   Returns the type of objects that can be written to or read from *stream*.

(stream-error-stream *condition*)   Function
   Returns the stream involved in the stream-error *condition*.

(stream-external-format *stream*)   Function
   Returns the external file format of *stream*.

(`streamp` *object*)   Function
    Returns true iff *object* is a stream.

(`synonym-stream-symbol` *synonym-stream*)   Function
    Returns the name of the special variable for whose value *synonym-stream* is a
    synonym.

(`terpri` &optional *stream*)   Function
    Writes a newline to *stream*.

(`two-way-stream-input-stream` *two-way-stream*)   Function
    Returns the input stream of *two-way-stream*.

(`two-way-stream-output-stream` *two-way-stream*)   Function
    Returns the output stream of *two-way-stream*.

(`unread-char` *character* &optional *stream*)   Function
    Undoes one `read-char` on *stream*. Can't be done twice without a `read-char`
    in between. Can't be done after a `peek-char`.

(`with-input-from-string` (*symbol string* &key *index start end*)   Macro
                     declaration* expression*)
    Evaluates the *expression*s with *symbol* bound to a string input stream made as
    if by passing *string* and the *start* and *end* arguments to `make-string-input-`
    `stream`. (There should be no assignments to this variable.) The stream exists
    only within the `with-input-from-string` expression, and it gets closed
    automatically when the `with-input-from-string` returns, or is interrupted.
    The *index* can be an expression (not evaluated) that could serve as the first
    argument to `setf`; if `with-input-from-string` terminates normally, the
    corresponding place will be set to the index of the first unread character in the
    string.

(`with-open-file` (*symbol path arg**) *declaration* expression**)   Macro
    Evaluates the *expression*s with *symbol* bound to the stream that would result
    from passing the *path* and *arg*s to `open`. (There should be no assignments to
    this variable.) The stream exists only within the `with-open-file` expression,
    and it gets closed automatically when the `with-open-file` returns, or is
    interrupted. In the latter case, if the stream was for output, no file should be
    left behind.

(`with-open-stream` (*symbol stream*) *declaration* expression**)   Macro
    Evaluates the *expression*s with *symbol* bound to the value of *stream*. (There
    should be no assignments to this variable.) The stream exists only within the
    `with-open-stream` expression, and it gets closed automatically when the
    `with-open-stream` returns, or is interrupted.

(`with-output-to-string` (*symbol* [*string*] `&key` *element-type*)   Macro
                         declaration* expression*)
> Evaluates the *expressions* with *symbol* bound to a string output stream. The
> stream exists only within the `with-output-to-string` expression, and it
> gets closed automatically when the `with-output-to-string` returns, or is
> interrupted. If no *string* is given, the `with-output-to-string` returns a
> string containing all the output written to the stream. If a *string* is given,
> it must be a string with a fill-pointer; output is appended to it as if by
> `vector-push-extend`, and the `with-output-to-string` returns the value
> of the last *expression*.

(`write-byte` *i stream*)   Function
> Writes *i* to *stream*, which must be a binary output stream. Returns *i*.

(`write-char` *character* `&optional` *stream*)   Function
> Writes *character* to *stream*.

(`write-line` *string* `&optional` *stream* `&key` *start end*)   Function
> Like `write-string`, but writes a newline afterwards.

(`write-sequence` *proseq* `&optional` *stream* `&key` *start end*)   Function
> Writes the elements of *proseq* to *stream*. The *start* and *end* are used as in
> sequence functions.

(`write-string` *string* `&optional` *stream* `&key` *start end*)   Function
> Writes *string* to *stream*. The *start* and *end* are used as in sequence functions.

(`yes-or-no-p` `&optional` *format* `&rest` *args*)   Function
> Like `y-or-n-p`, but requires an explicit `yes` or `no`, instead of a single letter.

(`y-or-n-p` `&optional` *format* `&rest` *args*)   Function
> Displays *format*, which should be a yes-or-no question but defaults to `""`, on
> `*query-io*` as if by calling `format` with *args* as the optional arguments.
> Then prompts for a single letter, returning true or `nil` depending on whether it
> corresponds to y or n, or prompting again if given an ambiguous response.

Printer

(`copy-pprint-dispatch` `&optional` *pprint-dispatch*)   Function
> Returns a copy of the pprint dispatch table *pprint-dispatch*, which defaults
> to `*print-pprint-dispatch*`. If *pprint-dispatch* is `nil`, copies the initial
> value of `*print-pprint-dispatch*`.

(`format` *dest format* `&rest` *args*)   Function
> Writes output to a location depending on *dest*: if it is a stream, to that stream;
> if t, to `*standard-output*`; if nil, to a string, which is returned. Returns
> nil if it does not return a string. The *format* can be either a string or the kind
> of function that `formatter` might return. If it is a function, it is applied to the
> *dest* and *args*. If it is a string, it may contain directives, which typically consist
> of a ˜, followed by prefix parameters separated from one another by commas,
> followed by optional : and @ modifiers, followed by some distinctive tag. A

prefix parameter can be: an integer; a character preceded by a single quote; a V or v, which represent the next argument (or the absence of a parameter if the argument is nil); or a #, which represents the number of arguments remaining. Prefix parameters can be omitted (leaving the commas), in which case they have default values. Trailing commas can also be omitted.

The possible directives are:

~w,g,m,pA

> Prints the next argument as if by *princ*, padded on the right (or left, with @) by at least *m* (default: 0) instances of *p* (default: #\Space), plus more instances of *p* added in groups of *g* (default: 1) until the total number of characters (including the representation of the argument) is *w* (default: 0) or more. With :, empty lists are printed as () instead of nil.

~w,g,m,pS

> Like ~A, but prints the argument as if by prin1.

~W

> Prints the next argument as if by write. With :, pretty-prints. With @, prints without limits on list length or nesting.

~C

> The next argument should be a character. If a simple character, it will be printed as by write-char. With :, non-printing characters are spelled out; :@ is similar but also explains how to type unusual characters. With @, characters are printed using #\ syntax.

~n%

> Prints *n* (default: 1) newlines.

~n&

> Like ~%, but the first newline is printed as if by fresh-line.

~n|

> Prints *n* (default: 1) page separators.

~n~

> Prints *n* (default: 1) ~s.

~r,w,p,c,iR

> The next argument should be an integer. It is printed in base *r* (default: 10), padded on the left by as many *p*s (default: #\Space) as needed to make the total number of characters at least *w*. With :, groups of *i* (default: 3) digits are separated by instances of *c* (default: #\,). With @, the sign is printed even for positive numbers.

> If none of the prefix arguments are given, ~R has a completely different interpretation—it displays integers in various non-digital forms. With no modifiers, 4 is printed as four; with :, as fourth; with @, as IV; and with :@, as IIII.

~w,p,c,iD

> Displays an integer in decimal. Equivalent to ~$10,w,p,c,i$R.

~w,p,c,iB

> Displays an integer in binary. Equivalent to ~$2,w,p,c,i$R.

~w,p,c,iO

> Displays an integer in octal. Equivalent to ~$8,w,p,c,i$R.

~w,p,c,iX

> Displays an integer in hexadecimal. Equivalent to ~$16,w,p,c,i$R.

~w,d,s,x,pF

> If the next argument is a rational, it will be printed as a floating-point number, shifted s digits to the left (default: 0), with d digits (default: as many as needed) after the decimal point. The number may be rounded to fit, but it is implementation-dependent whether up or down. If w is given, the number will be padded on the left by as many ps (default: #\Space) are needed to make the total number of characters equal to w. (If the representation of the number is already more than w characters, and an x is given, it is printed instead.) If both w and d are omitted, s is ignored. With @, the sign is printed even for positive numbers.

~w,d,e,s,x,p,mE

> Like ~F, but if the next argument is a rational, it will be printed as a floating-point number in exponential notation, with s (default: 1) digits before the decimal point, d digits (default: as many as needed) after it, and e (default: as many as needed) digits in the exponent. The m, if given, should be a character to use as the exponent marker.

~w,d,e,s,x,p,mG

> If the next argument is a rational number, it is printed using either ~F or ~E as appropriate based on its magnitude.

~d,n,w,p\$

> Intended for displaying amounts of money. If the next argument is a rational, it will be printed as a floating-point number with at least n (default: 1) digits before the decimal point, and d digits (default: 2) after it. At least w (default: 0) characters must be printed; if necessary the number will be padded on the left by ps (default: #\Space). With @, the sign is printed even for positive numbers. With :, the sign is printed before any padding.

> Like a call to **pprint-newline** with an argument that depends on the modifiers: none means :linear; @ means :miser; : means :fill; and :@ means :mandatory.

`˜<prefix˜;body˜;suffix˜:>`

Like a call to `pprint-logical-block` with the next argument as the list argument, the *prefix* and *suffix* as the `:prefix` (or `:per-line-prefix` if followed by `˜@;`) and `:suffix` arguments, and the *body* playing the role of the expressions in the body. The *body* can be any format string, and arguments for it are extracted from the list argument as by `pprint-pop`. Within *body*, the `˜ˆ` stands for `pprint-exit-if-list-exhausted`. If only two of *prefix*, *body*, and *suffix* appear, the *suffix* defaults to `""`; if only one of the three appears, the *prefix* defaults to `""` as well. With the `:` modifier, the *prefix* and *suffix* default to `"("` and `")"` respectively. With `@`, the list of remaining arguments becomes the argument to the logical block. If the whole directive ends with `˜:@>`, then a `:fill` conditional newline is inserted after each group of blanks in the body.

`˜nI`

Equivalent to `(pprint-indent :block n)`. With `:`, `(pprint-indent :current n)`.

`˜/name/`

Calls the function whose name is *name* with at least four arguments: the stream, the next argument, a value that is true if `:` was used, and a value that is true if `@` was used—plus any parameters given to the directive.

`˜m,nT`

Prints enough spaces to put the cursor in column m (default: 1), or if it is already past that column, into the nearest column that is a multiple of n (default: 1) columns past column m. With `@`, prints m spaces, then enough spaces to put the cursor in a column that is a multiple of n. With `:`, equivalent to `(pprint-tab :section m n)`. With `:@`, equivalent to `(pprint-tab :section-relative m n)`.

`˜w,n,m,p<+text0˜;...˜;textn˜>`

Displays the characters produced by the *texts* justified in a field w characters wide, with at least m (default: 0) extra instances of p (default: `#\Space`) introduced between the *texts* as necessary. If the width of the output with the minimum padding is greater than w, the limit is incremented by n until it will fit. With `:`, there will also be padding before the first *text*; with `@`, after the last. A `˜ˆ` within any *text* terminates processing of the directive.

If *text0* is followed by `˜a,b:;` instead of `˜;`, the characters yielded by *text0* will be output only if the remaining characters are more than b (default: the stream's line width, or 72) with a (default: 0) characters to spare.

`˜n*`

Ignores the next n (default: 0) arguments. With `:`, backs up n arguments. With `@`, makes the nth argument (zero-indexed) the current one.

~i[text0~;...~;textn~]

> Yields the text produced by *texti*. If *i* is not specified, the value of the next argument is used. If the last *text* is preceded by ~:; instead of ~;, then the last *text* is used if no other is selected. With a :, only two *texts* are expected: the second is used if the next argument is true, the first otherwise. With @, only one *text* is expected: if the next argument is true, the characters generated by the text are output and the argument remains for the next directive.

~n{text~}

> Like repeated calls to to format, with "*text*" as the string and the elements of the next argument, which should be a list, as arguments. Continues until the elements run out, or after *n* repetitions (default: no limit), whichever comes first. If the directive ends with ~:} instead of ~}, there will be at least one call to format, unless *n* is 0. If there is no *text*, the next argument (which must be a string) is used in place of it. A ~~ within the *text* terminates processing of the directive. With :, the argument should be a list of lists, and the elements of each become the arguments in successive calls to format. With @, instead of the next argument, the list of all the remaining arguments is used.

~?

> Equivalent to a call to format with the next argument as the string and the argument after that as a list of arguments. With @, the next argument is used as the string, but arguments are taken from the arguments in the current call to format.

~(text~)

> Prints *text* with case conversion, depending on the modifier: with none, converts all uppercase characters to lowercase; with : converts the first letter of each word to uppercase; with @, capitalizes the first letter of the first word and converts the rest to lowercase; and with :@, converts all lowercase characters to uppercase.

~P

> If the next argument is eql to 1 prints nothing, otherwise prints s; with :, backs up by one argument first. With @, if the next argument is eql to 1 prints y, otherwise prints ies; with :@, backs up by one argument first.

~a,b,c~

> Terminates the format (or the current directive, if used within one) under the following circumstances: if no prefix parameter is given; if one is given and it is zero; if two are given and they are equal; or if all three are given and (<= *a* *b* *c*).

If a ~ is followed by a newline, the newline and any whitespace following it are ignored. With @, the newline is ignored but not the whitespace.

(formatter *string*)   Macro

Returns a function that takes a stream and a rest argument, and applies format to the stream, *format*, and the rest argument, returning any leftover elements of the rest argument.

(pprint *object* &optional *stream*)   Function

Like print, but tries to indent its output nicely, and prints no final space.

(pprint-dispatch *object* &optional *pprint-dispatch*)   Function

Returns the highest priority function in *pprint-dispatch* for which *object* is of the associated type. If *pprint-dispatch* is not supplied, uses the current value of *print-pprint-dispatch*; if nil, uses its initial value. If no type in the dispatch table matches *object*, returns a function that prints it using print-object. Returns a second value true iff the first comes from a dispatch table.

(pprint-exit-if-list-exhausted)   Macro

For use within a pprint-logical-block. Terminates the block if there is nothing left to print; otherwise returns nil.

(pprint-fill *stream object* &optional *colon at*)   Function

Prints *object* to *stream*—in a distinctive way if it is a list and *print-pretty* is true. Prints as many elements of the list on a line as possible, surrounded by parentheses iff *colon* is true (the default). The *at* argument is ignored. Returns nil.

(pprint-indent *keyword r* &optional *stream*)   Function

If *stream* was created by pprint-logical-block and *print-pretty* is true, sets the indentation in the current logical block. If the *keyword* is :current, the indentation is set to the current position plus *r* ems; if :block, to the position of the first character in the current block plus *r* ems.

(pprint-linear *stream object* &optional *colon at*)   Function

Like pprint-fill, but prints the whole list on one line, or each element on its own line.

(pprint-logical-block (*symbol object*   Macro
                       &key *prefix per-line-prefix suffix*)
                       declaration* expression*)

Evaluates the *expressions* with *symbol* bound to a new stream (valid only within the pprint-logical-block expression) that sends output to the original value of *symbol* (which should be a stream). All output sent to the new stream is in the logical block associated with it. The *expressions* should not have side-effects on the surrounding environment.

The *object* should be a list that the *expressions* will print: if not, it is printed by write; if so, its elements will be available by calling pprint-pop. When the list is printed, shared and deeply nested components will be displayed as dictated by *print-circle* and *print-level*.

The keyword arguments, if given, should evaluate to strings. The *prefix* will be printed before the logical block, the *suffix* after it, and the *per-line-prefix* before each line of it. The *prefix* and *per-line-prefix* are exclusive.

(pprint-newline *keyword* &optional *stream*)   Function

> If *stream* was created by pprint-logical-block and *print-pretty* is true, writes a newline to *stream* depending on the *keyword*: :mandatory means always; :linear, if what the pretty printer wants to print on the current line won't fit; :miser, if the preceding and miser style is in effect; :fill if the preceding, or either the previous or next lines have to be broken.

(pprint-pop)   Macro

> Used within pprint-logical-block. If elements of the list being printed in the current logical block remain to be printed, returns the next element. If the remainder of the list is a non-nil atom, prints this atom preceded by a period, and returns nil. If *print-length* is true and that many elements have already been printed, prints an ellipsis and returns nil. If *print-circle* is true and the remainder of the list is shared structure, prints a period followed by #*n*#, and returns nil.

(pprint-tab *keyword* *i1* *i2* &optional *stream*)   Function

> If *stream* was created by pprint-logical-block and *print-pretty* is true, tabs as if by the ~T format directive, with *i1* and *i2* as the prefix parameters. The possible *keyword*s correspond to the variations of ~T: :line means ~T, :section means ~:T, :line-relative means ~@T, and :section-relative means ~:@T.

(pprint-tabular *stream* *object* &optional *colon at tab*)   Function

> Like pprint-fill, but prints the elements of a list so that they line up in columns. The *tab* (default: 16) is the intercolumn spacing in ems.

(princ *object* &optional *stream*)   Function

> Displays *object* on *stream* in a way that allows it to be read by people, if possible. No escape characters are displayed.

(princ-to-string *object*)   Function

> Like princ, but sends its output to a string, which it returns.

(print *object* &optional *stream*)   Function

> Like print1, but prints a newline first and a space afterward.

(print-object *object* *stream*)   Generic Function

> Called by the system to print *object* on *stream*.

(print-not-readable-object *condition*)   Function

> Returns the object that could not be printed readably in *condition*.

(print-unreadable-object (*object stream* &key *type identity*)   Macro
                          *expression**)

> For displaying objects in #<...> syntax. All arguments are evaluated. Writes
> #< to *stream*; then, if *type* is true, writes a type label for *object*; then evaluates
> the *expressions*, which should display *object* on *stream*; then, if *identity* is true,
> writes an identifying tag for *object*; finally writes >. Returns nil.

(prin1 *object* &optional *stream*)   Function

> Displays *object* on *stream* in a way that allows it to be read by *read*, if possible.

(prin1-to-string *object*)   Function

> Like prin1, but sends its output to a string, which it returns.

(set-pprint-dispatch *type function* &optional *r pprint-dispatch*) Function

> If *function* is true, adds an entry to *pprint-dispatch* (which defaults to *print-
> pprint-dispatch*) with the given *type*, *function*, and a priority of *r* (de-
> fault: 0). The *function* must take two arguments: a stream and an object to be
> printed on it. If *function* is nil, removes any entry for *type*. Returns nil.

(write *object* &key *array base case circle escape gensym length*   Function
                 level lines miser-width pprint-dispatch pretty
                 radix readably right-margin stream)

> Writes *object* to *stream* with each special variable *print-...* bound to the
> value of the corresponding keyword parameter.

(write-to-string *object* &key ...)   Function

> Like write, but sends its output to a string, which it returns.

Reader

(copy-readtable &optional *from* ⟨*to*⟩)   Function

> If *to* is nil returns a copy of the readtable *from* (default: *readtable*); if *to*
> is a readtable, returns it after copying *from* into it.

(get-dispatch-macro-character *char1 char2*   Function
                              &optional *readtable*)

> Returns the function (or nil if there isn't one) that is called in *readtable* when
> *char1* is followed by *char2* in the input.

(get-macro-character *char* &optional *readtable*)   Function

> Returns two values: the function (or nil if there isn't one) that is called in
> *readtable* when *char* is encountered in the input, and a second value true iff
> *char* can be read as part of a symbol name.

(make-dispatch-macro-character *char* &optional *nonterm*   Function
                               readtable)

> Makes *char* a dispatching macro character in *readtable*. If *nonterm* is true,
> *char* behaves like a normal character when used in the middle of a symbol.
> Returns t.

(read &optional *stream eof-error eof-value recursive*)   Function
    Parses one Lisp object from *stream* and returns it. If the end of file is en-
countered, either signals an error or returns *eof-value*, depending on whether
eof-error is true (the default) or false. The *recursive* argument will be true if
read was invoked by another input function.

(read-delimited-list *char* &optional *stream recursive*)   Function
    Like read, but continues parsing objects from *stream* until it encounters *char*,
whereupon it returns a list of all the objects parsed. Signals an error if no *char*
before the end of file.

(read-from-string *string* &optional *eof-error eof-value*   Function
                             &key *start end preserve-whitespace*)
    Like calling read on a stream containing the characters in *string*. Returns two
values: the object parsed and the position (zero-indexed) of the first unread
character in *string*. The *start* and *end* delimit the string as usual. If *preserve-
whitespace* is true, like read-preserving-whitespace rather than read.

(read-preserving-whitespace &optional *stream eof-error*   Function
                                      eof-value recursive)
    Like read, but leaves terminating whitespace in *stream*.

(readtable-case *readtable*)   Function
    Returns one of :upcase, :downcase, :preserve, or :invert, depending on
how *readtable* is set to handle case in the input. Settable.

(readtablep *object*)   Function
    Returns true iff *object* is a readtable.

(set-dispatch-macro-character *char1 char2 function*   Function
                               &optional *readtable*)
    Inserts an entry in *readtable* that says *function* is to be called when the reader
sees *char1* followed by *char2* (which is converted to uppercase and may not
be a decimal digit). The *function* should be a function of three arguments, the
input stream, *char1*, and *char2*, which returns either no value or an object read
from the stream. Returns t.

(set-macro-character *char function*   Function
                     &optional *nonterm readtable*)
    Inserts an entry in *readtable* that says *function* is to be called when the reader
sees *char*. The *function* should be a function of two arguments, the input stream
and *char*, which returns either no value or an object read from the stream. If
nonterm is true, the *char* behaves like a normal character when used in the
middle of a symbol. Returns t.

(set-syntax-from-char *to-char from-char*   Function
                      to-readtable from-readtable)
    Gives *to-char* the syntactic properties in *to-readtable* (default: *readtable*)
that *from-char* has in *from-readtable* (which defaults to the standard readtable).
Returns t.

(with-standard-io-syntax *expression**)   Macro
    Evaluates the *expression*s with all the special variables that control reading and
    printing (i.e. those whose names begin with *read- or *print-) bound to
    their initial values.

System Construction

(compile-file *path* &key *output-file verbose print external-format*) Function
    Compiles the contents of the file denoted by *path* and writes the result to the file
    denoted by the pathname *output-file*. If *verbose* is true, this fact is announced
    to *standard-output*. If *print* is true, information about top-level forms
    in the file is printed to *standard-output*. The default *external-format*
    (:default) is the only predefined external format. After the file is compiled,
    readtable and *package* are restored to their original values. Returns
    three values: the name of the output file (or nil if the file could not be written);
    a second true iff compilation generated errors or warnings; and a third true iff
    compilation generated errors or warnings other than style warnings.

(compile-file-pathname *path* &key *output-file*)   Function
    Returns the name of the output file that compile-file would create if given
    the same arguments. Allows other keys.

(load *path* &key *verbose print if-does-not-exist external-format*)   Function
    Loads the file denoted by *path*. If the file is a source file, like evaluating each ex-
    pression in order; similar if a compiled file, except that compiled-function-p
    will return true of functions defined in the file. If *verbose* is true, announces
    the loading of the file to *standard-output*. If *print* is true, describes the
    loading as it progresses to *standard-output*. If *if-does-not-exist* is true
    (the default), signals an error if the file does not exist; if it is nil, returns nil.
    The default *external-format* (:default) is the only predefined external format.
    Returns true if the file is loaded.

(provide *name*)   [Function]
    Adds the string *name* (or its name, if it is a symbol) to *modules*.

(require *name* &optional *paths*)   [Function]
    If the string *name* (or its name, if it is a symbol) is not in *modules*, tries
    to load the file containing the corresponding module. If *paths* is given, it
    should be a list whose elements are pathnames, streams, or strings, and the
    corresponding files will be loaded.

(with-compilation-unit ([:override *val*]) *expression**)   Macro
    Evaluates the *expression*s. Any warnings deferred by the compiler until the
    end of the file will be deferred until after the last *expression* is evaluated. A
    dynamically nested with-compilation-unit has an effect only the value of
    val is true.

Environment

(apropos *name* &optional *package*) Function
 Prints information about each interned symbol whose name contains *name* as
 a substring (or the name of *name*, if it is a symbol). If *package* is given, only
 that package is searched. Returns no value.

(apropos-list *name* &optional *package*) Function
 Like apropos, but prints nothing and returns the symbols in a list.

(decode-universal-time *i* &optional *time-zone*) Function
 Interprets *i* as a number of seconds since 0:00:00 (GMT), January 1, 1900,
 returning nine values: the second, minute, hour, date, month (1 = January),
 year, day of the week (0 = Monday), a value true iff daylight saving time is in
 effect, and a rational indicating the time zone as an offset from GMT. The *time-zone* should be a rational divisible by 3600 and between -24 and 24 inclusive;
 if a time zone is given explicitly, daylight saving time is not considered.

(describe *object* &optional *stream*) Function
 Writes a description of *object* to *stream*. Returns no value.

(describe-object *object* &optional *stream*) Generic Function
 Called by describe to describe *object* on *stream*.

(disassemble *fn*) Function
 Prints an indication of the object code generated for *fn*, which can be a function,
 a function name, or a lambda expression.

(documentation *object symbol*) Generic Function
 Returns the *symbol* documentation of *object*, or nil if there is none. Settable.

(dribble &optional *path*) Function
 If *path* is given, begins sending a transcript of the Lisp session to the file it
 denotes; if there is no argument, closes the file.

(ed &optional *arg*) Function
 Invokes the editor, if there is one. If *arg* is a pathname or a string, it indicates
 the file to be edited; if a function name, its definition is edited.

(encode-universal-time *second minute hour date month year* Function
 &optional *time-zone*)
 Like decode-universal-time in reverse.

(get-decoded-time) Function
 Equivalent to (decode-universal-time (get-universal-time)).

(get-internal-real-time) Function
 Returns the current system time in clock ticks, of which there are internal-time-units-per-second per second.

(get-internal-run-time) Function
 Like get-internal-real-time, but the return value is supposed to indicate
 something like the number of ticks used by the Lisp process.

(get-universal-time)   Function
    Returns the current time as a number of seconds since 0:00:00 (GMT), January
    1, 1900.

(inspect *object*)   Function
    An interactive version of describe that allows one to traverse complex objects.

(lisp-implementation-type)   Function
    Returns a string indicating the Lisp implementation, or nil.

(lisp-implementation-version)   Function
    Returns a string indicating the Lisp version number, or nil.

(long-site-name)   Function
    Like short-site-name, but verbose.

(machine-instance)   Function
    Returns a string indicating the particular computer on which this Lisp session
    is running, or nil.

(machine-type)   Function
    Returns a string indicating the general type of computer on which this Lisp
    session is running, or nil.

(machine-version)   Function
    Returns a string indicating the version of computer on which this Lisp session
    is running, or nil.

(room &optional (*arg* :default))   Function
    Prints an indication of state of memory. Terse if *arg* is nil; verbose if t.

(short-site-name)   Function
    Returns a string indicating the current physical site, or nil.

(sleep *r*)   Function
    Causes evaluation to pause for *r* seconds.

(software-type)   Function
    Returns a string indicating the general type of the underlying software (e.g. OS),
    or nil.

(software-version)   Function
    Returns a string indicating the version of the underlying software, or nil.

(step *expression*)   Macro
    Steps through the evaluation of *expression*, returning whatever value(s) it re-
    turns.

(time *expression*)   Macro
    Evaluates *expression*, returning whatever value(s) it returns, and also printing
    information to *trace-output* about how long it took to return.

(trace *fname**)   Macro
    Causes calls to the named functions to be announced to *trace-output*.
    May not work for functions compiled inline. Given no arguments, returns a
    list of the functions currently being traced.

(untrace *fname**)   Macro
    Undoes a call to `trace`. Given no arguments, untraces all traced functions.

(user-homedir-pathname &optional *host*)   Function
    Returns the pathname of the user's home directory, or `nil` if no home directory
can be found on *host*. The *host* argument is used as by `make-pathname`.

Constants and Variables

array-dimension-limit   Constant
    Positive fixnum one greater than the maximum number of elements there may
be in any one dimension of an array. Implementation-dependent, but at least
1024.

array-rank-limit   Constant
    Positive fixnum one greater than the maximum number of dimensions an array
may have. Implementation-dependent, but at least 8.

array-total-size-limit   Constant
    Positive fixnum one greater than the maximum number of elements an array
may have. Implementation-dependent, but at least 1024.

boole-1...boole-xor   Constants
    Positive integers for use as the first argument to `boole`.

break-on-signals   Variable
    A generalization of the old `*break-on-warnings*`. Its value should be a
type specifier. Whenever a condition of that type is signalled, the debugger is
invoked. Initially `nil`.

call-arguments-limit   Constant
    Positive integer one greater than the maximum number of arguments in a
function call. Implementation-dependent, but at least 50.

char-code-limit   Constant
    Positive integer one greater than the maximum value returned by `char-code`.
Implementation-dependent.

compile-file-pathname   Variable
    During the evaluation of a call to `compile-file`, the pathname made from the
first argument; otherwise `nil`.

compile-file-truename   Variable
    The truename of `*compile-file-pathname*`.

compile-print   Variable
    The default for the `:print` argument to `compile-file`. Initial value is
implementation-dependent.

compile-verbose   Variable
    The default for the `:verbose` argument to `compile-file`. Initial value is
implementation-dependent.

`*debug-io*`   Variable
>   Stream intended for interactive debugging.

`*debugger-hook*`   Variable
>   If non-nil, should be a function *f* of two arguments. When the debugger is about
>   to be invoked, *f* will be called with the condition and *f* itself as arguments. If
>   *f* returns normally, the debugger will be invoked. During the invocation of *f*,
>   `*debugger-hook*` will be bound to `nil`.

`*default-pathname-defaults*`   Variable
>   Used as the default value when a function like `make-pathname` is not given a
>   `:defaults` argument.

`short-float-epsilon`   Constant
`single-float-epsilon`   Constant
`double-float-epsilon`   Constant
`long-float-epsilon`   Constant
>   For each type of float, the smallest positive number in that format which, if
>   added to 1.0 in the same format, yields a result not = to 1.0. Implementation-
>   dependent.

`short-float-negative-epsilon`   Constant
`single-float-negative-epsilon`   Constant
`double-float-negative-epsilon`   Constant
`long-float-negative-epsilon`   Constant
>   For each type of float, the smallest positive number in that format which, if sub-
>   tracted from 1.0 in the same format, yields a result not = to 1.0. Implementation-
>   dependent.

`*error-output*`   Variable
>   Stream on which error messages are printed.

`*features*`   Variable
>   An implementation-dependent list of symbols representing features supported
>   by the current implementation. Such symbols can be used as the *test* component
>   in #+ and #-.

`*gensym-counter*`   Variable
>   A non-negative integer used by `gensym` to make symbol names. Initial value
>   is implementation-dependent.

`internal-time-units-per-second`   Constant
>   If the difference between two calls to `get-internal-real-time` is divided
>   by this integer, the result will represent the number of seconds of system time
>   between them.

`lambda-list-keywords`   Constant
>   A list of all the parameter list keywords (e.g. &optional, &rest, etc.) sup-
>   ported by the implementation.

`lambda-parameters-limit`   Constant
>   Positive integer one greater than the maximum number of variables in a pa-
>   rameter list. Implementation-dependent, but at least 50.

```
least-negative-short-float                                    Constant
least-negative-single-float                                   Constant
least-negative-double-float                                   Constant
least-negative-long-float                                     Constant
```
The negative floating-point number of smallest magnitude in each of the float formats. Implementation-dependent.

```
least-negative-normalized-short-float                         Constant
least-negative-normalized-single-float                        Constant
least-negative-normalized-double-float                        Constant
least-negative-normalized-long-float                          Constant
```
The negative normalized floating-point number of smallest magnitude in each of the float formats. Implementation-dependent.

```
least-positive-short-float                                    Constant
least-positive-single-float                                   Constant
least-positive-double-float                                   Constant
least-positive-long-float                                     Constant
```
The positive floating-point number of smallest magnitude in each of the float formats. Implementation-dependent.

```
least-positive-normalized-short-float                         Constant
least-positive-normalized-single-float                        Constant
least-positive-normalized-double-float                        Constant
least-positive-normalized-long-float                          Constant
```
The positive normalized floating-point number of smallest magnitude in each of the float formats. Implementation-dependent.

`*load-pathname*`   Variable

During the evaluation of a call to load, the pathname made from the first argument; otherwise nil.

`*load-print*`   Variable

Used as the default value of the :print argument to load. Initial value is implementation-dependent.

`*load-truename*`   Variable

The truename of *load-pathname*.

`*load-verbose*`   Variable

Used as the default value of the :verbose argument to load. Initial value is implementation-dependent.

`*macroexpand-hook*`   Variable

A function of three arguments—an expansion function, a macro call, and an environment—that is called by macroexpand-1 to generate macro expansions. Its initial value is a function equivalent to funcall, or the name of such a function).

`*modules*`   Variable

A list of strings built by calls to provide.

`most-negative-fixnum`   Constant
> The lowest possible fixnum. Implementation-dependent.

`most-negative-short-float`   Constant
`most-negative-single-float`   Constant
`most-negative-double-float`   Constant
`most-negative-long-float`   Constant
> The negative floating-point number of greatest magnitude in each of the float
> formats. Implementation-dependent.

`most-positive-fixnum`   Constant
> The highest possible fixnum. Implementation-dependent.

`most-positive-short-float`   Constant
`most-positive-single-float`   Constant
`most-positive-double-float`   Constant
`most-positive-long-float`   Constant
> The positive floating-point number of greatest magnitude in each of the float
> formats. Implementation-dependent.

`multiple-values-limit`   Constant
> Positive integer one greater than the maximum number of return values.
> Implementation-dependent, but at least 20.

`nil`   Constant
> Evaluates to itself. Represents false and the empty list.

`*package*`   Variable
> The current package. Initially `common-lisp-user`.

`pi`   Constant
> A long-float approximation of π.

`*print-array*`   Variable
> If true, arrays will be printed in a readable form. Initial value is implementation-
> dependent.

`*print-base*`   Variable
> An integer between 2 and 36 inclusive that determines the base in which
> numbers are printed. Initial value is 10 (decimal).

`*print-case*`   Variable
> Controls the printing of ordinary all-uppercase symbol names. The three
> possible values are: `:upcase` (the initial value), which yields all uppercase;
> `:downcase`, which yields all lowercase; and `:capitalize`, which prints sym-
> bol names as if returned by `string-capitalize`.

`*print-circle*`   Variable
> If true, shared structure will be displayed using the #n= and #n# read-macros.
> Initial value is `nil`.

`*print-escape*`   Variable
> If `nil`, everything is printed as if by `princ`. Initially `t`.

print-gensym   Variable

If true, #: is printed before uninterned symbols. Initially t.

print-length   Variable

Either nil (the initial value) or a positive integer. If an integer, up to that many elements of an object will be displayed, the rest being elided. If nil, there is no limit.

print-level   Variable

Either nil (the initial value) or a positive integer. If an integer, objects nested up to that depth will be displayed, the rest being elided. If nil, there is no limit.

print-lines   Variable

Either nil (the initial value) or a positive integer. If an integer, only that many lines will be shown when an object is pretty-printed, the rest being elided. If nil, there is no limit.

print-miser-width   Variable

Either nil or a positive integer. If an integer, pretty-printer prints in a compact style if fewer ems are available. Initial value is implementation-dependent.

print-pprint-dispatch   Variable

Either nil or a pprint dispatch table. If the latter, it controls pretty-printing. Initial value is a table that yields conventional output.

print-pretty   Variable

When true, objects will be pretty-printed. Initial value is implementation-dependent.

print-radix   Variable

If true, numbers will be printed with an indication of the radix in which they are displayed. Initial value is nil.

print-readably   Variable

If true, the printer must either generate readable output, or signal an error. Initially nil.

print-right-margin   Variable

Either nil (the initial value) or a positive integer representing a number of ems. If an integer, nothing will be printed past it; if nil, the right margin is set by the output stream.

query-io   Variable

Stream on which to ask for and receive user input.

random-state   Variable

An object representing the state of Common Lisp's random number generator.

read-base   Variable

An integer between 2 and 36 inclusive that determines the base in which numbers are read. Initial value is 10 (decimal).

`*read-default-float-format*`   Variable
> Indicates the default format for floats made by `read`. Must be a type-specifier for one of the types of float. Initial value is `single-float`.

`*read-eval*`   Variable
> If nil, `#.` signals an error. Initially `t`.

`*read-suppress*`   Variable
> If true, `read` becomes more accepting of syntactic diversity. Initially `nil`.

`*readtable*`   Variable
> The current readtable. Initially a readtable defining standard Common Lisp syntax.

`*standard-input*`   Variable
> Default input stream.

`*standard-output*`   Variable
> Default output stream.

`t`   Constant
> Evaluates to itself. Represents true.

`*terminal-io*`   Variable
> A stream representing the console, if there is one.

`*trace-output*`   Variable
> A stream on which traces are to be displayed.

`* ** ***`   Variables
> The first value returned by the last, next to last, and third to last expressions entered at the toplevel.

`+ ++ +++`   Variables
> The last, next to last, and third to last expressions entered at the toplevel.

`-`   Variable
> During the evaluation of an expression at the toplevel, that expression.

`/ // ///`   Variables
> List of the values returned by the last, next to last, and third to last expressions entered at the toplevel.

Type Specifiers

Type specifiers can be simple or compound. A simple type specifier is a symbol that is the name of a type (e.g. `integer`). A compound type specifier is a list of a symbol followed by one or more arguments. This section lists the possible compound type specifiers.

`(and `*type*`*)`   Type Specifier
> Denotes the intersection of the *type*s.

(array *type dimensions*)   Type Specifier
(simple-array *type dimensions*)   Type Specifier
    Denote the set of arrays whose :element-type is *type*, and with dimensions
    matching *dimensions*. If *dimensions* is a non-negative integer, it indicates the
    number of dimensions; if a list, the size of each dimension, as if in a call to
    make-array. Using simple-array restricts the set to simple arrays. A *
    appearing as the *type* or part of the *dimensions* indicates no restriction in that
    respect.

(base-string *i*)   Type Specifier
(simple-base-string *i*)   Type Specifier
    Equivalent to (vector base-character *i*) and (simple-array base-
    character (*i*)) respectively.

(bit-vector *i*)   Type Specifier
(simple-bit-vector *i*)   Type Specifier
    Equivalent to (array bit (*i*)) and (simple-array bit (*i*)) respectively.

(complex *type*)   Type Specifier
    Denotes the set of complex numbers whose real and imaginary parts are reals
    of type *type*.

(cons *type1 type2*)   Type Specifier
    Denotes the set of conses whose cars are of *type1* and cdrs of *type2*. A * in
    either position is equivalent to t.

(eql *object*)   Type Specifier
    Denotes a set of one element: *object*.

(float *min max*)   Type Specifier
(short-float *min max*)   Type Specifier
(single-float *min max*)   Type Specifier
(double-float *min max*)   Type Specifier
(long-float *min max*)   Type Specifier
    Denotes the set of floats of the designated type with values between *min* and
    max. The *min* and *max* may be either f (inclusive limit) or (f) (exclusive
    limit), where f is a float of the designated type; or *, which indicates no limit
    in that direction.

(function *parameters type*)   Type Specifier
    For use only in declarations. Denotes the set of functions whose arguments
    can be of the types indicated by *parameters*, and which return value(s) of type
    type. The *parameters* has the same form as a parameter list, but with variable
    names replaced by type specifiers, and keyword parameter types indicated by
    lists of the form (*key type*). A type specifier following &rest indicates the
    type of the remaining arguments, not the type of the rest parameter, which is
    always list. (See the values type specifier.)

(integer *min max*)   Type Specifier
    Like float, but for integers.

(member *object**)   Type Specifier
    Denotes the set of the *objects*.

(mod *i*)   Type Specifier
    Denotes the set of integers less than *i*.

(not *type*)   Type Specifier
    Denotes the complement of the *type*.

(or *type**)   Type Specifier
    Denotes the union of the *types*.

(rational *min max*)   Type Specifier
    Like float, but for rationals.

(real *min max*)   Type Specifier
    Like float, but for reals.

(satisfies *symbol*)   Type Specifier
    Denotes the set of all objects that satisfy the function of one argument whose
    name is *symbol*.

(signed-byte *i*)   Type Specifier
    Denotes the set of integers between -2^{i-1} and $2^{i-1} - 1$ inclusive. Equivalent
    to integer if *i* is *.

(string *i*)   Type Specifier
(simple-string *i*)   Type Specifier
    Denote the set of strings and simple strings, respectively, of length *i*.

(unsigned-byte *i*)   Type Specifier
    Denotes the set of non-negative integers less than 2^i. If *i* is *, equivalent to
    (integer 0 *).

(values . *parameters*)   Type Specifier
    For use only in function type specifiers and the expressions. Denotes the
    set of series of values that could be passed in a multiple-value-call to a
    function of type (function *parameters*).

(vector *type i*)   Type Specifier
(simple-vector *i*)   Type Specifier
    Equivalent to (array *type* (*i*)) and (simple-array t (*i*)) respectively.
    Note that a simple vector is not merely a simple array with one dimension; a
    simple vector must also be able to hold objects of any type.

Read Macros

The single-character read-macros are (,), ', ;, and `. All predefined dispatching read-macros have # as the dispatching character. They are:

#*c*	Denotes the character *c*.
#'*f*	Equivalent to (function *f*).
#(. . .)	Denotes a simple vector.
#*n*(. . .)	Denotes a simple vector of *n* elements. If fewer given, remaining positions filled with the last.
#*bbb*	Denotes a simple bit-vector.
#*n**bbb	Denotes a simple bit-vector of *n* elements. If fewer given, remaining positions filled with the last.
#:*sym*	Yields a new uninterned symbol whose name is that of *sym*.
#.*expr*	Yields the value of *expr* at read-time.
#B*ddd*	Binary number.
#O*ddd*	Octal number.
#X*ddd*	Hexadecimal number.
#*n*R*ddd*	Number in base *n*, which must be a decimal integer between 2 and 36 inclusive.
#C(*a b*)	Denotes the complex number *a+bi*.
#*n*A*expr*	Denotes an *n*-dimensional array, made as if '*expr* were the :initial-contents argument in a call to make-array.
#S(*sym*. . .)	Yields a structure of the type named *sym* in which each field contains the corresponding value, and unspecified fields default as if in a call to the constructor function.
#P*expr*	Yields the value of (parse-namestring '*expr*).
#*n*=*expr*	Equivalent to *expr*, but for the remainder of the outermost expression being read, the object yielded by *expr* is labelled as *n*.
#*n*#	Yields the object labelled as *n*.
#+*test expr*	If *test* succeeds, equivalent to *expr*, otherwise to whitespace.
#−*test expr*	If *test* fails, equivalent to *expr*, otherwise to whitespace.
#|. . .|#	Comment; ignored by the reader.
#<	Causes an error.

Backquote is easiest to understand if we define it by saying what a backquoted expression returns.° To evaluate a backquoted expression, you remove the backquote and each matching comma, and replace the expression following each matching comma with its value. Evaluating an expression that begins with a comma causes an error.

A comma matches a backquote if there are the same number of commas as backquotes between them, where *b* is between *a* and *c* if *a* is prepended to an expression containing *b*, and *b* is prepended to an expression containing *c*. This means that in a well-formed expression the outermost backquote matches the innermost comma(s).

Suppose that x evaluates to a, which evaluates to 1; and that y evaluates to b, which evaluates to 2. To evaluate the expression

``(w ,x ,,y)

we remove the first backquote and evaluate what follows any matching comma. The
rightmost comma is the only one that matches the first backquote. If we remove it and
replace the expression it's prepended to, y, with its value, we get:

`(w ,x ,b)

In this expression, both of the commas match the backquote, so if we were to evaluate
it in turn, we would get:

(w a 2)

   A comma-at (,@) behaves like a comma, except that the expression it's prepended
to must both occur within and return a list. The elements of the returned list are then
spliced into the containing list. So

``(w ,x ,,@(list 'a 'b))

evaluates to

`(w ,x ,a ,b)

A comma-dot (,.) is like comma-at, but destructive.

Notes

This section is also intended as a bibliography. All the books and papers listed here should be considered recommended reading.

viii Steele, Guy L., Jr., with Scott E. Fahlman, Richard P. Gabriel, David A. Moon, Daniel L. Weinreb, Daniel G. Bobrow, Linda G. DeMichiel, Sonya E. Keene, Gregor Kiczales, Crispin Perdue, Kent M. Pitman, Richard C. Waters, and Jon L White. *Common Lisp: the Language,* 2nd Edition. Digital Press, Bedford (MA), 1990.

1 McCarthy, John. Recursive Functions of Symbolic Expressions and their Computation by Machine, Part I. *CACM,* 3:4 (April 1960), pp. 184-195.

McCarthy, John. History of Lisp. In Wexelblat, Richard L. (Ed.) *History of Programming Languages.* Academic Press, New York, 1981, pp. 173-197.

Both were available at http://www-formal.stanford.edu/jmc/ at the time of printing.

3 Brooks, Frederick P. *The Mythical Man-Month.* Addison-Wesley, Reading (MA), 1975, p. 16.

Rapid prototyping is not just a way to write programs faster or better. It is a way to write programs that otherwise might not get written at all.

Even the most ambitious people shrink from big undertakings. It's easier to start something if one can convince oneself (however speciously) that it won't be too much work. That's why so many big things have begun as small things. Rapid prototyping lets us start small.

4 *Ibid.*, p. i.

5 Murray, Peter and Linda. *The Art of the Renaissance.* Thames and Hudson, London, 1963, p. 85.

5 Janson, W. J. *History of Art,* 3rd Edition. Abrams, New York, 1986, p. 374.

The analogy applies, of course, only to paintings done on panels and later on canvases. Wall-paintings continued to be done in fresco. Nor do I mean to suggest that painting styles were driven by technological change; the opposite seems more nearly true.

12 The names `car` and `cdr` derive from the internal representation of lists in the first Lisp implementation: `car` stood for "contents of the address part of the register" and `cdr` stood for "contents of the decrement part of the register."

17 Readers who have trouble with the concept of recursion may want to consult either of the following:

Touretzky, David S. *Common Lisp: A Gentle Introduction to Symbolic Computation.* Benjamin/Cummings, Redwood City (CA), 1990, Chapter 8.

Friedman, Daniel P., and Matthias Felleisen. *The Little Lisper.* MIT Press, Cambridge, 1987.

26 In ANSI Common Lisp there is also a `lambda` macro that allows you to write `(lambda (x) x)` for `#'(lambda (x) x)`. Since the use of this macro obscures the symmetry between lambda expressions and symbolic function names (where you still have to use sharp-quote), it yields a specious sort of elegance at best.

28 Gabriel, Richard P. Lisp: Good News, Bad News, How to Win Big. *AI Expert,* June 1991, p. 34.

46 Another thing to be aware of when using `sort`: it does not guarantee to preserve the order of elements judged equal by the comparison function. For example, if you sort `(2 1 1.0)` by `<`, a valid Common Lisp implementation could return either `(1 1.0 2)` or `(1.0 1 2)`. To preserve as much as possible of the original order, use instead the slower `stable-sort` (also destructive), which could only return the first value.

61 A lot has been said about the benefits of comments, and little or nothing about their cost. But they do have a cost. Good code, like good prose, comes from constant rewriting. To evolve, code must be malleable and compact. Interlinear comments make programs stiff and diffuse, and so inhibit the evolution of what they describe.

62 Though most implementations use the ASCII character set, the only ordering that Common Lisp guarantees for characters is as follows: the 26 lowercase letters are in alphabetically ascending order, as are the uppercase letters, and the digits from 0 to 9.

76 The standard way to implement a priority queue is to use a structure called a *heap.* See: Sedgewick, Robert. *Algorithms.* Addison-Wesley, Reading (MA), 1988.

81 The definition of `progn` sounds a lot like the evaluation rule for Common Lisp function calls (page 9). Though `progn` is a special operator, we could define a similar function:

```
(defun our-progn (&rest args)
  (car (last args)))
```

This would be horribly inefficient, but functionally equivalent to the real progn if the last argument returned exactly one value.

84 The analogy to a lambda expression breaks down if the variable names are symbols that have special meanings in a parameter list. For example,

```
(let ((&key 1) (&optional 2)))
```

is correct, but the corresponding lambda expression

```
((lambda (&key &optional)) 1 2)
```

is not. The same problem arises if you try to define do in terms of labels. Thanks to David Kuznick for pointing this out.

89 Steele, Guy L., Jr., and Richard P. Gabriel. The Evolution of Lisp. *ACM SIGPLAN Notices* 28:3 (March 1993). The example in the quoted passage was translated from Scheme into Common Lisp.

91 To make the time look the way people expect, you would want to ensure that minutes and seconds are represented with two digits, as in:

```
(defun get-time-string ()
  (multiple-value-bind (s m h) (get-decoded-time)
    (format nil "~A:~2,,,'0@A:~2,,,'0@A" h m s)))
```

94 In a letter of March 18 (old style) 1751, Chesterfield writes:

"It was notorious, that the Julian Calendar was erroneous, and had overcharged the solar year with eleven days. Pope Gregory the Thirteenth corrected this error [in 1582]; his reformed calendar was immediately received by all the Catholic powers of Europe, and afterwards adopted by all the Protestant ones, except Russia, Sweden, and England. It was not, in my opinion, very honourable for England to remain in a gross and avowed error, especially in such company; the inconveniency of it was likewise felt by all those who had foreign correspondences, whether political or mercantile. I determined, therefore, to attempt the reformation; I consulted the best lawyers, and the most skillful astronomers, and we cooked up a bill for that purpose. But then my difficulty began; I was to bring in this bill, which was necessarily composed of law jargon and astronomical calculations, to both of which I am an utter stranger. However, it was absolutely necessary to make the House of Lords think that I knew something of the matter; and also to make them believe that they knew something of it themselves, which they do not. For my own part, I could just as soon have talked Celtic or Sclavonian to them, as astronomy, and they would have understood me full as well; so I resolved to do better than speak to the purpose, and to please instead of informing them. I gave them, therefore, only an historical account of calendars, from the Egyptian down to the Gregorian, amusing them now and then with little episodes; but I was particularly attentive to the choice of my words, to the harmony and roundness of my periods, to my elocution, to my action. This succeeded, and ever will succeed; they thought I informed them, because I pleased them; and many of them said I had made the whole very clear to them; when, God knows, I had not even attempted it."

See: Roberts, David (Ed.) *Lord Chesterfield's Letters.* Oxford University
Press, Oxford, 1992.

95 In Common Lisp, a universal time is an integer representing the number of seconds since the beginning of 1900. The functions `encode-universal-time`
and `decode-universal-time` translate dates into and out of this format. So
for dates after 1900, there is a simpler way to do date arithmetic in Common
Lisp:

```
(defun num->date (n)
  (multiple-value-bind (ig no re d m y)
                       (decode-universal-time n)
    (values d m y)))

(defun date->num (d m y)
  (encode-universal-time 1 0 0 d m y))

(defun date+ (d m y n)
  (num->date (+ (date->num d m y)
                (* 60 60 24 n))))
```

Besides the range limit, this approach has the disadvantage that dates tend not
to be fixnums.

100 Although a call to `setf` can usually be understood as a reference to a particular
place, the underlying machinery is more general. Suppose that a `marble` is a
structure with a single field called `color`:

```
(defstruct marble
  color)
```

The following function takes a list of marbles and returns their color, if they all
have the same color, or `nil` if they have different colors:

```
(defun uniform-color (lst)
  (let ((c (marble-color (car lst))))
    (dolist (m (cdr lst))
      (unless (eql (marble-color m) c)
        (return nil)))
    c))
```

Although `uniform-color` does not refer to a particular place, it is both reasonable and possible to have a call to it as the first argument to `setf`. Having
defined

```
(defun (setf uniform-color) (val lst)
  (dolist (m lst)
    (setf (marble-color m) val)))
```

we can say

```
(setf (uniform-color *marbles*) 'red)
```

to make the color of each element of `*marbles*` be `red`.

100 In older Common Lisp implementations, you have to use `defsetf` to define how a call should be treated when it appears as the first argument to `setf`. Be careful when translating, because the parameter representing the new value comes *last* in the definition of a function whose name is given as the second argument to `defsetf`. That is, the call

```
(defun (setf primo) (val lst) (setf (car lst) val))
```

is equivalent to

```
(defsetf primo set-primo)
```

```
(defun set-primo (lst val) (setf (car lst) val))
```

106 C, for example, lets you pass a pointer to a function, but there's less you can pass in a function (because C doesn't have closures) and less the recipient can do with it (because C has no equivalent of `apply`). What's more, you are in principle supposed to declare the type of the return value of the function you pass a pointer to. How, then, could you write `map-int` or `filter`, which work for functions that return anything? You couldn't, really. You would have to suppress the type-checking of arguments and return values, which is dangerous, and even so would probably only be practical for 32-bit values.

109 For many examples of the versatility of closures, see: Abelson, Harold, and Gerald Jay Sussman, with Julie Sussman. *Structure and Interpretation of Computer Programs.* MIT Press, Cambridge, 1985.

109 For more information about Dylan, see: Shalit, Andrew, with Kim Barrett, David Moon, Orca Starbuck, and Steve Strassmann. *Dylan Interim Reference Manual.* Apple Computer, 1994.

At the time of printing this document was accessible from several sites, including `http://www.harlequin.com` and `http://www.apple.com`.

Scheme is a very small, clean dialect of Lisp. It was invented by Guy L. Steele Jr. and Gerald J. Sussman in 1975, and is currently defined by: Clinger, William, and Jonathan A. Rees (Eds.) *Revised[4] Report on the Algorithmic Language Scheme.* 1991.

This report, and various implementations of Scheme, were at the time of printing available by anonymous FTP from `swiss-ftp.ai.mit.edu:pub`.

There are two especially good textbooks that use Scheme—*Structure and Interpretation* (see preceding note) and: Springer, George and Daniel P. Friedman. *Scheme and the Art of Programming.* MIT Press, Cambridge, 1989.

112 The most horrible Lisp bugs may be those involving dynamic scope. Such errors almost never occur in Common Lisp, which has lexical scope by default. But since so many of the Lisps used as extension languages still have dynamic scope, practicing Lisp programmers should be aware of its perils.

One bug that can arise with dynamic scope is similar in spirit to variable capture (page 166). You pass one function as an argument to another. The function passed as an argument refers to some variable. But within the function that calls it, the variable has a new and unexpected value.

Suppose, for example, that we wrote a restricted version of mapcar as follows:

```
(defun our-mapcar (fn x)
  (if (null x)
      nil
      (cons (funcall fn (car x))
            (our-mapcar fn (cdr x)))))
```

Then suppose that we used this function in another function, add-to-all, that would take a number and add it to every element of a list:

```
(defun add-to-all (lst x)
  (our-mapcar #'(lambda (num) (+ num x))
              lst))
```

In Common Lisp this code works fine, but in a Lisp with dynamic scope it would generate an error. The function passed as an argument to our-mapcar refers to x. At the point where we send this function to our-mapcar, x would be the number given as the second argument to add-to-all. But where the function will be called, within our-mapcar, x would be something else: the list passed as the second argument to our-mapcar. We would get an error when this list was passed as the second argument to +.

123   Newer implementations of Common Lisp include a variable *read-eval* that can be used to turn off the #. read-macro. When calling read-from-string on user input, it is wise to bind *read-eval* to nil. Otherwise the user could cause side-effects by using #. in the input.

125   There are a number of ingenious algorithms for fast string-matching, but string-matching in text files is one of the cases where the brute-force approach is still reasonably fast. For more on string-matching algorithms, see: Sedgewick, Robert. *Algorithms*. Addison-Wesley, Reading (MA), 1988.

141   In 1984 Common Lisp, reduce did not take a :key argument, so random-next would be defined:

```
(defun random-next (prev)
  (let* ((choices (gethash prev *words*))
         (i (random (let ((x 0))
                      (dolist (c choices)
                        (incf x (cdr c)))
                      x))))
    (dolist (pair choices)
      (if (minusp (decf i (cdr pair)))
          (return (car pair))))))
```

141 In 1989, a program like Henley was used to simulate netnews postings by well-known flamers. The fake postings fooled a significant number of readers. Like all good hoaxes, this one had an underlying point. What did it say about the content of the original flames, or the attention with which they were read, that randomly generated postings could be mistaken for the real thing?

One of the most valuable contributions of artificial intelligence research has been to teach us which tasks are really difficult. Some tasks turn out to be trivial, and some almost impossible. If artificial intelligence is concerned with the latter, the study of the former might be called *artificial stupidity*. A silly name, perhaps, but this field has real promise—it promises to yield programs that play a role like that of control experiments.

Speaking with the appearance of meaning is one of the tasks that turn out to be surprisingly easy. People's predisposition to find meaning is so strong that they tend to overshoot the mark. So if a speaker takes care to give his sentences a certain kind of superficial coherence, and his audience are sufficiently credulous, they will *make sense* of what he says.

This fact is probably as old as human history. But now we can give examples of genuinely random text for comparison. And if our randomly generated productions are difficult to distinguish from the real thing, might that not set people to thinking?

The program shown in Chapter 8 is about as simple as such a program could be, and that is already enough to generate "poetry" that many people (try it on your friends) will believe was written by a human being. With programs that work on the same principle as this one, but which model text as more than a simple stream of words, it will be possible to generate random text that has even more of the trappings of meaning.

For a discussion of randomly generated poetry as a legitimate literary form, see: Low, Jackson M. Poetry, Chance, Silence, Etc. In Hall, Donald (Ed.) *Claims for Poetry.* University of Michigan Press, Ann Arbor, 1982. You bet.

Thanks to the Online Book Initiative, ASCII versions of many classics are available online. At the time of printing, they could be obtained by anonymous FTP from `ftp.std.com:obi`.

See also the Emacs Dissociated Press feature, which uses an equivalent algorithm to scramble a buffer.

150 The following function will display the values of the sixteen constants that mark the limits of floating point representation in a given implementation:

```
(defun float-limits ()
  (dolist (m '(most least))
    (dolist (s '(positive negative))
      (dolist (f '(short single double long))
        (let ((n (intern (string-upcase
                           (format nil "~A-~A-~A-float"
                                   m   s   f)))))
          (format t "~30A ~A~%" n (symbol-value n)))))))
```

164 The Quicksort algorithm was published by Hoare in 1962, and is described in: Knuth, D. E. *Sorting and Searching.* Addison-Wesley, Reading (MA), 1973.

173 Foderaro, John K. Introduction to the Special Lisp Section. *CACM* 34:9 (September 1991), p. 27.

176 For more detailed information about CLOS programming techniques, see the following:

Keene, Sonya E. *Object Oriented Programming in Common Lisp.* Addison-Wesley, Reading (MA), 1989.

Kiczales, Gregor, Jim des Rivieres, and Daniel G. Bobrow. *The Art of the Metaobject Protocol.* MIT Press, Cambridge, 1991.

178 Let's play that back one more time: *we can make all these types of modifications without even looking at the rest of the code.* This idea may sound alarmingly familiar to some readers. It is the recipe for spaghetti code.

The object-oriented model makes it easy to build up programs by accretion. What this often means, in practice, is that it provides a structured way to write spaghetti code. This is not necessarily bad, but it is not entirely good either.

A lot of the code in the real world is spaghetti code, and this is probably not going to change soon. For programs that would have ended up as spaghetti anyway, the object-oriented model is good: they will at least be structured spaghetti. But for programs that might otherwise have avoided this fate, object-oriented abstractions could be more dangerous than useful.

183 When an instance would inherit a slot with the same name from several of its superclasses, the instance inherits a single slot that combines the properties of the slots in the superclasses. The way combination is done varies from property to property:

1. The :allocation, :initform (if any), and :documentation (if any), will be those of the most specific classes.

2. The :initargs will be the union of the :initargs of all the superclasses. So will the :accessors, :readers, and :writers, effectively.

3. The :type will be the intersection of the :types of all the superclasses.

191 You can avoid explicitly uninterning the names of slots that you want to be encapsulated by using uninterned symbols as the names to start with:

```
(progn
  (defclass counter () ((#1=#:state :initform 0)))

  (defmethod increment ((c counter))
    (incf (slot-value c '#1#)))

  (defmethod clear ((c counter))
    (setf (slot-value c '#1#) 0)))
```

The progn here is a no-op; it is used to ensure that all the references to the uninterned symbol occur within the same expression. If this were inconvenient, you could use the following read-macro instead:

```
(defvar *symtab* (make-hash-table :test #'equal))

(defun pseudo-intern (name)
  (or (gethash name *symtab*)
      (setf (gethash name *symtab*) (gensym))))

(set-dispatch-macro-character #\# #\[
  #'(lambda (stream char1 char2)
      (do ((acc nil (cons char acc))
           (char (read-char stream) (read-char stream)))
          ((eql char #\]) (pseudo-intern acc)))))
```

Then it would be possible to say just:

```
(defclass counter () ((#[state] :initform 0)))

(defmethod increment ((c counter))
  (incf (slot-value c '#[state])))

(defmethod clear ((c counter))
  (setf (slot-value c '#[state]) 0))
```

204 The following macro pushes new elements into binary search trees:

```
(defmacro bst-push (obj bst <)
  (multiple-value-bind (vars forms var set access)
                       (get-setf-expansion bst)
    (let ((g (gensym)))
      '(let* ((,g ,obj)
              ,@(mapcar #'list vars forms)
              (,(car var) (bst-insert! ,g ,access ,<)))
         ,set))))
```

213 Knuth, Donald E. Structured Programming with goto Statements. *Computing Surveys*, 6:4 (December 1974), pp. 261-301.

214 Knuth, Donald E. Computer Programming as an Art. In *ACM Turing Award Lectures: The First Twenty Years*. ACM Press, 1987.

This paper and the preceding one are reprinted in: Knuth, Donald E. *Literate Programming*. CSLI Lecture Notes #27, Stanford University Center for the Study of Language and Information, Palo Alto, 1992.

216 Steele, Guy L., Jr. Debunking the "Expensive Procedure Call" Myth or, Procedural Call Implementations Considered Harmful or, LAMBDA: The Ultimate GOTO. *Proceedings of the National Conference of the ACM*, 1977, p. 157.

Tail-recursion optimization should mean that the compiler will generate the same code for a tail-recursive function as it would for the equivalent do. The unfortunate reality, at least at the time of printing, is that many compilers generate slightly faster code for dos.

217 For some examples of calls to `disassemble` on various processors, see:
Norvig, Peter. *Paradigms of Artificial Intelligence Programming: Case Studies
in Common Lisp.* Morgan Kaufmann, San Mateo (CA), 1992.

218 A lot of the increased popularity of object-oriented programming is more
specifically the increased popularity of C++, and this in turn has a lot to do with
typing. C++ gives you something that seems like a miracle in the conceptual
world of C: the ability to define operators that work for different types of
arguments. But you don't need an object-oriented language to do this—all you
need is run-time typing. And indeed, if you look at the way people use C++,
the class hierarchies tend to be flat. C++ has become so popular not because
people need to write programs in terms of classes and methods, but because
people need a way around the restrictions imposed by C's approach to typing.

219 Macros can make declarations easier. The following macro expects a type
name and an expression (probably numeric), and expands the expression so
that all arguments, and all intermediate results, are declared to be of that type.
If you wanted to ensure that an expression *e* was evaluated using only fixnum
arithmetic, you could say (`with-type fixnum e`).

```
(defmacro with-type (type expr)
  '(the ,type ,(if (atom expr)
                   expr
                   (expand-call type (binarize expr)))))

(defun expand-call (type expr)
  '(,(car expr) ,@(mapcar #'(lambda (a)
                              '(with-type ,type ,a))
                          (cdr expr))))

(defun binarize (expr)
  (if (and (nthcdr 3 expr)
           (member (car expr) '(+ - * /)))
      (destructuring-bind (op a1 a2 . rest) expr
        (binarize '(,op (,op ,a1 ,a2) ,@rest)))
      expr))
```

The call to `binarize` ensures that no arithmetic operator is called with more
than two arguments. As the Lucid reference manual points out, a call like

```
(the fixnum (+ (the fixnum a)
               (the fixnum b)
               (the fixnum c)))
```

still cannot be compiled into fixnum additions, because the intermediate results
(e.g. a + b) might not be fixnums.

Using `with-type`, we could duplicate the fully declared version of `poly` on
page 219 with:

```
(defun poly (a b x)
  (with-type fixnum (+ (* a (expt x 2)) (* b x))))
```

If you wanted to do a lot of fixnum arithmetic, you might even want to define a read-macro that would expand into a (with-type fixnum ...).

224 On many Unix systems, /usr/dict/words is a suitable file of words.

226 T is a dialect of Scheme with many useful additions, including support for pools. For more on T, see: Rees, Jonathan A., Norman I. Adams, and James R. Meehan. *The T Manual*, 5th Edition. Yale University Computer Science Department, New Haven, 1988.

The T manual, and T itself, were at the time of printing available by anonymous FTP from hing.lcs.mit.edu:pub/t3.1.

229 The difference between specifications and programs is a difference in degree, not a difference in kind. Once we realize this, it seems strange to *require* that one write specifications for a program before beginning to implement it. If the program has to be written in a low-level language, then it would be reasonable to require that it be described in high-level terms first. But as the programming language becomes more abstract, the need for specifications begins to evaporate. Or rather, the implementation and the specifications can become the same thing.

If the high-level program is going to be re-implemented in a lower-level language, it starts to look even more like specifications. What Section 13.7 is saying, in other words, is that the specifications for C programs could be written in Lisp.

230 Benvenuto Cellini's story of the casting of his *Perseus* is probably the most famous (and the funniest) account of traditional bronze-casting: Cellini, Benvenuto. *Autobiography.* Translated by George Bull, Penguin Books, Harmondsworth, 1956.

239 Even experienced Lisp hackers find packages confusing. Is it because packages are gross, or because we are not used to thinking about what happens at read-time?

There is a similar kind of uncertainty about defmacro, and there it does seem that the difficulty is in the mind of the beholder. A good deal of work has gone into finding a more abstract alternative to defmacro. But defmacro is only gross if you approach it with the preconception (common enough) that defining a macro is like defining a function. Then it seems shocking that you suddenly have to worry about variable capture. When you think of macros as what they are, transformations on source code, then dealing with variable capture is no more of a problem than dealing with division by zero at run-time.

So perhaps packages will turn out to be a reasonable way of providing modularity. It is *prima facie* evidence on their side that they resemble the techniques that programmers naturally use in the absence of a formal module system.

242 It might be argued that loop is more general, and that we should not define many operators to do what we can do with one. But it's only in a very legalistic

sense that loop is one operator. In that sense, eval is one operator too. Judged
by the conceptual burden it places on the user, loop is at least as many operators
as it has clauses. What's more, these operators are not available separately,
like real Lisp operators: you can't break off a piece of loop and pass it as an
argument to another function, as you could map-int.

248 For more on logical inference, see: Russell, Stuart, and Peter Norvig. *Artificial
Intelligence: A Modern Approach.* Prentice Hall, Englewood Cliffs (NJ), 1995.

273 Because the program in Chapter 17 takes advantage of the possibility of having
a setf form as the first argument to defun, it will only work in more recent
Common Lisp implementations. If you want to use it in an older implementation, substitute the following code in the final version:

```
(proclaim '(inline lookup set-lookup))

(defsetf lookup set-lookup)

(defun set-lookup (prop obj val)
  (let ((off (position prop (layout obj) :test #'eq)))
    (if off
        (setf (svref obj (+ off 3)) val)
        (error "Can't set ~A of ~A." val obj)))))

(defmacro defprop (name &optional meth?)
  '(progn
     (defun ,name (obj &rest args)
       ,(if meth?
            '(run-methods obj ',name args)
            '(rget ',name obj nil)))
     (defsetf ,name (obj) (val)
       '(setf (lookup ',',name ,obj) ,val))))
```

276 If defmeth were defined as

```
(defmacro defmeth (name obj parms &rest body)
  (let ((gobj (gensym)))
    '(let ((,gobj ,obj))
       (setf (gethash ',name ,gobj)
             #'(lambda ,parms
                 (labels ((next ()
                            (funcall (get-next ,gobj ',name)
                                     ,@parms)))
                   ,@body))))))
```

then it would be possible to invoke the next method simply by calling next:

```
(defmeth area grumpy-circle (c)
  (format t "How dare you stereotype me!~%")
  (next))
```

So far as the example goes, this looks simpler; but if `next` were implemented this way, we would have to add another function to do the job of `next-method-p`.

284 For really fast access to slots we would use the following macro:

```
(defmacro with-slotref ((name prop class) &rest body)
  (let ((g (gensym)))
    `(let ((,g (+ 3 (position ,prop (layout ,class)
                              :test #'eq))))
       (macrolet ((,name (obj) `(svref ,obj ,',g)))
         ,@body))))
```

It defines a local macro that refers directly to the vector element corresponding to a slot. If in some segment of code you wanted to refer to the same slot in many instances of the same class, with this macro the slot references would be straight `svref`s.

For example, if the `balloon` class is defined as follows,

```
(setf balloon-class (class nil size))
```

then this function pops (in the old sense) a list of balloons:

```
(defun popem (balloons)
  (with-slotref (bsize 'size balloon-class)
    (dolist (b balloons)
      (setf (bsize b) 0))))
```

284 Gabriel, Richard P. Lisp: Good News, Bad News, How to Win Big. *AI Expert*, June 1991, p. 35.

As early as 1973, Richard Fateman was able to show that the MacLisp compiler for the PDP-10 generated faster code than the manufacturer's FORTRAN compiler. See: Fateman, Richard J. Reply to an editorial. *ACM SIGSAM Bulletin*, 25 (March 1973), pp. 9-11.

399 It's easiest to understand backquote if we suppose that backquote and comma are like quote, and that `,x simply expands into `(bq (comma x))`. If this were so, we could handle backquote by augmenting `eval` as in this sketch:

```
(defun eval2 (expr)
  (case (and (consp expr) (car expr))
    (comma (error "unmatched comma"))
    (bq    (eval-bq (second expr) 1))
    (t     (eval expr))))

(defun eval-bq (expr n)
  (cond ((atom expr)
         expr)
        ((eql (car expr) 'comma)
         (if (= n 1)
```

```
              (eval2 (second expr))
              (list 'comma (eval-bq (second expr)
                                    (1- n)))))
        ((eql (car expr) 'bq)
         (list 'bq (eval-bq (second expr) (1+ n))))
        (t
         (cons (eval-bq (car expr) n)
               (eval-bq (cdr expr) n)))))
```

In eval-bq, the parameter n is used to determine which commas match the current backquote. Each backquote increments it, and each comma decrements it. A comma encountered when n = 1 is a matching comma.

Here is the example from page 400:

```
> (setf x 'a a 1 y 'b b 2)
2
> (eval2 '(bq (bq (w (comma x) (comma (comma y)))))))
(BQ (W (COMMA X) (COMMA B)))
> (eval2 *)
(W A 2)
```

At some point a particularly remarkable molecule was formed by accident. We will call it the *Replicator.* It may not necessarily have been the biggest or the most complex molecule around, but it had the extraordinary property of being able to create copies of itself.

Richard Dawkins
The Selfish Gene

We shall first define a class of symbolic expressions in terms of ordered pairs and lists. Then we shall define five elementary functions and predicates, and build from them by composition, conditional expressions, and recursive definitions an extensive class of functions of which we shall give a number of examples. We shall then show how these functions themselves can be expressed as symbolic expressions, and we shall define a universal function *apply* that allows us to compute from the expression for a given function its value for given arguments.

John McCarthy
Recursive Functions of Symbolic Expressions
and their Computation by Machine, Part I

Index